Everybody's Business

ROGER W. YOUNG
Headmaster of George Watson's College

Everybody's Business

This business is everybody's business
ALBERT CAMUS, *The Plague*

Oxford University Press

Oxford University Press, Ely House, London W. 1

GLASGOW NEW YORK TORONTO MELBOURNE WELLINGTON
CAPE TOWN IBADAN NAIROBI DAR ES SALAAM LUSAKA ADDIS ABABA
DELHI BOMBAY CALCUTTA MADRAS KARACHI LAHORE DACCA
KUALA LUMPUR SINGAPORE HONG KONG TOKYO

FIRST PUBLISHED 1968
REPRINTED 1970 (WITH CORRECTIONS), 1973

Reproduced and printed by photolithography and bound in
Great Britain at The Pitman Press, Bath

Preface

In my earlier book, *Lines of Thought*, I attempted to provide material for General Studies periods as an introduction to philosophical topics. The kindly reception of it led the Oxford University Press to suggest that I should collect some material on theological topics for Religious Instruction. As the book has developed, however, its scope has been widened, for reasons given below, and it should prove useful for General Studies as well, particularly since the distinction is tending to disappear. As in *Lines of Thought*, Part 1 deals mainly with specific and concrete problems, while Part 2 moves on to more abstract themes. The passages themselves, however, are here concerned, not with methods of reasoning, but with the actual issues of 'the human condition' on which our reasoning powers must be brought to bear.

The teaching of R.I. has dramatically altered in the last few years. Not only has there been a move away from instruction towards dialogue and discussion, but the subject matter itself has changed. Instead of starting from the Bible to see what light its insights shed on our lives, we are urged to begin with life as it is and probe it to the point where the biblical insights are found to take on new meaning and to have a real bearing on the issues which concern us today. This approach has determined the layout of the book and the relationship between its two parts.

Part 1 is concerned with personal, social, and political issues—examples of problems which senior pupils with any interest in the world around them are likely to be concerned about. My aim has been to choose writers of varying viewpoints who deal with matters of real importance which will call for actual decisions from our pupils when they go out into the world. For some these decisions will be based on Christian conviction; for others they will not. In either case the essential thing is to recognize that we cannot opt out. 'No man is an island'; for, as the title explains, 'this business is everybody's business'.

Since, however, many people's decisions are in fact grounded in the

Christian Faith, it is reasonable to ask what it is that Christians believe in and why. Part 2, therefore, examines and illustrates the basic tenets of the Christian Faith—its claims about Jesus Christ, about the work of the Holy Spirit and the Christian Community, and about the character of God. I have presented them in this order, because for many young people today the serious consideration of Christianity starts from the impact of the life and character of Jesus, which may then lead them on, through experience of the fellowship of believers, to face the ultimate questions of the reality and nature of God.

The book is designed for a two-year course, with approximately one year devoted to each Part; thus it should cover the fifth- and sixth-form years in a Scottish school and the two main years of the sixth in an English school. A wide range and variety of passages have been sought to give teachers and pupils plenty of choice; different passages will naturally suit different people best, and a number of the passages also help to set each other off. The list of references and the books suggested for further reading will, I hope, encourage exploration beyond the actual extracts, and, while much of the work will no doubt be done orally, there is plenty of scope for supplementary written work. Some heads of schools and chaplains may even find certain passages suitable for Morning Assembly.

It may well be that those who are concerned with the training of teachers, or with the teaching of ethics, politics, philosophy or theology in Colleges of Education, will find useful material for seminar work in this book. I have deliberately included a number of longer and more difficult passages not only to stretch the mind of the ablest sixth-former, but also to provide an intellectual challenge to the intending teacher. I have been encouraged to believe that those who are concerned with the professional education of teachers will welcome a book of this kind which raises some of the fundamental issues of our time.

My primary concern is not to instil a particular set of beliefs, but rather to awaken understanding and to help pupils see that there are serious questions in which they are inescapably involved. The danger of much present-day discussion is in leading people to suppose, first, that it is an end in itself and therefore a substitute for commitment; and, secondly, that, since it is often difficult to reach the truth, sincerity will serve in its place (but even bigots are sincere). Socrates would have abhorred both notions. For the object of Socratic dialogue is the discovery of the truth and hence of a way of life; and truth is only to be found by those who are open to new insights and who are willing to listen and think as well as talk. 'Insight has two moments: one, the moment of intuition; the other, the moment of reflective judgement as to whether the intuition meets the claims of the facts.'[1] My hope is that this book will help both to provide some moments of intuition and to make intelligible some of the evidence in support of the Christian's insight.

I find it difficult to acknowledge adequately my indebtedness to all those who have helped me in so many ways. Many, indeed, must go unnamed, though their guidance and teaching over the years may be found reflected in every part of the book. But I am glad to have this opportunity of thanking a number of others by name who have given direct assistance: Mr. Eric Anderson, Miss Pat McBryde, Mr. Glen Cavaliero, Miss Ruth Mary Young, Bishop Carey, the Revd. Eric Duncan, and Miss Margaret Bennett for their suggestions of material and their encouragement and comment; the fifth- and sixth-formers of Watson's who have proved most useful assistants in testing passages and sorting the wheat from the chaff; and my mother, Dr. Ruth Young, Miss Judith Carry, and Mrs. Betsy Snell for their untiring labours in preparing innumerable stencils and typing the text. More especially am I grateful to Dr. Walter Baston for his invaluable guidance at every stage of the work, and to Mr. Peter Spicer, whose original persuasiveness led me to undertake the book and whose skilful encouragement has brought about so many welcome improvements in it. Finally my greatest debt is to Bishop Cockin. His wise counsel, his many actual contributions to the text, acknowledged and unacknowledged, and his unfailing readiness to discuss both the general scheme and particular passages have made it almost as much his book as mine. For its shortcomings, however, I alone am responsible. In the hope that it may help to serve the cause of Christian education which he has espoused for so long and with such distinction I dedicate it to him with gratitude and affection.

R.W.Y.

Edinburgh, 1967

1. Michael Novak, *The Open Church* (passage 67, p. 262).

Contents

1. Learning from the world

There is, in principle, no encounter with the world which may not hold within itself an encounter with God.

ROBERT WALTON, *The Roots of Experience*

Community or chaos?

1. Life in death

In Pierre Boulle's book *The Bridge over the River Kwai* and the film which was based on it, the impression was given that British officers not only took part in building the bridge willingly, but finished it in record time to demonstrate to the enemy their superior efficiency. This was an entertaining story. But I am writing a factual account, and in justice to these men—living and dead—who worked on that bridge, I must make it clear that we never did so willingly. We worked at bayonet point and under the bamboo lash, taking any risk to sabotage the operation whenever the opportunity arose.

All these jobs were done by men who worked from Chungkai; but this camp was also the base for at least twenty-six smaller camps strung out westward along the river and the railroad for several hundred miles to the Three Pagodas Pass near the Burmese border. At the first Chungkai was a busy staging area, a mustering point for materials and fresh men; at the last, a fetid hospital camp where the broken returned to die. The crowded huts grew to forty. They housed nearly eight thousand at the peak, a battered population, but one that was ever-shifting, ever-changing. We lived in a constant state of flux, never knowing what the next day held for us or for our fellows. We were being slowly starved.

Our work was heavy, but our rations were light. Our diet was rice —nothing but rice—three times a day—and rice of the very poorest quality, the sweepings from the godowns. Much as we hated it, rice might have kept us going had there been enough of it. The most ever allotted officially was four hundred and twenty grams a day. This figure was purely hypothetical, however, for so many Japanese quartermasters dipped into the supply along the line that far less than that was left by the time the rice reached us. Rations were issued on the basis of heads counted for work; no rice whatever was allowed for the sick. It appeared to be the fixed policy of the Nipponese High Command to write them off as quickly as possible and to waste no rice on them while doing it. After a few months these scanty rations were further reduced, to provide, so we were told, better sustenance for the workers back in Japan. One can imagine that this made us very happy.

We thought much of escape, but escape was next to impossible. It was fairly easy to break through the flimsy twelve-foot bamboo fence.

Guards were stationed at several points around the perimeter of the camp; others patrolled at regular intervals. They could be eluded. But if a man broke through where was he to go? A thousand miles of jungle was the strongest fence that could surround any camp. To be caught outside meant death. Of those who attempted escape there is no record of any surviving.

Death called to us from every direction. It was in the air we breathed —it was the chief topic of our conversation. The rhythm of death obsessed us with its beat—a beat so regular, so pervasive, so inescapable that it made Chungkai a place of shadows in the dark valley.

Dying was easy. When our desires are thwarted and life becomes too much for us, it is easy to reject life and the pain it brings, easier to die than to live. It is an easy thing to adopt a philosophy of despair: to say, 'I mean nothing; there is nothing; nothing matters; I live only to die.' Those who decided they had no further reason for living, pulled down the shades and quietly expired. I knew a man who had amoebic dysentery. Compared to the rest of us, he was in good condition. But he convinced himself that he could not possibly survive and he did not.

As conditions steadily worsened, as starvation, exhaustion, and disease took an ever-growing toll, the atmosphere in which we lived was increasingly poisoned by selfishness, hatred, and fear. We were slipping rapidly down the scale of degradation. In Changi the patterns of army life had sustained us. We had huddled together because of our fears, believing there was safety in numbers. We had still shown some consideration for one another. Now that was gone, swept away. Existence had become so miserable, the odds so heavy against us, that nothing mattered except to survive.

When a man lay dying we had no word of mercy. When he cried for our help, we averted our heads. Everyone was his own keeper. It was free enterprise at its worst, with all the restraints of morality gone. Our captors had promised to reduce us to a level 'lower than any coolie in Asia'. They were succeeding all too well. Although we lived by the law of the jungle, the strongest among us still died, and the most selfish, the most self-sufficient, the wiliest and cleverest, perished with the weak.

Little acts of meanness, suspicion, and favouritism permeated our daily lives. Even the drawing of our meagre ration was a humiliating experience. To get our meals we formed a line in our huts. Our server would dip his can into the rice bucket and dump its contents on our mess tins. Another server would ladle out a watery stew of green leaves. We mistrusted not only the ones we could see, but also the ones we could not see. How much were the helpers in the cookhouse holding back? How much were they stealing for themselves? Suspicion gripped us.

The minute roll call was over in the evening, Japanese cooks would bring out swill pails and set them on the ground. Then they would stand back, fold their arms, and look on with self-satisfied smiles while prisoners pushed, kicked, and shoved one another out of the way as they fought for scraps from the enemy table. One evening a wretch broke away and stumbled towards me. In his hand he clutched a soggy mess of rice and stew. Bits of gravy dripped through his fingers. He had turned his back on the others, lest they should see what he had and be tempted to rob him. A wolfish leer contorted his face as he craftily licked at his spoils. He considered himself lucky.

'Rather than do that,' I thought to myself, 'I'd die!'

He passed me at a kind of trot, like an animal going to his lair, except that an animal would have had more dignity.

ERNEST GORDON, *Through the Valley of the Kwai*

1. 'Everyone was his own keeper', 'all the restraints of morality gone'. (*a*) What are the restraints of morality in your life? Are these external or internal? (*b*) What, ultimately, are the restraints of morality in general? (i.e. even if they appear to be, for example, social, what are the grounds for their being set up by society?) (*c*) How do you think you would have reacted to the situation in Chungkai? Would you have been your own 'keeper'? (*d*) How do you think you might have tried to reverse the descent to 'the law of the jungle'?

2. 'Might is right', it is said. Why shouldn't the Japanese have treated the P.O.W.s as they did?

3. 'I mean nothing; nothing matters; I live only to die'. What reasons would you have had for wanting to fight against disease and apathy, for nursing the will to live?

2. Freedom in school?

Summerhill was founded in the year 1921. Some children come to Summerhill at the age of five years, and others as late as fifteen. Children generally remain at the school until they are sixteen years old. We generally have about twenty-five boys and twenty girls. The children are housed by age groups with a House Mother for each group. One or two older pupils have rooms for themselves. The boys live two or three or four to a room, and so do the girls. The pupils do not have to stand room inspection and no one picks up after them. They are left free. No one tells them what to wear: they put on any kind of costume they want to at any time. Newspapers call it a 'Go-as-you-please school' and imply that it is a gathering of wild primitives who know no law and have no manners.

It seems necessary, therefore, for me to write the story of Summerhill as honestly as I can. Its merits will be the merits of healthy, free children whose lives are unspoiled by fear and hate.

Obviously, a school that makes active children sit at desks studying mostly useless subjects is a bad school. It is a good school only for those who believe in *such* a school, those uncreative citizens who want docile, uncreative children who will fit into a civilisation whose standard of success is money.

We set out to make a school in which we should allow children freedom to be themselves. In order to do this, we had to renounce all discipline, all direction, all suggestion, all moral training, all religious instruction.

My view is that a child is innately wise and realistic. If left to himself without adult suggestion of any kind, he will develop as far as he is capable of developing. For one thing, lessons are optional. Children can go to them or stay away from them—for years if they want to. There is a timetable—but only for the teachers. The children have classes usually according to their age, but sometimes according to their interests. We have no new methods of teaching, because we do not consider that teaching in itself matters very much. The child who *wants* to learn long division will learn it no matter how it is taught.

Strangers to this idea of freedom will be wondering what sort of mad house it is where children play all day if they want to. Many an adult says, 'If I had been sent to a school like that, I'd never have done a thing.' All the same, there is a lot of learning in Summerhill. Perhaps a group of our twelve-year-olds could not compete with a class of equal age in handwriting or spelling or fractions. But in an examination requiring originality, our lot would beat the others hollow. If, for some reason, a teacher cannot take his class on the appointed day, there is usually much disappointment for the pupils. A few years ago someone at a General School Meeting (at which all school rules are voted by the entire school, each pupil and each staff member having one vote) proposed that a certain culprit should be punished by being banished from lessons for a week. The other children protested on the grounds that the punishment was too severe.

To the children, I am no authority to be feared. I am their equal. It is not easy to describe this relationship between teacher and child, but every visitor to Summerhill knows what I mean when I say that the relationship is ideal. Rudd, the Chemistry man, is Derek. Other members of the Staff are known as Harry, and Ulla, and Pam. I am Neill, and the Cook is Esther.

In Summerhill, everyone has equal rights. No one is allowed to walk on my grand piano, and I am not allowed to borrow a boy's bicycle without his permission. At a General School Meeting, the vote of a child of six counts for as much as my vote does. But, says the knowing one, in practice of course the voices of the grown-ups count. Doesn't the child of six wait to see how you vote before he raises his hand? I wish he sometimes would, for too many of my proposals are beaten.

Free children are not easily influenced; the absence of fear accounts for this phenomenon. Our children do not fear our Staff. One of the School rules is that after ten o'clock at night there shall be quietness on the upper corridor. One night, about eleven, a pillow fight was going on, and I left my desk, where I was writing, to protest against the row. As I got upstairs, there was a scurrying of feet and the corridor was empty and quiet. Suddenly I heard a disappointed voice say, 'Humph, it's only Neill,' and the fun began again at once. When I explained that I was trying to write a book downstairs, they showed concern and at once agreed to chuck the noise. Their scurrying came from the suspicion that their bedtime officer (one of their own age) was on their track.

I emphasise the importance of this absence of fear of adults. A child of nine will come and tell me he has broken a window with a ball. He tells me, because he isn't afraid of arousing wrath or moral indignation. He may have to pay for the window, but he doesn't have to fear being lectured or being punished.

The most frequent remark that visitors make is that they cannot tell who is staff and who is pupil. It is true: the feeling of unity is that strong when children are approved of. There is no deference to a teacher as a teacher. Staff and pupils have the same food and have to obey the same community laws. The children would resent any special privileges given to the Staff. The function of the child is to live his own life—not the life that his anxious parents think he should live, nor a life according to the purpose of the educator who thinks he knows what is best. All this interference and guidance on the parts of adults only produces a generation of robots.

You cannot *make* children learn music or anything else without to some degree converting them into will-less adults. You fashion them into acceptors of the *status quo*—a good thing for a society that needs obedient sitters at dreary desks, standers in shops, mechanical catchers of the 8.30 suburban train—a society, in short, that is carried on the shabby shoulders of the scared little man—the scared-to-death conformist.

A. S. NEILL, *Summerhill*

Examine the author's ideas and arguments in turn and discuss their validity *per se* and within the framework of Summerhill itself. Now widen your discussion to consider:

1. Are the author's ideas applicable to your own school? Even if they **are**, would you like to see them adopted?

2. Are they dependent on a high staffing ratio (such as Summerhill has)?

3. Do you think they could or should be applied to the organization of schools throughout the country? (Bear in mind your answer to 2.)

4. What sort of staff/pupil relationship do you think should obtain in a school?

5. What place is there for punishment in a school, and of what kind?

6. Can you discern any influence stemming from the author's ideas in your own school now, and, if so, in what ways? (Remember that Summerhill was started in 1921.)

3. Murder in gambling casino

The following passage is a newspaper report which appeared as a result of two London murders. Imagine yourself as the editor of a newspaper or journal and write two editorials—one from an agnostic humanist's point of view, and one from a Christian point of view. You should include comments on the social as well as the moral aspects of this news item and discuss what action, if any, should be taken.

FREELANCE KILLERS STRUCK ON ORDERS FROM INTERNATIONAL SYNDICATE. MURDER POLICE SEEK HIRED GUNMEN

Hired killers are believed to have been responsible for last week's two gun murders in London. The young 'tearaways', picked from several hundred who offer their services without asking questions, were engaged by syndicates operating on an international scale. The murders were probably connected with the activities of at least two organisations. Their leaders have offices in the City and links with all parts of the world. They have large investments in Africa and dozens of carefully chosen criminals looking after the less ambitious schemes at home. Most of the leaders are known to Scotland Yard and Interpol but not necessarily to the men they employ. There is little the police can do to crush the organisations—particularly since in London alone there are as many as 45 lawyers whose practices are almost entirely devoted to advising and looking after the interests of these people and their henchmen.

It was the activities of these syndicates rather than the more old-fashioned local protection gang rivalries, which led to last week's gunplay.

The men who killed Richard Hart in Mr. Smith's Club in Catford were probably paid £50 each—the usual amount for a job of this kind. The killer of George Cornell, who was shot twice through the head in the Blind Beggar public house in Stepney, took greater chances and was paid more. He is thought to have received £1,000.

Two bystanders wounded in the Catford shooting, Edward Richardson and Francis Fraser, are in hospital. It is believed that they were on their way home from work (Richardson lives in Kent) and decided to stop off at Mr. Smith's Club for a meal. They sat at a table on a balcony. It seems that suddenly a group of young men started a fight. One acquaintance of Hart said last week: 'The attackers appeared to be a lot of young tearaways who show no fear of anybody.' The indications are, however, that the attack on Hart was not only premeditated but planned by someone who hired the gunmen.

The Blind Beggar incident was a supreme example of skilled murder. Cornell (also known as Myers) had been talking to two strangers at the bar. The narrow swing-doors of the pub opened and the gunman walked slowly in. He sauntered to the end of the bar and calmly fired three shots from a 9 mm. Luger. Two of them pierced Cornell's head, leaving a four-and-a-half inch break in his skull. As Cornell fell dying to the floor, the gunman walked just as slowly from the pub, still holding the gun. He got into a car parked at the pavement outside. The two men who had been with Cornell disappeared. These men have not yet been traced. As usual, police have encountered a lack of eye-witnesses.

While not ruling out the possibility that the murders were the result of a row over protection rackets, which are still a regular source of income for the syndicates, the indications are that bigger projects are involved. Lucrative though fruit machines are, they bring in only a fraction of the money controlled by the syndicates. Fruit machines (or 'one-armed bandits') are a source of friction in London. Many of them are installed in clubs through quite genuine contracts between club owners and fruit machine distributors. Others are installed by a method which forms a barely-veiled protection racket. Generally, the takings are split slightly in favour of the club owner (he gets 60 per cent. and the machine distributor gets 40), but in many cases pressure is sufficiently applied to produce a 50/50 split. In this case, a man with 300 fruit machines in various London clubs can expect a weekly income of £10,000.

One thing is certain, however. The sums of money currently being handled by big crime syndicates in London run into many millions of pounds. With so much at stake, the risk of killing over, say, a couple of hundred fruit machines, is much too big for the relatively small rewards.

There was a time when London gang leaders were not so particular; when the underworld gang wars were waged without the introduction of hired gunmen. Although the syndicates employ men notorious for their viciousness—one operating at the moment is a dangerous psychopath with a long prison record—they still prefer to hire freelance 'tearaways' for certain assignments. The result has been a wave of apparently unrestrained violence in London over the past two years, with police not much closer to the point of tackling the syndicate leaders directly. The pattern of organised crime has undergone revolutionary changes, but police methods have kept in step.

Until the end of the war, gangs, concentrating on the racecourses, were organised on a local basis. But in a few years, the underworld became a national sub-world, rather than a series of almost isolated city groups. Criminals from all over the country found themselves in the same prisons and acquired contacts they maintained after release. The emphasis shifted from racing to all forms of crime—theft, vice, drugs and clubs. Gambling is still an important source of crooked income. The recent relaxation of the gaming laws has led to an enormous business in fruit machines, casinos and gaming clubs all over the country. The protection racket flourishes in this atmosphere of legal gambling just as it has done in the United States.

But with the money coming easily, gang leaders began looking around for somewhere to invest it. The first step was property and today two men who got out of full-time crime a few years ago before the syndicates were formed, now own property worth £250,000 and run their own legal business as well.

The syndicates, however, established links in the United States and on the Continent and with vast sums at their disposal began looking for ways to increase their fortunes. One way was orthodox enough: smuggling and hi-jacking on an international scale. The other way looked even more lucrative—the exploitation of African countries. Many of the business ventures on the African continent sponsored from London are financed partly by money accrued from protection rackets in Britain.

Because of their greater commitments and the need for a veneer of respectability the syndicates moved away from the traditional image of violence while still maintaining valuable contacts in the underworld. To do this they adopted the idea of hiring people for violent jobs and today, unencumbered by loyalties, the freelance gunman flourishes. They appear to be concentrated in South London. Ironically, the business is now so lucrative that a large number of them south of the Thames look like getting together and forming a single organisation.

CAL MCCRYSTAL, in the *Sunday Times*, 13 March 1966

4. Trouble at harvest time

God's Way is like this.

It was harvest time, and the farmer went out to the market square to hire workmen for his vineyard. He settled with them for the proper wage for the day—a pound—and sent them out to work.

About nine o'clock he went out again. Men were hanging about the square with nothing to do.

'You, too, can go and work in the vineyard,' he said, 'and I'll pay you the proper wage.'

Off they went to work.

At noon and at three o'clock in the afternoon he went out to the market square again, and the same thing happened.

About five o'clock he went out again to the square. Men were still hanging about.

'Why are you hanging about all day doing nothing?' he asked.

'Nobody has taken us on,' they said.

'You can go into the vineyard with the others,' he told them.

By now it was evening. The farmer spoke to his foreman.

'Call the workmen in,' he said, 'and pay them their wages. And start with the last ones we took on.'

Those who started work at five o'clock in the afternoon came up and got a full day's wage—a pound.

Then those who had started work at six o'clock in the morning came up; they expected to get more than that. They, too, got a full day's wage—a pound.

They began to go for the farmer.

'These fellows who started last have only done an hour's work!'

'And you are treating them like us!'

'We've had to do all the hard work!'

'And we've had the scorching sun to put up with as well!'

The farmer tackled their leader.

'My dear man,' he said, 'I'm not treating you badly. Didn't you settle with me for a proper day's wage? Take your money and get out. I'm going to give these fellows who started at five o'clock the same wage I'm giving you. Can't I use my own money as I want to? Does my generosity make you jealous?'

ALAN DALE's translation of The Gospel according to St. Matthew, 20:1–15

1. This story is not fundamentally about wages. What is it about? What is your reaction to the picture of 'God's way' which it gives us? How far ought it to be *our* way of treating people? Consider it also in relation to your discussion of the next two passages, 5 (*a*) and (*b*).

2. Despite the 'parabolic' nature of the story, can it be seen as in any sense a Christian prescription for work and wages? If so, what kind of 'economy' do you see based on it? What would be its good points? What would be its bad ones in your view, whether practical or moral?

3. How far is our present wage structure a fair one? What are its weaknesses and strengths?

5. Strikes

These two passages are both about strikes: the first passage is set in France in 1949–52; the second in London in 1967. Try to sort out the fundamental issues at stake in the two passages. What difference is there between them? Are some more important than others? Why? Which do you think justified or did not justify strike action? Again, why?

In the first passage do you think it is significant that a Jesuit priest (who was also a worker) was at the centre of the dispute and negotiations? Ought the Church to get involved in management/labour relations? How?—or why not?

In the second passage *either* Write an imaginary dialogue between the union and British Railways leaders in the course of the negotiations, *or* Write an editorial article as for a serious weekly journal discussing the implications of the strike for management/labour relations.

(a) Priest-worker at the Isère-Arc dam

Isère-Arc. These two words were destined to become famous, not only because of the immense dam completed in 1953 after about six years' work, but also because of the strike that broke out on the worksite soon after Henri's[1] arrival at the end of 1951. 'Le Monde' described the work as follows.

'The construction of the Isère-Arc tunnel and the generating station at Radens is one of the main aspects of the work centred around the upper course of the river Isère. The dam, situated at the egress of the Pont-Seran gorges, creates a little lake some 70 feet deep. The pipeline begins by following the banks of the Isère, flanking the slope first, then underground over a total length of nearly ten miles. The pipeline is of reinforced concrete 20 feet in diameter. The powerhouse, which is entirely underground, is composed of two stations.'

Further information on the work is provided in the preface written by Henri Perrin for the book of photographs published by the C.G.T. (the largest French trades union organization, Communist-dominated) at the time of the completion of the work.

'A dam and a tunnel are not only technical achievements; they are first and foremost a creation of men, a crystallization of the thought, the will, and the efforts of thousands of men. . . . The work was often carried out in exceptionally difficult conditions because of the water and the heat, as well as the inadequacy of the pay at first. The miners had to contend with mountain conditions and all the risks that they entail. And the work underground, which continued night and day, was of a nature to undermine the health of the hardiest. The 'dam-boys' were also up against the nomadic life of huts and canteens, which gradually wears a man out as surely as factory life. . . . The photographs in this book are more than landmarks in a great technical achievement. They are reminders of many human things we do not want to forget. Alas, they are also reminders of the accidents that were the price of our achievement, and they commemorate the thirteen men who paid for the tunnel with their lives.'

The following, from the Journal of the C.G.T., January 1954, is a rough account of the disputes between the management and the workers up to the time of the 42-day strike at the beginning of 1952:

1. Henri Perrin, one of the Jesuit priest-workers in France in the 1950s.

'In 1947 pay was poor, 55 francs an hour, with no extras. Numbers of the workers soon began to agitate, and this led to the foundation of a union group which included Balmain, Allemand, and Franchino. They claimed a 4½ per cent bonus because of geographical situation. In 1948 and 1949, as the work got under way, the workers' "township" was set up—canteens, workshops, dormitories. It was work for coolies; the men were waist deep in water, their tools were of the roughest, and there were no bonuses to speak of. The struggle began for a water bonus. Arguments began with the management and by August, 1949, a strike had broken out, voted unanimously, with pickets out. Better conditions of work were obtained, but the movement only achieved its aims with "the agreement of November, 1949," fixing conditions in general.

The year 1950 passed calmly. The bonuses began to be worth while. Wages averaged between 12– and 15,000 francs per fortnight. In 1951, there started an endless story of "sabotage", and the police were brought in by the management to question the union leaders, which in no way diminished the combativeness of the latter. At the beginning of 1952 a new strike started which lasted 42 days and ended in a victory for the unions.'

A worker who went to Isère-Arc some months after Henri Perrin, wrote as follows:

'The B. worksite at Notre-Dame-de-Briançon was, at the beginning of May, 1952, emerging from a long and severe strike which had lasted 42 days. My first impression was extremely unfavourable. I had never before worked in conditions like these and had never come across a boss with so little respect for the workers and their organization. Never before had I seen union leaders so timid toward the management, nor men working like convicts at the cost of life and health in an atmosphere of humidity, extreme changes in temperature, gas, dust, and mud, to the infernal noise of the pneumatic drills and cement mixers. Never before had I had the experience of leaving work wet through, in winter, and finding nothing in the huts to dry the clothes you had to put on again next morning. And the men who'd been there for several years said: "If you'd been here before our strike you would have found it much worse." Sometimes it is hard to believe that in a country like ours there are still bosses like B. to whom the machinery is more important than the men.'

A collective letter from Henri Perrin to his friends:

'. . . The firm of Borie employs over 400 men at each end of the tunnel. Of all nationalities, they are accommodated in the sort of barracks I know well. Work goes on night and day, including Sundays. I worked last Sunday for the first and last time. My minimum is a 51-hour week for a basic wage of 115 to 125 francs an hour. . . . I've been put in a dormitory with four people. It is over-heated and entirely decorated with Paris-Hollywood nudes. There is a good old Spanish grandfather, a half-caste, and two young fellows from Romans. There are a lot of North Africans here. During these last days I've kept feeling that I must be mad to be doing this. It's true. Before I left, one of my friends told me that at times I hadn't got both my feet on the ground; but, hang it all, who would say that the Church has both feet on the ground when she asks us to do it ! This cheers me up, and in the last three days I've not felt depressed at all.'

'Notre-Dame-de-Briançon,
January 20, 1952

My dear Friends,

We are out on strike. I enclose the text of the appeal which will be forwarded to the press tomorrow. You will think that I'm at the bottom of this ! But you'll be wrong. Until last Friday I didn't think any prolonged opposition would be possible. But now it's happened, and we're up to our necks in it. I found myself elected to the committee, and for the last three days I've been acting as its typist. In addition, of course, I'm a member of the solidarity commission. What is so exciting, and so moving, is the sudden trust that has suddenly come into the eyes of my workmates. As for the committee, I take off my hat to it. It contains a dozen worthwhile militants, and their own conflicts and resentments have been melted by the strike like snow in summer. And there's no question of our being "led by the nose". Anyway, read our declaration. I'll keep in touch with you about it. Pray for us as I do for you. With all my affection.'

Here is the text to which Henri Perrin refers :

'Strike at the Isère-Arc tunnel. It is our duty to explain why over 1,000 workers are prepared to accept hardships and to fight to be treated like men. For months the workers have been trying to obtain a statute which recognizes the work involved in constructing the largest tunnel in Europe. During the last ten days the workers' representatives have been trying to reach a solution. On Friday an unrestricted strike was decided on at Notre-Dame-de-Briançon.

Why is this? Because pay is too low, especially in view of the dangers involved. Because the conditions of work and accommodation, of hygiene and safety are inadequate and unfit for human beings. Because the management fails to fulfil its commitments, or hoodwinks its employees with promises that never materialize.

Who can deny our right to demand human conditions, and especially for the foreigners that France has taken in? Who can deny the right of men to be respected and not reduced to mercenaries or slaves?

As a result of these things, we are claiming a pay increase of 20 per cent, the signing of collective agreements to guarantee our work, and the application of a sliding rule to guarantee the stability of our wage in relation to the cost of living. We are claiming living conditions in which a human being can at least have some rest, since he cannot return to his family at night. We are claiming solid guarantees proportionate to the risks we run in serving the community.

Because we know that our struggle is everyone's struggle, we call on everyone for solidarity. We appeal to everyone to help us in our struggle.'

As the strike continued, Henri Perrin rapidly became to all intents and purposes the committee secretary. It is largely to his pen that we owe the almost daily communiques issued by the committee.

The Isère-Arc strike had wide repercussions beyond the locality, and was widely discussed in France. On February 19, 1952, 'La Croix' said: 'When one reads of these living conditions, one is astonished that the revolt did not occur earlier.' The Bishops of Annecy, Chambery, and Moutiers issued their own special communiqués. The sympathetic response among the local population resulted in hundreds of workers, hitherto regarded as 'foreigners', being absorbed friendlily into the life of the region. In this, as in many other events, we can see the influence of Henri Perrin and a few associates.

On January 28, the thirteenth day of the strike, the committee argued for ten hours with the management in the presence of officials from the Ministry of Works. But the management refused to give way on the principal claims of the workers.

Letter from Henri Perrin to the management of worksite B.

'Sirs. At the conclusion of the fourth week of a dispute that you deplore as much as we do, and in view of the slow pace of negotiations which the strikers, more than anyone, have reason to wish rapidly concluded, I would like to make a summary of the past four weeks of the strike.

The Strike Committee wishes to lodge a bitter complaint regarding the slowness of negotiations. It is intolerable that the first commission of employers should have delayed ten days before hearing us, and the second commission twelve days. This happened at a time when 1,100 families were affected by the strike. We think that many of these points should have been gained without any need for striking.

As regards the "township", no one denies the lack of amenities which has resulted in the present state of things. We have been offered a standard indemnity for our discomforts—600 francs. But we would like to point out that at an earlier stage the management charged 128 francs a day for the hire of a bed in our rooms.

As regards the bonus for output, the workers are unable to forget that it has remained unchanged since 1949, except for an increase of 8 francs last year. Every day it becomes more deflated as compared with wages which, as you yourselves have admitted, have increased during the same period by 70 per cent. And, as you yourselves have admitted, wages are not yet in line with the increased cost of living.

The workers would like to repeat that when they resort to exceptional means, such as a strike, they do so at the price of great sacrifices and with the determination to achieve such substantial changes as will allow them to live a decent life and one with some relationship to the risks they run. At the beginning of the strike you said you always wanted to do the maximum for the workers. In our opinion you now have an opportunity to do so.'

Negotiations which took place from February 22 to 25 led to an agreement in principle. On February 26 the General Assembly of the strikers ratified the work of their representatives and were back on the job the following morning. A communique, drafted by the Strike Committee and Henri Perrin, was sent to the press announcing the end of the dispute.

'. . . The strike has achieved three essential gains. Regarding the reorganization of the "township", the victory has been almost complete. Regarding displacement, a bonus has been obtained for major displacements in the cases where this applies; and regarding the output bonus, a 60 per cent increase has been obtained—with all bonuses indexed to wages. Various other increases have also been won.'

The events leading up to the second strike, which broke out on June 16, 1953, are best described in a collective letter:

May 13, 1953.

'. . . Life goes on at the worksite, but it's slowing down. No large-scale dismissals yet, but the boys are going off in driblets. In view of our worksite's folding up, we have to be more watchful over our union life. Never a day passes without some friction with the boss. Union life is becoming more and more the operative point in the workers' consciousness. More and more one is obliged to listen to, love, and wrestle with one's workmates, and they are grateful and responsive. My life from many points of view is still poor, humble, obscure, and sorrowful. The redemption has to be like that.'

June 10.

'More news. First of all, we had our thirteenth fatal accident on May 27. The responsibility of the management for the lack of safety precautions was flagrant. I felt obliged to say something about it at the graveside—briefly, but it went home.

At the same time I was anticipating an event which soon followed. A list of dismissals appeared on June 2 which included my name. All my mates think, and rightly, that this has been done deliberately, and they're saying, "If you go, we might as well pack up too, because there'd be no more defence for us on the worksite." '

June 14.

'Up to date, things don't seem to be going too well regarding the dismissals. We have only three more cards to play. The first has already been played; the second is that of the conciliation commission; and the third and last is a strike. Provisionally, we have decided on a strike, to begin next Thursday morning.

My morale is fine, all the more so as today we had a splendid meeting with the other priest-workers. Still, these endless days of squabbling are tiring.'

A general strike began on June 16. This second strike was not as long as the 1952 one; it lasted twenty-two days. It was also less complex. Yet it was harder, the management was tougher, and personal feelings ran higher. Its causes couldn't have been more clear and just. This is how they were announced to the people:

'After sixteen months, the workers on worksite B., Isère-Arc, are again embarking on an unrestricted strike. They are forced to do so by the stubborn obstinacy of a boss whose incompetence becomes more manifest every day. They do so only after having forewarned the management, throughout ten days, of their obligation to strike if their rights were not respected.

Their rights? First and foremost these are concerned with respect for the rules and regulations governing dismissals. Collective dismissals have been going on for two months without the authorization of the Inspectorate of Labor, and bypassing its demands.

Their rights? These concern also an increase in basic wages. . . .

Their rights? These concern also small matters of bonuses and grave matters of security to safeguard the lives of the workers. . . .'

An account of the strike was given by Maurice Verdy, in typical Communist language. It should be quoted here:

'Long shall I remember the splendid strike of last June when the management had violated in all hypocrisy the law concerning the Joint Production Committee by illegally dismissing our secretary, Comrade Perrin. In general assembly all the workers voted for an unrestricted strike to defend both the union rights and *the best man among us*—the man whom all the workers loved and respected for his uprightness and sincerity, the man who succeeded in uniting all our workmates. I myself am rather ashamed today, for at first *I used to reproach him with being too soft with the management.*

I can still see our strike pickets and the motorized police with machine guns on their shoulders coming up to us and saying: "You on strike to defend a priest! I can't understand it." And when we explained that the union includes men of all political and religious views, they went off, shrugging their shoulders.'

On Thursday, July 2, on the order of the Prefect of Savoy, the meeting of the conciliation commission took place.

The management did not accept the terms, but a modification of them.

Henri Perrin recounts: '. . . There's to be no revision of basic wages. . . . But the workers dismissed on June 2 are to be re-employed except for two North Africans and . . . me! I won't be taking up my workshop duties any more, but I shall continue with my union activities, and assure the continuation of my job as representative and secretary—if the boss doesn't put spokes in the wheels, which he seems determined to do. This is the text of the motion which has been handed to the boss: "The workers have unanimously decided that the representative and secretary of the Joint Production Board, Perrin, will remain on the worksite and shall by every means continue to carry out the mandate which they have entrusted to him and which is guaranteed by law." There's the working class for you.'

The men went back to work on July 9.

At the end of the strike a collection was made 'to guarantee Perrin's livelihood after he had wrongfully and illegally been dismissed by the firm, and to date has realized 80,000 francs at Notre-Dame-de-Briançon.' Henri was accepted as pay clerk of the social security pay office at Chambery. It enabled him to join even more closely in the life of his workmates and to get a grasp of their personal and family problems.

Henri Perrin considered that he owed the union 40,000 francs for the wages it provided him during this period. He intended to return it as soon as he won the case he had brought up against the management for illegal dismissal. But the firm did not give in so easily. It appealed against the decision.

The firm [was involved in various other cases as well, but it] lost all the cases in which it was involved.

Priest and Worker: the Autobiography of Henri Perrin (tr. BERNARD WALL)

(b) Rail freight strike

RAIL FREIGHT STRIKE COVERS ALL LONDON

The freight liner terminal strike spread yesterday to all London goods depots except Nine Elms. By last night 3,265 men at 18 depots had stopped work. Mr. Leonard Neal, labour relations officer for the railways board, said this meant that goods handling in almost the whole of London was stopped. 'This is in spite of the N.U.R. letter last night advising the branches that this spreading is unofficial and not in conformity with the executive's policy', he said.

The dispute is over a union claim that only railwaymen should be employed at the £1,500,000 freight terminal at Stratford, E. Only the strike there is recognized as official. About 10,000 tons of freight a day is handled in the 18 depots.

Mr. Neal said that he had spoken to Mr. Sidney Greene, general secretary of the N.U.R., and hoped to meet his union's executive to explain the 'writing on the wall'. This was that the loss of traffic caused by the strike could only lead to further unemployment. 'I cannot emphasize too much that a retreat in the direction of the men's proposal is no solution to their problems. I am not trying to threaten or pressurize people but merely reporting that if we lose work it may be we shall have greater problems of unemployment than we contemplated.' The possibility of depots other than Stratford losing work could not be dismissed.

Mr. George Atkinson, a member of the N.U.R. executive, and one of those concerned in the Stratford dispute, said yesterday that the strike could spread to the passenger staff. He claimed that between 8,000 and 10,000 men were involved in strike action.

If railwaymen did not act firmly over the employment of outsiders at the international freight terminal, Stratford, E., 'it will blossom everywhere'. This view was expounded by the Irish checker picketing the gate at another London depot yesterday. He was manning the gates in the name of the unofficial strikers, while his mate patrolled the other entrances by bicycle. 'Strikes do nobody any good, neither the management nor the workers. But we have to do it to stick up for our rights.' The dispute, in which 3,000 goods-handling staff at depots in the London region have come out in sympathy with their colleagues officially on strike at Stratford, reminded him of the Middle East. Theirs was another territorial conflict.

There was very little sign of life at the affected railway depots yesterday. The pickets stood around and the police maintained a discreet presence. Railwaymen outside the new British Railways terminal at Stratford were turning back the odd lorry and van at the gates. The occasional driver drove into the depot. One jumped out of his cab and chased a striker but most accepted the situation. Several vans entered the gates without interruption. These belonged to companies with their own sheds at the terminal. Nine of these had been leased to forwarding agents and only one being operated by British Railways. This raised the fear of redundancy, which started the strike. 'The forwarding agents want to use their own men to load and unload', a driver said. 'Having the right to use private hauliers, they will need only engine drivers, guards and shunters.' It was, they assured me, the thin end of the wedge. The young pickets passionately argued their rights. It was 1 p.m. and time to be relieved after their two-hour stint.

Before they left, one of them said the present strike had come too late. The railwaymen should have dug in on the liner train issue. They should never have given way on the principle of allowing private hauliers to use railway terminals. The anxieties of the railwaymen were not lightened by an advertisement in an east London newspaper seeking men to work for the forwarding agents.

The Times, Thursday 22 June 1967

STRIKE AT RAIL DEPOTS MADE OFFICIAL

The strike of more than 4,000 men at 21 London goods and parcels depots was last night made official by the national executive of the National Union of Railwaymen. Aware that attempts may be made to spread the strike unofficially throughout Britain, Mr. Sidney Greene, general secretary of the union, said last night that the executive had 'reviewed the position to try to contain and control it'. He said the union negotiating committee would meet representatives of the British Railways Board this morning. The union had no intention of extending the strike, although the situation would be reviewed after the meeting with the board. The union had not altered its position over the Continental freight terminal at Stratford, E. It blacklisted the terminal, which opened on Monday, in protest at workers other than railwaymen being employed there. Since then there have been sympathetic stoppages at the other London depots and it is these that have been declared official.

Mr. Greene said there had been a lot of misrepresentation over what the dispute was about. If British Railways built a new station the people working in it should be railwaymen. When a station was closed, it was railwaymen who lost their jobs. They should be entitled to the jobs when new stations were built. 'When you build a new coal mine, you do not ask the coal distributors to go down and hack it out', he said.

The Times, Friday 23 June 1967

RAIL FREIGHT STRIKE SPREADS

Nearly 1,000 more men were out on strike in London yesterday as the rail freight dispute spread to another four goods depots. British Railways said last night that more than 5,000 men were out. Twenty-six depots in the London area were affected. Mr. Leonard Neal, industrial relations member of the British Railways Board, said the dispute was causing a loss of revenue of about £50,000 a day. Usually about 10,000 tons of freight was handled each day at the affected depots.

Talks between the National Union of Railwaymen and the British Railways Board dragged on yesterday until a late hour without sign of a settlement. Mr. Sidney Greene, N.U.R. general secretary, said last night that he was not pessimistic, but no progress had been made on the principle of employing only railwaymen inside the Stratford terminal. 'If we could have that accepted, then we could end the strike,' he said.

After three hours' discussion between Mr. Greene, the union's negotiating committee and Sir Stanley Raymond, chairman of the board, the union side returned to its headquarters to consult the full executive. The British Railways Board said that Sir Stanley had offered to provide employment for all the 35 men surplus at Stratford. He gave an undertaking that the establishment for the terminal would not fall below the existing number.

The Times, Saturday 24 June 1967

BITTER RAILMEN SEE STRATFORD AS STAND AGAINST EXTINCTION

'It looks like a dog kennel on the edge of a housing estate.' This was how a member of the National Union of Railwaymen's executive described the only shed for his members' use when he toured the new £1,500,000 freight terminal at Stratford, London, a few weeks ago. It sums up the bitterness all railwaymen feel: that the streamlining of their industry is to everyone's advantage but their own.

Canute-like, they have decided to make a stand. They insist, not without justice, that if non-railwaymen are allowed to work at Stratford the precedent will be extended to the other 10 freight depots which are planned for the provinces. Less work for fewer railwaymen —the process seems inexorable. In the last five years, railway staff have declined by 150,000, a loss of over 30 per cent. Some 80,000 of these belonged to the N.U.R.

The flashpoint in the Stratford crisis is the employment of outside workers in a British Railways terminal. The forwarding agents, who have leased 90 per cent of it, are determined to use their own men for loading and unloading. The N.U.R. is equally determined they shall not. Railwaymen feel they have given way enough and that no one can accuse them of being unreasonably obstructive. The N.U.R., they argue, has been giving full co-operation in the running down of the railways. In 1962 there were 29 railway workshops; now there are 16. In one area, the work of 175 signal boxes is now done by three. 'Modernisation has happened with our help,' an N.U.R. spokesman said, 'but naturally we scrutinise everything the Railways Board proposes. Last year we told the management we didn't like the plan for employing outside staff at the terminal. The work was traditionally railway work.'

The Stratford plan was the phoenix born out of the fire three years ago at the old Bishopsgate goods depot. The idea was to speed up the import and export of freight. Instead of a jumble of small depots scattered round the East End, there would be one efficient central point, directly linked to Channel ports and offering shippers on-the-spot Customs clearance. Stratford is part of a much more ambitious plan— the Harwich-Zeebrugge container traffic scheme, costing between £8–£9 million, which will be in operation by next year. Goods packed in containers on the Continent will not have to pass Customs till they reach Stratford.

Rubbing their hands at the hoped-for profit this master-plan would bring (and at the change it might make to the current £135 million deficit), British Railways managers played down the growing signs of railwaymen's discontent. Warnings were voiced at every level in the union. Mr. Ted Bowers, the 46-year-old lorry driver at the centre of the Stratford dispute, said last week: 'We warned the management six months ago that they were pushing the men too hard on every front. I told them that sooner or later there would be trouble, but I don't think they took it seriously.'

For over two years, the Eastern Region has been cajoling and persuading N.U.R. officials to accept its plans for Stratford. But with a national background of increasing redundancies on the railways, discontent about pay, and the reluctant acceptance of the liner train principle, the task was extremely difficult. In spite of all the management efforts, the N.U.R. declared Stratford 'black' last February. Negotiations now became somewhat frantic—though they didn't dispel the perhaps rather wishful management feeling that everything would be all right on the day. Their confidence was bolstered when the union gave in on the liner train issue last March and the N.U.R. executive members were each soundly kissed by Mrs. Barbara Castle, 'my happiest moment since becoming Minister of Transport'. All the same, the management was worried enough to send a letter to the staff on May 24 appealing to them to recognise where their own interests lay. 'Many jobs,' it urged in capitals, 'could well be in jeopardy unless common sense prevails. This is a very important matter.'

By the first week in June, the management was confident it had N.U.R. agreement to the opening of Stratford—in return for a 'no redundancy' pledge. The day after this meeting, 16 of the 24 members of the N.U.R. executive visited Stratford at the invitation of Mr. Leonard Neal, the Railways Board industrial relations director. It was on this occasion that the 'dog kennel' remark was made, and shortly afterwards the executive voted unanimously to continue blacking

Stratford—advertised as 'Britain's most modern inland terminal for rail and road traffic'.

By then there were doubts that the 'most modern inland terminal' could keep its promise to open last Monday. All along, the Board has been forced to agree to the forwarding agents' insistence that they should be allowed to use their own men. If the Board had resisted this, it could not have leased the sheds and B.R.'s 1967 baby would have been stillborn. However, the Board wasn't fighting too hard; the more men the agents employed, the less burden on the railways' wages bill. Mr. Peter Kunzler, chairman of the agents' committee, said last week: 'The old system was inadequate. It took up to a week to get goods loaded and dispatched. Because of this, some agents who wanted to increase their business started to recruit their own loaders.' By advertising locally for men to fill new jobs at Stratford, the agents antagonized the N.U.R., and the Stratford men had no difficulty in drumming up the sympathy strikes which now paralyse 26 London goods depots.

It is difficult to see a way out of the deadlock; compromise would be expensive for both sides. Ted Bowers, chairman of the N.U.R.'s joint departmental committee, is tough and cheerful and commands the absolute loyalty of his men. He is also a man who is amenable to argument, and it is with resignation rather than anger that he says: 'This time we're hard up against it.' Bowers's superior on the N.U.R. executive, Mr. George Atkinson, feels the same way. 'We are trying to protect our future,' he says. 'It's not just this incident that we are fighting for. We are fighting what amounts to extinction.'

Somehow, Mr. Leonard Neal will have to reconcile these powerful emotions with the economic arguments of the Board. His past as a trade unionist (until 1955 he was a senior official in the Transport and General Workers' Union) only makes him a tougher negotiator now. He gave no indication last week that he was prepared to compromise. Yet it is clear that he badly underestimated the strength of rank-and-file feeling among the railwaymen. The situation in Stratford is serious enough. Neither side is likely to give way easily. Both sides know that the settlement will mould the pattern for the future.

The Observer, Sunday 25 June 1967

6. The valley of humiliation

The old lady's crumbling house was infested with lice, but she accepted it with broken fatalism: 'It may be bad but God has willed us to live here.' She even thanked us for coming: 'It makes dying a little easier.' Yet all we could do was to visit her regularly and to chat for half an hour. Words—a strange lifeline, but the only one we had to offer.

That we were there at all was due to a Community Service Volunteer who was first established in East Manchester in 1963. He asked the Manchester Grammar School Service Group to help in visiting old people in the twilight areas of the city. At first only the odd sixth-former was involved, then there were more of us, and last year our own project amalgamated with the Lord Mayor's Youth and Community Scheme.

A typical case was Mrs Watson. She lived in a derelict street facing a railway goods yard, a widow and a cripple. She was in her eighties, helpless without her hearing aid, and totally reliant on the weekly visits of her son for food and provisions. Of her neighbours, only two took any interest in her unless she was ill, when people tended to rally round. As a study in the loneliness of the aged there is little extraordinary in Mrs Watson—a fact sad in itself. But the aspect which the three of us who visited her found most horrifying was the failure of the Welfare State. We have only knowledge of a few old ladies, but they are all badly served.

Not that Mrs Watson was a simple character. Born in the early 1880s, she lived in her home community for 40 years. In the 1930s, however, her whole family moved to a more prosperous part of Manchester. The area, she complained, was too noisy, so after the death of her husband, she moved into a flat in South Manchester. But this was too quiet, so 1950 saw her voluntary return to the slums where she had been brought up.

Her house there was owned by a Manchester estate company, to which she paid nearly one third of her old-age pension. She dealt with the agent who called for her rent every Monday. The actual landlord seemed to her to be a mighty and legendary figure. The first time that we visited her, she was guarded and told us little, but she laid great stress on the fact that 'I haven't always lived here, d'you see?' Apart from this point about her home she struck me as a mild, cheerful little woman, not easily broken by anything or anybody.

On the second visit she told us more. She was an invalid and could not go upstairs, but her son told her that her front bedroom was in a dangerous condition. Bad tiling on the roof and the absence of guttering caused the rain to seep in and the plaster to fall off the walls heavily on to the ceiling of the room below. It was far beyond her own means to repair this, and the rent collector could only promise to pass on the message. On going upstairs it was found that the room was worse than she had described; it was deteriorating with every rainfall. 'I don't want to cause anybody any bother, I just wish somebody would plaster it up,' she said.

Third visit. The room was hopelessly waterlogged and we decided that to ask the Service Group to plaster it up could serve no purpose since the same thing was sure to happen again. The room was a health hazard and to make it safe would have cost at least £50. For years, said Mrs Watson, whenever she had spoken to the landlord's representative he had given her the same ready answer. 'You'll have to wait. These houses are to come down shortly.'

Fourth visit. One of us went upstairs to inspect the room, punched the wall, and a brick fell out. The outside wall was sodden and in urgent need of renovation. Mrs Watson had spoken to the rent collector again. Reply as before. Her attitude was changing. 'I don't mind telling, I'm getting fed up.'

Fifth visit. This time I was alone. Mrs Watson greeted me unenthusiastically, looking tired and ill. She was unsteady on her legs, even with her stick. Her eyes were bloodshot and heavy. She sent me upstairs to inspect the bedroom, now in an almost irreparable state, a thick covering of broken plaster over the floor. Afterwards she asked me to sit down and she began to complain about her house. She was finding her two downstairs rooms damp and draughty, and she had difficulty in getting outside to her lavatory. She lay awake waiting for the slightest drop of rain for when it rained she could hear the plaster dropping heavily on to the ceiling above her head. 'I know it's going to come through. It might fall on my bed. And if it does, there's nobody.' She had not slept at all for a fortnight. 'If it goes on much longer, I shall collapse, I know I will.'

The doctor called occasionally, gave her pills for her legs and some ineffective sleeping pills. A year before we started our visits, she had enquired about going to a home. After four months' delay she was informed that her name had been placed at the bottom of the waiting list and that it could well be at least two years—or more—before it became her turn. Mrs Watson, remember, was in her eighties.

Alarmed by her general condition, I wrote to her doctor, asking him to go to see her as soon as possible. I persuaded her to give the Service Group power to lodge an official complaint about her property at the town hall, and this broke her fear of the landlord—too often in these areas a basic and vicious fear, for the rent man is even today no cartoon strip cliché. Only one person in 20 owns his own home; the shelter of the others depends on a mysterious and unseen potentate.

In the case of Mrs Watson, the town hall sent a health official to inspect the property. He decided it was a health hazard and the landlord was instructed to make repairs. A grotesque wrangle ensued of several months' duration, with the corporation going to the full extent of its powers and threatening compulsory purchase. Eventually, the landlord made repairs, but not the extensive renovations necessary. The inspector ruled the condition of the property was still unsatisfactory and the landlord made more token repairs. And so it dragged on.

Meanwhile, the doctor had paid a visit to Mrs Watson and pre-
scribed more sleeping pills. Constant worry over the property brought
her to the verge of collapse. Nine days later, a neighbour noticed three
bottles of milk on her doorstep. She broke in and found her on the floor
where she had been since she had begun to vomit, 36 hours earlier,
powerless to summon help. The neighbour at first took her for dead,
but Mrs Watson showed signs of slight movement. A doctor was
called in and he diagnosed chronic pneumonia. Later that day, when
being moved in her bed (there was no room in the local hospital), she
suffered a heart attack. It was touch-and-go for 48 hours, and for a
further three days Mrs Watson was in a critical condition. She survived and gradually recovered some of her strength, but it was
obvious that unless she was taken into a home as a matter of priority,
she was destined to die in a hospital geriatric ward. When Mrs Watson
left for the home, after help from a sympathetic city welfare officer,
the corporation and her landlord were still at loggerheads, and the
landlord immediately rented the property to someone else.

A further example was Miss Norris. She was a fine little lady of 70,
a diabetic who was gradually going blind and who had no other company than a much-battered tom cat, on which she lavished all she had.
She ate scraps and the cat ate tinned chicken. He was never allowed
to go out for fear of his meeting a premature end, and he filled her
front room with a peculiarly pungent odour; but to all the shortcomings of her only living companion she was entirely impervious.

She was a real person—warm, hospitable, and incredibly cheerful.
We visited her just before Christmas and found her in excellent
spirits. Her only worry was her fire—it was freezing weather, but a
brick was stuck in her chimney and thick smoke filled her front room
when the fire was lit. She had contacted the landlord a week before
and he had promised to send somebody. She was trying to decide
whether to have the sweep in the meantime or to buy a Christmas
chicken for herself and her cat; she could not afford both, and eventually she decided on the chicken. The landlord had again promised to
come tomorrow or the next day, so there was no point wasting money
on something she had a right to, free. We parted.

When we visited her house again soon after Christmas, it was empty
and closed. The landlord had never been. Miss Norris had sat help-
lessly, first in dense smoke, then without a fire through the worst
weather of December. Ten days before Christmas she contracted
bronchial pneumonia and two days later she died. (A workman called
the next day: 'We're very busy at this time of year.') Miss Norris's
cat was destroyed, and two people followed her coffin. When we came
a fortnight later it was as if she had never lived.

It leaves you with a strange feeling, this kind of work. We get angry because we know that it is not our responsibility. But whose responsibility is it? The State's? *Who is the State?* The physical squalor is often terrible, and welfare frighteningly insufficient; yet the degradation of some of these old people goes deeper than welfare. Too many are destitute in every way—remote and hopeless, because we wait until people are old before we start bothering about their condition. Our problem, in the shape of thousands of old people, is not even simply going to die out—whole generations, their children and grandchildren, have already grown up in the slums of Manchester. What about them?

DAVID LAWTON in the *Guardian*, 7 April 1966

1. 'We get angry because it is not our responsibility.' (*a*) But whose responsibility is it? The State's? (*b*) Who is the State? (*c*) Who else has a responsibility? How do you think they could be made to fulfil it?

2. (*a*) What are the philosophical/moral/theological grounds of the writer's criticism of the Welfare State and the landlords? What view of man and human relationships does it presuppose? (*b*) Do you agree with his outlook? If not, state your own view. (*c*) Why *should* we, or anyone else, help these old people anyway?

3. (*a*) The problem of Mrs Watson and Miss Norris is 'the problem of old age'. What action(s) do you feel should be taken by the country to solve it? (*b*) What about those who have already grown up in the slums of your city? (See the last sentence of the passage.)

4. The writer belonged to a school service group. (*a*) Do you think this is a good idea? (*b*) Does the article suggest to you that such a group is not of much use or that the need for it is all the greater? (*c*) What would you do yourself, in your present position, faced with the problem of Mrs Watson and Miss Norris?

7. What is the meaning of this city?

The Word of the Lord came unto me, saying:
O miserable cities of designing men,
O wretched generation of enlightened men,
Betrayed in the mazes of your ingenuities,
Sold by the proceeds of your proper inventions:
I have given you hands which you turn from worship,
I have given you speech, for endless palaver,
I have given you my Law, and you set up commissions,
I have given you lips, to express friendly sentiments,
I have given you hearts, for reciprocal distrust.
I have given you power of choice, and you only alternate
Between futile speculation and unconsidered action.
Many are engaged in writing books and printing them,
Many desire to see their names in print,
Many read nothing but the race reports.
Much is your reading, but not the Word of GOD,

Much is your building, but not the House of GOD.
Will you build me a house of plaster, with corrugated roofing,
To be filled with a litter of Sunday newspapers?

1st male voice

A Cry from the East:
What shall be done to the shore of smoky ships?
Will you leave my people forgetful and forgotten
To idleness, labour, and delirious stupor?
There shall be left the broken chimney,
The peeled hull, a pile of rusty iron,
In a street of scattered brick where the goat climbs,
Where My Word is unspoken.

2nd male voice

A Cry from the North, from the West, and from the South
Whence thousands travel daily to the timekept City;
Where My Word is unspoken,
In the land of lobelias and tennis flannels
The rabbit shall burrow and the thorn revisit,
The nettle shall flourish on the gravel court,
And the wind shall say: 'Here were decent godless people:
Their only monument the asphalt road
And a thousand lost golf balls'.

Chorus

We build in vain unless the LORD build with us.
Can you keep the City that the LORD keeps not with you?
A thousand policemen directing the traffic
Cannot tell you why you come or where you go.
A colony of cavies or a horde of active marmots
Build better than they that build without the LORD.
Shall we lift up our feet among perpetual ruins?
I have loved the beauty of Thy House, the peace of Thy sanctuary,
I have swept the floors and garnished the altars.
Where there is no temple there shall be no homes,
Though you have shelters and institutions,
Precarious lodgings while the rent is paid,
Subsiding basements where the rat breeds
Or sanitary dwellings with numbered doors
Or a house a little better than your neighbour's;
When the Stranger says: 'What is the meaning of this city?
Do you huddle close together because you love each other?'

What will you answer? 'We all dwell together
To make money from each other'? or 'This is a community'?
And the Stranger will depart and return to the desert.
O my soul, be prepared for the coming of the Stranger,
Be prepared for him who knows how to ask questions.

O weariness of men who turn from GOD
To the grandeur of your mind and the glory of your action,
To arts and inventions and daring enterprises,
To schemes of human greatness thoroughly discredited,
Binding the earth and the water to your service,
Exploiting the seas and developing the mountains,
Dividing the stars into common and preferred,
Engaged in devising the perfect refrigerator,
Engaged in working out a rational morality,
Engaged in printing as many books as possible,
Plotting of happiness and flinging empty bottles,
Turning from your vacancy to fevered enthusiasm
For nation or race or what you call humanity;
Though you forget the way to the Temple,
There is one who remembers the way to your door:
Life you may evade, but Death you shall not.
You shall not deny the Stranger.

T. S. ELIOT, Chorus III from The Rock

1. Describe in your own words: (a) The character of Western urban society as the poet sees it. (b) The message the poet is giving to this society.

2. (a) Do you think the poet is fair to our society? What would you claim should be said 'on the other side' to redress the pessimism of this passage? (b) Do you think that what you have adduced under 2 (a) takes away the point and force of the 'judgement' in 1 (b) above? (c) Do you agree, in any case, with this 'judgement'? Give the reasons for your answer.

3. (a) When the Stranger says: 'What is the meaning of this city?', 'what will you answer?' (b) When the Stranger says: 'Do you huddle close together because you love each other?', 'what will you answer?'

4. (a) What do you understand by the term 'a community'? (b) Is your own city a 'community'? (c) If you do not believe it is, what do you think needs to be done to make it one?

5. Who is 'the Stranger'?

6. (a) What is meant by 'Life you may evade, but Death you shall not'? (b) Do you believe that what the line is trying to say is true? Give arguments and/or examples to support your answer.

Personal encounters

8. Parents: are they human?

Over 500 schools participated in this 'Sixth Form Opinion Poll', representing the opinions of some 16,000 sixth-formers, which is a completely sound statistical sample (indeed, excessively so). The proportions of boarding schools to day, boys to girls and so on, have been accounted for. As well as public schools and grammar schools, we have had replies from technical, convent, 'experimental' and 8-stream comprehensive schools. All individual answers were given anonymously.

Noticeable in preparing the poll's findings for publication has been the abstention of some schools and individuals from certain questions —usually because they were 'too personal'. In no case have such phenomena been widespread or consistent enough to affect the validity of the results.

All figures quoted are percentages.

1. Do you think you are, on the whole, treated as a person of your age should be by your

(a) father?

	BOYS	GIRLS
Ayes	76·8	71·1
Noes	16·8	23·8
Don't know	6·4	5·1

(b) mother?

	BOYS	GIRLS
Ayes	68·9	81·8
Noes	23·5	16·4
Don't know	7·6	1·8

2. Do your parents ban

(a) smoking?

	BOYS	GIRLS
Ayes	24·8	32·8
Noes	75·2	67·7

(b) drinking?

	BOYS	GIRLS
Ayes	25·4	22·0
Noes	74·6	77·0

3. Do you *have* to go to church, chapel, synagogue, etc. (i.e. more than you would otherwise go)?

	BOYS	GIRLS
Ayes	9·2	4·6
Noes	90·8	95·4

4. Until what hour are you normally allowed out?

	BOYS	GIRLS
Before 10 p.m.	1·3	1·6
10 p.m.	3·0	5·9

	BOYS	GIRLS
10.30 p.m.	9·9	18·1
11 p.m.	18·0	24·2
11.30 p.m.	9·4	8·5
12 p.m.	7·5	4·1
No restrictions	46·5	33·2
Don't know or varies	4·4	4·4

The greater strictness in Northern Ireland and Scotland in this and the two preceding questions was most marked.

5. Do you have to ask permission to go out at night?

	BOYS	GIRLS
Ayes	25·9	52·4
Noes	71·5	46·9
Don't know or depends	2·6	0·7

6. Are you pumped (however nicely) on your activities?

	BOYS	GIRLS
Ayes	63·4	64·2
Noes	36·6	35·8

7. (If yes) do you really mind being pumped?

	BOYS	GIRLS
Very much	22·1	13·2
Mildly	47·2	47·5
No	30·7	39·3

8. Do you think you are nagged by
   (a) your father?   (b) your mother?

	BOYS	GIRLS			BOYS	GIRLS
Ayes	19·1	21·5	Ayes		51·2	48·2
Noes	80·9	78·5	Noes		48·8	51·8

   (c) both?

	BOYS	GIRLS
Ayes	17·2	16·8
Noes	82·8	83·2

9. Do you possess your own house-key?

	BOYS	GIRLS
Ayes	58·8	58·2
Noes	41·2	41·8

10. Are you allowed to use the family car?

	BOYS	GIRLS
Ayes	26·8	28·9
Noes	28·9	32·6
No car or no licence	44·3	38·5

11. Do you, on the whole, share your parents' views on
    (a) Religion?

		BOYS	GIRLS
Father:	Ayes	51·9	56·2
	Noes	37·5	38·6
	Don't know	10·6	5·2
Mother:	Ayes	57·0	65·8
	Noes	37·8	38·6
	Don't know	5·2	2·8

(b) Politics?

Father:	Ayes	52·0	56·8
	Noes	38·0	34·9
	Don't know	10·0	8·3
Mother:	Ayes	49·4	60·5
	Noes	43·4	32·7
	Don't know	7·2	6·8

(c) Sex?

Father:	Ayes	45·8	47·2
	Noes	42·1	38·9
	Don't know	12·1	13·9
Mother:	Ayes	41·1	64·6
	Noes	47·8	31·6
	Don't know	11·1	3·8

(d) Aesthetics?

Father:	Ayes	32·1	38·0
	Noes	58·0	54·2
	Don't know	9·9	7·8
Mother:	Ayes	39·2	51·6
	Noes	54·4	43·7
	Don't know	6·4	4·7

(e) Your career?

Father:	Ayes	68·8	71·4
	Noes	24·0	21·6
	Don't know or undecided about career	7·2	7·0
Mother:	Ayes	72·0	76·9
	Noes	22·6	19·2
	Don't know or undecided about career	5·4	3·9

12. Do you have a regular allowance from your parents?

(a) Those with part-time jobs:

	BOYS	GIRLS
Ayes	63·1	62·1
Noes	36·9	37·9

(b) Others:

	BOYS	GIRLS
Ayes	79·1	76·8
Noes	20·9	23·2

13. After deducting *essential* clothes, fares, meals, etc., from allowance, about how much is left as 'pocket money' weekly?

	BOYS	GIRLS		BOYS	GIRLS
5s. and under	21·6	39·7	to 30s.	1·9	0·5
to 10s.	45·6	46·3	to 35s.	0·5	0·5
to 15s.	16·5	9·3	to £2	0·9	0·5
to £1	9·5	3·1	over £2	0·6	0·5
to 25s.	2·9	1·1			

14. Have you got a room of your own?

	BOYS	GIRLS
Ayes	83·2	83·4
Noes	16·8	16·6

15. Do your parents confide in you?

Father:

	BOYS	GIRLS
Ayes	54·0	34·0
Noes	41·4	59·5
Don't know	4·6	6·5

Mother:

	BOYS	GIRLS
Ayes	70·0	77·9
Noes	25·9	19·8
Don't know	4·1	2·3

16. Did either tell you about sex?

	BOYS	GIRLS
(a) In a formal talk	16·0	20·5
(b) Ad hoc in answer to questions?	21·7	46·2
(c) Not at all?	53·3	30·3

17. Do they ever punish you?

	BOYS	GIRLS
Ayes	28·9	37·6
Noes	71·1	62·4

18. To whom would you prefer to go with a personal worry?

	BOYS	GIRLS		BOYS	GIRLS
Father	17·1	3·5	Keep it to yourself	24·9	34·4
Mother	30·7	31·2			

	BOYS	GIRLS		BOYS	GIRLS
Person of			Person of		
about own age	22·1	27·4	about parents'		
			age or older	3·4	3·2
Write to a					
magazine	0·8	0·3			

19. Do you think you will, on the whole, bring your children up the way you have been brought up?

	BOYS	GIRLS
Ayes	62·3	65·3
Noes	29·7	29·8
Don't want any	8·0	4·9

20. Do you still go on family holidays?

	BOYS	GIRLS
Ayes	51·2	59·4
Noes	48·8	40·6

If 'yes', do you still enjoy them?

	BOYS	GIRLS
Very much	42·8	44·9
Mildly	48·7	43·2
No	4·4	8·9
Hate	4·1	3·0

21. Are you allowed to holiday with a group of boys *and* girls of your own age?

	BOYS	GIRLS
Ayes	76·4	72·0
Noes	16·3	22·3
Don't know	7·3	5·7

If 'yes', do you think either parent worries?

	BOYS	GIRLS
Ayes	53·8	61·4
Noes	46·2	38·6

22. Does either parent try to direct your choice of friends?

	BOYS	GIRLS
Ayes	35·4	34·8
Noes	64·6	65·2

23. Do you freely invite people home?

	BOYS	GIRLS
Ayes	73·5	80·6
Noes	26·5	19·4

Consider the proportion who don't and read on.
  If no,

	BOYS	GIRLS
For lack of parental encouragement?	29·7	34·8
Apprehensive about parental reactions?	41·8	38·1
Apprehensive about friends' reactions?	28·5	27·1

24. (a) Did your parents want very much to get you into your present type of school?

	BOYS	GIRLS
Ayes	88·9	84·6
Noes	11·1	15·4

(b) Do they tend to look down on other types of school?

	BOYS	GIRLS
Ayes	26·8	21·9
Noes	73·2	78·1

Do you?

	BOYS	GIRLS
Ayes	26·8	21·9
Noes	73·2	78·1

25. Would you leave school now if your parents would let you?

	BOYS	GIRLS
Ayes	9·8	10·9
Noes	85·2	86·0
Undecided	5·0	3·1

If 'yes', do you feel strongly about it?

	BOYS	GIRLS
Ayes	51·4	42·2
Noes	48·6	57·6

26. Do your parents

	BOYS	GIRLS
(a) over-estimate your potential?	30·1	28·3
(b) underestimate it?	12·9	9·1
(c) know you pretty well?	57·0	57·0

27. What sort of a job, taking them together, are they making of parenthood? (Giving them marks.) (See diagram below. Those who

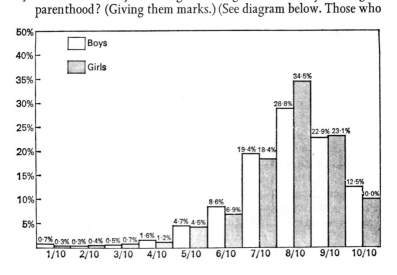

gave 0/10 have been counted with those who gave 1/10 as we
regard the effort to produce a child as meriting at least one mark.)
GERALD JONES and JOHN PENYCATE in *Sixth Form Opinion*,
No. 4, 20 June 1962

1. The tables given above are presented without comment. Discuss (*a*) the
questions: Are they tendentious or misleading? Have any important questions
on sixth former/parent relationships been left out? What are your own
answers to these and to those given in the questionnaire? (*b*) the answers:
Which figures do you find significant, and why? What general conclusions do
you draw from this poll?
2. What do you think are the main problems (*a*) for parents and (*b*) for their
children which militate against the establishment of successful family relationships? How do you think each party can help to overcome them?

9. Nicky's story

'I was mostly in the streets because my parents had customers coming
where we lived. They were spiritualists, my parents, they would talk
with the dead and cure sickness, and they would also give advice
about money and family problems. . . .

'There was only one room at home, so us kids were in the street. At
first the other kids beat me up and I was afraid all the time. Then I
learned how to fight and they were scared of me and they left me
alone. After a while I got so I liked it better in the street than I did at
home. At home I was the youngest one. I was nothing. But in the
street they knew who I was.

'My family moved a lot and mostly it was on account of me. If there
was any trouble the police would come around asking questions and
then the superintendent wherever we lived would go to my parents
and say we had to move.

'I didn't know why I acted like I did. There was a thing inside me
that scared me. It worried me all the time but I couldn't stop it. It
was this feeling I got if I saw a cripple. It was a feeling like I wanted to
kill him. If someone had crutches I would kick them or if an old man
had a beard I would try to pull it out and I would rough up little kids.
And all the while I would be scared and wanting to cry, but the thing
inside me was laughing and laughing. The other thing was blood. The
minute I saw blood I would begin to laugh and I couldn't stop it.

'When we moved into the Fort Greene Projects, I went in with the
Mau Maus. They wanted me to be President. But in a rumble the
President has to give orders and I wanted to fight. So they made me
Vice-President. I was also Sergeant-at-Arms. That meant I was in
charge of the arsenal. We had garrison belts and bayonets and switchblades and zip guns. I liked to go in and just look at these things. But
for rumbling I liked a baseball bat. I'd cut a hole in a garbage can to
see out, then I'd put it over my head and swing the bat.

'I also learned how to stick with a knife, which is when you cut someone but don't kill him. I stuck sixteen people, and I was in jail twelve times. Some of these times my picture was in the paper. When I walked down the street everybody knew me and the mothers would call their little kids.

'The gangs knew me too. One day when I was waiting for a subway five guys came up behind me. They got a leather belt round my neck and kept twisting it. I didn't die, but I used to wish I had because after that I could never talk right. There was a funny noise in my throat. I had this hate of people who had anything wrong with them, and now it was me. I had to bop all the time, after that, to keep respect.

'Our gang controlled the turf as far as Coney Island and Ralph Avenue. We had red jackets with MM on them and we wore continental heels, which are good in a fight. One day we were in a candy store on Flatbush Avenue. There were six of us, drinking soda, when seven Bishops walked in. The Bishop gang was at war with the Mau Maus.

'One of the Bishops went up to the candy counter like he owned it. My boys were watching me. I walked over and I shoved him. He shoved back and then everyone was fighting. The owner's wife started screaming. All the other customers ran out on the side-walk. There was a butcher knife on the counter. One of my boys picked it up and cut a Bishop five times through the scalp. I saw the blood and I started to laugh. I knew he was dead and I was scared but I couldn't stop laughing. The owner's wife was telephoning the police. Another one of my boys picked up that butcher's knife and hit her right in the stomach. Then we ran.

'I never touched the knife so I didn't go to jail. But my parents had to go to the court and I guess it was the first time they looked at me. They got scared when they saw what I was. They decided to get out of New York and go back to Puerto Rico. My brother and I went to the airport to say good-bye to them. On the way back from the airport in his car he gave me a ·32 pistol. He said, "You're on your own, Nick."

'The first thing I had to do was find a place to sleep. I held up a guy with the gun and got ten dollars. I rented a room on Myrtle Avenue. I was sixteen then. That's how I lived after that, holding up guys for money or something to hock. During the day it was all right. I was with the gang. Whatever the President and I told them to do they would do. But at night, when I had to go into that room, it was terrible. I would think about the two dead people in the candy store. I would bang my head on the floor to stop thinking about them. I started waking up in the night, crying for my mother.'

DAVID WILKERSON, *The Cross and the Switchblade*

1. State frankly your reaction to Nicky as a person.

2. Does an understanding of his background and home circumstances (or lack of them) make any difference to your attitude? In what way?

3. Suppose you have a concern for Nicky and his fellow-gangsters, and want to see them off the streets, away from 'rumbles', and usefully employed, how would you set about it? Suppose, further, that you succeeded, what sort of job do you think Nicky might usefully do, and why? (See no. 71 for what some-one actually did for Nicky.)

4. Nicky lives in New York. He and the Mau Maus might live in, say, Manchester or Glasgow. What responsibility does our society have for Nicky and his fellow-gangsters? What actual steps (social, legal, educational, etc.) do you think should be taken to discharge that responsibility?

10–12

In the three following passages a variety of attitudes to personal relationships are expressed. Social, moral, emotional, and theological issues are raised in considering how we should behave towards the opposite sex. Here are a number of questions which are explicitly or implicitly posed by the various writers, and they should provide a useful starting point for discussing the passages. Other questions will arise as you study them further, and as you try to work out your own decisions about love, sex, friendship, and marriage.

1. What is real love? Is it the same as being 'in love'; if not, how does it differ from it? Is it different from 'lust'?

2. Can sexual relations properly be separated from 'personal' relations? What responsibilities have we in our sexual activity—to ourselves? and to others? Are there any differences between 'fornication', 'promiscuity', 'going to bed with' your boy friend/girl friend?

3. What is marriage? In what ways is it different from 'being engaged' or being friends with someone? What responsibilities have we to our *prospective* wife/husband?

4. What are the grounds on which you make decisions about the way you treat your boy friend/girl friend or casual acquaintances in matters of sex? Do you do what 'everyone else' does or what your emotions or instincts prompt you to? Is any of these a good basis for your actions? What place, if any, have your religious or non-religious beliefs in determining how you act?

5. What is the place of a moral code in matters of sex? How are ideals related to the actual situations and problems of individual people? What place has the law in regulating personal relations? What should be the connection between moral and legal rules? What is the difference between upholding moral 'standards' and 'judging' other people? Is it important?

10. What are we to do?

Characters: ROSE PEMBERTON—'A girl of about twenty, with . . . a face which depends for its prettiness on youth.'

FATHER JAMES BROWNE: Rose's uncle, 'a man of about 65', an invalid in a wheel chair for 20 years.

MICHAEL DENNIS—'a man in the middle forties', married to an hysterical wife.

(*Rose enters, and looks from one to the other*)

Rose. What's happened? What's it all about? You, both of you. . . .

James. He wants you to pack your bag.

Rose. (*to Michael*) You mean—go away? They know all about us? Do you want me to go away now, today? (*She speaks with excitement and no apprehension.*)
  (*Michael watches her with growing uneasiness. She is too young and unprepared.*)
How lucky I never unpacked the trunk. I can be ready in a few minutes. (*She turns to her uncle with sudden remorse.*) Oh, Uncle, you must think we are very wicked.

James. No. Just ignorant. And innocent.

Rose. (*with pride*) Not innocent. . . . I know it's wrong, but I don't care. Uncle we're going to be happy.

James. Is he?
  (*Rose looks quickly at Michael. He doesn't look a happy man*)

Rose. Darling, is anything the matter?

Michael. My wife knows.

Rose. (*with the glibness and unfeelingness of youth*) It had to happen sooner or later. Was she very angry?

Michael. Not exactly angry.

Rose. You've had an awful time.

Michael. Other people are having an awful time.

Rose. Yes, of course. It's terribly sad, but we'll be all right. You'll see. And people get over everything.

Michael. She cried a great deal. I left her crying.

James. Please open the door. I feel like an accomplice.

Rose. I'm sorry, Uncle. (*She opens the door for his chair to pass.*)

James. Come and see me when you've done.

Rose. You don't think I'd go away without saying goodbye? (*Turning to Michael after shutting the door*) Darling, tell me what you had planned.

Michael. My plans haven't been a success. My wife won't divorce me. We may never be able to marry.

Rose. (*with momentary disappointment*) Oh ! (*She sweeps her disappointment aside.*) It doesn't really matter, does it? It wouldn't have been a real marriage, anyway. And—somebody may die.

Michael. You're a Catholic. I never knew any Catholics before— except your mother.

Rose. Perhaps I'm only half one. Father wasn't.

Michael. You never knew him, did you?

Rose. No. But I've seen lots of photographs. He had a nose rather like yours.

Michael. (with bitterness) I never noticed that.

Rose. Shall I pack now?
> (*She begins to get her things together in a small suitcase*
> *as the dialogue continues.*)

Michael. You don't mind—about the Church?

Rose. (*lightly*) Oh, I expect it will come all right in the end. I shall make a deathbed confession and die in the odour of sanctity.

Michael. Our children will be illegitimate.

Rose. Bastards are the best, so Shakespeare says. . . .

Michael. Your aunts won't let you come back here.

Rose. Do you think I care? Darling, I can't bear this house. It gives me the creeps. . . . You aren't angry about something, are you? I'll do anything you say. Just tell me where to go, and I'll go. Like Ruth. 'Your people shall be my people.' I suppose your people are all psychologists.

Michael. Not all.

Rose. I've read Freud in Penguin. 'The Psychology of everyday life'.

Michael. You have, have you?

Rose. Darling, something's fretting you. You haven't fallen in love with another woman?

Michael. No. I finished all that with you.

Rose. I shall never be sure of that. You didn't waste much time with me.

Michael. I haven't much time to waste.

Rose. You are worrying, just like yesterday. What *is* the matter?

Michael. Only a damned sense of responsibility. Listen, Rose, this is serious. Have you really thought . . .?

Rose. I don't *want* to think. You *know* about things, I don't. Darling, I've never been in love before. You have.

Michael. Have I?

Rose. Your wife.

Michael. Oh, yes.

Rose. You know the way around. Tell me what to do. I'll do it. I've packed my bag, but I'll unpack it if you want it a different way. I'll do anything, darling, that's easier for you. Tell me to come to Regal Court, now, this minute, and I'll come.

Michael. Regal Court?

Rose. It's where people go to make love. So everybody says. I'll go there and come back here. I'll meet you there every day. Or I'll take my bag and go away with you—for years.

Michael. Only years?

Rose. Just say what you want. I'm awfully obedient.

Michael. Dear, it's not only you and me . . . you have to think.

Rose. Don't make me think. I warned you not to make me think. I don't know about things. They'll all get at me if they have a chance. They'll say, 'Did you ever consider this? Did you ever consider that?' Please don't do that to me too—not yet. Just tell me what to do.

Michael. You're very dear to me.

Rose. Of course. I know.

Michael. I don't want you to make a mistake.

Rose. A mistake wouldn't matter so much. There's plenty of time. . . .

Michael. 'You're not a cruel man' your uncle said to me. I don't know much about the young. I've caused a lot of trouble in the last few weeks, breaking in. . . .

Rose. And haven't I? Dear, don't worry so. Worries bring worries, my nurse used to say. Let's both give up thinking for a month, and then it will be too late.

Michael. I wish I could.

Rose. But you can.

Michael. You can live in the moment because the past is so small and the future so vast. I've got a small future, I can easily imagine— even your uncle can imagine it for me. And the past is a very long time and full of things to remember.

Rose. You weren't so horribly wise yesterday.

Michael. Put up with my 'wisdom'.

Rose. Of course, if I have to. (*Shutting her case.*) Shall we go?

Michael. I have to go home first—and say goodbye.

Rose. That's hard for you.

Michael. (*harshly*) Don't waste your sympathy on me. After all these years she had the right to feel secure.

Rose. I'm sorry.

Michael. Oh, it's not you I'm angry with. I'm angry with all the world who think one doesn't care. . . .

Rose. You won't let her talk you round, will you?

Michael. No.

Rose. She's had you so long. She'll have the right words to use. I only know the wrong ones.

Michael. You don't need words. You're young. And the young always
   win in the end. (*He draws her to him*.)

Rose. Where shall we meet?

Michael. Lancaster Gate Station, in an hour.

Rose. (*She is worried by his reserve*.) You do still want me?

Michael. Yes.

Rose. I mean like yesterday?

Michael. I still want you in just the same way.

Rose. I wasn't much good, but I'm learning awfully fast.

Michael. You've nothing to fear. (*He kisses her*.) You've got the whole
   future.

Rose. I only want one as long as yours.

Michael. (*going*) In an hour.

Rose. Goodbye, my heart!

GRAHAM GREENE, The Living Room, Act I scene ii

11. Alfie's aphorisms

I am the same as any other man where women are concerned, I'm
only interested in the pleasure. When it comes to the pain I just don't
want to know. You can't blame me—you can only blame human
nature.

I must say like any other normal man, I love a woman you can take
out and show off. It's half the pleasure. I mean it don't half make these
other geezers envy you.

I don't know any feeling much nicer than you're saying goodbye to
one bird to go off to meet another. Whoever said a change was as good
as a rest must have had birds in mind. It sort of re-charges all your
batteries.

The mistake I made with Gilda was getting involved. Never get yourself involved with a bird beyond what you do together. Let her little
life when you're not with her be all her own. Then you always come
fresh to one another. Chat her up, of course, and listen to her—but in
one ear and out the other, if you see what I mean. I was having a
beautiful little life and couldn't see it. Has it ever struck you that you
only see what pleasure you had in something when they take it away?
I was living a full carefree life.
   There was this little fat young bird from the Dial.
   I'd this chiropodist woman, Daphne, whom I could slip in of a

Saturday afternoon. . . . Then on Sunday afternoons dancing at the Locarno I'd usually pull in a bird to go out with that same night. . . . And yet with all this marvellous life going on I have to get myself involved with Gilda.

I begin to wonder is this love lark really worth it. I mean, when I look back on my little life, and I think of the birds I've known, and of all each of those little birds has done for me, and of how little I've ever done for them—yet they couldn't have cost me more or took more out of me if I'd given them everything I had. That's the rub.

BILL NAUGHTON, *Alfie*

12. The new family of man

(*a*) First I would like to state briefly my view that the family of our own day is a great moral improvement upon the family-types of the past. Taking into account all the social changes which have altered the family-types of Victorian Britain, we can say that, by contrast, the modern British family tends to be:

1. Of long duration, since it is founded at an early age;
2. Small in size, as a consequence of birth control;
3. Separately housed in an improved material environment;
4. Economically self-providing, and therefore independent of aid from wider kindred;
5. Founded and maintained by partners of equal status, enjoying a marital relationship based increasingly upon mutuality of consideration;
6. Democratically managed, in that husband, wife, and children are all taken into account in arriving at family decisions;
7. Centrally and very responsibly concerned with the care and upbringing of children, and, finally;
8. Aided in achieving health and stability by a wide range of public provisions both statutory and voluntary.

Now, if these characteristics of the family in contemporary Britain and all that they entail are considered fully it is clear beyond doubt that they represent a considerable improvement upon family types of the past. . . . The modern family is the type of family appropriate to the conditions of a complex industrial society. . . . I believe that the great majority of British families are of the kind I have described, and that they do in fact cope successfully with all the internal and external demands made up on them: successfully, in the way in which families do—with much conflict, difficulty, irritation, with much which is not only trying but positively exasperating, but with firm loyalties, with ties which go deeper than is often known and acknowledged, with abiding attachments, with much happiness, and engendering a core of character which is a strength in all their members.

Some families, however, do not. . . . Is it really difficult to understand why some marriages break down and why some families are problematical and badly managed? Surely the chief reason is that marriage is tough—the most exacting, demanding, difficult—though, if it succeeds, the most richly rewarding—of all the relationships we have to work out.

The other reason is (apart from making mistakes—and it is not that some make mistakes and others do not; we all make mistakes, the question is how big they are and how we shape up to them) that some people do not possess the personal qualities required. They haven't got what it takes. Good relationships are harder to maintain than bad ones.

The other point I wish to emphasise is : *how new this type of family is in the history of man. Never before* have men, women and children both within and beyond the family enjoyed such personal freedom, equality of status, and mutuality of consideration within the context of helpful provisions of sympathetic government. In our own society, this is not more than 35 years old; and, of course, *much* more has still to be done in this direction. But all this is so new that even our parents did not enjoy it, and we ourselves are not acclimatised to it.

Now there are a few points upon which I wish to lay strong emphasis in considering the forward-looking task of consolidating and improving our situation, and in justifying my large title: The New Family —not of Britain only—but of Man.

(1) Firstly, in our concern to remedy unhappiness, I think we are in danger of focussing our attention too narrowly upon the family. . . .

The family is not self-contained. Though a group within which our deepest satisfactions are found, the family is also, for the child, an introduction to life in the wider society, and, for the adult, a basis for life within the wider society. Family relationships may positively suffer from too inward-looking, too self-contained, too enclosed an attitude to the family, and in this context I believe there is a positive danger in emphasising sex, love, and romanticism in general, to the exclusion of other qualities and activities. There are—if it does not sound too simple-minded—other things in life. Sex and love are pretty good— but we cannot be forever folded in one another's arms. And a perpetual embrace is in danger of becoming a stranglehold.

There is another aspect of this which is important. If we examine the matter fully, it becomes clear that there is no such thing as the ethics of sex and family education at all. The ethical principles in the light of which we should regulate our sexual and family relationships are the same as those on which we should base *all* our conduct in *all* human relationships. They are, for example, that we should always:

1. Try to increase happiness and diminish pain;
2. Treat other individuals as persons, as ends in themselves, and never only as a means to some end of our own;
3. Behave towards others as we think it right that they should behave towards us;
4. Seek to attain the highest level of excellence of which we are capable in any task to which we commit ourselves, and;
5. To seek to secure, in society, those human rights which these principles entail, and which *require* to be secured for their fulfilment.

And it is this mention of society which matters. If we are concerned to improve the family and marriage in society, we cannot do this by concentrating on the family alone, but only by concerning ourselves with the attainment of social justice and the improvement of human relationships throughout the whole of our society; in factories, schools, government and all other institutions. Consequently, it is not education for sexual and family relationships which we want, it is education in the widest sense for responsible citizenship, within which sexual and family relationships will have their proper, but not an all-embracing, place.

(2) My second point is that—in clarifying the best nature of marriage and family life in accordance with the ethical principles we have stated—we still have revolutionary ideas to face. . . . One is with regard to sexual morals. The idea that marriage is the only relationship within which sexual intimacy is morally justifiable must go. It is not tenable. I do not want to enter into all the ethical questions relating to pre-marital or extra-marital sex, but only to show that the conception of marriage as a legitimation of sex, is itself immoral.

Now that sex is dispossessed of sinfulness and is regarded as a natural and enjoyable impulse and experience, and now that contraceptive techniques make possible the experience of sexual intimacy without reference to procreation, sexual intimacy and marriage are no longer going to be thought synonymous. Furthermore, if sexual intimacy is entered into with responsibility and mutual consideration (and let us note that our ethical principles clearly condemn inconsiderate promiscuity) then there is no reason why this should not be so. It is true that sex is one of the important bases of a happy marriage, and, consequently, of a happy family life—but *this is just why* people should be as clear in mind and experience about it as possible before they commit themselves to the serious status and duties of marriage, entailing, centrally, the having and rearing of children. Also, though important, sex is far from being the only important thing in marriage. Married love includes sex, but it is certainly not to be equated with sex, and it is much more than romanticised sex. It is of the very greatest importance that young people should not enter into marriage on the grounds of the mounting pressure of the desire to sleep with each other.

When people totally reject the propriety of any experience of sexual intimacy before marriage, it is usually on the grounds (*a*) that marriage is a sacrament in its own right, (*b*) that people may make a disastrous mistake in involving themselves so deeply before marriage, and it is therefore better to avoid sex until the partners are actually committed in marriage, and (*c*) that sex before marriage entails the possibility of deception and the exploitation of one partner by the other for his or her own gratification. Let us examine these points.

If, because of a belief that marriage is a sacrament in its own right, men and women are to be bound together throughout their lives no matter what mistakes they may have made, no matter what misery they may be suffering through whatever maladjustment (that is, unless they have committed a matrimonial offence), this is clearly to treat human individuals not as ends in themselves but as a means only—in this case, a means to the correct observance of religious law, or even the divine law. It is interesting to notice that if God exists, and is a moral being, He could not want it so. He could not treat a person as a means only, even if it were as a means to the maintenance of His own law, or even to His own greater glory. This religious law, therefore, falls very far short of our ethical standards. Secondly, though it is true that people may make mistakes and suffer deception and exploitation in sexual relations before marriage, it is equally true that the same things can happen *within* marriage. The truth is that people in general never think about the ethics of sex *within* marriage, only outside it. And their attitude has a rather appalling implication that once marriage has occurred less concern need be felt about these matters: sex is now safely confined, firmly controlled, hedged round with social and legal safeguards. But this, too, clearly involves treating individuals not as ends in themselves but only as a means to what is thought to be a socially necessitous regulation of sex.

In short, such a conception of marriage, as a kind of social or religious impounding of the sexual impulse, only to be allowed out on presentation of a licence, is itself immoral. In our new conception of marriage, the legitimation of sex is going to be—rightly so—a diminishing factor. Increasingly, marriage will be regarded as an entry into family life, and a growing, deepening companionship centering about the joy of shared parenthood.

RONALD FLETCHER in *Marriage Guidance*, November 1963

(b) Dr Fletcher's two[1] 'revolutionary ideas' were: (1) 'The idea that marriage is the only relationship within which sexual intimacy is morally justified must go. It is not tenable'; and (2) 'There is no doubt that we must consider again the reform of the divorce law—to take into account the question of mutual consent as a ground for divorce.'

These two statements were made in the course of a larger argument, which began by suggesting that 'we are in danger of focusing our attention too narrowly upon the family ... in isolation,' that 'family relationships may positively suffer from too inward-looking, too self-contained, too enclosed an attitude to the family'; and claimed that 'if we examine the matter more fully, there is no such thing as the ethics of sex and family education at all. The ethical principles in the light of which we should regulate our sexual and family relationships are the same as those on which we should base *all* our conduct in *all* human relationships.'...

It is only fair to Dr Fletcher that we should consider his more controversial statements in their wider context, and indeed, we shall spare ourselves a good deal of trouble if we begin by saying that, just as we found no difficulty in going along with him in the opening part of his lecture, so even in this controversial section there was much with which we could agree. We shall all agree (certainly Christians will) that the family must not be treated 'in isolation' from its social setting. We shall agree, too, that the ethics of sex and family relations are the same as those of all human relationships. ('Love thy neighbour as thyself' covers boy-friend, girl-friend, husband, wife, parents and children as well as the rest of our neighbours.) We may feel that he was a little careless in saying that 'there is no such thing as the ethics of sex and family education at all' when what he clearly meant was not that they do not exist but that they do not exist in isolation; but we may allow him the rhetorical emphasis without making too much fuss about it.

Even in his statement of his 'revolutionary ideas' we can agree with a good deal. The difficulty here is first that his presentation of them is so short, and second that it is so muddled. In respect to pre-marital relationships, for instance—Dr Fletcher mentions extra-marital relations but does not discuss them—he presents us with the statement that 'the conception of marriage as the legitimation of sex is itself immoral'. It is a little difficult to see just what he means by this. Neither society nor the Church regards pre-marital sexual activities as *illegal* in themselves (except in terms of age, degree of relationship, consent or the lack of it, and so on) but rather as *extra-legal*. Marriage does, of course, in its legal aspect, bring about a state in which the re-

1. Editor's note: The second idea has been omitted from passage (a) and its rejoinder from passage (b).

lationships of man and woman, including their sexual relation and its outcome, possess legal status. Dr Fletcher can scarcely mean that he regards this as immoral. He must mean that marriage does not in itself render sexual relationships *moral*, and that to claim that it does is immoral. If this *is* what he means, we may heartily agree (a brutal husband enforcing his rights upon an unwilling wife is not behaving morally). But he is not concerned to argue this but its converse—that sexual relations outside marriage are or may be moral—and this does not follow; it is not proved or even helped by the statement. The case remains to be stated.

Dr Fletcher sets out to state it in some very questionable propositions. That sex should be 'dispossessed of sinfulness and . . . regarded as a natural and enjoyable experience' might be described as a pious hope, but not as a present fact by anyone with any knowledge of human problems. That 'contraceptive techniques make possible the experience of sexual intimacy without reference to procreation' has still only a limited truth at the most superficial level, for even the Family Planning clinics and the specialists in the field will admit their failures (even if they blame them on their patients !). But at the deeper level of emotional or personal reference, the statement can only be described as wishful thinking, and that of a kind largely indulged in by the male sex. That 'sexual intimacy and marriage are no longer going to be thought synonymous' leaves one asking 'Whenever were they?'—and, more seriously, 'Is a valid morality dependent on what people think?' (to which the answer is, in one sense Yes, in another No).

We now come upon a glimmering of light. We may be grateful that Dr Fletcher's ethical principles 'clearly condemn inconsiderate promiscuity'—but then there is a relapse. 'If sexual intimacy is entered into with responsibility and mutual consideration . . . then there is no reason' (why sexual intimacy should be restricted to marriage). None that Dr Fletcher has stated, certainly, but then he has stated so little, and this so inadequately. We may agree with him when he goes on to say that because sex is one of the most important bases of a happy marriage (though not the only one) 'people should be as clear in mind and experience about it as possible before they commit themselves to the serious status and duties of marriage. . . . It is of the very greatest importance that young people should not enter into marriage on the grounds of the mounting pressure of desire to sleep with each other'. Yes, indeed—yet the operative words here are the words 'as possible'. Is it possible?—how far is it possible?—to enter into sexual intimacy before marriage, not in 'inconsiderate promiscuity', but 'with responsibility and mutual consideration'? This is precisely the question that needs to be answered, and Dr Fletcher has offered us very little help in considering it. A *non sequitur*, three half truths and a sprinkling of *obiter dicta* do not constitute much of an argument.

Dr Fletcher does not in fact offer any further consideration of this issue, for although he has a good deal more to say under his first head, what he says turns out to be concerned either with objections to the doctrine of the indissolubility of marriage, or else with a repetition of the argument that marriage does not solve all the moral problems. If we ask why he should imagine that considerations of this kind should support the case for pre-marital sexual experience—as we have seen, this does not follow—we are left to guess.

He says, for instance, that to enforce marriage on sacramental grounds as a life-long union whatever happens, is 'to treat human individuals not as ends in themselves but as means only—in this case a means to the correct observance of religious law, or even the divine law. It is interesting to notice that if God exists and is a moral being, He could not want it so'; we may be inclined to agree that there is truth in this, but to wonder what is its relevance to pre-marital sex. Our guess is that what Dr Fletcher is protesting against is an arbitrary 'revealed law' which not only proclaims that marriage is indissoluble but also forbids sexual activity beforehand; and that what really annoys him is its arbitrariness.

Now here we may admit that some Christians and others have sometimes taught in this way and laid themselves open to this charge. The main stream of Christian teaching, however, has always been concerned not only with 'revealed law' but also with 'natural law', and has always claimed that these are not contradictory but complementary. What Christian teaching says about pre-marital sex is not merely 'God forbids it' (and in so far as it does say this it also adds 'although He leaves people free to decide for themselves whether or not to obey Him'): it also says 'and in fact it is not in the best interests of the couple concerned, of their potential children, or of society as a whole'. This is why, within the Marriage Guidance Movement, Christians join hands with non-Christians to uphold the importance for morality both of the freedom of choice and also of the understanding of the best interests of all concerned. The undoubted fact that people can suffer and cause suffering within marriage as well as before marriage *is*, as Dr Fletcher says, good reason for caring about sexual ethics *within* marriage. It is no reason at all for drawing the conclusion that therefore sex before marriage can be just as good. But this is the case which he is supposed to be arguing.

It is precisely because we do agree with Dr Fletcher that human beings should be treated as ends in themselves and not as means only that we take leave to doubt whether this is possible in pre-marital sexual relationships, if these are undertaken experimentally or with a view to gaining experience (and still more to lessen a mounting pressure of sexual desire). What is lacking in such relationships is the element of total commitment to each other as persons who are 'ends in themselves' and not merely means even to a mutual gratification in bed. If Dr Fletcher says that such a total commitment may be present even before marriage, we may reply that the intention may be—the moral problem is certainly less if what we are discussing is strictly the anticipation of marriage—but that it is not always possible for human beings to fulfil their best intentions. Has he ever met a pregnant girl whose fiancé has been killed in a motor accident, for instance? If he says that total commitment is not always present even in marriage we shall agree, but go on insisting that this is irrelevant to the point at issue. Marriage may or may not embody the intention: what is certain is that the intention is not embodied without it.

CHARLES DAVEY, ibid. January 1964

Face to face with yourself

13. Two of the Ten Commandments

EIGHT. Thou shalt not steal.

TWO. Thou shalt not make unto thee any graven image, or any likeness . . .
thou shalt not bow down thyself to them, nor serve them : . . .

Look at the writers' expansions of these two commandments, and ask yourself 'Why (really *why*) not?' Do your answers have any common basis?

EIGHT. So all right, we are not shop lifters, are we? not bag-
snatchers, smash-and-grab raiders, bank-robbers, pay-bandits. . . . No,
we are strictly honourable in all our dealings—aren't we?

WORDS TO THE WISE

Buy on the cheapest and sell on the dearest.
A buyer's market is a seller's graveyard.
Supply and demand, this is the law and the profits.
Nothing for nothing, and twenty-nine and eleven for thirty bob if you
    can manage it without being caught.
Close to the wind the money's loose.
Sooner lose a friend than a deal.
Borrow at six per cent, lend at seven, and sleep easy.
Invest where the returns are best, and, if necessary, weep all the way
    to the bank.
Put as much as you can in your wife's name, and then, when you have
    to go, go bankrupt.
All things are possible on an Expense Account.
Fiddling Income Tax is different.
Pinching from the Firm is different, too.
Everybody else does it.
A tanner too much change, and that's his look-out : a penny short and
    report him to the Manager.
If he doesn't bother to collect my fare. . . .
The threat of Industrial Action backing a legitimate demand for a
    substantial wage increase, with one hundred per cent solid Union
    Membership in a closed shop.
A million unemployed, and see who's Master then.
They can afford it.
Plenty more where that came from.
Business is business.

They won't miss one.
They'd do exactly the same.
Pay it back next week.
All you have to do is pick eight draws and you stand to win two
    hundred and fifty thousand quid.
Capital Appreciation.
Property Development.
Skimming the cream.
. . . .(*Insert own favourite expression and/or excuse*)

GEORGE TARGET, We, the Crucifiers

TWO. 'What shape is an idol?'
I worship Ganesa, brother, god of worldly wisdom, patron of shop-
    keepers. He is in the shape of a little fat man with an elephant's
    head; he is made of soapstone and has two small rubies for eyes.
    What shape do you worship?
I worship a Rolls-Royce sports model, brother. All my days I give it
    offerings of oil and polish. Hours of my time are devoted to its
    ritual; and it brings me luck in all my undertakings; and it estab-
    lishes me among my fellows as a success in life. What model is your
    car, brother?
I worship my house beautiful, sister. Long and loving meditation have
    I spent on it; the chairs contrast with the rug, the curtains har-
    monize with woodwork, all of it is perfect and holy. The ash trays
    are in exactly the right place, and should some blasphemer drop
    ashes on the floor, I nearly die of shock. I live only for the service
    of my house, and it rewards me with the envy of my sisters, who
    must rise up and call me blessed. Lest my children profane the
    holiness of my house with dirt and noise, I drive them out of doors.
    What shape is your idol, sister? Is it your house, or your clothes, or
    perhaps even your worth-while and cultural club?
I worship the pictures I paint, brother . . . I worship my job; I'm the
    best darn publicity expert this side of Hollywood . . . I worship my
    golf game, my bridge game. . . . I worship my comfort; after all,
    isn't enjoyment the goal of life? . . . I worship my church; I want
    to tell you, the work we've done in missions beats all other de-
    nominations in this city, and next year we can afford that new
    organ, and you won't find a better choir anywhere . . . I worship
    myself. . . .
What shape is *your* idol?

JOY DAVIDMAN, Smoke on the Mountain

14. The addict

What is this thing called drug addiction?

It took me four years to put into focus a picture of the complex threat that lies behind the single word 'narcotics'. But the picture that finally emerged is staggering.

According to the latest official estimates, there are more than 30,000 addicts in New York City alone, and these statistics are based only on the records of those who are hospitalized, jailed or committed to an institution. Thousands of others are 'breaking in' on heroin by sniffing and 'skin popping': thousands of men, women, and children condemned to what Linda vividly called 'death on the instalment plan'.

One boy (Joseph), whom I got to know very, very well, told me how this works.

'A pusher[1] gets you into his car, Davie, and maybe he's got one or two kids from your class in there smoking pot. "Marijuana won't hurt you", they say. Then they tell you it isn't habit-forming. Which it isn't: but marijuana leads to habit-forming drugs. The pusher tries to get you to take a smoke, and if you hesitate, the other boys start to laugh and call you "chicken" and in the end maybe you give in and take one of his cigarettes. That's how I got started.'

Joseph's story is typical. The child takes a puff in the back seat of some pusher's car. He learns that you don't inhale marijuana like you do tobacco; you sniff it till the fumes make you feel giddy. That first day, when the boy returns to school, he is untroubled by his problems. Most narcotics addicts are lonesome, frustrated, angry and usually come from a broken home. One sampling of the wonderful weed and the boy discovers what it would be like to be permanently happy. He forgets his drunken father and wandering mother, he is unruffled by the total lack of love in his life, by the stifling poverty which forces him to sleep in the same bed as his two sisters and in the same room as his parents. He forgets all this. He is free, and that is no small thing.

The next day the obliging pusher is on hand to suggest another little sample of heaven. When the boy is ready, he is introduced to stronger stuff: heroin. Here, too, the pattern is followed: a free gift of the drug the first time, the first two times. The pusher is happy to make the investment because he knows that *only fifteen days of continuous heroin use produces addiction!*

Now comes the truly fiendish part of this story.

Heroin costs from three to fifteen dollars a 'deck'—a deck is a tiny

---

1. Dope-pedlar.

cellophane container of the drug, sufficient for a single intravenous shot.

'Davie,' one twenty-year-old girl told me during a heroin shortage, 'it costs me sixty dollars a day to support my habit. I've heard of users hooked to the tune of a hundred dollars a day.' More typical, I found, would be a twenty-five or thirty dollars a day habit. Where is a teen-ager who is given twenty-five cents a day lunch money going to find twenty-five dollars?

He might turn to crime. But the boy only gets one-third of the value of his theft when he sells it to a receiver of stolen goods. So to support a twenty-five dollar a day habit, he must steal seventy-five dollars worth of goods. The director of the Narcotics Bureau in New York, Inspector Edward Carey, estimates that drug addiction is responsible for $200,000,000 a year in stolen goods in this city alone.

Theft, though, is not really the answer for a boy who has become addicted. It takes too much ingenuity and too much effort, and there is always the risk involved. A much simpler solution is to become a seller.

On a dark street corner, one night, a teen-age boy told me how this happened to him. Karl is eighteen. He has been mainlining for three years. When he first realised that his habit was going to cost him fifteen dollars a day, then twenty dollars a day, then twenty-five, he went to his supplier and offered to help him sell.

'Oh no, boy. If you want to sell you have to find your own cus-tomers.' And in this sentence lies the reason for the steady spread of addiction.

Karl, to pay for his own drugs, pressed narcotics on younger boys. He used the same technique that had been used on him. He passed off the habit as being 'worth the couple bucks it costs'. He chose the more sensitive, hurt, withdrawn boys to pressure. He called them 'chicken' when they wouldn't smoke marijuana. And in the end Karl succeeded in building up a business for himself. Into the chain of ever-widening addiction not one but ten new boys were added.

One of the questions I asked these boys was, 'Why don't you just stop?'

Suppose that a boy did choose to stop. This is what he faces. About two hours after the effect of the final shot wears off, the boy begins withdrawal symptoms. First there is a deep craving which pulls at his body from every pore. Then the boy begins to sweat. He shakes with chills, while his body temperature rises higher and higher. He begins to vomit. He retches for hours on end. His nerves twang with ex-cruciating pain from foot to hair roots. He suffers hallucinations and nightmares more horrible than the worst ever imagined by an alcoholic.

This lasts for three full days. And unless he is helped, he just won't make it. Even with help, the chances are nine to one that he will never be free from his habit. Each year 3,500 addicts are admitted to the United States Public Health Service Hospital in Lexington. More than six hundred doctors and staff members try to help the addict free himself from the habit. Yet a twenty-year study, carried out between 1935 and 1955, showed that sixty-four per cent of the addicts returned! Many more went back on drugs without returning to the hospital. Between eighty-five and ninety per cent of the addicts, says Dr Murray Diamond, Chief Medical Officer at the hospital, eventually return to their habit.

'Once you are hooked, man,' a boy who had been to Lexington told me, 'you are hooked for good. I got me a fix within five minutes after getting out of that place.'

DAVID WILKERSON, The Cross and the Switchblade

1. Drug addiction has been on the increase in the U.K. (*a*) Why is this a matter for concern? (*b*) What steps, if any, do you think society should take to deal with traffic in drugs and drug addiction? (*c*) How would you answer an addict who said 'It's my own private life. You've no right to interfere'?

2. In the light of this passage discuss the cogency of the following pleas as a basis for taking drugs: 'You should try anything once'; 'I do it for the kicks'; 'Live now; pay later'.

3. What arguments would you use to try to dissuade someone tempted to start taking drugs from doing so? Don't confine yourself to practical arguments or ones based on expediency; take it deeper.

15. In praise of chastity

'What we need are new social taboos to replace the old ones we have lost: but to be effective they must be generated by society itself. While that urgently needed process is taking place we must guard against the crime of producing children without parents. And it certainly is easier to teach contraception than chastity.'

These three sentences, part of a Comment on sexual morality, published in the *Observer*, on Dec. 6th, are as good a summary as any I have read of your recent pronouncements on the subject. Presumably they are also a summary of the opinions of many secular humanists.

Frequently in your columns you warn against the danger of isolating sexual immorality from social immorality. Far more frequently and with persistent vigour, you condemn *apartheid* as an outrageous violation of social morals. It is because I so wholeheartedly agree with you in your attitude to *apartheid* that I find your attitude to sexual ethics so distressing—and so unintelligent. For in fact you have stated

as clearly as Dr Verwoerd has ever done the *moral* justification for
the present policy of the South African Government.

What is *apartheid* but 'new social taboos . . . generated by society
itself'? And, 'while this process is taking place' (that is, the creation
of new Bantu institutions of equal quality with white institutions;
the emergence of a Bantu middle class; the ultimate emergence of
Bantustans) South Africa 'must guard against the crime of producing
children of mixed parentage. And it is certainly easier to teach (and
practise) *apartheid* than integration'. So, in the name of the new
morality, let South Africa get on with the job.

This, sir, is the logic of your pronouncement on sexual morality—
that because chastity is hard it should not be attempted. I wish to
state quite simply that, just because it is hard, it is in fact the only
thing worth attempting. And I want further to suggest that because
England is stifling in the fumes of an emergent secular-humanist
ethic, her voice is unlikely to be heard effectively when major moral
issues (such as *apartheid*) are being debated in the world forum.

This ethic will always avoid what is hard and choose the soft option.
It cannot do otherwise, for it is based solely on a pragmatic view of
human behaviour. Man in himself and for himself is alone worth consideration. Society must be ordered, not to any ultimate good, but to
a present, immediate comfort and satisfaction. And because the human
passions clamour so, let them be pacified—'contraception is easier
than chastity'.

I do not believe you really know what chastity is. I am certain you
do not know what Christians mean by it. But I fear that, even if you
did, you would reject it as too hard.

Christian chastity is not a prohibition but an affirmation—the
affirmation that soul and body are so closely interrelated, the body so
essentially expressing, influencing and being influenced by the soul
that it must be treated as having an eternal and infinite dignity. We
believe in the resurrection of the body: not in the immortality of the
soul alone.

Therefore, we know, and we rejoice in knowing, that the conflicts
and tensions, the joys and sorrows, which are part of our human condition here, are not meaningless disconnected experiences, but are the
very stuff of Love. And amongst them the needs for self-discipline and
restraint are recognisably of supreme importance. Without them, love
can degenerate into lust; affection into selfishness; surrender into
defeat.

The artist has his vision, and it is obscured by a failure in discipline.
The musician, too, has his vision, and it is muffled by a refusal of discipline.

Man is made for the vision of God—that is all he *is* made for. And chastity is the discipline of love by which he attains it, not in Heaven but here and now. It is certainly harder than contraception, but rather more worth while.

T R E V O R   H U D D L E S T O N in *The Observer*, 24 April 1966

1. What does the writer mean by 'chastity'?

2. (*a*) In what way does he see *The Observer*'s attitude to apartheid at odds with its attitude to sexual morals? (*b*) What are the presuppositions of its attitude to the latter? (*c*) What are the presuppositions of the writer's attitude? (*d*) With which do you agree, and why?

3. In what way does the writer see the question of chastity as ultimately a matter of personal integrity? What is the relevance of his analogies from art and music? Can you think of any others?

16. Samaritans against suicide

The new Christian resembles his grandfather even less than he re-sembles the Apostles. He is committed to the same Christ, the same yesterday, today and for ever, but has to represent and re-present Him in a different world.

The new Christian knows that he himself is, with his brethren in the Church, a continuation of the Incarnation and an agent of Christ's Redemption, and that only through him can Christ make a relation-ship with people today.

In many situations, communication by speech, or by speech alone, is ineffective. One can only usefully *be*, or *act*, or *suffer*. In His in-fancy, Christ was; in the face of sickness, He acted; before Pilate, He was silent; often, and supremely on the Cross, He suffered. Vital as His words were and are, His deeds (including His suffering) spoke louder—and still will. The new Christian knows he is called to be Christ in his world, to let Christ act and suffer in and through him. He seeks opportunities to take the form of a servant.

He finds more and more of these opportunities in our day outside the church premises and the normal parochial activities, and, most significant of all, he finds himself working, in mutual respect, along-side colleagues who do not profess his Faith. Amongst these oppor-tunities is one with a clearly Christian task and a great variety of Christian and non-Christian personnel—The Samaritans.

Although the idea of an emergency telephone for potential suicides who were not at this stage seeking medical aid started in the less dis-ciplined part of the mind of an Anglican priest, and many of the 68 centres in the U.K. are, like the original London centre at St. Stephen Walbrook, in premises attached to a church, the Samaritans are not a Church organisation.

In Christian countries, the great majority of the Samaritans are at least nominal members of one of the larger Christian denominations, but this is not true of the Branches in (say) India, Pakistan and Turkey; and in U.K. Branches there are also Jews, Moslems, Hindus, Buddhists, Agnostics and Humanists. None of the Samaritans tries to convert either the 'clients' or fellow-members, and a volunteer frequently becomes a close friend of another through shared duties without knowing or caring from what very different starting points they have reached their common vocation.

For the Christians, the work of the Samaritans is the most Christian thing they do; for the Humanists, it is the most human thing they do; and *what* they do, at its best, is the same thing, though the conscious motive and inspiration seem quite different. Only if a client not merely *has* a religious problem (most people have) but is also aware of it and wants to talk about it, does the Agnostic hand over to someone who can meet this particular need; and can one imagine it more graciously and encouragingly put than 'I don't happen to be very well up in theology, but I've a friend here who is, and you'll get on just as well with him as you have done with me'? The kind of militant atheist who couldn't say this is not enlisted, for precisely the same reason as the compulsive evangeliser; neither can shut up and listen, and then humbly go where the client is and try to help him there.

What started as an emergency counselling service by one man answering MANsion House 9000 in November 1953 had changed early in 1954 into an emergency befriending service by a group of lay people who used the first contact by telephone to win the callers' confidence to the point where they would almost always come to the office.

There, about a third of the clients were found to need only the kind of understanding friend the hand-picked Samaritans are, and most of the rest needed a friend as well as some counselling or arrangement to see a psychiatrist. Those who urgently needed psychiatry but wouldn't accept this more often agreed to it after a while because of the concern of their friend rather than as a result of professional urging.

For nearly the whole of the twelve years of the Samaritans' existence theirs has been a lay ministry, with parsons and doctors and other professional social workers kept firmly in their place. This 'place' is very important: the Samaritans require someone to select them, instruct them, supervise them, deal with their anxieties, make decisions they aren't qualified to make, supplement their heartwarmingly amateur ministrations with professional ones—and sack them if necessary.

But these Directors and Consultants have no function apart from the lay volunteers who outnumber them about fifty to one and who do the work for which the Samaritans exist.

All round the clock and the calendar, something like 7,000 Samaritans are keeping about 80 emergency telephones manned and not only being there at a moment's notice for perhaps 500 new clients a week, but also spending uncounted hours in private homes or public places with literally thousands of existing clients who haven't yet found other friends. They also write interminable letters and make innumerable phone calls. Sometimes their work is dramatic, more often it is a matter of patient plodding on. They receive all kinds of confidences which they keep strictly confidential, and though they occasionally receive thanks, they are accustomed to being whipping boys for people's frustrations and disappointments.

When a client rings up, the person who answers is the one he wants: an understanding and accepting person who will listen with all his attention and bear his burdens with him. If, as is usually the case, someone can subsequently be found who can help to solve some of his problems, this is a bonus; all the Samaritans offer is their loving concern and sympathy, and this saves many lives. In the larger towns, the Samaritan the client first encounters is unlikely to be the one who is allocated to continue the befriending (the volunteer may not be of the sex, age or background the client needs anyway), but whenever he rings or comes, he must be sure of finding one of the many forms of 'Samaritan' voice or face. Naturally, some Samaritans appear from the Director's bird's eye view of the flock to be more certainly and generally 'Samaritans' than others, and these will be entrusted with the most disturbed clients; but to the client, any of the volunteers is the-person-who-cares-when-he-thought-nobody-did, and the one who befriends him usually becomes in his mind the *best* befriender.

The relationship is not a psychotherapeutic one calculated to produce transferences and other complications, but in its 'ordinary', comfortable way is markedly therapeutic. One of the things the volunteers are taught is how to befriend those who are, and those who are not, being treated or counselled by an expert.

Even in the London Branch, to which over 15,000 clients have come, only a fraction of the number of the socially isolated are helped. What of the others? Is it too much to expect that while the Samaritans specialise in the crises which may lead to suicide, and which require experience and organisation, less desperate cases, including those of long-term chronic inadequacy, should find their befriending in the parishes in which they live? One thing is clear from the experience of the Samaritans: if you set out to give, with no thought of reward other than the inescapable blessedness of the giving, God is enabled to grant many rewards which could not have been had for the seeking.

The Samaritans were not started, and have not spread so widely and fast, in order to 'make the Church relevant', or to 'promote fully ecumenical co-operation', or to set Christians and Jews, religious and non-religious, West and East, black and white, working together lovingly; though all these things have been added unto them—surely because they exist simply and solely to dedicate such compassion as they have 'to help those tempted to suicide or despair'.

C H A D   V A R A H in *New Christian*, 4 November 1965

1. What moral issues are raised by suicide: (*a*) for the prospective suicide? (*b*) for the community?

2. How do you think suicide should be treated?

3. In what way do Samaritans who profess the Christian Faith feel their Christian convictions illuminate/affect their work?

4. Does it matter at all what motive and/or justification lies behind the work of the Samaritans?

17. (*a*) Gyges' ring

First, I shall state the common opinion on the nature and origin of justice; second, I shall show that those who practice it do so under compulsion and not because they think it good in itself. What they say is that our natural instinct is to inflict wrong or injury, and to avoid suffering it, but that the disadvantages of suffering it exceed the advantages of inflicting it; after a taste of both, therefore, men decide that, as they can't have the ha'pence without the kicks, they had better make a compact with each other and avoid both. They accordingly proceed to make laws and mutual agreements, and what the law lays down they call lawful and right. This is the origin and nature of justice. It lies between what is most desirable, to do wrong and avoid punishment, and what is most undesirable, to suffer wrong without redress; justice and right lie between these two and are accepted not as being good in themselves, but as having a relative value due to our inability to do wrong. For anyone who had the power to do wrong and called himself a man would never make any such agreement with anyone—he would be mad if he did.

This then is the account they give of the nature and the origins of justice; the next point is that men practise it against their will and only because they are unable to do wrong. This we can most easily see if we imagine that a just man and an unjust man have each been given liberty to do what they like, and then follow their subsequent careers. We shall catch the just man in exactly the same pursuits as the unjust, led by self-interest, the motive which all men naturally follow if they are not forcibly restrained by the law and made to respect each other's claims.

The best illustration of the liberty I am talking about would be if we supposed them to be possessed of the power which Gyges, the ancestor of the famous Lydian, had in the story. He was a shepherd in the service of the then king of Lydia, and one day there was a great storm and an earthquake in the district where he was pasturing his flock and a chasm opened in the earth. He was much amazed, and descended into the chasm and saw many astonishing things there, among them, so the story goes, a bronze horse, which was hollow and fitted with doors, through which he peeped and saw a corpse of more than human size. He took nothing from it save a gold ring it had on its finger, and then made his way out. He was wearing this ring when he attended the usual meeting of shepherds which reported monthly to the king on the state of his flocks; and as he was sitting there with the others he happened to twist the bezel of the ring towards the inside of his hand. Thereupon he became invisible to his companions, and they began to refer to him as if he had left them. He was astonished, and began fingering the ring again, and turned the bezel outwards; whereupon he became visible again. When he saw this he started experimenting with the ring to see if it really had this power, and found that every time he turned the bezel inwards he became invisible, and when he turned it outwards he became visible. Having made his discovery he managed to get himself included in the party that was to report to the king, and when he arrived seduced the queen and with her help attacked and murdered the king and seized the throne.

Let us now imagine there to be two such rings, one for the just man, and one for the unjust. There is no one, it would be commonly supposed, who would have such iron strength of will as to stick to what is right and keep his hands off other people's property. For he would be able to steal from the shops whatever he wanted without fear of detection, to go into any man's house and seduce his wife, to murder or to release from prison any one he felt inclined and generally behave as if he had supernatural powers. And in all this the just man would differ in no way from the unjust, but both would follow the same course. This, it would be claimed, is strong evidence that no man is just save under compulsion, and that no man thinks justice pays him personally, since he will always do wrong when he gets the chance. Indeed, the supporter of this view will continue, men are right in thinking that injustice pays the individual better than justice; and if anyone who had the liberty of which we have been speaking neither wronged nor robbed his neighbour, men would think him a most miserable idiot, though of course they would pretend to admire him in public because of their own fear of being wronged.

PLATO, *The Republic*, Book II

(*b*) Franz Jagerstatter

The facts of Franz' life are these: He was born May 20, 1907, in St. Radegund, a little village in upper Austria. His daily life was like that of most Austrian peasants. In nineteen thirty six he married a girl from a nearby village and she is credited with changing him from 'a beloved, lusty youth', 'an accomplished and enthusiastic fighter' into a strongly religious man. But his wife to-day denies this and says his religious awakening came about gradually around the time of his marriage. They went to Rome on their honeymoon.

She had met him at a dance at Ach where she herself had been working as a waitress. Later, in addition to running the family farm, Franz became sexton of the parish church. When Hitler's troops moved into Austria in 1938, Jagerstatter was the only man in the village to vote against the *Anschluss*. Before this he had served his military training and had not been interested in politics nor was he involved in any political organization. After Hitler's occupation he refused to contribute in any way to Hitler's collections or to receive any benefits. It was necessary, he said, to dissociate oneself from the Nazi Folk Community and make no contributions to it. 'Anyone who wishes to practise Christian Charity in his deeds can manage to provide the poor with something for their sustenance without Winter Relief Collection or the People's Welfare Fund.' He renounced all claims to the official Family Assistance Programme under which he would have been entitled to cash allotments for his children; and after a disaster to the crops, he refused the emergency cash subsidies offered the farmers by the government. He was alone in this refusal.

The family was living at a level described as being near the point of poverty; nevertheless he distributed foodstuffs to the poor.

Franz remained openly anti-Nazi and refused to fight in Hitler's war. He was finally called up in February, 1943 and was imprisoned first at Linz, then at Berlin. After a military trial he was beheaded August 9, 1943.

There is an interesting comparison between St Thomas More and his witness and that of the humble peasant, the 'great man' and the 'little man', and the comparison may perhaps enhance rather than diminish the significance of the latter's sacrifice. 'For the very fact that none would notice or be likely to be affected by what he did serves to reduce the issue to the individual and his conscience in silent and inner confrontation with God. Certainly this is what it meant to Franz Jagerstatter himself. That same confrontation existed for St Thomas More, but to the extent to which he knew that others would take account of what he did, he was not alone. As far as the St Radegund peasant knew, the choice he made would pass unnoticed by the world and would completely fade from human memory with the passing of the handful of people who had known him personally.'

How did Franz Jagerstatter get that way? The few simple facts that we know are that his religious awakening came about because of a retreat. He had lived of course in the simple religious atmosphere of an Austrian village, where all were Catholic, and close to the church where he was sexton, which meant daily contact with the Holy Eucharist. He was poor, he led a life of hard work. He read the Scriptures and the Lives of the Saints (which included St Thomas More and the Curé of Ars, who was what one would call to-day a 'draft dodger').

There was no chance at all of his affecting the policies of the State, or influencing the lives of others as far as he knew. No one encouraged Franz in his act of disobedience to the orders of the state. Every one argued against what he was doing, even the most sympathetic of priests, who could only see his resistance as futile, and even bad for the institutionalised Church.

DOROTHY DAY in *The Catholic Worker*, July/August 1965

1. What do you think is the relevance of passage (a) to passage (b)?

2. What would you have done if you had possessed Gyges' ring?

3. Do you think that 'no man is just save under compulsion'? Does the fable actually show that honesty is not in itself the best policy?

4. (a) The writer of the first passage takes 'I'm all right, Jack' as his rule in life. Is it yours? Support your answer (Yes *or* No) with the reasons which lead you to hold it. (b) Do you think that Franz Jagerstatter was a 'miserable idiot' (end of passage (a)) for taking the opposite view? Was his resistance 'futile'? What were the grounds of his stand against the Nazis?

5. Do these passages help you to understand what is meant by 'integrity'? Try to express its meaning in your own words. Is it important that you should have integrity? Why?

18. Dying we live

(Extracts from letters written by two German prisoners executed by the Nazis.)

(a) Kim: cabin boy and seaman

The press bureau of the chief of the S.S. and the police force in Denmark on Sunday, 8 April 1945, issued the following announcement:

Condemned to death: Seaman Kim Malthe-Bruun, born on July 8, 1923, in Saskatchewan, Canada, resident in Copenhagen, as a member of an illegal organisation, annexed a revenue service boat and took it to Sweden. In addition he procured arms for his organisation and took part in transporting arms. The death sentence was carried out by a firing squad.

January 13, 1945

'The Gestapo is made up of very primitive men who have gained considerable skill in outwitting and intimidating feeble spirits; if you
observe them a little more closely during one of their interrogations,
you will see them displaying a look of violent dissatisfaction, as if
they were obliged to muster all their self-control and as if it were an
act of mercy on their part not to shoot you down on the spot for not
telling them more. But if you look into their eyes, you see that they
are enormously satisfied with anything they have succeeded in squeez-
ing out of their victim. The victim himself realises only much later
that he has allowed himself to be led by the nose.

'Confront them calmly, showing neither hatred nor contempt, because both of these goad their over-sensitive vanity beyond endurance.
Regard them as human beings and use their vanity against them.'

On March 2, after being tortured, Kim was carried back unconscious to his cell. The next day he wrote:

March 3, 1945

'Since then I have been thinking about the strange thing that
actually has happened to me. Immediately afterwards I experienced
an indescribable feeling of relief, an exultant intoxication of victory,
a joy so irrational that I was as though paralysed. It was as if the soul
had liberated itself completely from the body, as if soul and body were
gambolling like two detached beings, the one in a completely un-
fettered supernatural ecstasy, the other, severely earthbound, writhing
in a passionless convulsion. Suddenly I realised how incredibly strong
I am. When the soul returned once more to the body, it was as if the
jubilation of the whole world had been gathered together here. But
the matter ended as it does in the case of so many other opiates: when
the intoxication was over, a reaction set in. I became aware that my
hands were trembling, that there was a tension within me. It was as
if a cell in the depths of my heart had short-circuited and were now
very swiftly being discharged. It was like an addict consumed by his
addiction. Yet I was calm and spiritually far stronger than I have ever
been.

'However, though I am unafraid, though I do not yield ground, my
heart beats faster every time someone stops before my door. This must
be something purely physical, even though it is indisputably a sense
of perception that evokes it.

'Immediately afterwards it dawned upon me that I have now a new
understanding of the figure of Jesus. The time of waiting, that is the
ordeal. I will warrant that the suffering endured in having a few nails
driven through one's hands, in being crucified, is something purely
mechanical that lifts the soul into an ecstasy comparable with nothing
else. But the waiting in the garden—that hour drips red with blood.

'One other strange thing. I felt absolutely no hatred. Something happened to my body; it was only the body of a boy, and it reacted as such. But my soul was occupied with something completely different. Of course it noticed the little creatures who were there with my body, but it was filled so with itself that it could not closely concern itself with them.'

March 27, 1945

'Since then I have often thought of Jesus. I can well understand the measureless love he felt for all men, and especially for those who took part in driving nails into his hands. From the moment when he left Gethsemane, he stood high above all passion.'

Farewell letter to his mother.

'Western Prison, German Section, Cell 411
April 4, 1945

Dear Mother:

To-day, together with Jorgen, Nils, and Ludwig, I was arraigned before a military tribunal. We were condemned to death. I know that you are a courageous woman, and that you will bear this, but, hear me, it is not enough to bear it, you must also understand it. I am an insignificant thing, and my person will soon be forgotten, but the thought, the life, the inspiration that filled me will live on. You will meet them everywhere—in the trees at springtime, in people who cross your path, in a loving little smile. You will encounter that something which perhaps had value in me, you will cherish it, and you will not forget me. And so I shall have a chance to grow, to become large and mature. I shall be living with all of you whose hearts I once filled.

Finally, there is a girl whom I call mine. Make her realise that the stars still shine and that I have been only a milestone on her road. Help her on: she can still become very happy.

In haste—your eldest child and only son,
Kim.'

(b) Dietrich Bonhoeffer: theologian

Dietrich Bonhoeffer, born on 4 February 1906, in Breslau, was a lecturer at the University of Berlin and the philosopher among the pastors of the evangelical Confessional Church. The intellectual sensitivity and world perspective of his religious life produced in him not weakness but clear-sightedness. When he saw both his church and his fatherland in mortal danger, the learned theologian placed himself in the front line of action. 'When a madman is tearing through the streets in a car,' he said, 'I can, as a pastor who happens to be on the scene, do more than merely console or bury those who have been run over. I must jump in front of the car and stop it.'

In 1942, as spokesman for both the Confessional Church and the German resistance, he tried unsuccessfully to win the co-operation of the British War Cabinet in overthrowing the Hitler government, and with this end in view he met in secret at Stockholm Dr. George Bell, Bishop of Chichester. Bonhoeffer was arrested on 5 April 1943. He died on 9 April 1945, in the concentration camp at Flossenburg.

God's Role in History

I believe that God can and intends to let good spring from everything, even from what is most evil. For this he needs human beings who know how to turn all things to the good. I believe that God purposes to give us in every crisis as much power of resistance as we need. But he does not give it to us in advance, in order that we shall rely not on ourselves but on him alone. In such faith, all fear of the future would necessarily be overcome.

On Suffering

It is infinitely easier to suffer in obedience to a human command than to suffer in the freedom of an act undertaken purely on one's own responsibility. It is infinitely easier to suffer in community than to suffer in loneliness. It is infinitely easier to suffer openly and in honour than to suffer apart and in shame. It is infinitely easier to suffer by risking one's physical life than to suffer in spirit. Christ suffered in freedom, in loneliness, apart and in shame, in body and in spirit, and many Christians have since suffered with him.

On Danger and Death

It would not be entirely correct to say that we would die willingly, though there is probably no one who has not known that lassitude— to which, however, one must on no account submit. The truth is that we are too curious still for that, or, to put it more seriously, that we should like to get a better view of the meaning of our confused life. We do not idealise death, either; life is far too great and precious to us for that. Above all we refuse to see the meaning of life in courting danger; for this, we are not despairing enough and know too well the benefits of life; we know too well what it is to fear for one's life, and all the other destructive effects of a persistent threat to existence. We still love life, but I believe that death can no longer surprise us very much. It is not external circumstances, but we ourselves that will each make of his death what it can be, a death by free consent.'

1. (a) Describe the attitude of these two writers to death. (b) What is the basis of their attitude? (c) What is your attitude to death? (d) On what more general beliefs is it based?

2. Try to imagine honestly how you might have acted had you been a German citizen under the Nazi regime. How would you have explained your stance to a sympathetic inquirer? Be quite frank.

3. Does the vicarious experience of these two victims of Nazi persecution help you to understand better the relevance and meaning of Christ's death and their faith in Him? In what ways?

19. The plague

What has yet to be recorded before coming to the culmination, during the period when the plague was gathering all its forces to fling them at the town and lay it waste, is the long, heartrendingly monotonous struggle put up by some obstinate people like Rambert to recover their lost happiness, and to balk the plague of that part of themselves which they were ready to defend in the last ditch.

Rambert fought to prevent the plague from besting him. Once assured that there was no way of getting out of the town by lawful methods, he decided, as he told Rieux, to have recourse to others. It was not until he happened to meet Cottard at Rieux' place that he made a little headway. On that day he and Rieux had been talking again about his unsuccessful efforts to interest the authorities in his case, and Cottard heard the tail-end of the conversation.

Some days later, Cottard met him in the street.

'Hullo, Rambert! Still no luck?'

'None whatever.

'It's damned difficult.'

'Yes,' Cottard replied. 'It certainly is. However. . .'.

He, however, knew a way to go about it, and he explained to Rambert that he had learnt of the existence of an 'organization' handling this sort of business.

[*Editor's* note. After being handed from one 'introduction' to another, Rambert, who is a journalist, succeeds in making arrangements for his escape, though it is all most devious, time-consuming, and frustrating for him. He tries to fill in time by seeing two acquaintances, Dr. Bernard Rieux the physician, and M. Jean Tarrou, a visitor to Oran of private means, caught there by the plague and now helping Rieux in his work.]

To Rambert the next two days seemed endless. He looked up Rieux and described to him the latest developments, then accompanied the doctor on one of his calls.

'I hope Tarrou will be up in time,' Rieux murmured. He looked worn out.

'Is the epidemic getting out of hand?' Rambert asked.

Rieux said it wasn't that; indeed the death-graph was rising less steeply. Only they lacked adequate means of coping with the disease.

'We're short of equipment. In all the armies of the world a shortage of equipment is usually compensated for by manpower. But we're short of man-power, too.'

'Haven't doctors and trained assistants been sent from other towns?'

'Yes,' Rieux said. 'Ten doctors and a hundred helpers. That sounds a lot, no doubt. But it's barely enough to cope with the present state of affairs. And it will be quite inadequate if things get worse.'

Rambert, who had been listening to the sounds within the house, turned to Rieux with a friendly smile.

'Yes,' he said, 'you'd better make haste to win your battle.' Then a shadow crossed his face. 'You know,' he added, in a low tone; 'it's not because of *that* I'm leaving.'

Rieux replied that he knew it very well, but Rambert went on to say:

'I don't think I'm a coward—not as a rule, anyhow. And I've had opportunities of putting it to the test. Only, there are some thoughts I simply cannot endure.'

The doctor looked him in the eyes.

'You'll see her again,' he said.

'Maybe. But I just can't stomach the thought that it may last on and on, and all the time she'll be growing older. At thirty, one's beginning to age, and one's got to squeeze all one can out of life. But I doubt if you can understand.'

Rieux was replying that he thought he could, when Tarrou came up, obviously much excited.

'I've just asked Paneloux to join us.'

'Well?'

'He thought it over, then said "Yes".'

'That's good,' the doctor said. 'I'm glad to know he's better than his sermon.'

'Most people are like that,' Tarrou replied. 'It's only a matter of giving them the chance.' He smiled and winked at Rieux. 'That's my job in life—giving people chances.'

'Excuse me,' Rambert said, 'I've got to be off.'

[Three more days pass; more 'introductions', more procrastinations, but the final appointment is fixed.]

Next day on his way to his bedroom Rambert met Tarrou coming down the stairs at the hotel.

'Like to come with me?' he asked. 'I'm just off to see Rieux.'

The journalist pondered. Then, 'Look here,' he said. 'If you've any time to spare after dinner, never mind how late, why not come to the hotel, both of you, and have a drink with me?'

'That will depend on Rieux,' Tarrou sounded doubtful. 'And on the plague.'

At eleven o'clock that night, however, Rieux and Tarrou entered the small, narrow bar of the hotel. Some thirty people were crowded into it, all talking at the top of their voices. Coming from the silence of the plague-bound town, the two newcomers were startled by the sudden burst of noise, and halted in the doorway. They understood the reason for it when they saw that spirits were still to be had here. Rambert, who was perched on a stool at a corner of the bar, beckoned to them.

'Any luck?' Rieux had to raise his voice.

'I'm getting on,' Rambert replied. 'In the course of the week, perhaps.'

'A pity!' Tarrou shouted.

'Why?'

'Oh,' Rieux put in, 'Tarrou said that because he thinks you might be useful to us here. But, personally, I understand your wish to get away only too well.'

Tarrou stood the next round of drinks.

Rambert got off his stool and looked him in the eyes for the first time.

'How could I be useful?'

'Why, of course,' Tarrou replied, slowly reaching towards his glass, 'in one of our sanitary squads.'

The look of brooding obstinacy that Rambert so often had came back to his face, and he climbed again on to his stool.

'Don't you think these squads of ours do any good?' Tarrou had just taken a sip of his glass and was gazing hard at Rambert.

'I'm sure they do,' the journalist replied, and drank off his glass.

Rieux noticed that his hand was shaking, and he decided, definitely, that the man was far gone in drink.

[The contact fails to turn up for the 'final appointment'; Rambert is forced to start the whole devious procedure from the beginning again; at last a certain Gonzales agrees to introduce Rambert to two of the sentries, who will effect his escape.]

When the two friends entered Rambert's room that night, they found him lying on the bed. He got up at once and filled the glasses he had ready. Before lifting his to his lips, Rieux asked him if he was making progress. The journalist replied that he'd started the same round again and got to the same point as before; in a day or two he was to have his last appointment.

He asked Rieux how the sanitary groups were functioning. Five teams were now at work, and it was hoped to form others. Sitting on the bed, the journalist seemed to be studying his fingernails. Rieux was gazing at his squat, powerfully built form, hunched up on the edge of the bed. Suddenly he realized that Rambert was returning his gaze.

'You know, doctor, I've given a lot of thought to your campaign. And if I'm not with you, I have my reasons. No, I don't think it's that I'm afraid to risk my skin again. I took part in the Spanish civil war.'

'On which side?' Tarrou asked.

'The losing side. But since then I've done a bit of thinking.'

'About what?'

'Courage. I know now that man is capable of great deeds. But if he isn't capable of a great emotion, well, he leaves me cold.'

'Tell me, Tarrou, are you capable of dying for love?'

'I couldn't say, but I hardly think so—as I am now.'

'You see. But you're capable of dying for an idea; one can see that right away. Well, personally, I've seen enough of people who die for an idea. I don't believe in heroism; I know it's easy and I've learnt it can be murderous. What interests me is living and dying for what one loves.'

Rieux had been watching the journalist attentively. With his eyes still on him, he said quietly:

'Man isn't an idea, Rambert.'

Rambert sprang off the bed, his face ablaze with passion.

'Man *is* an idea, and a precious small idea, once he turns his back on love. And that's my point; we—mankind—have lost the capacity for love. Let's wait to acquire that capacity or, if really it's beyond us, wait for the deliverance that will come to each of us anyway, without his playing the hero'.

Rieux rose. He suddenly appeared very tired.

'You're right, Rambert. However, there's one thing I must tell you; there's no question of heroism in all this. It's a matter of common decency. That's an idea which may make some people smile, but the only means of fighting a plague is—common decency.'

'What do you mean by "common decency"?' Rambert's tone was grave.

'I don't know what it means for other people. But in my case I know that it consists in doing my job.'

'Your job! I only wish I were sure what my job is!' There was a mordant edge to Rambert's voice. 'Maybe I'm all wrong in putting love first.'

Rieux looked him in the eyes.

'No,' he said vehemently. 'You are *not* wrong.'

He went out.

Tarrou followed, but seemed to change his mind when he reached the door. He stopped and looked at the journalist.

'I suppose you don't know that Rieux's wife is in a sanatorium, a hundred miles or so away.'

Rambert showed surprise, and began to say something; but Tarrou had already left the room.

At a very early hour the next day Rambert rang up the doctor.

'Would you agree to my working with you until I find some way of getting out of the town?'

There was a moment's silence before the reply came.

'Certainly, Rambert. Thanks.'

During the first part of September Rambert had worked conscientiously at Rieux's side. He had merely asked for a few hours' leave on the day he was due to meet Gonzales and the two youngsters outside the Boys' School.

Gonzales kept the appointment and, while he and the journalist were talking, they saw the two boys coming towards them, laughing. They said they'd had no luck last time, but that was only to be expected. Anyhow, it wasn't their turn for sentry-go this week. Rambert must have patience till next week.

It turned out that he had a fortnight to wait, as the periods of sentry-duty were extended to two weeks, to reduce the number of shifts. During the fortnight Rambert worked indefatigably, getting every ounce out of himself, with his eyes shut, as it were, from dawn till night. He went to bed very late and always slept like a log. This abrupt transition from a life of idleness to one of constant work had left him almost void of thoughts or energy. He talked little about his impending escape. Only one incident is worth noting; after a week he confessed to the doctor that for the first time he'd got really drunk. It was the evening before; on leaving the bar he had an impression that his groin was swollen and he had pains in his armpits when he moved his arms. I'm for it! he thought. And his only reaction—an absurd one, as he frankly admitted to Rieux—had been to start running to the Upper Town and when he reached a small square, from which if not the sea, a fairly big patch of open sky could be seen, to call to his wife with a great cry, over the walls of the town. On returning home and failing to discover any symptoms of plague on his body, he had felt far from proud of having given way like that. Rieux, however, said he could well understand one's being moved to act thus. 'Or, anyhow, one may easily feel inclined that way.'

'Monsieur Othon was talking to me about you this morning,' Rieux suddenly remarked, when Rambert was bidding him good night. 'He asked me if I knew you, and I told him I did. Then he said, "If he's a friend of yours advise him not to associate with smugglers. It's bound to attract attention."'

'Meaning—what?'

'It means you'd better hurry up.'

'Thanks.' Rambert shook the doctor's hand.

In the doorway he suddenly swung round. Rieux noticed that, for the first time since the outbreak of plague, he was smiling.

'But why don't you stop my going? You could easily manage it.'

Rieux shook his head with his usual deliberateness. It was none of his business, he said. Rambert had elected for happiness, and he, Rieux, had no argument to put up against him. Personally he felt incapable of deciding which was the right course and which the wrong in such a case as Rambert's.

'If that's so, why tell me to hurry up?'

It was Rieux who now smiled.

'Perhaps because I, too, would like to do my bit for happiness.'

On Wednesday Marcel announced: 'It's for tomorrow night, at midnight. Mind you're ready on time.' He could count on them to see it through. Rambert thanked them.

The next day was very hot and muggy and a heat-mist veiled the sun. The total of deaths had jumped up. Rambert kept prowling round like a caged animal, without speaking. Abruptly, at four in the afternoon, he announced that he was going out.

'Don't forget,' Marcel said. 'At midnight sharp. Everything's set.'

Rambert went to the doctor's flat. Rieux's mother told him he would find the doctor at the hospital in the Upper Town. As before, a crowd was circling in front of the entrance gates. 'Move on, there!' a police-sergeant with bulging blue eyes bawled every few minutes. Rambert showed his pass to the sergeant, who told him to go to Tarrou's office.

Tarrou was sitting at a black-wood desk, with his sleeves rolled up, mopping up with his handkerchief a trickle of sweat in the bend of his arm. The office, a small, white-painted room, smelt of drugs and damp cloth.

'Still here?' Tarrou seemed surprised.

'Yes. I'd like to have a word with Rieux.'

'He's in the ward. Look here! Don't you think you could fix up whatever you've come for, without seeing him?'

'Why?'

'He's overdoing it. I try to spare him as much as I can.'

Rambert gazed thoughtfully at Tarrou. He'd grown thinner, his eyes and features were blurred with fatigue, his broad shoulders sagged. There was a knock at the door. A male attendant, wearing a white mask, entered. He laid a little sheaf of cards on Tarrou's desk and, his voice coming thickly through the cloth, said 'Six', then went out. Tarrou looked at the journalist, and showed him the cards, spreading them fanwise.

'Neat little gadgets, aren't they? Well, they're deaths. Last night's takings.' Frowning, he slipped the cards together. 'The only thing that's left us is—accountancy!'

Taking his purchase on the table, Tarrou rose slowly to his feet.

'You're off quite soon, I take it?'

'To-night, at midnight.'

Tarrou said he was glad to hear it, and Rambert had better look after himself for a bit.

'Did you say that sincerely?'

Tarrou shrugged his shoulders.

'At my age one's got to be sincere. Lying's too much effort.'

'Excuse me, Tarrou,' the journalist said, 'but I'd greatly like to see the doctor.'

'I know. He's more human than I. All right, come along.'

'It's not that . . .' Rambert stumbled over his words, and broke off in mid-phrase. Tarrou stared at him; then, unexpectedly, his face broke into a smile.

Tarrou took Rambert into a small room, all the wall-space of which was occupied by cupboards. Opening one of these, he took from a sterilizer two masks of cotton-wool enclosed in muslin, handed one to Rambert, and told him to put it on.

The journalist asked if it was really any use. Tarrou said 'No,' but it inspired confidence in others.

They opened the glazed door. It led into an enormous room all the windows of which were shut, in spite of the great heat. Electric fans buzzed near the ceiling, churning up the stagnant, overheated air above two long rows of grey beds. Groans shrill or stifled rose on all sides, blending in a monotonous dirge-like refrain. Men in white moved slowly from bed to bed under the garish light flooding in from high, barred windows. The appalling heat in the ward made Rambert ill at ease, and he had difficulty in recognizing Rieux, who was bending over a groaning form. The doctor was lancing the patient's groin, while two nurses, one on each side, held his legs apart. Presently Rieux straightened up, dropped his instruments into a tray that an attendant held out to him, and remained without moving for some moments, gazing down at the man, whose wound was now being dressed.

'Any news?' he asked Tarrou, who had come beside him.

'Paneloux is prepared to replace Rambert at the quarantine station. He has put in a lot of useful work already. All that remains is to re-organize Number Three Group, now that Rambert's going.'

Rieux nodded.

'Castel has his first lot of the vaccine ready now,' Tarrou continued. 'He's in favour of its being tried at once.'

'Good,' Rieux said. 'That's good news.'

'And Rambert's come.'

Rieux looked round. His eyes narrowed above the mask when he saw the journalist.

'Why have you come?' he asked. 'Surely you should be elsewhere?'

Tarrou explained that 'it' was fixed for midnight. To which Rambert added : 'That's the idea, anyhow.'

Whenever any of them spoke through the mask the muslin bulged
and grew moist over the lips. This gave a sort of unreality to the conversation; it was like a colloquy of statues.

'I'd like to have a word with you,' Rambert said.

'Right. I'm just going. Wait for me in Tarrou's office.'

A minute or so later, Rambert and Rieux were sitting at the back of
the doctor's car. Tarrou, who was at the wheel, looked round as he let
in the gear.

'Petrol's running out,' he said. 'We'll have to foot-slog it tomorrow.'

'Doctor,' Rambert said, 'I'm not going. I want to stay with you.'

Tarrou made no movement; he went on driving. Rieux seemed
unable to shake off his fatigue.

'And—what about *her*?' His voice was hardly audible.

Rambert said he'd thought it over very carefully, and his views
hadn't changed, but, if he went away, he would feel ashamed of
himself, and that would embarrass his relations with the woman he
loved.

Showing more animation, Rieux told him that was sheer nonsense;
there was nothing shameful in preferring happiness.

'Certainly,' Rambert replied. 'But it may be shameful to be happy
by oneself.'

Tarrou, who had not spoken so far, now remarked, without turning
his head, that if Rambert wished to take a share in other people's
unhappiness, he'd have no time left for happiness. So the choice had
to be made.

'That's not it,' Rambert rejoined. 'Until now I always felt a stranger
in this town, and that I'd no concern with you people. But now that
I've seen what I have seen, I know that I belong here whether I want
it or not. This business is everybody's business.' When there was no
reply from either of the others, Rambert seemed to grow annoyed. 'But
you know that as well as I do, damn it! Or else—what are you up to
in that hospital of yours? Have *you* made a definite choice, and turned
down happiness?'

Rieux and Tarrou still said nothing, and the silence lasted until they
were nearing the doctor's home. Then Rambert repeated his last question in a yet more emphatic tone.

Only then Rieux turned towards him, raising himself with an effort
from the cushion.

'Forgive me, Rambert, only—well, I simply don't know. But stay
with us if you want to.' A swerve of the car made him break off for
a moment. Then, looking straight in front of him, he said: 'For nothing in the world is it worth turning one's back on what one loves.
Yet that is what I'm doing—though *why* I do not know.' He sank back
on the cushion. 'That's how it is,' he added wearily, 'and there's

nothing to be done about it. So let's recognize the fact, and draw the conclusions.'

'What conclusions?'

'Ah,' Rieux said, 'a man can't cure and know at the same time. So let's cure as quickly as we can. That's the more urgent job.'

At midnight Tarrou and Rieux were giving Rambert the map of the district he was to keep under surveillance. Tarrou glanced at his watch. Looking up, he met Rambert's gaze.

'Have you let them know?' he asked.

The journalist looked away.

'I'd sent them a note'—he spoke with an effort—'before coming to see you.'

ALBERT CAMUS, The Plague

1. Rambert, Tarrou, and Rieux have different attitudes to the plague. Try to distinguish them.

2. It was a criminal offence with severe penalties to escape or try to escape from the plague-stricken city. (a) Would you have run the risk of being caught in order to escape? If not, why not? (b) Would you have left the city, supposing there was no risk of being caught? Would it have made any difference to your answer if you had been a journalist, like Rambert, or a visitor, like Tarrou, or a physician, like Rieux? (c) Rambert was breaking the law, it is true. But apart from that, why shouldn't he have tried to escape? Can you give any reasons? Do you think they are good reasons or poor ones? compelling reasons or inconclusive ones?

3. (a) Why did Rambert change his mind? (b) What had he learnt through his experiences of the plague-stricken city which he had not realized before?

4. Is he telling the truth in the last line? If not, why not?

5. What relevance has this passage got to your understanding of Life and your decisions on how to live your own life?

20. The dilemma of morality

People are genuinely puzzled as to which actual types of behaviour and courses of action are right and which are wrong. Moral classifications won't stay put. Things which an earlier generation approved of are now regarded as old-fashioned conventions; and bad conventions at that. Things which an earlier generation condemned are now regarded as quite normal conduct.

Deeper and more serious than this is the widespread doubt as to the nature of the ground, the sanction, on which such distinctions between lines of conduct are based. Who says that this is right and this is wrong? By what authority do they say it? And is that authority a valid one? The old traditional sanctions have broken down. 'It's forbidden in the Ten Commandments', 'the Church says it's wrong', even 'it's condemned by all decent people', no longer have any com-

pelling force for perhaps the majority. And we find ourselves in a
welter of conflicting claims and counter claims. It's a matter of
personal taste; it depends on how you were brought up; it's condi-
tioned by the economic set-up; right and wrong are determined by the
will of the State; it's all a question of glands.

From that it's not a long step to the third stage at which the validity
of the very distinction between right and wrong is impugned. There
is no such thing as an absolute distinction; and we are reduced to an
ethical scepticism which, by abandoning the problem as insoluble,
probably leaves the issue to be decided between epicureanism and
brute force.

'There was no ruler in Israel.' The old authority has abdicated or is
dead. The throne is empty. But no: it isn't. Seats of moral authority
don't remain empty for long. And already we can see pretty clearly
the shape of some of the claimants to the vacant throne.

There is irrationalism, the despair of reason and the flight from it,
making itself felt in ethics as elsewhere; the relapse into an emotional
response to stimulus. That is one: and hedonism is another. I use the
word in its more general sense, as an attitude which follows only too
easily from the other, the substitution of the pleasant for the good,
the disagreeable for the evil. How common it is to hear people say in
reply to criticism of their conduct—But there's nothing wrong in it:
it doesn't *hurt* anybody. Oh, I assure you that we are scrupulously
careful to see that no one suffers. And we ourselves get so much
satisfaction out of it; no, not just a kick; real happiness.

I know. It sounds so considerate, so tolerant, so enlightened; so
much more attractive than the narrow strait-laced Puritanism which
talks bluntly about 'fornication and all other deadly sin', and is old-
fashioned enough to believe that such things come under the judgement of God.

It is, I need hardly say, not only in the sphere of sexual morality
that this insidious hedonistic influence makes itself felt. It shows
itself in the training and discipline of children—the tearful mother
in the Juvenile Court: 'Well I'm sure we've done our best for him;
we've always given him everything he asked for'. It shows itself in a
good deal of our social legislation. We can all find traces of it in the
personal choices and decisions which we all make in our daily life.
Nobody knows what is right and what is wrong. Everybody can tell
the difference between pleasant and unpleasant; so it's easy.

And that of course leads straight into a third distortion of true
ethical judgment; indeed it may be said to be only a particular form
of it. That is the acceptance of a purely relativist, individual standard
of judgement, as the only alternative to the discarded idea of an absolute universal standard. The whole thing resolves itself into what is

really a matter of taste, or of early habituation and training. No, I don't happen to like dishonesty, or unchastity, or self-assertion. But then I suppose I'm made like that. Odd, I know, but there it is. Of course I shouldn't dream of suggesting that you would necessarily feel the same, still less that you *ought* to; I'm not so narrow-minded as to want to impose my particular outlook on you. And after all, who knows which of us is right—if there is such a thing?

The crux of the question is surely whether we can find any firm standing ground on which to base our moral judgement, a standard which is not a matter of'taste or convention, but which so to speak compels our acknowledgment.

For myself I am convinced that it is at this precise point, the providing of a fixed point, a firm standing ground amid the shifting tides of moral tastes and moods, that the recognition of God has something definite—I would say the one essential and decisive thing—to say.

Turn for a moment to the situation presented not by our personal moral perplexities, but by the large scale moral issues involved in international politics. The nations are looking, pretty desperately, not just for a formula of agreement, not just for a *modus vivendi*, but for a basis of co-operation, and for a principle of control of such co-operation, which carries a really effective sanction and authority. If I read the evidence aright there is going to be no hope of finding that except on the basis of the common acknowledgment of an authority which stands above, and is recognised as standing above, the likes and dislikes, the ambitions and fears, the *amour propre*, the national interest of any and every nation; the recognition of which involves, as its price, the deliberate surrender of some measure of national sovereignty.

The good European, or the good world citizen, would say that that authority can only be super-national. The Christian would say that it can only be super-natural. For he pushes his diagnosis of the disease to a deeper level, and discovers the root of the trouble not in the particular iniquity of Russia or America or Britain, but in that radical defect of human nature which consists in the refusal to admit to, to submit to, any final and unquestionable moral authority which just *is not* subject to amendment, revision, repudiation because it doesn't happen to suit our particular plan at any given moment.

And the same Christian insight insists that there is no answer to the indeterminism, the scepticism, or moral relativism except in the recovery of the sense of *obligation*, obligation to a law, law not as the arbitrary fiat of a despot, human or divine, but as the expression of the order of man's being, the way human nature was made to work.

Of course it will come to all of us at certain points with the feeling of law in the sense of restriction, prohibition, commandment. But that

is inevitable, since our own natures are not attuned to the true order
of our nature. But when truly seen it is recognised not as the imposi-
tion of something alien, arbitrary, capricious; but as the expression of
that which we know and acknowledge as our true good, because it is
not made by us, but is the expression of the purpose for which we
were made. It is not, that is, vitiated by the imperfection of our
fallible and sinful individualisms. It is the perfect law of liberty.

That is the kind of obligation which the Christian finds in that which
is described paradoxically, but with absolute truth, as the fear *and*
love of God. It is an obligation the content of which he may not clearly
apprehend in detail; he has his moral perplexities like anyone else—
What *is* right, and can I be sure? But it is an obligation the existence
and authority of which is *not* in doubt. To know God is to know what
the fear of God means. It is to know that that phrase which we use so
casually: 'I'll be damned if I do that', is a phrase which can be strictly
and literally true.

You remember that tremendous and terrible passage in Mr. C. S.
Lewis' *The Weight of Glory* (see No. 88) where he writes: 'We are
warned that it may happen to any one of us to appear at last before
the face of God and hear only the appalling words: "I never knew
you. Depart from me." To realise what we have lost, and that we have
lost it through our own choice, that is damnation.'

But to know God is also to know the love of God. For the reason why
the possibility of damnation matters, why it is worth bothering about,
is that it means the loss of that which, in our moments of true insight,
we know to be the one thing supremely worth having.

I [have elsewhere spoken] of the discovery of the reality of God, not
as the end term in a balancing of probabilities, but as the finding ourselves confronted by one in whom we are compelled—morally compelled—to recognise and acknowledge a self-authenticating authority
which gives a quite new depth of meaning to these words: 'Never
man spoke as this man'.

Will you try to relate that to the line of thought we have just been
following? Cast your minds back for a moment to those claimants for
the empty throne of moral authority of which we were thinking.
Irrationalism. But there is no trace of that in the Gospel. Instead
there is the impression of relentless unshakeable purpose—the expression in human life of that all-embracing creative purpose which is the
very nature of God. 'My Father is at work up to this moment, and so
am I.' 'It's meat and drink for me to do my Father's will and finish his
work.' 'I have a baptism to be baptised with, and how am I straitened
until it is accomplished.' There is no fumbling, no vacillation, no surrender to an emotional reaction here; there is just the clear-sighted,
deliberate, rational following of a coherent purpose.

Hedonism. But what conceivable sense can you make of that life, still more of that death, if the pleasant is the good, if suffering, not evil, is the real enemy, if all that we are required to do is to see that we don't hurt anybody? If hedonism is true then let us drop all this high-sounding language about a great redemptive act of sacrifice, and call the Crucifixion what, on this reckoning it is, a piece of obstinate and useless idealism. Relativism: just a matter of taste. But again you just cannot make sense of that life on those terms; for the thing which stands out from it is the terrible sense of obligation to a law, which yet, freely accepted, is the highest good. And further you cannot escape the realisation that that life communicates to you its own sense of obligation. What we think about that life is *not* a matter of taste; it is a matter of moral discernment which we know touches the heart of our own integrity.

Countless Christians in every age in this encounter have found just precisely what we are looking for. They find, I find myself, there is no getting away from the conviction that here we are face to face with an authority which we cannot question. I cannot demonstrate to you the truth of this conviction; no one can. We have got to test it for ourselves and come to our own conclusion. We have got to put ourselves, with all our moral perplexity, with all the shifting relative values of our moral judgements, over against that clear imperative certainty, and see what the effect is.

F. A. COCKIN, *Christianity in Common Speech*

1. Can you suggest any further 'claimants to the vacant throne' of 'moral authority' which are not mentioned by the writer? What are the grounds of their claims?

2. Comment on the writer's assessment of the moral dilemma of our time.

3. (a) What arguments can you adduce in favour of irrationalism, hedonism, and relativism respectively as a basis for moral decision and judgement. (b) What arguments can be adduced against each of them? Bear in mind some of the situations and answers which you have discussed in earlier passages.

4. Discuss the claims of the alternative 'standing ground' expounded by the writer.

5. What is your own personal basis for personal conduct? Is it relevant to the 'large-scale moral issues' referred to by the writer? In what ways?

American or Negro?

21. Fifth Avenue, Uptown[1]: a letter from Harlem

The avenue is elsewhere the renowned and elegant Fifth. The area I am describing, which, in to-day's gang parlance, would be called 'the turf', is bounded by Lenox Avenue on the west, the Harlem River on the east, 135th Street on the north, and 130th Street on the south. We never lived beyond these boundaries; this is where we grew up. All along the block, for anyone who knows it, are immense human gaps, like craters. These gaps are not created merely by those who have moved away, inevitably into some other ghetto; or by those who have risen, almost always into a greater capacity for self-loathing and self-delusion; or yet by those who, by whatever means—World War II, the Korean war, a policeman's gun or billy, a gang war, a brawl, madness, an overdose of heroin, or, simply, unnatural exhaustion—are dead. I am talking about those who are left, and I am talking principally about the young. What are they doing? Well, some, a minority, are fanatical churchgoers, members of the more extreme of the Holy Roller sects. Many, many more are 'moslems', by affiliation or sympathy, that is to say that they are united by nothing more—and nothing less—than a hatred of the white world and all its works. They are present, for example, at every Buy Black street-corner meeting—meetings in which the speaker urges his hearers to cease trading with white men and establish a separate economy. Neither the speaker nor his hearers can possibly do this, of course, since Negroes do not own General Motors or RCA or the A&P, nor, indeed, do they own more than a wholly insufficient fraction of anything else in Harlem (those who *do* own anything are more interested in their profits than in their fellows). But these meetings nevertheless keep alive in the participators a certain pride of bitterness without which, however futile this bitterness may be, they could scarcely remain alive at all. Many have given up. They stay home and watch the TV screen, living on the earnings of their parents, cousins, brothers, or uncles, and only leave the house to go to the movies or to the nearest bar. There are further retreats, of course, than the TV screen or the bar. There are those who are simply sitting on their stoops, 'stoned', animated for a moment only, and hideously, by the approach of someone who may lend them the money for a 'fix'. Or by the approach of someone from whom they

1. 'Downtown' in the U.S.A. means the main city centre.

can purchase it, one of the shrewd ones, on the way to prison or just coming out.

And the others, who have avoided all of these deaths, get up in the morning and go downtown to meet 'the man'. They work in the white man's world all day and come home in the evening to this fetid block. They struggle to instill in their children some private sense of honor or dignity which will help the child to survive. This means, of course, that they must struggle, stolidly, incessantly, to keep this sense alive in themselves, in spite of the insults, the indifference, and the cruelty they are certain to encounter in their working day. They patiently browbeat the landlord into fixing the heat, the plaster, the plumbing; this demands prodigious patience; nor is patience usually enough. In trying to make their hovels habitable, they are perpetually throwing good money after bad. Such frustration, so long endured, is driving many strong, admirable men and women whose only crime is colour to the very gates of paranoia.

Now I am perfectly aware that there are other slums in which white men are fighting for their lives, and mainly losing. I know that blood is also flowing through these streets and that the human damage there is incalculable. People are continually pointing out to me the wretchedness of white people in order to console me for the wretchedness of blacks. But an itemized account of the American failure does not console me and it should not console anyone else. The people, however, who believe that this democratic anguish has some consoling value are always pointing out that So-and-So, white, and So-and-So black, rose from the slums into the big time. The existence—the public existence—of, say, Frank Sinatra and Sammy Davis, Jr., proves to them that America is still the land of opportunity and that inequalities vanish before the determined will. It proves nothing of the sort. The determined will is rare—at the moment, in this country, it is unspeakably rare—and the inequalities suffered by the many are in no way justified by the rise of a few. Not all of these people, it is worth remembering, left the world better than they found it. The determined will is rare, but it is not invariably benevolent. Furthermore, the American equation of success with the big time reveals an awful disrespect for human life and human achievement. This equation has placed our cities among the most dangerous in the world and has placed our youth among the most empty and most bewildered. The situation of our youth is not mysterious. Children have never been very good at listening to their elders, but they have never failed to imitate them. They must, they have no other models. That is exactly what our children are doing. They are imitating our immorality, our disrespect for the pain of others.

All other slum dwellers, when the bank account permits it, can

move out of the slum and vanish altogether from the eye of persecution. No Negro in this country has ever made that much money and
it will be a long time before any Negro does. The Negroes in Harlem,
who have no money, spend what they have on such gimcracks as they
are sold. These include 'wider' TV screens, more 'faithful' hi-fi sets,
more 'powerful' cars, all of which, of course, are obsolete long before
they are paid for. Anyone who has ever struggled with poverty knows
how extremely expensive it is to be poor; and if one is a member of a
captive population, economically speaking, one's feet have been placed
on a treadmill forever. One is victimized, economically, in a thousand
ways—rent, for example, or car insurance. Go shopping one day in
Harlem—for anything—and compare Harlem prices and quality with
those downtown.

The people in Harlem know they are living there because white
people do not think they are good enough to live anywhere else. No
amount of 'improvement' can sweeten this fact. Whatever money is
now being earmarked to improve this, or any other ghetto, might as
well be burnt. A ghetto can be improved in one way only: out of
existence.

Similarly, the only way to police a ghetto is to be oppressive. None
of the Police Commissioner's men, even with the best will in the world,
have any way of understanding the lives led by the people they
swagger about in twos and threes controlling. Their very presence is
an insult, and it would be, even if they spent their entire day feeding
gumdrops to children. They represent the force of the white world,
and that world's real intentions are, simply, for that world's criminal
profit and ease, to keep the black man corraled up here, in his place.
The badge, the gun in the holster, and the swinging club make vivid
what will happen should his rebellion become overt. Rare, indeed, is
the Harlem citizen, from the most circumspect church member to the
most shiftless adolescent, who does not have a long tale to tell of police
incompetence, injustice, or brutality. I myself have witnessed and
endured it more than once.

It is hard, on the other hand, to blame the policeman, blank, good-
natured, thoughtless, and insuperably innocent, for being such a perfect representative of the people he serves. He, too, believes in good intentions and is astounded and offended when they are not taken for the
deed. He has never, himself, done anything for which to be hated—
which of us has?—and yet he is facing, daily and nightly, people who
would gladly see him dead, and he knows it. There is no way for him
not to know it: there are few things under heaven more unnerving than
the silent, accumulating contempt and hatred of a people. He moves
through Harlem, therefore, like an occupying soldier in a bitterly
hostile country; which is precisely what, and where, he is, and is the

reason he walks in twos and threes. And he is not the only one who knows why he is always in company: the people who are watching him know why, too. Any street meeting, sacred or secular, which he and his colleagues uneasily cover has as its explicit or implicit burden the cruelty and injustice of the white domination. He is exposed, as few white people are, to the anguish of the black people around him. Even if he is gifted with the merest mustard grain of imagination, something must seep in. He cannot avoid observing that some of the children, in spite of their color, remind him of children he has known and loved, perhaps even of his own children. He knows that he certainly does not want *his* children living this way. He can retreat from his uneasiness in only one direction: into a callousness which very shortly becomes second nature. He becomes more callous, the population becomes more hostile, the situation becomes more tense, and the police force is increased. One day, to everyone's astonishment, some one drops a match in the powder keg and everything blows up. Before the dust has settled or the blood congealed, editorials, speeches, and civil-rights commissions are loud in the land, demanding to know what happened. What happened is that Negroes want to be treated like men.

Negroes want to be treated like men: a perfectly straightforward statement, containing only seven words. People who have mastered Kant, Hegel, Shakespeare, Marx, Freud, and the Bible find this statement utterly impenetrable. The idea seems to threaten profound, barely conscious assumptions. A kind of panic paralyses their features, as though they found themselves trapped on the edge of a steep place. I once tried to describe to a very well-known American intellectual the conditions among Negroes in the South. My recital disturbed him and made him indignant; and he asked me in perfect innocence, 'Why don't all the Negroes in the South move North?' I tried to explain what *has* happened, unfailingly, whenever a significant body of Negroes move North. They do not escape Jim Crow: they merely encounter another, not-less-deadly variety. They do not move to Chicago, they move to the South Side; they do not move to New York, they move to Harlem.

Northerners indulge in an extremely dangerous luxury. They seem to feel that because they fought on the right side during the Civil War, and won, they have earned the right merely to deplore what is going on in the South, without taking any responsibility for it; and that they can ignore what is happening in Northern cities because what is happening in Little Rock or Birmingham is worse. Well, in the first place, it is not possible for anyone who has not endured both to know which is 'worse'. I know Negroes who prefer the South and white Southerners, because 'At least there, you haven't got to play any guessing games !' The guessing games referred to have driven more than one Negro into the narcotics ward, the madhouse, or the river. I know another Negro, a man very dear to me, who says, with conviction and with truth, 'The spirit of the South is the spirit of America.' He was born in the North and did his military training in the South. He did not, as far as I can gather, find the South 'worse'; he found it, if anything, all too familiar. In the second place, though, even if Birmingham *is* worse, no doubt Johannesburg, South Africa, beats it by several miles, and Buchenwald was one of the worst things that ever happened in the entire history of the world. The world has never lacked for horrifying examples; but I do not believe that these examples are meant to be used as justification for our own crimes. This perpetual justification empties the heart of all human feeling. The emptier our hearts become, the greater will be our crimes. Thirdly, the South is not merely an embarrassingly backward region, but a part of this country, and what happens there concerns every one of us.

Neither the Southerner nor the Northerner is able to look on the Negro simply as a man. They are two sides of the same coin and the South will not change—*cannot* change—until the North changes. The country will not change until it reexamines itself and discovers what it really means by freedom. It is a terrible, an inexorable, law that one cannot deny the humanity of another without diminishing one's own: in the face of one's victim one sees oneself. Walk through the streets of Harlem and see what we, this nation, have become.

JAMES BALDWIN, *Nobody knows my Name*

1. Why is Harlem a ghetto?

2. What are the attitudes to the problem presented here of (*a*) the whites, (*b*) at least two different groups of Negroes, (*c*) the police, according to the writer?

3. What is your own attitude to the situation described above? What do you think should be done about it? Do you agree that 'a ghetto can be improved in one way only: out of existence'?

4. What are the differences and likenesses between the Southern and Northern attitudes of the whites to the Negro? Does the writer discriminate between his moral judgements of the two?

5. According to the writer, what are the Negroes asking for? Do you think they have a right to it or not? and on what grounds? In what ways do you think the writer envisages its being accorded to his fellow Negroes?

6. Try to describe how you would see yourself reacting to living in Fifth Avenue, Uptown, as a Negro. What would be the basis of your particular choice of response to this situation?

22. The black man's burden

The relationship with Negroes is so bewildering to most white Americans, because our ability to judge them accurately, and to react to them generously, has been severely crippled by a conditioning in racial myth, by emotional malformation, and by a theological preparation which has done little for the development of compassion. Let it be admitted that we are not above the ignorant conviction that the Negro is something of a black parasite upon the national body, someone given by history as a test of our magnanimity, someone that we are literally stuck with, since a return to slavery or deportation would be out of the question. I would like to devote this article to the Negro contribution to this country, so that we may better recognize the Negro as one of our first immigrants, as devoted and stalwart soldier, as pioneer in the East, South and West, as journeyman in field and factory, as citizen in slavery and segregation, as carrier of white burdens and atoner for white crimes, an innovator of protest and non-violent resistance, as giving the lie to our classlessness, as hope to our religion, as friend and brother.

It may startle some of us to know that Negroes arrived in this country a year before the Mayflower landed at Plymouth in 1620, to begin the greatest forced migration in human history, the sorriest chapter in the annals of our nation, and what has already been adequately proved as the most valuable contribution of one continent to another, one people to another, one race to another. The original twenty Negroes of Jamestown, Virginia were not slaves, but indentured servants, who were prompt in discharging their servitude, earning their freedom and mingling with the other settlers on the basis of equality. This relatively happy state could not last however. White greed saw to that. Virginia and Maryland were the first colonies to legalize slavery in the 1660's, and it was not long before color became a badge of servitude in all of the colonies, stripping Negroes of all rights of personality. In contrast, the poor whites and Indians who had experienced the indentured state with the Negro, had the protection of government or tribe, or they could easily escape; while the Negroes had no recourse to law, could not hide or escape, and, as the Spanish used to say, were worth four times their number of Indians. By 1710, there were fifty thousand Negroes in America; when the Declaration of Independence was signed, there were half a million; by 1860, there were four million.

'The Western world,' Eric Williams contends, 'is in danger of forgetting today what the Negro has contributed to Western civilization. London and Bristol, Bordeaux and Marseilles, Cadiz and Seville, Lisbon and New England, all waxed fat on the profits of the trade in the tropical produce raised by the Negro slave. Capitalism in England, France, Holland and colonial America received a double stimulation—from the manufacture of goods needed to exchange for slaves, woollen and cotton goods, copper and brass vessels, and the firearms, handcuffs, chains and torture instruments indispensible on the slave ships and on the slave plantations.' W. E. B. DuBois takes a different tack, and, ignoring what the Negro has given to this country, he concentrates on what it cost to give it: 'Raphael painted, Luther preached, Corneille wrote, and Milton sang; and through it all, for four hundred years, the dark captives wound to the sea amid the bleaching bones of the dead.'

Ironically enough, Negroes fought in the American Revolution for the freedom of their masters, a freedom nonetheless denied them. Crispus Attacks, a Negro, was the first man killed in the Boston Massacre; the two Salems, Peter Salem and Salem Poor, were among the most valiant men of the war. Before the Revolution ended, some five thousand Negroes, both slaves and freemen, had taken up arms to defend a liberty that could not be theirs.

Though the Revolutionary War did much to eliminate strict slavery in the North, it had little effect upon the South, where an implacable decision had been made to make the Negro the flesh and blood prop of a Way of Life, causing in turn an introverted and demented folk culture and an economic totalitarianism. Historians of the period tell us that for two hundred years 'a social system as coercive as any yet known' was built on the unreal foundations of 'the most implacable race consciousness yet observed in virtually any society'. It has been called, with a great deal of justice, the 'Cotton Curtain'. Individual, family and collective rights were arbitrarily and totally stripped away —it was a crime to teach Negroes to read and write, a crime to give them a Bible. Children were sold from their mothers, and fatherhood was, in practice, outlawed. A Mississippi court ruled that the rape of a slave woman was outside the scope of common or civil law. 'The father of a slave,' said a Kentucky court, 'is unknown to our law.' Children were often herded to the fields at five and six years, women were prized more for their breeding qualities than for their ability to perform massive drudgery under a burning sun. Seldom did a slave live out his life without a flogging of anywhere from thirty-nine to a hundred lashes from a cowskin whip, and it was not infrequent that 'kind' masters would flog the skin from their slaves' back and wash them down in brine. The toil in the fields was long, unremitting and harsh; ten or fifteen minutes at noon for a crust and a lump of bacon; work until dark; cut wood, feed mules and swine; cook supper and eat it without the simple amenities of knife, fork or skillet; go to bed at midnight with a prayer that the morning horn be not overslept, since this would mean twenty lashes. Protest was common—escape, revolt, suicide—while among all Negroes who took none of these measures there was a vast, seething hate which kept the South apprehensive and unrestful before an unconfronted fear. 'Slavery time was tough, boss,' said one ex-slave, 'you just don't know how tough it was.'

Yet the Negro endured under slavery, he survived and did more than that, he waxed strong through the simple fight for existence. Alternatives were simple and utterly real: either develop qualities of soul which would transform oppression into life, or die. He decided to live, and in living founded the wealth of this country, which rested, as Lincoln believed, 'on the 250 years of unrequited toil of Negro men and women'. Frederick Douglass, the great Negro abolitionist, spoke of this decision to live, and the stake in this country that Negroes gained in result. 'We are here, and here are we likely to be. To imagine that we shall ever be eradicated is absurd and ridiculous. We can be remodified, changed, and assimilated, but never extinguished. We repeat therefore, that we are here and that this is our country. We shall neither die out, nor be driven out; but shall go with this people, either as a testimony against them, or as an evidence in their favour throughout their generations.'

Furthermore, the Negro contribution did not end in slavery—his efforts to preserve the Union which had done so little for him were even more significant. Outside of Richmond in 1864, a Negro division swept away entrenched Confederate opposition, suffered bloody losses, and won for twelve of its men the Medal of Honor, most of which were awarded posthumously. The willingness to fight on the part of the Negroes, and their capability to do so, long preceded the indecisiveness of Lincoln and the Federal Government as to the use of Negro troops. Men like Generals Butler, Lane and Hunter, however, unofficially organized Negro regiments and brigades. At one point, in 1863, Butler heard of fourteen hundred free Louisiana Negroes, who of themselves had organized a regiment. He sent for their leaders and asked if they would fight. Their answer was classic. 'General,' their spokesman said, 'we come of a fighting race. Our fathers were brought here because they were captured in war, and in hand to hand fights too. We are willing to fight. Pardon me, General, but the only cowardly blood we have got in our veins is the white blood.' And so they fought. Acceptance in the Union Army was tenuous, pay was often half of what the white soldiers received, and capture by the Confederates meant almost certain death, often after inhuman torture. Yet, fifty thousand Negro soldiers served the Union Army by the end of 1863, and at key engagements at Port Hudson, Miliken's Bend, Fort Wagner, Poison Spring, Olustee, Nashville, Petersburg, and four hundred and forty other places, they hurried the end of the bloodiest war in American history.

It is not my intention to give an exhaustive history of the Negro response to this country, in face of constant dehumanization, brutality, terror and death. What I am trying to do is establish a pattern of what the Negro has received from White America, and what he has, in turn, given. Reference can be made, for example, to what has been termed 'the Terrible Nineties', the 1890's, when a Negro was lynched every two days or so, only seldom for alleged rape, usually for other 'crimes' like testifying against a white man in court, seeking other employment, failing to use 'Mister' when speaking to whites, arguing over the price of blackberries, attempting to vote, accepting a job as postmaster, or just being too prosperous. Lerone Bennett, the Negro historian, sums up the pitiable and inhuman spectacle of those days in this fashion: 'To work from sun up to sun down for a whole year and to end owing "the man" $400 for the privilege of working; to do this year after year and to sink deeper and deeper into debt; to be chained to the land by bills at the plantation store; to be knocked down in the streets and whipped for not calling a shiftless hillbilly "Mister"; to be a plaything of judges and courts and policemen; to be without understanding, to not know why it is happening; to not know where to go and what to do to stay the whip and the rope and the chain; to give in finally; to bow, to scrape, to grin; to hate oneself for one's servility and weakness and blackness—all this was a Kafkaian nightmare which continued for days and nights and years.'

Yet, from all of this has come a donation to the American scene as paradoxical as it is intense. Southern historians have long been puzzled over the tyranny that Negroes held over the customs and manners of the South, and they wonder at the resilience of lives which can, under slavery and under a mockery of citizenship, influence others as strongly as they are influenced. When C. G. Jung visited America, he immediately noticed the imprint of the Negro. 'The mark of the Negro,' he said, 'was apparent in the walking, singing, dancing and even the praying of white Americans.' Beyond that, the Negro has been, even under slavery, the only American who has constantly made an issue of democracy—his presence has forced us to rewrite our Constitution, and to constantly re-evaluate what has been so blithely and inaccurately called the American dream of equality. He himself is evidence that what we believe ourselves to be is so largely a myth, and what we take such pride in doing is so largely worthless.

Negroes presently supply the only example of heroism under oppression that this country can claim; and it is a tragic loss to our youth that so-called educators pass over in silence the spectacle of twelve-year olds in jail, or Negroes praying for Sheriff Jim Clark, or students facing dogs, cattle prods and firehoses. Negroes have so assaulted the ears and sensibilities of white Americans with human rights and human dignity that the whole country has been led unwillingly into the debate; and were it not for the Negro revolution, it is hard to see how Jews, Puerto Ricans, immigrant workers and even some poor whites would now be faring as well as they are. Negroes have led the churches from an apathetic lethargy of religiosity and lip service to the Gospel, and it is no fantasy to say that the future of Christianity in this country rests squarely upon our reaction. Negroes have done more for ecumenism in the United States than any other force, and they have oddly collaborated with Pope John in helping us to understand that people are not to be feared but loved. Negroes have shook the whole religious, governmental, economic and social bureaucracy of the country, forcing it to look at itself, forcing it to lengths of justice and efficiency otherwise impossible, forcing it to the sullen and stubborn admission that, as it stands now, it has neither sympathy, room nor provision for any people but whites, and that this condition cannot remain. Negroes have been the catalyst for justice and human unity that the Christian Church is supposed to be, but never has been. Negroes finally, and perhaps most importantly, have written the death notices for the white man. True, he has received help from Auschwitz and Buchenwald, from Hiroshima and Nagasaki, even as he receives help from Vietnam today. But the local obituaries have nonetheless come from Harlem, Birmingham, Albany, Georgia, and Selma, Alabama. We can observe that the white man is dead as a notion of superiority and selected mission; dead as a person with an assumed mandate from God to coerce and limit the lives of men of darker skin; dead as one who considered himself the ruler of the earth, the heir of its wealth, the beneficiary of its fruits. The color of mankind has indeed changed, and with this phenomenon comes a terrifying freedom for whites particularly, since it invites us to abandon those foul and dark enclosures of mind whose walls are our myths and delusions and fears, and whose restless interiors are indication enough of our fragility, limitation and dependence.

PHILIP BERRIGAN, S.S.J., in *The Catholic Worker*, April 1965

1. (*a*) Summarize the benefits the writer claims the Negro has conferred on his country since 1619. (*b*) Can you suggest any other contribution which Negroes have made to the world today? (*c*) Summarize the different kinds of injustice meted out to the Negro in the U.S.A. according to the writer.

2. (*a*) What arguments are said to have been put forward in defence of the whites' paternalism and injustice? (*b*) How does the writer believe his countrymen ought to regard the Negro?

3. (*a*) Why does the writer regard the continued existence of the Negro in American society as of such peculiar importance? (*b*) In what sense is 'the white

man' said to be 'dead'? What evidence is given in support of this view? Do you
agree with it, and why? If not, why not?

4. What do you think would be the implications of an acceptance of the thesis
outlined in the passage for the social and political life of (*a*) Negroes and (*b*)
whites in the U.S.A.?

5. Explain in what ways this indictment might be considered to be of special
importance to the Christian? In what way would his/her assessment and
reaction differ from those of a humanist or communist or Negro nationalist
(for example, Black Muslim)?

23. Black like me

I caught the bus into town, choosing a seat halfway to the rear. As we
neared Canal, the car began to fill with whites. Unless they could find
a place to themselves or beside another white, they stood in the aisle.
A middle-aged woman with stringy gray hair stood near my seat. Her
face looked tired and I felt uncomfortable. As she staggered with the
bus's movement my lack of gallantry tormented me. I half rose from
my seat to give it to her, but Negroes behind me frowned disapproval.
I realized I was 'going against the race' and the subtle tug-of-war
became instantly clear. If the whites would not sit with us, let them
stand. When they became tired enough or uncomfortable enough, they
would eventually take seats beside us and soon see that it was not so
poisonous after all. But to give them your seat was to let them win.
I slumped back under the intensity of their stares.

But my movement had attracted the white woman's attention. For
an instant our eyes met. I felt sympathy for her, and thought I de-
tected sympathy in her glance. The exchange blurred the barriers of
race (so new to me) long enough for me to smile and vaguely indicate
the empty seat beside me, letting her know she was welcome to accept
it.

Her blue eyes, so pale before, sharpened and she spat out, 'What're
you looking at me like *that* for?'

I felt myself flush. Other white passengers craned to look at me.
The silent onrush of hostility frightened me.

'I'm sorry,' I said, staring at my knees. 'I'm not from here.' The
pattern of her skirt turned abruptly as she faced the front.

'They're getting sassier every day,' she said loudly. Another woman
agreed and the two fell into conversation.

My flesh prickled with shame, for I knew the Negroes rightly resented me for attracting such unfavourable attention. I sat the way I
had seen them do, sphynxlike, pretending unawareness. Gradually
people lost interest. Hostility drained to boredom. I learned a strange
thing—that in a jumble of unintelligible talk, the word 'nigger' leaps
out with electric clarity. You always hear it and always it stings. And

always it casts the person using it into a category of brute ignorance.

I left the bus on Canal Street. Other Negroes aboard eyed me not with anger, as I had expected, but rather with astonishment that any black man could be so stupid.

On Derbigny Street I had coffee in a small Negro cafe called the Two Sisters Restaurant. A large poster on the wall caught my attention:

Desegregate the Buses with the 7 point Program:

1. Pray for guidance.
2. Be courteous and friendly.
3. Be neat and clean.
4. Avoid loud talk.
5. Do not argue.
6. Report incidents immediately.
7. Overcome evil with good.

Sponsored by Interdenominational Ministerial Alliance

Rev. A. L. Davis, *Pres.*

Rev. J. E. Poindexter, *Secretary*

I walked to the same shoeshine stand in the French Quarter that I had been visiting as a white man. My friend Sterling Williams sat on an empty box on the sidewalk. He looked up without a hint of recognition.

'Shine?'

'I believe so,' I said and climbed up on the stand.

He hoisted his heavy body on his crutch and hobbled over to begin the work. I wore shoes of an unusual cut. He had shined them many times and I felt he should certainly recognize them.

'Well, it's another fine day,' he said.

'Sure is.'

'You're new in town, aren't you?'

'Yeah—just been here a few days,' I said.

'I thought I hadn't seen you around the quarter before,' he said pleasantly. 'You'll find New Orleans a nice place.'

'Seems pretty nice. The people are polite.'

'Oh . . . sure. If a man just goes on about his business and doesn't pay any attention to them, they won't bother you. I don't mean any bowing or scraping—just, you know, show you got some dignity.' He raised his glance to my face and smiled wisely.

'I see what you mean,' I said.

He had almost finished shining the shoes before I asked, 'Is there something familiar about these shoes?'

'Yeah—I been shining some for a white man—'

'A fellow named Griffin?'

'Yeah.' He straightened up. 'Do you know him?'

'I am him.'

He stared dumbfounded. I reminded him of various subjects we had discussed on former visits. Finally convinced, he slapped my leg with glee and lowered his head. His shoulders shook with laughter.

I went into one store after the other. In every store their smiles turned to grimaces when they saw I meant not to buy but to cash a check. It was not their refusal—I could understand that; it was the bad manners they displayed. I began to feel desperate and resentful. They would have cashed a travelers check without hesitation for a white man. Each time they refused me, they implied clearly that I had probably come by these checks dishonestly.

Finally, after I gave up hope and decided I must remain in New Orleans without funds until the banks opened on Monday, I walked toward town. Small gold-lettering on the window of a store caught my attention: CATHOLIC BOOK STORE. Knowing the Catholic stand on racism, I wondered if this shop might cash a Negro's check. With some hesitation, I opened the door and entered. I was prepared to be disappointed.

'Would you cash a twenty-dollar travelers check for me?' I asked the proprietress.

'Of course,' she said without hesitation, as though nothing could be more natural. She did not even study me.

I was so grateful I bought a number of paperback books—works of Maritain, Aquinas and Christopher Dawson. With these in my jacket, I hurried toward the Greyhound bus station.

In the bus station lobby, I looked for signs indicating a colored waiting room, but saw none. I walked up to the ticket counter. When the lady ticket-seller saw me, her otherwise attractive face turned sour, violently so. This look was so unexpected and so unprovoked I was taken aback.

'What do you want?' she snapped.

Taking care to pitch my voice to politeness, I asked about the next bus to Hattiesburg. She answered rudely and glared at me with such loathing I knew I was receiving what the Negroes call 'the hate stare'. It was my first experience with it. It is far more than the look of disapproval one occasionally gets. This was so exaggeratedly hateful I would have been amused if I had not been so surprised. I framed the words in my mind: 'Pardon me, but have I done something to offend you?' But I realized I had done nothing—my color offended her.

'I'd like a one-way ticket to Hattiesburg, please,' I said and placed a ten-dollar bill on the counter.

'I can't change that big a bill,' she said abruptly and turned away, as though the matter were closed. I remained at the window, feeling strangely abandoned but not knowing what else to do. In a while she flew back at me, her face flushed, and fairly shouted: 'I *told* you—I can't change that big a bill.'

'Surely,' I said stiffly, 'in the entire Greyhound system there must be some means of changing a ten-dollar bill. Perhaps the manager—'

She jerked the bill furiously from my hand and stepped away from the window. In a moment she reappeared to hurl my change and the ticket on the counter with such force most of it fell on the floor at my feet. I was truly dumbfounded by this deep fury that possessed her whenever she looked at me. Her performance was so venomous, I felt sorry for her. It must have shown in my expression, for her face congested to high pink. She undoubtedly considered it a supreme insolence for a Negro to dare to feel sorry for her. I stooped to pick up my change and ticket from the floor. I wondered how she would feel if she learned that the Negro before whom she had behaved in such an unladylike manner was habitually a white man.

With almost an hour before bus departure, I turned away and looked for a place to sit. The large, handsome room was almost empty. No other Negro was there, and I dared not take a seat unless I saw some other Negro also seated. A Negro porter sidled over to me. I glimpsed his white coat and turned to him. His glance met mine and communicated the sorrow, the understanding.

'Where am I supposed to go?' I asked him.

He touched my arm in that mute and reassuring way of men who share a moment of crisis. 'Go outside and around the corner of the building. You'll find the room.'

In the colored waiting room, which was not labeled as such, but rather as COLORED CAFE, presumably because of interstate travel regulations, I took the last empty seat. The books I had bought from the Catholic Book Store weighed heavily in my pocket. I pulled one of them out and, without looking at the title, let it fall open in my lap. I read: '. . . it is by justice that we can authentically measure man's value or his nullity . . . the absence of justice is the absence of what makes him man' (Plato). I have heard it said another way, as a dictum: 'He who is less than just is less than man.'

They called the bus. We filed out into the high-roofed garage and stood in line, the Negroes to the rear, the whites to the front. An army officer hurried to get at the rear of the white line. I stepped back to let him get in front. He refused and went to the end of the colored portion of the line. Every Negro craned his head to look at the phenomenon. I have learned that men in uniform, particularly officers, rarely descend to show discrimination, perhaps because of the integration of the armed forces.

At Slidwell we changed into another Greyhound bus with a new driver—a middle-aged man, large-bellied, with a heavy, jowled face filigreed with tiny red blood vessels near the surface of his cheeks.

A stockily built young Negro, who introduced himself as Bill Williams, asked if I minded having him sit beside me. 'People come down here and say Mississippi is the worst place in the world,' Bill said. 'But we can't all live in the North.'

'Of course not. And it looks like beautiful country,' I said, glancing out at giant pine trees.

Seeing that I was friendly, he offered advice. 'If you're not used to things in Mississippi, you'll have to watch yourself pretty close till you catch on,' he said. The others, hearing, nodded agreement. I told him I did not know what to watch out for.

'Well, you know you don't want to even look at a white woman. In fact, you look down at the ground or the other way.'

A large pleasant Negro woman smiled at me across the aisle. 'They're awful touchy on that here. You may not know you're looking in a white woman's direction, but they'll try to make something out of it,' she said. 'If you pass by a picture show, and they've got women on the posters outside, don't look at them either.'

'Is it that bad?'

Another man said: 'Somebody's sure to say, "Hey, boy—what are you looking at that white gal like *that* for?"' I remembered the woman on the bus in New Orleans using almost the same expression.

'And you dress pretty well,' Bill continued, his heavy black face frowning in concentration. 'If you walk past an alley, walk out in the middle of the street. Plenty of people here, white and colored, would knock you in the head if they thought you had money on you. If white boys holler at you, just keep walking. Don't let them stop you and start asking you questions.'

I thanked him for telling me these things.

'Well, if I was to come to your part of the country, I'd want somebody to tell me,' Bill said. He told me he was a truck driver, working out of Hattiesburg. He asked if I had made arrangements for a place to stay. I told him no. He said the best thing would be for me to contact a certain important person who would put me in touch with someone reliable who would find me a decent and safe place.

It was late dusk when the bus pulled into some little town for a stop. 'We get about ten minutes here,' Bill said. 'Let's get off and stretch our legs. They've got a men's room here if you need to go.'

The driver stood up and faced the passengers. 'Ten-minute rest stop', he announced. The whites rose and ambled off. Bill and I led the Negroes toward the door. As soon as he saw us, the driver blocked our way. Bill slipped under his arm and walked toward the dim-lit shed building.

'Hey, boy, where you going?' the driver shouted to Bill while he stretched his arms across the opening to prevent my stepping down. 'Hey, you, boy, I'm talking to you.' Bill's footsteps crunched unhurriedly across the gravel.

I stood on the bottom step, waiting. The driver turned back to me. 'Where do you think you're going?' he asked, his heavy cheeks quivering with each word.

'I'd like to go to the rest room.' I smiled and moved to step down.

He tightened his grip on the door facings and shouldered in close to block me. 'Does your ticket say for you to get off here?' he asked.

'No, sir, but the others—'

'Then you get your ass back in your seat and don't you move till we get to Hattiesburg,' he commanded.

'You mean I can't go to the—'

'I mean get your ass back there like I told you,' he said, his voice rising. 'I can't be bothered rounding up all you people when we get ready to go.'

'You announced a rest stop. The whites all got off,' I said, unable to believe he really meant to deprive us of rest-room privileges.

He stood on his toes and put his face up close to mine. His nose flared. Footlights caught silver glints from the hairs that curled out of his nostrils. He spoke slowly, threateningly: 'Are you arguing with me?'

'No, sir . . .' I sighed.

'Then you do like I say.'

We turned like a small herd of cattle and drifted back to our seats. The others grumbled about how unfair it was. The large woman was apologetic, as though it embarrassed her for a stranger to see Mississippi's dirty linen. 'There's no call for him to act like that,' she said. 'They usually let us off.'

I sat in the monochrome gloom of dusk, scarcely believing that in this year of freedom any man could deprive another of anything so basic as the need to quench thirst or use the rest room. There was nothing of the feel of America here. It was rather some strange country suspended in ugliness. Tension hung in the air, a continual threat, even though you could not put your finger on it.

'Well,' I heard a man behind me say softly but firmly, 'if I can't go in there, then I'm going in here. I'm not going to sit here and bust.' He walked in a half crouch to a place behind the last seat, where he urinated loudly on the floor. Indistinguishable sounds of approval rose around me—quiet laughter, clearing throats, whispers.

'Let's all do it,' a man said.

'Yeah, flood this bus and end all this damned foolishness.'

Bitterness dissolved in our delight to give the bus driver and the bus as good as they deserved. The move was on, but it was quelled by another voice: 'No, let's don't. It'll just give them something else to hold against us,' an older man said. A woman agreed. All of us could see the picture. The whites would start claiming that we were unfit, that Negroes did not even know enough to go to the rest room—they just did it in the back of the bus; never mentioning, of course, that the driver would not let us off.

The driver's bullish voice attracted our attention. 'Didn't you hear me call you?' he asked as Bill climbed the steps.

'I sure didn't,' Bill said pleasantly.

'You deaf?'

'No sir.'

'You mean to stand there and say you didn't hear me call you?'

'Oh, were you calling me?' Bill asked innocently. 'I heard you yelling "Boy", but that's not my name, so I didn't know you meant me.'

Bill returned and sat beside me, surrounded by the approval of his people. In the immense tug-of-war, such an act of defiance turned him into a hero.

JOHN HOWARD GRIFFIN, Black Like Me

1. The writer 'became a Negro' for a while to see what it was like to be treated as a Negro in the Southern States of America. Comment on the implications of this experiment for those who believe in segregation or apartheid. Is the fact that he was 'really a white man' significant?

2. (a) Pick out from the passages the ways in which white folk show their scorn for Negroes as 'inferior', without actually breaking the law. (b) Have you ever come across similar practices in Great Britain? Of what kind? (c) Why shouldn't the whites act in this way?

3. Why was Bill's act of defiance effective when the suggestion to 'flood' the bus would not have been?

4. Do you see any signs of hope for better black/white relationships in the future in either of these two passages? What are they? Could they be built on? How?

Apartheid

24. Darkest Africa

One may, if one wishes to, see in the arrangement of the Anglican grounds something symbolic of the Church's past mistakes and present dilemma. In one corner stands the Rectory, and in the corner diagonally opposite lie the remains of a church school, defunct and silent since Dr. Verwoerd's Native Affairs Department took African education under its wing. Of the remaining two corners, the one near the town holds the Church of St. John the Baptist—for Europeans; and the corner nearest the location holds the Church of St. Augustine—for Africans. The one is well panelled and carpeted; the other a little nearer, it may be, to Bethlehem—a slightly better fit for the eye of a needle, with its creaking benches, its mud floors, its flat hassocks, and its lovely altar ornaments, made from motor-car scrap, standing red, gold and black against pale-blue East End walls, with a brown Christ on the cross lifted above the sky line.

Through all these years—and St. John's is the oldest Anglican church in the Transvaal—the congregations of St. John and St. Augustine have not once met to worship God together; and what began as an unwise expedient, based on a difference of language, has been perpetuated as a fundamental attitude, almost as an Article of Faith. Blacks here, whites there, and heaven protect us from the day when any whites get 'communistic ideas', or the blacks get 'cheeky'. When we arrived in Zeerust the idea of African and European meeting together to worship God was unthinkable.

It still is.

On our first Sunday there, having preached a rather conventional New Year's sermon on the need to take stock of one's life from time to time, I met the parish council of St. John's in my study at the Rectory. I made the suggestion that, since I had a divided function, being both missionary and parish priest, it would be fitting for the mission council of St. Augustine's Church to be present at my institution in St. John's. I invited comment.

Nobody spoke. The senior churchwarden dozed placidly at my side; but a tendency on the part of the other councillors to avoid each other's eyes, and mine, made me reluctant to accept his acquiescent verdict. I tried to provoke some reaction.

'Please, I don't want to steamroller this. I am aware that there might be misgivings. The decision would be mine; but one of my privileges is to be advised by you, and I'd be grateful if you would express what may be on your minds.'

A throat was cleared; but no words came. Somebody stirred uneasily in his chair, somebody shuffled her feet. At length I gave up. 'Since you seem to have no objection, I shall invite the mission council. But I should have been glad to hear your comments.' The churchwarden woke up, the meeting came to an end.

The Second Major Disaster was our tour of the Reserves. In order to suit our convenience, my predecessor withdrew on the condition that I take over his belated Christmas rounds in the Reserves. Within a week, though we did not realise this, it again appeared that we were 'giving preference to natives'. We were visiting the Reserves before we had paid calls on white parishioners; to say nothing of duty calls, of the obligation of which we were ignorant, on Zeerust's Leading Families. And that after I had preached a sermon which, it seems, meant that I intended to 'stand St. John's on its head'; and had declared that I would 'invite all the natives to my institution'.

We returned to Zeerust. On my desk lay two letters. It was the end of the honeymoon.

The first terse letter informed me without preamble that, in view of my 'intention to start mixed services in our church', the eight council members in whose name the churchwarden signed, together with the congregation whom they represented, would be absent from my institution. (Two of the 'eight councillors' later told me that, at this time, they had knowledge neither of this document nor of its contents.) There was no suggestion of meeting or of discussion.

By this time I had already invited the mission council to be present at the institution. The choice was, therefore, my resignation; the withdrawal of the invitation, which would have been a breach of faith; or trouble. I rejected the first, refused to consider the second, and so chose the third. The prospect did not promise pastoral delights.

The second letter was written by the ubiquitous Anon, who on this occasion sought to disguise his anonymity under the handwriting of a backward child. 'Sir,' he wrote mendaciously, 'as a nonmember of St. John's Church Zeerust I am writing this letter to warn you that I am making it my business to collect as much information as I possibly can and that I intend making a report to Mr. C. R. Swart, Minister of Justice for South Africa to have both your name and your wife's put on the list as Communists. Yours The Local Communist Investigator.' I was glad that, at the moment of writing, the Local Communist Investigator had the grace to dissociate himself from St. John's; but the malice and hostility contained in his composition—as though one were to encounter a wet alligator in the dark—were new to us.

My answer to the first letter, written in some detail, elicited no reply.

In this somewhat inauspicious setting, occurred the Third Major Disaster. Coming from an unforeseeable source, it took everybody by surprise.

At eight o'clock on a Sunday morning, after a dawn Eucharist in St. Augustine's Church, I went to say Mass in St. John's for the second time since our arrival. The service was almost over before I realised that our problems in Zeerust had acquired a new and piquant ingredient. Kneeling at the Communion rail, at the end of the queue, were a man and a woman whom I did not know. What gave them a significance of which they themselves were unconscious, was their being of mixed forebears. They were what South Africa calls 'Coloureds'. In St. John's Church, Zeerust. In 'our dear little church', albeit rather empty.

As I turned back to the altar, their presence brought some temporary comfort. They clarified the issue. Here was a problem—for I had no doubt that there *was* a problem—not of my making in any sense; and a situation on which the ruling of the Church was clear, and, alike on people and priest, binding. A matter (so I thought) of principle.

I discovered that the new arrivals came from Mafeking, forty miles away. The man was a school-teacher who had been transferred to Zeerust. It being Sunday he and his wife acted as they had been accustomed to do in Mafeking. They came to church to worship, and to make their communions, having found out the time and place of worship. Nothing else happened. But the day the Coloureds came turned out to be decisive in the affairs of the Church of St. John the Baptist.

Reaction came swiftly. In the Sunday School that morning there was barely a handful of children. At Evensong, there were barely a dozen people.

I had learned from a well-disposed parishioner that the congregation was that evening to meet in the home of a certain councillor to plan their next move. My letters remaining unanswered, and my suggestion of discussion having been, as far as I was aware, ignored, I decided after Evensong to make my way to this house in the hope of being admitted; and, if admitted, of trying to reach some common understanding. As I approached I noticed a row of cars; and, through the lighted windows, a gathering of the absentee flock. That was all I saw. The owner of the house met me outside.

There was a meeting in the end.

The discussion went on for over two hours, with rather less sense of direction than a mole on a dance floor. It amounted simply, to this: either I withdraw my invitation to the African mission council, and

inform the coloured school-teacher and his family that they were not
to worship in St. John's Church, or the congregation would withdraw,
and, what was more strongly urged, end their contribution in money.

'I think,' I ventured, 'one point is this: I did at the council meeting
ask you to state your views. You withheld them, and now I have
issued the invitation.'

'Well, withdraw it.'

'That would be a breach of faith. And a discourtesy.'

'Yes,' asked another, 'but why make all this trouble over twelve
natives?'

'I might say the same. Why not extend a courtesy?'

'If you had lived here as long as we have you'd know you can't do
this here. You Englishmen walk into this country with a lot of liberal-
istic ideas and think—'

'But,' I interpolated, 'I'm a South African. Born and bred. So is my
wife.' There was a few seconds' silence.

'But you *can't* be!' breathed an incredulous voice. 'You *can't* expect
us to believe *that*!'

I must have shown my surprise. One of the less blunt councillors
rushed in hurriedly.

'Well, all right then,' he said, conceding us our citizenship, 'but
you're getting everybody's back up when you don't need to. Isn't it
better,' he reasoned, 'that the natives should stay away rather than
you offend a hundred church members?'

'If I withdraw this invitation I offend a thousand—not that the
number's the point. And they're also church members.'

'Yes, but,' objected somebody, 'they're natives.'

'Well!' expostulated the burly man heavily. 'I came here to hear
something different. A man can always make a mistake and I'll be the
first to forgive him. But a man who sticks to his mistakes is his own
worst enemy!'

'But look here,' said a woman councillor with some accuracy, 'this
isn't getting us anywhere. What I want to know is, why can't these
coloureds go to the natives' church?'

'Well, as I explained, even the Archbishop lacks the power to make
them do that.'

'But just tell them to.'

'I haven't the right. And even if I had, they don't understand
Tswana. They're English-speaking.'

'Yes, but they aren't Europeans.'

'Nor are they Bechuana. The real point is: they're Anglicans. And
people. Like us. St. Peter and St. Paul worked the whole thing out
centuries ago.'

'Well, we can't build a separate church for two coloureds. And if we let them come to St. John's it will be the thin end of the wedge.'

CHARLES HOOPER, *Brief Authority*

1. (a) If you had been in the writer's place what would your reaction to the Three Disasters have been? Give the grounds of your answer. (b) If you had been a resident of Zeerust in sympathy with the writer what do you think would have been the result of your support of him? Would you in fact have supported him openly or secretly or not at all? (c) What would you have done if you had been the coloured schoolteacher or his wife and had discovered the effect of your attending Communion?

2. Do you think the actual situation in Zeerust shows that apartheid was a sensible, practical policy in the circumstances, or that opposition to apartheid was even more necessary? Give your reasons.

3. The situation described in the passage did not appear to involve legal issues, but rather psychological and social problems. (a) What are these latter? (b) What evidence in the passage suggests that they were not amenable to rational refutation? (c) What do you think could have been done to overcome them?

4. Suppose that you supported the view of the European in Zeerust: (a) how far would you feel one was justified in extending and maintaining 'separation'? (b) how would you justify your 'separatist' view (the use of emotive language or abuse against the rector is disallowed)?

5. (a) On what grounds did the writer break with his predecessor's practice? Was he right to do so? (b) What results do you gather the writer's stand achieved? What results do you think may actually have been achieved? Is this an important or relevant question to ask about his Ministry?

25-8

Here are four more passages about the racial issue in South Africa, and the social, political, personal, moral and practical problems raised by it.

1. Compare and contrast the kind of stand taken by the different writers; indicate which facets of the situation each regards as having the greatest importance; which do you think seems to carry the most weight?

2. Two of the passages support 'separate development'; two are 'anti-apartheid'. (a) Take each 'side' in turn, and examine the cogency, relevance and validity of the points made by each. In particular, note any emotive phrases and say how far, if at all, they are justified by the evidence adduced. (b) Do you see any possibility of reconciliation between the two viewpoints?

3. Dr. Verwoerd once challenged a British audience with the words: 'What would *you* do?' Indicate what you would do if you were (a) in Dr. Verwoerd's position; (b) a Communist Q.C. practising in South Africa; (c) a British-stock white voter; (d) an educated black South African; (e) a newspaper editor in South Africa.

25. The meaning and basis of apartheid

South Africa's policy is based on these fundamental considerations:

Throughout their history of three centuries the peoples of South Africa have *never* been a single homogeneous nation.

The 3,500,000 people of European stock are a nation in their own right, with their own nationalism—the *first* of all the African nationalisms.

The 12 million Bantu comprise several distinctive nations, each with its own language and customs. Among these are the Xhosas (3.5 million) and the Zulus (3 million).

History has shown all nationalisms to be exclusive: one is not readily blended with another and none will be placated by artificial formulas.

Thus Black African peoples have so far refused to be pseudo-Europeans. Instead, they insist on an 'Africanisation' that is not watered down by any foreign influence.

Therefore, despite many attempts, there is as yet no *true* multi-racialism anywhere in Africa.

Recent events still suggest that in Africa the European and African personalities cannot be reconciled in one political system, but that either the one or the other will predominate.

If all South African peoples were to share *one* political system, there would inevitably follow a clash of nationalisms in which one must eventually dominate all others.

But if all African peoples are entitled to rule themselves, the White South African nation *must* be entitled to continue to rule itself and must not be subjected to a new colonialism.

The policy of apartheid provides for the separate development of South Africa's disparate peoples, avoiding a struggle for supremacy among them.

In the first place, apartheid safeguards the long established nationhood of the White people in that part of South Africa that has always been theirs and which they have not taken from anyone.

At the same time this policy provides for the progress of the Bantu peoples to full self-government.

The focal point of this political progress is the homelands of the Bantu peoples—those parts of the country (larger than England and Wales) which they originally settled and which are still theirs today.

The basis of all political progress for the Bantu is what is familiar to them—their own traditional systems of government. These are being developed to carry the full burden of modern statehood.

In order that their political autonomy may have substance, apartheid also calls for the full social and economic progress of the Bantu peoples.

Indeed, separate development means that the Bantu peoples will as far as possible be self-sufficient in all spheres of activity. They will provide their own doctors, teachers, civil servants and business men. The Transkei, homeland of the Xhosa people, is the epitome of this development. Of her 2,500 civil servants, for instance, nearly 2,000 are already Bantu.

There is no ceiling to all this development. Apartheid envisages a number of self-governing Bantu nations alongside, and in co-operative association with, the White nation—a South African commonwealth.

SOUTH AFRICA HOUSE, *South Africa In Fact*, October 1965

26. That hideous system

Mr Abram Fischer, Q.C., one of South Africa's leading barristers and grandson of a former President of the Orange Free State Republic, will be sentenced tomorrow (9 May 1966) on the nine charges under the Suppression of Communism Act and the Sabotage Act in which he has been convicted. Mr Fischer, now 59, broke bail in January, 1964, and eluded arrest for more than a year while he tried to mobilise underground opposition to the South African Government's policies. We print here extracts from his own defence speech, setting out the reasons which prompted him—an Afrikaner who was once an 'earnest believer' in segregation—to throw up his lucrative practice to identify himself with the struggle to achieve a democratic South Africa.

'I am on trial for my political beliefs and for the conduct to which those beliefs drove me. Whatever labels may be attached to the charges brought against me, they all arise from my having been a member of the Communist Party and from my activities as a member. I engaged upon those activities because I believed that, in the dangerous circumstances which have been created in South Africa, it was my duty to do so.

I accept the general rule that for the protection of a society laws should be obeyed. But when laws themselves become immoral and require the citizen to take part in an organised system of oppression— if only by his silence or apathy—then I believe that a higher duty arises.

These laws were enacted not to prevent the spread of Communism, but for the purpose of silencing the opposition of the large majority of our citizens.

In my mind there remain two clear reasons for my approach to the

Communist Party. The one is the glaring injustice which exists and has existed for a long time in South African society, the other, a gradual realisation as I became more and more deeply involved with the Congress Movement, that is, the movement for freedom and equal human rights for all, that it was always members of the Communist Party who seemed prepared, regardless of cost, to sacrifice most; to give of their best, to face the greatest dangers in the struggle against poverty and discrimination.

The glaring injustice is there for all who are not blinded by prejudice to see. All white South Africans can see it. The vast majority of them remain unmoved and unaffected. They are either oblivious to it or, despite all its cruelty, condone it on the assumption, whether admitted or not, that the non-white of this country is an inferior being with ideals, hopes, loves and passions which are different from ours.

It is true that *apartheid* has existed for many decades with all that it entails in shapes ranging from segregation and the deprivation of rights to such apparently trivial things as the constant depiction in our Afrikaans newspaper cartoons of the African as a cross between a baboon and a nineteenth-century American coon.

What is not appreciated by my fellow Afrikaner, because he has cut himself off from all contact with non-whites, is that the extreme intensification of that policy over the past 15 years is laid entirely at his door. He is now blamed as an Afrikaner for all the evils and the humiliation of *apartheid*.

Hence today the policeman is known as a 'Dutch'. That is why, too, when I give an African a lift during a bus boycott, he refuses to believe that I am an Afrikaner.

All this bodes ill for our future. It has bred a deep-rooted hatred for Afrikaners, for our language, our political and racial outlook amongst all non-whites—yes, even among those who seek positions of authority by pretending to support *apartheid*. It is rapidly destroying among non-whites all belief in future co-operation with Afrikaners.

To remove this barrier will demand all the wisdom, leadership and influence of those Congress leaders now interned and imprisoned for their political beliefs. It demands also that Afrikaners themselves should protest openly and clearly against discrimination.

All the conduct with which I have been charged has been directed towards maintaining contact and understanding between the races of this country. If one day it may help to establish a bridge across which white leaders and the real leaders of the non-whites can meet to settle the destinies of all of us by negotiation and not by force of arms, I shall be able to bear with fortitude any sentence which this court may impose upon me. It will be a fortitude strengthened by this knowledge at least, that for 25 years I have taken no part, not even by passive acceptance, in that hideous system of discrimination which we have erected in this country and which has become a byword in the civilised world today.'

The Observer, 8 May 1966

27. South Africa's ethnic problem

It would, of course, have been impossible to keep South African gold production profitable, had not the hiring of Bantu migratory workers contributed to keep labor costs relatively low. Here again we are confronted with the ethnic problem, which outweighs all others. Already the fact that, within the borders of the Republic, there is a population of 3·25 million Whites as opposed to 11·64 million Bantu, not to mention 1·65 million mulattos (who are referred to as 'Coloureds') and 522,000 Indians, is a difficult enough problem. The situation is aggravated because South Africa, through the development of its industry, its mines and its large cities, has become a country in which the majority—consisting of an extremely different race—has filtered into white settlements and in some cases already outnumbers the white people there. This has given rise to a problem which, to be fair, we must admit has no parallel elsewhere in the world.

In order to understand the issue and its unique nature, one must start with the indisputable fact that the Whites of South Africa have not merely a doubtful right to the land which they have settled and brought to the highest prosperity, but, rather, they are completely justified in owning and controlling it. When the Europeans, starting from the Cape, began to settle there in the middle of the 17th century, they came to a practically empty country at approximately the same time as the Bantu tribes from Central Africa, to the north, arrived in South Africa from the opposite direction. During the course of the succeeding centuries, the Whites have become just as much Africans as the other Europeans, who went westwards across the Atlantic Ocean, became Americans. The sole difference is that the white South Africans, contrary to the white Americans, did not at first—and later to a far lesser degree—crowd out the original inhabitants of the country.

Nor must we lose sight of the fact that the South African Bantu is not only a man of an utterly different race but, at the same time, stems from a completely different type and level of civilization. One of the most shocking signs of the intellectual confusion of our times is that too few seem to ask themselves if it is at all possible to weld a nation worthy of the name out of such utterly different ethnic-cultural groups and, on top of that, to organize it politically as a

democracy. It is all the more necessary to keep in mind the words of
Ernest Renan, in his classic work 'Qu'est-ce qu'une nation?' (1882):
'A nation is a spiritual principle, resulting from the deep complications
of history; a spiritual family, not a group determined by the geographical shape of the land in which it lives. Man does not improvise
himself. A nation, like an individual, is the end result of a long past
filled with effort, sacrifice and devotion.' If this truth serves us as a
premise, we must admit that seldom has there been a group of men
who, by virtue of their completely heterogeneous cultural and ethnic
heritage, were so unsuitable for the building of a nation, to say nothing of a democracy, as that composed of the white and black men of
South Africa. An uncommon measure of ideological passion is required, in order to ignore these differences—and an even more uncommon one to dispute the elementary truth expressed by Renan after
it has been pointed out.

It is here that the tremendous difference between the South African
ethnic problem and that of the Negro question in the United States
stands out. The South Africans could actually envy the Americans;
their Negro question being merely one of a minority representing no
danger for the majority and one which has more or less been assimilated into the great mass of the population during the course of centuries. This problem could be solved without jeopardizing the very existence of the nation as a whole. The South Africans are therefore right
when they express a desire for an understanding of South Africa's
ethnic problem most of all by the Americans, especially since the latter
have not even been able to solve their far easier and less dangerous
problem. The Bantu problem in South Africa stems not so much from
an inheritance of the slavery system, but is rather the consequence of
the ever-increasing power of attraction of European industry and
urban culture which, as continued immigration from northern Africa
proves, has spread far into the continent toward the north.

'Apartheid' concerns a separation of the races, by means of which
the South African government is trying to solve, or at least render
bearable, the ethnic problem of the country. We, as outsiders, should
make an honest effort to understand the true nature of the issue—its
uniqueness and the heaviness of the burden it represents. What—
possibly in unattractive fashion—this Dutch word is meant to convey
is the effort, at the cost of great sacrifice, to do something completely
reasonable, that is to say, keep apart the immiscible ethnic groups
through the setting up of autonomous areas reserved for the Bantu, the
first of which has now been given over to the Xhosa nation under the
name of 'Transkei'.

If we find it hard, in principle, to reach a just verdict, we should
remember other cases in which the separation of ethnically hetero-

geneous groups, painful as the operation generally is, is considered today as unavoidable. The banishment of the Greeks from Turkey after the first World War was surely, for those concerned, a terrible thing and cannot, in its rigor, be compared to the current apartheid in South Africa. Every one will admit that, if Turks and Greeks still had to live together in Asia Minor, problems would arise which would far overshadow those on Cyprus. Further they would concern the political symbiosis of groups much closer to each other than the Whites and Bantu in South Africa. The Jews in Israel, to cite another example close to us, own that they would be faced with a completely insoluble problem if Israel were forced by the United Nations to accept the return of hundreds of thousands of Arab refugees into the land they left in 1948, in a sort of spontaneous 'apartheid', which Israel itself recognises as inevitable. Finally, it must be borne in mind that the division of the Indian subcontinent into India and Pakistan, which was accomplished with hideous sacrifices and still represents the cause of great enmity between the incompletely and unsatisfactorily separated races, is, basically, nothing other than a particularly brutal form of apartheid. This in no way hinders those responsible for it from making South Africa the butt of their most severe opprobrium, even though that country is trying to reach a milder and more equitable application of a principle which, in general, is tacitly accepted.

Apartheid means that certain appropriate possibilities for development will be given the two ethnic groups in South Africa, black as well as white, through the establishment of 'Bantustans'. This is the specific form in which South Africa pursues the policy of 'decolonializing' and 'development aid', which corresponds to this country's needs. No expense is being spared and all the experience of the Whites who have had contact with the Bantu for centuries is being utilized. One of the major aims of this policy is to raise the educational standards of the Bantu, already higher than in any other part of Africa, and to teach them modern agricultural methods.

One may judge the chances of success of this policy as good or not, but it could hardly be called stupid or evil. Its leading concepts were epitomized a year ago by former Swiss Ambassador F. Kappeler, in a talk before the Swiss-South African Association in Zurich, as follows:

1. Because a mixed white and black racial community is not possible in view of experiences both in South Africa and elsewhere, but is, on the contrary, undesirable to the overwhelming majority on both sides, a common seat of power cannot be achieved;
2. a continuation of white supremacy with merely limited representation of the black population through the Bantu will be no longer accepted;

3. a transferral of power by the white to the black majority will be
   nearly unanimously refused;
4. equal rights for both races, with the right to vote for those who
   qualify, must, in the end, given progressive schooling and development, lead equally to black supremacy;
5. it must be concluded that the generally-demanded right to vote and
   self-government of the Bantu can today be realised only through
   separation of white and black areas.

Here is the proper place to mention the idea given a focal position
by R. Wertheimer. Without rejecting apartheid as such, this authority
accepts it, in that he relies on its serving, through training and development of the Bantu population within an appropriate framework,
to prepare for a future in which whites and blacks, after overcoming
their excessive racial consciousness, will be able to work together in
such a way that the whites could then grant the blacks equality
without destroying themselves and South Africa in the process (as
they would today, a fact which must be granted by all informed
persons). Whether Wertheimer's hopes will be fulfilled remains to be
seen. In any case, apartheid as such would not preclude them.

May I emphasize that a fair judgement of this policy is rendered
even more difficult by a circumstance of great importance. A difference
must be drawn between the 'actual' or 'big' apartheid and that of the
'little' or 'small' apartheid. The latter is the often humbling, petty
and exasperating degradation of the black within the white settlements. Here there is little to excuse and less to defend and the government in Pretoria would be well advised, in the interest of its policy
of 'big' apartheid, to undertake a thorough revision of its methods.

Justice demands refutation of the idea that South Africa's Bantu,
as a whole, are a persecuted and unhappy mass of people. In view of
the cold war being waged against that country by the entire world,
but above all by the propagandistically least scrupulous governments,
all unfavourable reports about this country should be viewed with
the greatest scepticism. It would be best to count them either untrue
or grossly exaggerated, until the opposite is proved. I, personally, have
the liveliest and most pleasant memories of the happily-waving children in the native villages; the humorous farmer from the northern
Transvaal, who earned sufficient money to buy another cow by working in our hotel for several months as an elevator boy, and the magnifi-
cent dances put on by the individual tribes represented among the
seasonal workers in the gold mines. These were their great Sunday
entertainments at which they merely tolerated the presence of their
white employers, whom they caricatured drastically in a refreshingly
disrespectful way. All statistics prove, in addition, that nowhere in

Africa is the black so well paid, provided with such good living quarters, so well fed and so well dressed as he is in South Africa. Nowhere is as much done for his education and health as in South Africa, and Giniewski reminds us that that country has never had a lynching.

If we weigh all the factors, 'small' apartheid remains a saddening affair and a source of unhappiness for countless individuals. But, the smugness with which so many people the world over regard the South Africans (the Boers and the English are drawn closer together through campaigns against their country) is morally hardly on a higher level. These self-satisfied people sit in judgement, although they are lucky enough not to have in their own countries, whether they are Swiss, German or Scandinavian, such a unique and terrible problem as the ethnic problem of South Africa, and are probably not even capable of imagining its dimensions.

This Phariseeism, so difficult to take, is one of the main reasons why perspectives are here again grotesquely twisted. It would be ludicrous, were it not scandalous, to compare conditions in South Africa with, for instance, the genuine genocide and culture murder in Tibet or even only with the fate of the Baltic peoples and others within the boundaries of the Communistic supercolonial empire. But many of those desirous of forcing South Africa out of the community of nations, who do not even wish to sit at the same table with South Africans in order to discuss questions of social insurance, vaccination or the tourist trade, are the very same ones who would like to invite into the United Nations the people responsible for the crushing of Tibet, not to mention their flirtation with the colonial rulers in Moscow.

W I L H E L M R Ö P K E, in the *Schweitzer Monatshefte*, May 1964

28. Inside Verwoerd's trap

At a golf tournament near Johannesburg the other day the usual Government officials were present to see that the rules of *apartheid* were strictly observed. Their orders were to prevent the space reserved for white spectators from being used by Coloureds, Indians, Chinese, or Malays, if any. For some reason the orders did not say what to do about Africans. Possibly the department had assumed that Africans would not be interested in a game requiring poise and self-control; or had forgotten that the under-employed are, like the over-rich, an infinitely leisured class; or it had escaped notice that Africans are curious about happenings as such. They turned up by the dozen. The result was confusion, an all-colours rush down the fairway, and a hopeless intermingling at the greens. It proved to be the first multi-racial sporting occasion for some years in the Republic of Dr Verwoerd.

For the stranger to South Africa what registers most is that sceptical-minded people here need to tell this kind of story over and over again, as though it gave some special relief, offered the whisper of a chance that a rigid control must sometime, somewhere, break down. It also leaves the visitor puzzled to know how even Dr Verwoerd's Government, the most efficient on the African continent, backed by a first-class Civil Service, ever finds time for anything besides racial matters when even golf-watchers must be watched.

Perhaps 80 per cent of parliamentary and administrative time must be occupied in enforcing the cleavage between the various racial groups, and in matters of defence and foreign policy that spring from it. The part of the plan which prescribes the removal of some 250,000 Africans from their present homes in the Western Cape area to distant homelands in the east is now getting under way. A number of whites are having to move out of 'black' areas to the places allotted to them on the map, and so are Indians, Chinese and others who are not in their proper racial sector.

It must be fairly added that some non-whites even welcome the moves, either because they may get a better and newer house (the Government puts a good deal of effort into its housing schemes) or because the shipping out of Africans protects their particular group from too much job competition. But some of the decrees handed down from Pretoria have surprised South Africans in their bold dismissal of traditions.

One example is the declaration that the old and celebrated (or notorious) coloured quarter of Cape Town, 'District Six', is to be converted into an all-white area, despite the hot opposition of the city council. The town-planners and the police may rejoice that this over-crowded, boozy, blowsy, paint-peeled, banjo-strumming, Damon Runyon sort of place will be elevated to a whiter respectability. It does not sound like security of tenure for any non-white, however deep his roots.

After eighteen years of Nationalist rule apartheid is not so much a code as an ingrained habit. About the time they are picking up the twice times table non-white children learn from their parents which bus seats and benches not to use, where to exit and enter in public buildings, how to be inconspicuous on white territory. The reasons why—as obscurely interesting as the facts of life—come later. So do the devious adjustments of personality needed to cope with it: the hard, probing, cynical wit of the Johannesburg African; the muddled sycophancy of many Cape Coloureds; the respectful, almost affectionate, subservience of black farm-hands for a masterful Afrikaner boss; the hangdog resentment of teenage political thinkers, born to trouble.

'To understand the Afrikaner,' said one leading Cape figure to me, 'you must like him. No, I don't mean sentimentally: just sympathise a little with his character, antecedents and predicament.' For the enquiring stranger it is hard to pass this test first time. The harshness of the solution adopted, the intricate social mechanism of Dr Verwoerd's response to the challenge, continually distract the eye from the depth and difficulty of the problem behind it.

The code of domestic law which regulates almost every aspect of the African's life, defining the non-existence of his right to be anything more than a unit of work-capacity in white areas (which cover 87 per cent of the land space of the country), now fills a thousand-page book which few lawyers have entirely grasped. It continues to grow as each tiny loophole which might allow racial mixing is plugged.

It is an offence for a white and a non-white to have tea together in any café in South Africa unless they have obtained a permit. If any non-white sits on a whites-only bench as a protest against *apartheid* he risks a fine of up to £300, or three years imprisonment, or ten strokes of the whip, or any two of these. Penalty for an African taking part in a strike: fine of up to £500, or three years jail, or both . . . and so on.

For the doctrine's sake nothing is too much trouble or too trivial. The African who is staying illicitly without a job or permit in a so-called white area among the teeming thousands of African migratory workers may feel safely lost among the vague, dark crowd. But not at all. Some official cares deeply about him. To lose just one numeral may mean getting the whole sum wrong. The interloper may escape attention for months. But then he will and must be found, punished by a court, and then 'endorsed out' to some tribal area which may be totally new to him and where he will almost certainly find no job.

The Government will allow no blurring of edges, at least openly. There is the example of the beaches. Until recently the sands along the Cape coast were open to everyone. In practice most were 'whites only' places, anyway, since poorer people without cars could not reach them easily; and when non-whites did turn up they made a habit of sitting deferentially out of the way, knowing their place. This was seen not to be in the strict spirit of the plan, so the Government has now allotted separate beach areas, and presumably the portions of sea in front of them, to different racial groups.

The Coloureds—that is people of mixed racial parentage—had also been allowed the privilege of using white cinemas, though seated separately in the balcony. One new order prohibits this; another prevents Coloured taxi-owners from carrying white passengers, obviously the major part of their business. Since many Coloured people felt that they enjoyed some status in the community, as business or professional men, with a deep yearning to be treated on a level with whites, and are closely tied to the Afrikaner way of life, these rejections cut them to the quick.

There was also resentment from the Indian community which includes a prosperous shopkeeper class, when they found that they were being moved to residential areas up to 30 miles from the cities, away from their white customers. And there was dismay among the Chinese community (which contains many professional men, and counts more graduates per head than any other racial group) to find they were being moved to less privileged areas and categorised as 'non-white', while the Japanese can stay in the white areas (*apartheid* has many subtleties of this kind). The reason the Japanese have been made 'honorary Aryans'—as happened to them in Hitler's Germany—is that their trade with South Africa now ranks second in importance, after Britain's.

The sweeping victory of the Nationalists in the election was primarily a vote for Dr Verwoerd's tough and shrewd leadership. With security as their main preoccupation, a large body of English-speaking voters, increasingly racialist in their views, added their weight to the party's solid Afrikaner support.

While the Prime Minister's first priority will be to strengthen the economy against sanctions by investing even more in oil-prospecting, synthetic fuel, aircraft and munitions, his big internal challenge over the next five years will be to show that separate development can work—not only in the 'pinprick' *apartheid* represented by separate beaches, bus-seats and so on, but in the major experiment of the Transkei. This large east coast province, with its rolling downland, hills and over-worked maize and millet patches, is meant to be the first Bantustan or African homeland. Dr Verwoerd's radical wing want to be shown evidence that this large empty territory can absorb a good part of the African masses and check their migration to the 'white' cities and towns. The party's right-wingers, on the other hand, will be breathing over his shoulder to see that he does not spend a penny too much on 'Kaffirs' and that he is not unknowingly creating a bridge-head for Communists.

Either way it will be a stern test of Dr Verwoerd's command of the art of the impossible. A commission has already shown that the Transkei cannot even offer a subsistence living to its present population, far less take any more. Dr Verwoerd has firmly resisted suggestions that the Bantustans should be given a bigger share of the land or that white capital should be allowed inside them to create work (there is hardly any, so far). His probable first step will be to encourage more industries to move from the Johannesburg industrial complex down to the Transkei border (strictly on the white side of it) where they will get very cheap labour and help to support the Transkeians.

Dr Verwoerd has warned against 'over-hastiness'; so the prospects are that he will again be seen to be travelling skilfully without ever quite arriving. Now that the Republic has been brought under a tight political control, he may be able to afford a more leisurely domestic pace. With a massive operation by the security police over the last few years the illegal opposition parties and their sympathisers have been eradicated, intimidated or otherwise reduced to a frozen silence. Those overseas critics who, after Sharpeville and the subsequent Poqo risings, predicted a series of eruptions leading to a final explosion cannot have bargained for so relentless an attack by the security forces. Their net has been used without compunction to pull in a wide variety of potential dissidents: not only the obvious ones who were planning some demonstration or act of violence but also those who, years ago, belonged to some group of moderate protest, or anyone tenuously connected with a group.

In the Eastern Cape province, once the breeding-ground of the most able African leaders, the eradication of every rank-and-file member of the banned nationalist parties is now more or less completed. No quarter was given. More than 800 have been brought to trial so far and sentences averaging five or six years imposed. Some of the methods employed to ensure conviction—the rehearsing of prosecution witnesses, their use in case after case, the re-arrest and re-charging of anyone acquitted, the hindrances put in the way of the defence—showed the police in a mood of unforgiving conquest. A couple of years ago—about the time optimistic forecasts of downfall were being made—they were relying more on muscle than sophistication. Now, under the expert direction of the Minister of Justice, Mr Vorster, they have been trained to a high degree of professionalism. A wide network of informers, enrolled by the usual world-wide methods of intimidation or promise of favour, keeps the security police in a state of near-omniscience about any important rumblings below the surface. They move in all circles. 'Go out to dinner,' said one liberal, 'and you will find one talking Shakespeare to the hostess.'

Several lawyers told me that they thought judges and magistrates were still admirably standing in the middle between State and accused in spite of the pressures. Others were more doubtful and said that as more political appointees came to the Bench there was an increasing priority for 'protection of the State' in their judgements. Fair or not, the courts can now be by-passed by a wide variety of 'administrative' rulings. There are 25 different kinds of banning order under the Suppression of Communism Act, ranging from house arrest downwards. The Minister of Justice's decision cannot be challenged—on what he regards as 'Communist', for example. A ban normally lasts for five years. In its effect it means that the banned person cannot talk to anyone outside his family circle or his doctor, and it is hard to find a job that suits all the conditions.

About 420 people have been banned so far, including 40 members of the Liberal Party (the only party which proposes a universal, all colours, franchise). The effect of all these rulings, and of the Minister's powers of ordering virtually indefinite detention under the 180-day law, has been to reduce even the moderate non-violent stand against racialism to a shadow of what it was. Those who remain, out of a sense of duty or because, strangely enough, they are attached to South Africa, live in an atmosphere of increasing isolation and uncertainty. 'There's just no one left to talk to', said one liberal to me, in a voice that mixed scorn and self-pity. I asked him how many close acquaintances were now missing from his company. His list came to about 50, either gone into exile, in jail, or under banning orders.

The Government's attack, which has had no failures so far, may now be turning on the English-language Press. Its effort to discredit the *Rand Daily Mail* and its editor-in-chief, Lawrence Gandar, its most persistent newspaper critic, is now moving towards its climax. All the informants who helped the paper to produce a series of articles on prison conditions have since been pounced on, flaws discovered in their stories and records, charges laid and convictions secured. Action may now be taken against Mr Gandar and the reporter who prepared the series—though it did, in fact, secure an improvement in prison conditions.

The Government no doubt hopes that its discrediting technique will persuade the public to draw the conclusion that the paper's demand for an enquiry into jail conditions was baseless and unnecessary. This would not be true. If the discouragement of potential witnesses had not been so effective, ample evidence could be produced from lawyers and other people of credibility and standing to show that an enquiry was overdue. Sworn affidavits exist from Africans who have been given electric shock treatment to extract information; suffocation treatments (the bag over the head, sometimes with smoke pumped in); or the bucket or oil-drum over the head, persistently beaten until the prisoner talks; or the method, largely reserved for white detainees, of enforced standing for hours—all these have been used on large numbers of prisoners and, occasionally, brought to light by a vigilant magistrate.

If they have largely dropped out of use it is perhaps because they are no longer needed; they worked. Apologists say, 'Look, some of those Kaffirs have been trained in Algeria. They could do worse than that. What do you expect?'

The white man-in-the-street, who hears relatively little of the methods involved, is mostly conscious only of the magical stability that Dr Verwoerd has produced and of the fact that if he is living in a trap, as some outsiders say, then the Benefactor has made it a very prosperous and privileged trap. The walls have been made thicker and the bolts stronger. For white South Africans this circumscribed world is complete in itself. Only occasionally do they worry that the view ahead is so limited and always uncertain.

R O Y P E R R O T, in *The Observer*, 24 April 1966

Integrating immigrants?

29. (*a*) 'Sorry, we will not be able to use you'

At the Demobilisation Centre I had been interviewed by an officer whose job it was to advise on careers. On learning that I had a science degree and varied experience in engineering technology, he expressed the opinion that I would have no difficulty in finding a good civilian job. He had given me a letter of introduction to the Higher Appointments Office in Tavistock Square, London, where I was interviewed by two courteous, impersonal men who questioned me closely on my academic background, service career and experience in industry. I explained that after graduating I had worked for two years as a Communications Engineer for the Standard Oil Company at their Aruba Refinery, earning enough to pay for post-graduate study in England. At the end of the interview they told me that I would be notified of any vacancies suitable to my experience and qualifications.

I was nervous as I stood in front of the Head Office in Mayfair; this firm had a high international reputation and the thought of being associated with it added to my excitement. The uniformed commissionaire courteously opened the large doors for me, and as I approached the receptionist's desk she smiled quite pleasantly.

'Good morning.' Her brows were raised in polite enquiry.

'Good morning,' I replied. 'My name is Braithwaite. I am here for an interview with Mr Symonds.'

I was wearing my best suit with the right shirt and tie and pocket handkerchief; my shoes were smartly polished, my teeth were well brushed and I was wearing my best smile—all this had passed the very critical inspection of Mr and Mrs Belmont with whom I lived. I might even say that I was quite proud of my appearance. Yet the receptionist's smile suddenly wavered and disappeared. She reached for a large diary and consulted it as if to verify my statement, then she picked up the telephone and, cupping her hand around the mouthpiece as if for greater privacy, spoke rapidly into it, watching me furtively the while.

'Will you come this way?'

At the second floor we stepped out into a passage on to which several rooms opened; pausing briefly outside one of them she said, 'In there', and quickly retreated to the lift. I knocked on the door and entered a spacious room where four men were seated at a large table.

One of them rose, walked around to shake hands with me and introduced his colleagues, and then indicated a chair in which I seated myself. After a brief enquiry into my place of birth and R.A.F. service experience, they began to question me closely on telecommunications and the development of electronics in that field. The questions were studied, deliberate, and suddenly the nervousness which had plagued me all the morning disappeared; now I was confident, at ease with a familiar subject. They questioned me on theory, equipment, circuits, operation; on my training in the U.S.A., and on my experience there and in South America. They were thorough, but I was relaxed now; the years of study, field work and post-graduate research were about to pay off, and I knew that I was holding my own, and even enjoying it.

And then it was all over. Mr Symonds, the gentleman who had welcomed me, leaned back in his chair and looked from one to another of his associates. They nodded to him and he said:

'Mr Braithwaite, my associates and I are completely satisfied with your replies and feel sure that in terms of qualification, ability and experience, you are abundantly suited to the post we have in mind. But we are faced with a certain difficulty. Employing you would mean placing you in a position of authority over a number of our English employees, many of whom have been with us a very long time, and we feel that such an appointment would adversely affect the balance of good relationship which has always obtained in this firm. We could not offer you that post without the responsibility, neither would we ask you to accept the one or two other vacancies of a different type which do exist, for they are unsuitable for someone with your high standard of education and ability. So, I'm afraid we will not be able to use you.' At this he rose, extending his hand in the courtesy of dismissal.

I felt drained of strength and thought; yet somehow I managed to leave that office, navigate the passage, lift and corridor, and walk out of the building into the busy sunlit street. I had just been brought face to face with something I had either forgotten or completely ignored for more than six exciting years—my black skin. It had not mattered when I volunteered for aircrew service in 1940, it had not mattered during the period of flying training or when I received my wings and was posted to a squadron; it had not mattered in the hectic uncertainties of operational flying, brothered to men who like myself had no tomorrow and could not afford to fritter away today on the absurdities of prejudice; it had not mattered when, uniformed and winged, I visited theatres and dance-halls, pubs and private houses.

I had forgotten about my black face during those years. I saw it daily yet never noticed its colour. I was an airman in flying kit while on his Majesty's business, smiled at, encouraged, welcomed by grateful civilians in bars or on the street, who saw not me, but the uniform and its relationship to the glorious, undying Few. Yes, I had forgotten about my skin when I had so eagerly discussed my post-war prospects with the Careers Officer and the Appointments people; I had quite forgotten about it as I had jauntily entered that grand, imposing building.

Now, as I walked sadly away, I consciously averted my eyes from the sight of my face reflected fleetingly in the large plate glass shop windows. Disappointment and resentment were a solid, bitter, rising lump inside me; I hurried into the nearest public lavatory and was violently sick. I realised at that moment that I was British, but evidently not a Briton, and that fine differentiation was now very important.

1. Was there any excuse for the treatment the writer received from Mr Symonds and his fellow directors? What excuse did they offer? Do you think it at all cogent? Was it a 'smokescreen'? If so, what was the *real* reason? (Try to state it from Mr Symonds' point of view.)

2. Why did the war make a difference to the writer's acceptance by his white colleagues? Was this valid only in wartime (if so, why?), or not?

3. Is there any reason why a firm should not choose its staff as it pleases? Do you think there should be legislation to prevent colour-discrimination in appointing people to jobs? Suppose that you do: what kind of legislation do you think it would be practical to enact?

(b) 'Don't you mind?'

Thursday, November 18th, was Gillian's birthday. On the Monday evening I had been to Foyle's and bought her a book of poems. During mid-morning recess on Tuesday she came into my classroom, where I was, as usual, surrounded by a group of chattering youngsters.

'May I see you for a moment, Mr Braithwaite?'

'Certainly, Miss Blanchard.' We walked to the rear of the class out of earshot of the smiling, whispering group.

'Got a surprise for you.'

'Oh, yes? What is it?'

'Thursday is my birthday.'

'No surprise, I already knew.'

'I've ordered dinner for two at the "Poisson d'Or". Special, with wine. Supposed to be very good; you know—*très élégant*.'

'Good. I'm fond of *très élégant*.'

'That's fine then. We can see *Paisan* at the Academy and dine afterwards.'

'Right, it's a date.' Smiling she hurried out.

I waiked back to the group of children and into a barrage of questions.

'Is Miss Blanchard your girl-friend?' Tich Jackson queried. 'She's smashing, isn't she?'

By agreeing that Miss Blanchard was smashing I managed to parry the first part of the question. The girls began to discuss Gillian's hair, clothes and shoes, and the conversation was steered into smoother water.

When Thursday came I felt excited as a sandboy.

Gillian looked very lovely in an ensemble of light grey with a ridiculous little black hat perched saucily on her head. We caught a bus and changed to another at Aldgate, where we sat in front on the upper deck. Gillian immediately linked her arm in mine and we were together in a private, wonderful world of pleasant, whispered, unimportant talk about anything and everything which caught our attention en route.

The film was wonderful and we left the cinema somewhat subdued by the artistry and sheer reality of it, and walked through Piccadilly Circus to catch a bus for Chelsea.

The 'Poisson d'Or' was, as Gillian had said, *très élégant*. The Maître d'hôtel came forward and directed us to our table, with a questioning glance at me. We sat down and chatted quietly, both of us very much aware of the special something between us, recognised, but waiting to be acknowledged. Eventually we both realised that the service was being exceptionally slow, especially to our table, for the other diners seemed to have waiters hovering around them all the time.

Presently a waiter brought us a bill of fare which he placed on the table, and departed. Annoyance was large in Gillian's eyes, but I took it up and we spent a little time carefully choosing the food. The waiter returned and took our order, his manner casual with an implied discourtesy, and he was so long in returning that I became really uneasy and annoyed. What was the fellow playing at?

He came at last with the soup. Whether by accident or design, some of the soup was spilled from my plate on to the cloth. I sat back expecting that he would do something about it as good service demanded, but he merely stood there looking at me, with a faint sneer on his face. Gillian reacted suddenly. With a swift movement she gathered up her gloves and handbag. 'Let's go, Rick.'

Outside she turned to me, her eyes like coals in her pale face.

'Will you take me home, please?'

What had I done? Was the waiter's stupid discourtesy to be blamed on me? She had chosen the place, yet at the first sign of bother she had turned on me. Was that all that our friendship meant to her? The taxi stopped at her direction outside a block of flats in a quiet street

near the embankment. She got out and hesitated while I paid the
driver, then turned and ran up the steps. I watched her, expecting that
she would disappear forever inside, but she turned and said: 'Aren't
you coming?' in a tight angry voice. This Gillian was a stranger,
a cold, hateful stranger. I was tempted to hurry away from her, but
she meant too much to me. I'd see it through, whatever it was. I
followed her inside. Her flat was on the ground floor. Everything
here was in harmony except ourselves. Gillian threw hat, handbag
and gloves on to the sofa with an impatient gesture and invited me to
sit, then began to move about the room idly fixing and straightening
the things on the top of the bookcases. At last with a few quick strides
she pushed open one of the doors and was gone.

I took the book of poems from my briefcase and laid it on a low
coffee table; the whole evening was irretrievably spoilt, and this was
certainly not the time to present my gift as I had planned.

In a few minutes she returned, apparently calmer. She was about to
sit down when she saw the little package; she picked it up, tore off the
wrappings, and looked at it. Then her hands dropped by her side in an
attitude of despair.

'Damn you, damn you.' Each word was torn out of her like a dry,
painful cough. 'Why did you just sit there and take it?'

'What was I supposed to do, hit him? Did you want a scene in that
place?'

'Yes, I wanted a scene. I wanted a big, bloody awful scene.' The
words sounded foul coming from her. She was glaring at me, her body
bent forward at the waist, her arms raised slightly backwards like an
agitated bird.

'What good would that have done?'

'I don't know and I don't care. I wanted you to hit him, to beat him,
down, down . . .' She was nearly incoherent with anger and sobbing.

'It wouldn't help, it never helps.'

'Why not? Just who do you think you are? Jesus Christ? Sitting
there all good and patient? Or were you afraid? Is that it? Were you
afraid of that damned little waiter?'

'You're being hysterical, Gillian; beating people up never solves
anything.'

'Doesn't it? Well, you tell me what does. You've been taking it and
taking it, don't you think it's time you showed a little spirit?' She was
becoming quite shrill now, like a fishwife. 'Was I supposed to stand
up for you to-night?'

I felt tired, awfully tired of the whole thing.

'Let's not talk any more about it.'

'That's right, run away from it.'

'Oh, let's forget it.'

'Forget it? Do you know what to-day is? I'd planned and planned for it to be nice and wonderful for us. To-day of all days. I could have gone somewhere else or done something else, but no, I had to be with you, and you calmly tell me to forget it. Oh I hate you, I hate you, you damn black . . .'

With a scream she hurled the book at me and followed behind it, her hands stiff and clawing, like a demented creature. I led her to a chair and she sat sideways, crying softly. I sat nearby, nervously watching her, knowing in my heart that this was the end; knowing that I ought to leave her now, but loath to go. Presently she turned to me and asked :

'What are we going to do, Rick?'

'I don't know, Gillian.' What could I say? There was a small flutter of hope in my heart and I held my breath, waiting for her next words.

'Is that the sort of thing we'd be faced with, all the time?'

She was speaking about us, both of us.

'Do you mean the waiter thing?'

'Yes, does it happen to you often?'

'Not often, hardly ever really. You see, it never happened to me while I was in the R.A.F., and since becoming a civilian I have not been anywhere socially, until, well, until we started going out together.'

I sat watching her, uncertain what to say. She was English and had spent all her life in England; was she truly free from the virus of racial intolerance?

'Didn't you know that such things happened?' I asked.

'Not really. I have heard and read about it in a vague sort of way, but I had never imagined it happening to me.'

'It wouldn't have if you hadn't been with me.'

She looked up quickly, the hurt still strong in her dark eyes.

'What does that mean, Rick?'

'It need never happen to you again.' In spite of myself, in spite of the love tearing at my inside, I was saying these things, not wanting to, but saying them.

'Is that what you want, Rick?'

'No, Gillian, that's not what I want.'

My mind was seeing the dangers and the difficulties, but my heart was answering boldly and carelessly. She rose and came over to sit on the arm of my chair.

'I love you, Rick.'

'I love you, Gillian.'

'But I'm afraid, Rick, terribly afraid now. Everything seemed all right before, but now it's all a bit frightening. How do you take it so calmly, Rick? Don't you mind about it?'

'Mind? Oh yes, I do mind, but I'm learning how to mind and still live. At first it was terrible, but gradually I'm learning what it means to live with dignity inside my black skin.'

And then I told her about my life in Britain, the whole thing, everything which led to my becoming a teacher and meeting her. She listened quietly, not interrupting but soon, somehow, her hand was in mine, its firm, gentle pressure supporting, comforting, uplifting.

'I'm sorry, Rick,' she murmured when I had finished.

'Don't be sorry about it, my dear. I just thought I should let you know the sort of thing which happened and is probably still likely to happen.'

'Oh, not about that, about the things I said to you to-night.'

'I understand; it is forgiven—it was nothing.'

For a while we sat united in our thoughts, needing no words, no further reassurance.

'I'll write to Mummy tomorrow. I've told her so much about you she won't be surprised.'

'Won't she mind?'

'I suppose she will but she's very understanding really. We talked about it last time I was at home.'

'And your father?'

'Mother will get to work on him, I expect. I think we can be happy together, Rick.'

'We'll try.'

Others had met this problem before and had succeeded in rising above it. God willing, I'd try to do the same. We'd both try.

E. R. BRAITHWAITE, *To Sir, with Love*

1. What is noticeable about the children's relationship to the writer? What do you think brought it about? Can this throw any light on the general question of race relations?

2. (a) Why did the waiter behave as he did? (b) How do you think his behaviour to Rick and Gillian should have been dealt with by them? (c) How could this kind of behaviour towards coloured people be countered in general?

3. (a) Suppose Gillian Blanchard were your sister. What would your reaction be to her telling you she was going to marry Rick? (b) Suppose further that you were against the marriage. What would you say to Gillian? What do you think would be your reasons for your objection, and would they be well-grounded or really prejudice of one kind or another?

30. Immigration and integration

The ease of integration varies inversely with the number of immigrants. And, in every situation, there is a threshold of safety. On one side lies a relatively smooth process of absorption, on the other the danger of open conflict between immigrant and host. Where that threshold lies must vary with circumstance, but it's nearly always there and should be demarcated. One might use the analogy of a blood transfusion. Each human body can take so much of someone else's blood and no more. If you overdo the transfusion, and the patient's body cannot absorb so much alien blood so quickly, reactions are set up which can, and do, prove fatal. On the other hand, the same quantity dripped in gradually will strengthen the patient. It is the same with host and immigrants.

In schools and Universities, in factories and public services, a ratio of immigrant to British—which generally means of coloured folk to whites—is often unofficially observed. In schools, the threshold is widely considered to be somewhere between one quarter and one third immigrant. Some schools have a roll two thirds immigrant or even higher. And here the lamb whose flag proclaims integration, finds himself, strangely, lying down with the lion who roars apartheid. Too many immigrants don't integrate, they 'clot', and set up, of their own volition, their own communities, quarters and ghettos. In so far as this depends on housing, there seems to be little we can do about it except, wherever possible, to 'spread the load'. If birds of a feather prefer to flock together, it is hard to keep them apart.

And have we the right to do so? This brings us to the wishes of the immigrants themselves. Some of the newcomers have no desire whatsoever to become assimilated, integrated, absorbed, or anything else. They want to make their pile and go home.

But many will stay, *malgré lui* in most cases; and what about them? Will they integrate? Those few who intermarry will doubtless do so. At the other extreme are the Chinese who keep themselves so much to themselves that their assimilation seems improbable. In between, the process seems likely to be slow.

Apart from the Chinese, the most anti-integrationist community are the Pakistanis, perhaps because they are Muslims and Islam's cloth has always incorporated a strong xenophobic strand. Hitherto insufficient Muslim families have settled here to provide an answer to the question of whether the minds of children sent to English schools will be cast in a different mould.

It is the West Indians who most want to integrate. Amongst most communities of African origin a pale skin carries prestige. Conquering and ruling races pressing down from the North have generally been lighter in pigment than the true Negro; so pallor and prestige have forged a link. In the Caribbean, it is smarter to be light-skinned than coal-black. Inter-marriage with white people, the former masters, is in general smiled and seldom frowned upon.

It therefore appears that the group farthest away from us in physical appearance and pigmentation is the one we are most likely to assimilate. They share our language, faith and culture and, as a community, do not object.

Between Chinese and Pakistanis on the one hand, and Caribbeans on the other, lies a number of communities who really want a half way house. Such are the Italians and Cypriots, Hungarians and Ukranians, and above all the Poles and the Jews, who came as exiles but need no longer be so if they wish; they have a country, now, to which most could repair. But very few will. They know they are settlers and must settle, and yet they want—many Poles and Jews want with passion— to hold on to their identity, to preserve a nucleus at least of their religion, to keep their language, and not to be dissolved entirely in the all-devouring, all-pervading blood stream of the host.

It can be done, and the Jews are here to prove it. Their diaspora lasted nearly two thousand years, and they have kept their identity. If the Jews can do it, so, perhaps, can Poles. There is the French Canadian example. India is a parcel of separate races, not a unity. In Ceylon there are Singhalese and Tamils; in Cyprus Greeks and Turks; the instances are legion. Full integration is probably the exception, not the rule.

Should we object to this? Obviously not, if we believe in freedom; yet any large undigested lump of foreigners lies heavy on the stomach of all nations at all times. It presses on some nerve that signals danger; unity is strength, separateness an invitation to conflict. (Look at Cyprus.) From this arises the threat to all minorities, of religion, of race, of ideology; Catholics or Protestants, Jews or Huguenots, Albigensians or Gnostics, Negroes or Armenians. Minorities have been persecuted either because they are small enough to bully, successful enough to pillage, or large enough to be feared. In Britain, some are small enough, and some sufficiently successful, to qualify for persecution; instead, they are being absorbed. None is, as yet, large enough to be feared, but this may need watching; and here we come back to the margin of safety, the threshold.

So much comes back to the schools. We too easily assume that, because children have no sense of race or colour when they are little, racial co-education will solve all. It doesn't. As children grow older, they draw apart. They absorb their parents' outlook and prejudices, and these harden like cysts in their growing minds. With adolescence comes sex rivalry; the young cocks sparring, the male urge towards violence in this turbulent third age of man, the transference of frustrations, and your own failures, to the image of the alien, the eternal scapegoat. Here, at adolescence, where the flashpoint is nearest, efforts to unite and blend the various communities have met with least success.

Can more be done? For a start, perhaps, sharpen curiosity. Here are all these people from exotic backgrounds in all corners of the world, full of strange lore and peculiar ways. Most of us take no interest in them at all. We are idle; language can be a barrier; on top of that, we are shy. But, fundamentally, lazy. A television programme on Barbados or Nigeria, a feature on Sicilian politics or the Warsaw rising, is less trouble, and more informative, than a halting conversation with the family next door. It's all pre-digested, and the neighbour's English is poor. The human being tends nowadays to be a sort of filter, something that gets in the way.

Those who do take the trouble tend to do so from a sense of duty rather than of exploration; taking pity on strangers in a strange land. There's no need to pity them. They came of their own free will—at least, all but the political refugees—in their own self-interest, and most of them are doing well. They don't want charity, and don't need or deserve it. They are not the lame ducks, but the energetic ones. 'The most enterprising of their race', it has been said, 'live amongst the least enterprising of ours.'

Our idealists, progressives and reformers, the activists of our society, who march with banners to Aldermaston, squat in Trafalgar Square, sign petitions and letters to *The Times*—these individuals leave us in no doubt of the wickedness of apartheid in South Africa, of segregation in America, of the Portuguese in Africa who won't gracefully bow themselves out. They condemn with equal spirit, in their native land, colour-conscious landladies, protesting parents, local officials who shy away from turbans, any sign of colour prejudice wherever it may rear its head. Fair enough. But I sometimes wonder how many of the paraders, demonstrators, petitioners, and inveighers have ever asked a Jamaican bus conductor, a Pakistani factory hand, an Indian shop-keeper, a Cypriot café-owner, a Polish tool-maker, a Nigerian nurse or a Lithuanian ward-maid home to tea.

ELSPETH HUXLEY, *Back Street New Worlds*

1. (a) Have we the right to press immigrants towards integration? On what grounds? (b) Do we want them to be assimilated? What are your reasons, for or against?

2. This passage provides one rational argument for limitation of immigrants. What is it? Are there any others? In the light of all these discuss the rights and wrongs of the Commonwealth Immigration Bills, giving your own attitude to them and saying why you come down on this or that side.

3. Race has tended to be discussed in terms of coloured people and whites. This passage suggests that the problem is much wider, Jews and Poles being among the most difficult to assimilate wholly. Try to find out about immigrants in your area. From what races do they come? What patterns of work and housing are discernible for the different racial groups? What kind of local action, if any, needs to be taken on their behalf? How many do you know personally?

Encounters with Communism

31. God's beloved East Zone

A few weeks ago a student who is now studying outside our Zone, but who is determined to return here, wrote me a long letter. He told with gratitude about that other world in which he had been allowed to live without a care for a year, but added that precisely in this other world he had come to realise what gifts God continually bestows on us in the Zone, so that he believed one should never again speak of the 'East Zone', but only of 'God's beloved East Zone'.

Let me take this word as the theme on which to report to you a bit about us; above all, however, about that which happens to us by God's goodness and under his forgiveness, and how God does his work among us, even where we Christians fail again and again in the time of testing. Many lead a dangerous double existence: on the one side in the Bible Study hour, in public worship, communion and cell group; on the other side in the public life of a student. With time one becomes accustomed to this double life and one finds it no longer unbearable; or one emigrates spiritually in secret, to the West, and hopes for the Americans, i.e. for American bombers and tanks—a strange hope for us in Germany! Alongside of this runs a deep, only too understandable, human bitterness and national hate, which longs for the day when the foreign tormentors will be beaten, and the German tormentors will hang from the gibbet.

Next to the man with his fist clenched in his pocket, stands the Marxist fanatic, who in his idealism (whether opportunistic or honestly come by) is out to improve the world, and doesn't even notice that he is leading himself and many others towards an abyss.

Every Christian shares in some way the guilt of this unhealthy development, just as does every East Zone resident as well.

So it was with a girl student, who held her ground bravely for a while. She came to know the gospel with wonder and surprise during a long spell in hospital, through the Christian students who visited there, and through it she came to believe. She found in the Christian fellowship her greatest joy; until the day of temptation came. A Communist functionary on the faculty explained to her that she could never expect to be admitted to an examination unless she joined a party. In conscious falsehood she joined the SED (Socialist Unity Party —Communist), and then came to the pastor with the words: 'Now I can no longer participate in the life of the Christian fellowship, because I lie continually.' He pointed out to her that precisely now she needed the comfort of the Word of God, and therefore she ought more than ever to come to the Bible study hour. So she attended both Party and Christian fellowship, torn in spirit, and ever more miserable. One day this girl declared to me: 'I can't stand this any longer. I can't pray, I can't read the Bible, I can't take communion. Even if I end up as a charwoman, I won't live with this lie any longer.' So she handed in her resignation to the SED, with such a natural inner peace that it seemed almost a matter of course. This is the greatest miracle, that Christ can and will draw men to himself, that they become free from themselves, to go their way in his forgiveness with joy, though they can only see the way a yard ahead.

What happened next shows us that God not only shelters his people under his cross, but often does so quite publicly as a sign for many. At the parting interview in the Party headquarters, six functionaries argued with her: 'Think what will happen to you. You are completely dependent on your scholarship.' She answered: 'Because I was afraid for myself, I came to you. Because God has made me free from myself, I am leaving now.' They looked at her in amazed silence. Shortly afterwards another functionary spoke to her: 'What you did, so shortly before examination time, was unbelievably courageous. We need people like you. The riff-raff and the opportunists we will shake off one day in any case. Couldn't you make up your mind, after all, to become a Marxist?' And as the examination came, the responsible authorities declared: 'We must admit this girl. She has shown unusual character in resigning from the Party before examination time.' She passed the examination and suffered no material loss.

This is our condition, we Christians in the East Zone—upheld only by the reality of Christ, who was crucified and is risen for us. He is a fool who believes that it is possible, by high political cooperation here in our Zone, to hold up the course of events. But he is a hundredfold a fool who does not see with amazement and joy that the Almighty Creator and Father of Jesus Christ here also, and precisely here, performs his healing and saving acts; that he uses us to perform them; and that when we believe and obey, many an early possibility opens up miraculously for us.

In the first years after the war we often lived next to the developing Marxists without contact. It bothered our conscience that we were holding ourselves so critically aloof, showing ourselves so indifferent, towards those new fanatics who are so much wiser and more tolerant than the Nazis. Christ was there for us; we knew that from experience. But it was hidden from us that he died and rose again for all people. So the Student Christian Fellowship put on a play, *The Sign of Jonah*, with an overwhelming attendance. They toured the congregations by the dozen. Party functionaries woke up and listened. Thus we came—finally!—to meetings about the Marxist understanding of man, to which we invited the functionaries. Six months later we heard a remarkable echo from these conversations. Functionaries complained that their best men were being made uncertain, and were even becoming Christians. This must stop. A plan was made there and then to infiltrate the Student Christian Fellowship, to awaken dissatisfaction with the leadership and thereby to destroy the Fellowship from within. The plan remained on paper. 'Those we send on this errand come back to us as Christians!' one party leader is reported to have complained.

Then we found that here and there a few of us were beginning to talk to half and full Marxists with love. With love—that means undiplomatically, in all frankness and freedom, yet not self-righteously or moralistically. And almost everywhere where that happened we saw that the evil spirits stole away and the sea became still. In the place of their dialectically grounded desire to liquidate us (for the moment largely in rhetoric) came human respect and the assurance that they wouldn't do us any harm because we were really 'good honest people' whom one protects and defends. Then, here and there, something quite different occurred. Suddenly the mask, which looks so deceivingly like a real face, fell and revealed a helpless man who sinks under his load of sin and guilt, and who clings to the Christian who has treated him with a bit of love, who hasn't lied to him like the others. I have been in meetings where all the signs promised storm, and one held one's breath: will there be an explosion? And lo, it not only went well, but the political meeting transformed itself into a brotherly talk around the question of God's grace and commandment.

Where people take their place in this self-movement of the gospel, there opens, usually by surprise, a door by which they can get on in their earthly life. To be sure this door is only visible, most of the time, in the last moment. One must have enough faith to run against a doorless wall up to the last centimetre, in the certain hope that God who leads one in this way will not allow his people to break their heads. So it happens in that last moment often, that a Nicodemus or a Gamaliel appears to hold his protecting hand over people who would otherwise be lost. Somehow or other these men break, inwardly, out of the bonds of their doctrine and give a secret answer to a call which has moved them. A professor seeks students for assistance in his research, a paid job, 'Please,' he says, 'send me Christians. They are the only ones I can rely on.' Several were helped thus on their way. An assistant is the only one who discusses with reason and facts, in the compulsory weekly Marxist training courses for assistants. The other seventy keep still or make fun of it. In private they say to him : 'Why do you expose yourself? You can't get anywhere in any case.' One day he was suspended. Why was he so careless? The case was heard before the local union officials. With some anxiety he defended his position. Result : a few days later he was reinstated. To be sure—for how long? But all seventy greeted him respectfully and warmly. Often this is how people begin a little to praise their Father in Heaven, because they see good works which point to him. And out of this, as a by-product, comes a bit more room for honest work in a profession. In this case also some room was gained for free science and scholarship; if only more people would move with conviction into this room ! One student, for example, speaking to a group of a hundred students, twelve functionaries and a Communist state secretary : 'We cannot give our allegiance to the National Front, because so much goes on in it that violates the Christian conscience.' Or another student, before a similar group : 'This election was so dominated by fear that we could not take part in it.' Another time the whole school question was brought out in the open. None of our great and powerful can complain that their inhumanities have not been held before them. And sometimes they correct these inhuman acts. Naturally these corrections seem to be insignificant, and they are so. But they show how, even with all the distortion and perversity in these men's minds and hearts, they have yet a certain awe which keeps them from completely ignoring this warning voice of the Word of God, or from silencing it.

You understand that because of this the gospel every day takes away from us the hope we have from the West, and we allow it to be taken. We experience how God's living word makes bound men here and now so free that they begin and end with his praise. God has something in mind for these Communists whom no one wishes any good and no one trusts to do anything good.

We are privileged to be there when he works, and to be used by his grace. Our one concern is that we resist what God is doing, not that we be relieved of our task by bombs and tanks. For 'it is a great thing to live in the East Zone'. My wife and I say that sometimes, in different tones of voice : now questioning, now bitter, now despairing or scornful, but ever again joyful. The old Adam would often prefer it otherwise and he looks every morning towards the West. But the joyful message of God himself points us back to the living people here, and makes it clear to us that he has given up no single one of them. Why should the Communists be lost?

There is no defence against the gospel. One discovers this usually just where all the preconditions for it seem to be lacking. So it was with the young and timid girl who talked with me today. She worked in a factory with 900 employees. One day a resolution was to be drawn up against the 'capitalist and warmongering West', and above all against America. Her fiancé advised her the night before to withhold her vote when the matter came up, and if she were questioned, to say, 'The vote came as too much of a surprise to me. I wasn't able to think it through beforehand.' And so it went, all according to plan. First a propaganda speech, full of hate and incitement against America. Then came the call for an open vote on the resolution. No one voted against it. Only she withheld her vote, and answered to questioning as planned. But then things took an unexpected turn. Two Communists demanded that the group immediately decide to fire the girl from her job, for it was impossible that upstanding fighters for peace work together any longer with such a person. To be sure, only five of the 900 voted in favour of this proposal, but the girl had to justify her refusal to vote before the whole meeting. She stood on the platform and had to speak.

'This resolution,' she said slowly, 'breathes hate. Do you think that peace can come from hate? From hate comes only fighting, strife, blood and tears. Real peace between man and man, and between nation and nation, comes from God, who has brought peace to us all. Where his peace is accepted, peace arises among human beings. But the resolution says nothing of all this.'

Applause; laughter; objection. The manager, a Communist, dec ded that she should answer for her opinions on the next day before twenty organization leaders. She left the room amid friendly and respectful greetings from all sides. One functionary said softly to her in passing, 'That was well done.' A woman told her on the side, 'I'm a Christian, too. But I have a boy I have to take care of.'

The next day she was questioned for a full hour. They tried in vain to set traps for her, to trick her into statements which could be used against her. 'What do you think of the Soviet Union?'

'The Soviet Union is a nation like all other nations. It has a commission from God, as have all other lands, and will answer to him, as they do.'

Then she was sent out of the room. As she heard later, the assembled leaders were in great perplexity over what they should do with her. There were no grounds for firing her. On the other hand the Party declared that she must leave the plant that very day. Otherwise the whole propaganda campaign threatened to collapse. Everywhere people were talking about this courageous girl. The Party decided finally so to intimidate her that she would resign her job of her own accord. This she did under pressure, for she was planning to marry not many months hence.

Half an hour after she resigned, one of the leading Communists of the plant summoned her to his office. And as she entered the room, she froze to the spot with amazement. For there at his desk sat the official, his head on the blotter, weeping. Slowly he looked up. 'What a criminal I am,' he said. 'Is there still help for me anywhere?'

All evening this man sat with the girl and her husband-to-be and confessed to them his past—horrible tales, one after the other, of his crimes against humanity.

'What brings you,' asked the future bridegroom, shaken and over-awed, 'to put so much confidence in us?'

The Communist pointed to the small symbol which the young man was wearing in his lapel. 'Because,' he said, 'I trust your cross.'

Shortly afterwards the man became seriously ill and was forced to leave the key position which had enabled him to commit his crimes. A girl spoke the truth in an open meeting, against her plan and will, and a man began, for the first time in his life, to fear God. This is the power of the gospel, against which no other force can prevail. If only we Christians would reckon with God !

JOHANNES HAMEL, A Christian in East Germany

1. Why does the writer call the East Zone of Germany 'God's beloved East Zone'?

2. In what ways does he see God calling him and his fellow-Christians to act in their difficult situation? In particular, what virtues does he see as pre-eminently needed if God is to 'use us to perform his healing and saving acts'?

3. 'We cannot give our allegiance to the National Front, because so much goes on in it that violates the Christian conscience'. What goes on, according to the passage, which would 'violate the Christian conscience'?

4. Supposing you were a student in the East Zone and were neither a Communist nor a Christian, (a) what 'stance' would you take up vis-à-vis the State, and in particular vis-à-vis the 'party functionaries' and your studies and examinations? and (b) upon what grounds would your decisions be based?

32. Simply human

The 'I' in this extract from a novel is a certain Sebastian Ionesco. He is a Security officer of the Communist Party in Rumania, who is gathering evidence for a Commission of Inquiry into anti-Communist activities. Having served in the Rumanian army against the Russians, he was taken prisoner, and eventually went over to Communism. He joined the Russians in their defeat of the Germans and in the setting up of the Communist Government in Rumania. He has just won promotion, together with Mitu Bussuioc, for his services. Romeo Romanesco was his closest friend in the Rumanian army and as a prisoner of war, but he refused to accept Communism. Thus the two friends were separated before the end of the war.

Partisan risings occurred in the mountain districts. I was sent on a mission. I found Mitu Bussuioc, wearing a heavy overcoat and an automatic in his belt, in a village town hall among forest clad hills.

'You've arrived just when the party's over,' said Mitu grinning.

'I've still got to put in a report.'

'Well, you'd better come with me. I'm going up there.'

We got into a jeep fitted inside with racks for rifles and machine guns, and set off for the forest. We Communists had become hunters, after being for so long the quarry; and now the quarry was anyone who was not prepared to accept us. We came to a clearing occupied by soldiers with tent canvasses draped over them like cloaks, just as a party of prisoners was brought in with their hands on their heads. They were ragged and unshaven.

One of the prisoners met my eye and pulled up abruptly. It was Romeo Romanesco. A soldier jabbed him in the ribs with his rifle. He staggered and nearly fell, recovered himself and moved on. And I— like when one has just killed someone, or inflicted some great injury on oneself—I felt nothing.

I saw Romeo again at his trial in Bucharest; but at least I did not have to do so in connection with that Commission of Inquiry. I sat at a table with Panait Petre, Mitu and other officers. Spotlights had been rigged up behind us so that their beams passed over our heads to concentrate on a bare wall opposite. A man stood facing us on the concrete floor. He hadn't shaved for weeks, his hair was long and tangled, his face dirty and his shirt stained with the blood, long since dried, that had flowed from his nose and mouth. He was gazing towards us with apprehensive, blood-shot eyes, unable to see us because of the glare of the lights.

'Look at yourself, Citizen!' said Panait Petre. 'You look shameful and disgraceful. And it's entirely your own doing. You're a bourgeois. But we're only too willing to explain the present social and historical position to you, and to help you to understand the laws of history. You'll be punished in any event, but if you answer our questions frankly and honestly, it will be taken into account at your trial. Well, what have you to say?'

'Nothing,' said the young man.

'You admit that you have borne arms against the power of the people?'

'No. We're the ones who are fighting for the people.'

'If you refuse to understand we shall have to use other methods,' Panait said in a very matter-of-fact voice.

The prisoner smiled faintly and again shrugged his shoulders.

'Take him away,' said Panait. 'Bring in the next.'

I did not see Romeo face the spotlights because I was sent off on another job. Before leaving I said to Panait:

'Comrade Panait, are they going to torture them?'

'If they can't be made to talk in any other way,' he answered sourly. 'But Socialism—how do you reconcile that with torture? The bourgeois Secret Police used torture, and now we're doing the same.'

'It's a question of the objective. That's where we differ from the bourgeoisie. We're working for the people, for mankind. If we handle this riff raff with kid gloves we'll get nothing out of them, and good comrades may lose their lives, or important projects fail. The coming of Socialism might be delayed. Are you prepared to incur that responsibility?'

I could find nothing to say.

The only torturer I have known at all well was a certain Major Bulz. He said to me once, sitting with his chair tilted back:

'The essential ingredient of torture could not be more simple: all you need is a collective, a constituted group operating on a man in isolation. The group, as we know, is stronger than the individual, and torture is the first way of proving it. Torture is also the first of the experimental sciences. All it calls for is a pair of bare hands and a gang to hold the patient down and assist in the experiment.'

He was eating a pastry, pulling a face as he did so. He always ate with an air of repugnance, and repugnantly. He went on:

'The people in my outfit never talk about these things; the fact is, they're never quite happy in their minds. They feel they're doing wrong. But why? According to our principles, everything that speeds up the coming of Socialism and Communism is good, and everything that delays it is bad. So? And yet, I don't know why, my people have fits of nervous depression, migraine, God knows what. Curious, isn't it? Do you think it's because they are still worried by bourgeois prejudice?'

He was smiling calmly at me but with a hint of uncertainty in his eyes. I will not say unease—uncertainty. I laughed at him.

'We can't afford to be sentimental! If you're asking my opinion, I haven't got one—I haven't reached one—not entirely.'

'When you do I hope you'll tell me. I'd be interested,' said Major Bulz.

I attended the trial of the group of partisans to which Romeo Romanesco belonged. They had been kept awake for many nights, which gave them a bloodless look. When it was Romeo's turn, the presiding judge asked him his name, age and last address. Romeo did not answer.

'Accused, why don't you say anything?'

The prosecutor arose.

'Comrade President, the accused has refused to speak for the past six months, on the pretext that he has been ill-treated.'

'Is that true?' the presiding judge asked.

'Of course not, Comrade President,' the prosecutor replied calmly.
I did not listen any more. Romeo was condemned to death and shot
—it was the price of the Socialist Industrialisation of our country.

Terror is a generalised state affecting all society. At the extreme of
suffering a terrorist society sees in terror a possible solution of its
problems; terror is the criterion of a nation's immorality. Terror is the
measure of universal cowardice: terrorists have to inspire fear in others
because they are afraid themselves. When we no longer fear God, and
are not humbled by our imperfections, our limitations and our sins,
God reminds us of His existence by showing one of His less smiling
faces. In any country with the simplicity of spirit to fear God, Hitler
and Stalin would have failed. We are all guilty of terror, and not one
of us can escape it: Stalin, taken with a stroke in the barred solitude
of his *dacha*, lay groaning on the floor till morning, when his old
servant was authorised to ring his bell. At the end we come to fear
God in the person of men—in human folly and cruelty, those disguises
which He adopts when we refuse to name His name, or to accord Him
the fear which is His due.

I speak from experience, for shortly after this I was summoned to
appear before Comrade Panait Petre, now a deputy minister.

'Sit down,' he said. 'We propose to entrust you with a particularly
difficult and responsible task. It is this. You are to go straight from
here to the office of Comrade Colonel Bussuioc and arrest him.'

My expression must have changed.

'I will explain to you why this is necessary,' Panait went on; 'we
are entering upon a new stage in the building of Socialism. There must
be rigid discipline in our ranks. Mitu has a tendency to question his
orders, or to interpret them as he sees fit. You are a man capable of
rising above that sort of petty-bourgeois behaviour. That is why the
Party trusts you. Have you got a revolver? Mitu's a good shot—I've
seen him at work.'

Panait concluded with a grim smile in which there was still a gleam
of affection for Mitu. They had fought together in Spain, in the international brigades; they had been like brothers for fifteen years.

I got up, saluted and left the room. Out in the corridor I stood
motionless, knowing that I was going to be sick. I went into the toilet,
spewed up my breakfast, washed my face and rinsed my mouth, and
then went straight to Mitu's office.

'Comrade Colonel, you are under arrest!'

Mitu stood up slowly, stupefied with amazement.

'Have you gone crazy? I'm under arrest? But why? What have I
done?'

I shrugged my shoulders and signed to him to come out from behind his desk; and like a sheep he obeyed me. He was a head taller than I, twice my weight and twice as strong, but he showed only one feeble flicker of revolt.

'On whose orders are you doing this?'

'By order of Comrade Panait Petre,' I said, looking him in the eye. I hated him for letting it be done to him, for getting involved in this shameful machinery that was now going to crush him; but I hated myself even more.

'Panait? I don't understand,' he said in a low voice.

I nodded to him to go in front of me and he did so, suddenly weak and helpless, his broad back become nothing but human flesh, so fragile, so vulnerable—like the backs of even the most feared and dangerous men.

A number of officers of different ranks were arrested on that same day. Then there was a pause, and then another wave of arrests. I heard nothing about what happened to them. In any case, I no longer talked to anyone, except in the way of duty. Months later one of the Comrades said to me:

'You remember Bulz? It seems he wasn't shot, he's in the Central Hospital for Nervous Disorders.'

I was not interested in Bulz; but on a sudden impulse I called at the hospital some days later and asked, as a former colleague, if I might be allowed to see him. The Doctor to whom I had sent a message beckoned to me to follow him and remarked as we went along the corridor:

'We get a good many patients from your outfit, Comrade Major.'

'My friend, Bulz,' I said. 'What's his trouble?'

'He's a manic-depressive. I needn't bother you with technicalities. You'll see.'

He left me alone with Bulz, who was sitting up in his bed staring blankly into space. I addressed him by name, but he did not seem to hear. Without raising my voice I asked:

'Bulz, what happened to Mitu Bussuioc?'

A smile of imbecile craftiness came over his face.

'Don't know. Nothing to do with me.'

'Is he alive?'

'If he's dead he's lucky,' Bulz said. 'And I'm lucky—very lucky indeed.'

He said this so clearly and rationally that I asked:

'In what way—lucky?'

'I went sick. I said to them, let me alone or else I'll—'

His voice had suddenly sunk. He mumbled confusedly, staring at his grey counterpane. Then he fell silent.

I got up and left. The Doctor was waiting for me in the corridor.

'Is he mad,' I asked, 'or is he shamming?'

'He wanted to go mad—probably because it was the only way out for him. We're giving him tonics to restore the nervous system, but his body doesn't respond.'

On my way home I thought—I, a Communist? a servant of the Socialist State? I? No more. Never again. Not I. I had done too much already. 'If it's still possible, try if you can to be human. Simply human.' It would be very hard, things having gone so far. But it had to be tried. Simply be human. No more.

PETRU DUMITRIU, Incognito

1. (a) Trace the course of Sebastian's disillusionment in this passage; what are the significant moments or events? (b) What would your own reactions have been in his place?

2. (a) Analyse the grounds for Sebastian's break with the Communist Party. (b) Discuss whether you think these grounds constitute a good case for rejecting Communism or not.

3. What is the writer trying to tell us about terror? What are your views on this? How is it to be dealt with if it becomes an instrument of political power or of government?

4. Explain the part played by Bulz in illuminating the novelist's theme?

5. What do you think the prosecutor understands by 'true'? Is the concept of truth important in understanding or counteracting Communism?

6. (a) What do you think Sebastian means by being 'simply human'? Why would it be 'very hard'? (b) What do you understand by the phrase? (c) On what presuppositions is your view based?

33. Vietnam: a case history

(a) Basic Vietnam: a simple guide to the world's most complicated crisis

Vietnam is the story of two wars and a peace that failed. The first war began in 1946 with the French attempt at reconquest in Indo-China, which had been part of their empire since 1883. It ended with the armistice agreements signed in Geneva in 1954, which left Vietnam divided between North and South along the 17th parallel.

The second war began to develop, with the breakdown of the armistice, as a civil war in the South. Communist North Vietnam and the United States gradually joined in on opposing sides. Like the French in 1946, the South Vietnam Government with American support now faces what is virtually another war of reconquest to try to recover the large area of South Vietnam which is now controlled either fully or partially by the rebels.

Attempts to end the war by negotiation have so far failed. To understand why there is still a war and still no peace one needs to ask and answer some wider questions.

Who are the Vietnamese?

They are the most numerous and vigorous of the peoples of the Indo-China peninsula which forms a cultural and linguistic watershed between the civilisations inspired by China and India.

The Laotians and Cambodians are on the Indian side of the divide and the Vietnamese on the Chinese side. They came originally from southern China into the northern part of what is now Vietnam (which means 'Far South').

A thousand years of Chinese rule from 111 B.C. left the Vietnamese with a Chinese-based culture but with their national identity intact. Their history is dominated by their resistance to Chinese conquest and their own expansion south and west.

Of the population of 30,000,000 in the whole of Vietnam today some 4,500,000 are minority groups. In the South are more than one million Khmers (Cambodians), and a million Chinese, as well as aboriginal mountain tribes. In addition there are strong groups of Catholics, and religious sects, such as the Caodaists and the Hoa Hao, who are ethnically Vietnamese.

How did the French get involved?

First, through Catholic missionaries in 1615. Then, in the eighteenth century, a French bishop called in French mercenaries from India to help one of his Vietnamese royal protégés in a civil war. Vietnam later tried and failed, like China, to withdraw into isolation from Western contact. French intervention culminated in complete conquest of Indo-China in 1883, at the height of the great European imperialist scramble and the commercial assault on the Far East.

What has happened since 1941?

1941—Vichy Government gives Japan permission to use French Indo-China as base in Second World War. Resistance groups formed to overthrow both French and Japanese fascists, and to win Independence.

1945—When Japan collapses, Communist Ho Chi-Minh controls the only organised troops in northern part of Vietnam and sets up Democratic Republic.

1946—War breaks out between Ho Chi-Minh and French determined to restore colonial empire in South.

1954—French surrounded by Ho's forces at Dien Bien Phu. 14-nation conference on Indo-China meets at Geneva and settles cease-

fire in June. Vietnam partitioned. Many Communist soldiers
left south of the armistice line. Vietnam was to be united after
free elections; Laos and Cambodia to be independent and
neutral. All countries signing at Geneva not to send troops to
the region. John Foster Dulles refuses to sign, for the United
States.

1955—South Vietnam having refused to hold elections, the temporary
partition solidifies into Ho Chi-Minh's Hanoi regime in the
North and that of the Catholic nationalist, Ngo Dinh Diem,
at Saigon in the South. The Diem regime was corrupt but
Western-inclined. Dulles sends in men and materials to prop
it up.

1960—Communists in South Vietnam set up a National Liberation
Front. Its guerillas are referred to in Saigon Government's
statements as Vietcong.

1961—President Kennedy, on taking office, decides to step up U.S.
commitment in arms and men.

1963—Vietcong claim to control two-thirds of South Vietnam and
half the population. In May Buddhists there riot against discrimination by the Roman Catholic minority. Suicides by fire.
In October the U.S. decides to withdraw all its forces by 1965.
Next month a military junta overthrows Diem regime.

1964—Confusion between rival military and civilian leaders in South.
400,000 South Vietnam troops now in combat against 100,000
Vietcong, who are supplied with arms from North along 'Ho
Chi-Minh trail'. North Vietnam attacks U.S. warships; Americans retaliate with bombing raids on North Vietnamese military targets.

1965—More confusion in South. Marshall Ky emerges as Prime
Minister. U.S. claims that North Vietnam has turned down
many peace moves, but later admits that it turned down opportunity of having peace talks under U.N. auspices. War acceler-
ates. U.S. and South Vietnamese fly 11,880 sorties against
North. From May to June, 100,000 U.S. troops landed on east
coast. By end of year, 190,000 U.S. men in Vietnam. Christmas
time diplomatic 'peace offensive' by President Johnson fails.

1966—Escalation continues. Growing anxiety in U.S.A. about Ameri-
can policy. Buddhist opposition to military government in
South Vietnam grows, and 'war within a war' develops, with
Americans cautiously treading tightrope. Marshall Ky crushes
Buddhist rebels at Danang. Next stage : ? ? ?

What is the Ho Chi-Minh trail?

It is a network of roads and paths through the jungle and mountains of southern Laos along which supplies and men move from North to South Vietnam.

What is the American aim?

The United States says it wants a negotiated settlement for South Vietnam but is determined to prevent 'aggression from the North' from succeeding. It reckons that if it did not do so, its other allies round the world would lose faith in American promises, Chinese Communist influence would spread in Asia, other South-East States might collapse 'like a row of dominoes', and the technique of aggression by subversion would be tried elsewhere. President Johnson's recent 'peace offensive' was backed by fourteen Points for a settlement based on the Geneva agreements.

But if Ho Chi-Minh also says he wants the Geneva agreements applied, why are they still fighting?

The chief problem still seems to be the relative status of the Saigon Government and the Vietcong and the kind of Government South Vietnam might have if the fighting stopped. If the South Vietnamese are really able to elect their own Government freely, whose military force is to hold the ring?

What is Russia's interest in Vietnam?

The Russians would like a negotiated settlement but they have so far been unable to persuade the North Vietnamese to go to peace talks. Russia and China are struggling for influence in Hanoi, with China urging a continuation of the war. The North Vietnamese have tried to remain neutral in the Russian-Chinese dispute. Recently they seemed to be moving closer to Moscow, but in the end they made their own decisions about peace or war.

Ho Chi-Minh's four points

On April 10th, 1965, the North Vietnamese National Assembly passed a resolution calling for a political settlement based on four points, claimed to be in accordance with the Geneva agreements.

1. All United States troops must withdraw from South Vietnam.
2. Pending peaceful reunification of Vietnam, the 1954 military agreements must be respected and North and South remain neutral.
3. Internal affairs must be settled by the South Vietnamese themselves, 'in accordance with the programme of the South Vietnam National Liberation Front', without any foreign interference.

4. Peaceful reunification of Vietnam to be settled by Vietnamese people in both zones without foreign interference.

In January, 1966, Ho Chi-Minh added a fifth condition for talks; that the National Liberation Front (Vietcong) be recognised as the sole spokesman of the people of South Vietnam.

Johnson's fourteen points

A White House statement on January 3rd, 1966, listed fourteen basic points of United States policy for South-East Asia.

1. The Geneva agreements of 1954 and 1962 are adequate basis for peace.
2. The United States would welcome a conference on S.E. Asia or any part of it.
3. The United States would welcome 'negotiations without pre-conditions' as proposed by seventeen non-aligned countries.
4. The United States would welcome 'unconditional discussions'.
5. A cease-fire could be first item on a conference agenda or be subject of preliminary talks.
6. Hanoi's four points could be discussed along with others.
7. The United States wants no bases of her own in S.E. Asia.
8. The United States does not want to keep troops in South Vietnam after peace is assured.
9. The United States supports free elections in South Vietnam.
10. Reunification of Vietnam should be determined by Vietnamese through their own free decisions.
11. The countries of S.E. Asia can be non-aligned or neutral if they choose.
12. If there is peace, North Vietnam could take part in regional economic reconstruction to which the United States would be willing to contribute.
13. The Vietcong could be represented at talks 'if Hanoi for a moment decides she wants to cease aggression'.
14. The United States could stop the bombing of North Vietnam as a step towards peace although Hanoi has given no hint as to what she would do if the bombing stopped.

The Observer, 14 February 1965 and 6 February 1966

(b) Buddhist monk wages peace

Thich Nhat Hanh, a chief spokesman for peace among Vietnamese Buddhist monks, had come simply to tell the American people of the torture of his people, who, for the past twenty years, have been caught in relentless wars. He had no political axe to grind and he spoke of people, not ideologies. Also he was a scholar by temperament more fitted for scholarly research than for militantly opposing government policy. He has come to be considered by the Buddhist lay people and religious leaders to be the philosopher of the Movement. He edits the major Buddhist magazine in Vietnam, a weekly which has a circulation of twenty thousand, an impressive number in a country where the population is small and the illiteracy rate high. He also founded the first Buddhist University in Vietnam and is the director of the Youth for Social Service School. It is the latter that qualifies Thich Nhat Hanh to speak honestly about the Vietnamese peasant, since his work with the Social Service programme requires him to travel in the rural parts of the country.

As Thich Nhat Hanh says about the project, 'Our people receive no salary and carry no weapons. They are young people devoting themselves to the spiritual rebirth of Vietnam. Already, in only a year, they are having some success. The government agents and the Vietcong both hate our youth workers, but the people see that we are sincere and are beginning to protect us. This is the way Vietnam can be saved—by restoring a sense of humanity to Vietnamese life after twenty years of war and hatred. Neither guns nor foreigners can do this for us.

'We only ask the freedom to make our own mistakes rather than to die for the mistakes of others. Is this not what freedom means?' Over and over in a tone of voice that had about it a sad and determined wisdom he spoke of the suffering of his people. 'We weep to see so many of our countrymen die, but we weep even more to see Vietnam's social fabric destroyed by the war. Many of our people have learned to love money too much and will do anything, say anything, to get money. Today in Vietnam dollars will buy everything: politicians, generals, guns, girls, even religious leaders. The size of our national economy is decided by the American Congress. We are not free people.'

He spoke of how the most virulent anti-communists in Saigon did little to improve the social conditions that Communism seeks to answer and he said, with a smile, that he was not anti-communist because he was afraid of losing a car since he had none to lose. But he did fear Communism because he personally saw in the philosophy little room for spiritual growth. Yet he did feel that ninety per cent of the peasants were for the Vietcong, and that the difference between the Buddhists and the Vietcong was psychological. Given a climate of peace in Vietnam they could, hopefully, work together in the reconstruction of their country. His plea was simple: 'Let us try to work out a Vietnamese solution because we now see that the foreign solutions do not work. In this way you can also keep the affection of the Vietnamese people.'

This is part of the greatness of the man, that he can still speak in terms of the American and Vietnamese being able to love one another. He spoke of the American clergymen who visited Vietnam in a reconciliation effort and of the American workers in International Voluntary Service who do social work among the people. I only heard hardness come into his voice once when he was asked by someone about the possibilities of 'doing the job right', as it were, by sending in more troops and escalating the bombing. His comment was an unusually terse, 'You should go there yourself and see the bombing.'

We must put our faith in the Vietnamese people, since they are willing to risk peace. We must have faith in the goodness of men such as Thich Nhat Hanh and take courage from the history of Buddhist non-violent resistance in South Vietnam. It is the Buddhists who are non-violently quaking the government of Premier Ky, not the Vietcong, just as they quaked and toppled the government of Diem. They have as part of their religious orientation all the qualities which should grace a non-violent soldier. The Buddhist priests and peasantry often seem to possess the ingredients for a massive non-violent resistance movement yet the fact remains that the longer we remain in Vietnam the stronger will the Vietnamese commitment be toward a guerilla war. One thing becomes more and more clear and that is that we must stop this genocidal war and allow the Vietnamese people the freedom, as Thich Nhat Hanh said, 'to make their own mistakes.'

NICOLE D'ENTREMONT in *The Catholic Worker*, June 1966

(c) Vietnam: a personal impression by Lady Alexandra Metcalfe during a visit in February 1966 on behalf of The Save the Children Fund

Saigon is a large well laid-out city, very French in influence with wide boulevards, tree-lined avenues, streets of good but run down shops and attractive houses in gardens full of flowering trees and shrubs. At the back of this is the usual teaming squalor of an Asian city. The traffic, which never seems to cease, except for a few blessed hours between 2 a.m. and 5 a.m., is an incredible mixture. Exquisite ladies, traditionally dressed in satin trousers with long tight sheaths of flowered silk or chiffon, flowing black hair and high-heeled sandals, ride pillion on motor bikes or bicycles, weaving in and out of military lorries, trucks, jeeps, cars and peddicabs of every vintage. In the blazing sky are planes of all types, the airport is the busiest in the world. International passenger jets, monster military transports, camouflaged streamlined fighter bombers and helicopters (those most incongruous but life-saving of planes) all on their missions of mercy or destruction. The crunch of bombs, the blast of rockets or the boom of guns are often heard, but mostly at night when the noise of the traffic has dimmed. The Vietcong hold the country around the city so that the fighting is very near.

This is the life of Saigon. The war is on their doorstep. The two hospitals, Choo Ray and Nhi Dong (400 children in-patients and 500 out-patients) have insufficient beds to deal with the flood of patients even in normal times. Now with the wounded and the refugees they are having to put two or three people to a bed. The nursing staff is also inadequate and inexperienced, so that the few qualified personnel, Vietnamese and foreign, have to work day and night. It is to the Nhi Dong hospital that the team from Great Ormond Street Hospital in London is going. Children with limbs blown off, peppered with gun shot or burnt by Napalm, sometimes the only one of a family left alive, are sights which one cannot forget. Their courage is incredible.

The Vietcong terrorism and intensified military action have created a serious refugee problem, with as many as 600,000 people coming over into Government held territory. Many of the families have men fighting in the Government forces; others have been killed, or are being held by the Vietcong.

The conditions in the camps vary. Sometimes a vast camp of 10,000 people consists of huts made of bamboo, sacking, cardboard or tin with nothing to protect them from the rains except a little thatch. Narrow lanes of mud run between the huts; there are a few wells and no sanitation. I saw a large go-down housing 2,000 people, without even a curtain for privacy. In another camp the refugees had individual jerry built houses but these had been built on swampy ground which gets flooded in the monsoon. These people have lost everything, and very often their menfolk as well; but they smile and laugh as one tries to talk to them.

The Government policy is to protect and resettle the refugee families in secure rural areas, therefore they are reluctant to make the conditions in the refugee camps any better for fear they will create a longstanding problem.

In Saigon there are many crêches for babies. Some of these are true orphans, others have only one surviving parent, others are abandoned. They also vary greatly. A few are very well run while others leave much to be desired, but at least the problem of the children is foremost in everyone's mind.

A great deal of aid in various forms is coming into Saigon, so I was determined to try and find a place outside the city where Save the Children Fund could work. I flew up to Qui Nhon which is on the coast about 250 miles north of Saigon.

The province is the most heavily infested of all by the Vietcong. They have burnt most of the villages to the ground and the whole area is controlled by them, so that the flood of refugees into the town is enormous. There are four refugee camps and two hospitals. The Hospital of the Holy Family with 40 beds and 100 out-patients is run by Catholic nuns of the Medical Missionary Sisters—wonderful women doing first class work. At the Provincial Hospital a New Zealand team of doctors and surgeons have been working for some years under very difficult conditions. The main trouble is the almost total lack of trained nursing staff so that the patients have to be cared for by their families. One goes into ward after ward of post-operated and seriously ill patients without ever seeing a nurse. One little girl who had been badly burnt from head to foot had had 12 skin grafts. Her whole body was raw, she was lying on a dirty bed, open to any infection from dust and flies, in the charge of an aged old granny.

If there has been fighting the wounded start coming in, in the afternoon, brought by every known method : helicopter, bicycle, slung in hammocks or carried pick a back. The surgeons begin operating, both theatres going till far into the night.

The USAID programme for the civilian population is gigantic, the country is being kept alive by it and I have nothing but praise for the way I saw it being used. The U.S. troops are also lending a hand and helping the civilians and refugees in every possible way; there is nothing they are not willing to do. Those in command with whom I talked I found exceptionally intelligent, wise and understanding.

LADY ALEXANDRA METCALFE in *The World's Children*, Summer 1966

Perhaps a good point to begin discussion is a consideration of the two extreme views of the Vietnam war.

The extreme 'Left' position
U.S. imperialism is the sole cause of the war in Vietnam. The National Liberation Front is morally and militarily superior and will win the war. Because of the crimes committed daily in this savage war by the U.S. aggressors, they should be forced to leave South-east Asia immediately.

The extreme 'Right' position
War is terrible. But the U.S.A. must remain in Vietnam until its superiority is evident and gives it a strong position in negotiations. A Communist victory must be avoided, because it would result in a strengthening of world Communism and disturb the balance of power. Free elections in South Vietnam should be avoided in order to prevent the extension of the Communist camp.

What is your position? Why?

Haves and have-nots

34. The world of inter-related nations

Our shrinking world has been described many times and in many language games during recent decades. The call to internationalism is also not new. We still hear ringing in our ears the triumphant rhetoric of the politicians one hundred years ago: 'A specter is haunting Europe—the specter of Communism. All the powers of old Europe have entered into an unholy alliance to exorcise this specter: Pope and Czar, Metternich and Guizot, French radicals and German police-spies. . . . Communists everywhere support every revolutionary movement against the existing social and political order of things. . ., they labour everywhere for the union and agreement of the democratic parties of all countries. . . . The proletarians have nothing to lose but their chains. They have a world to win. Working men of all countries, unite!'[1]

Scientists are less given to rhetoric, but their description is no less passionate than the flamboyance of the political man: 'The technological capabilities of the modern world have bound together all men, one species in one community, and this interdependence is creating a climate of opinion in which the older dependence of the have-nots on the benevolence of the haves is being replaced by a new idea of partnership in the use of technology.'[2]

The artists, poets, novelists and musicians have sung their hymns of praise and fear of world unity: ' I am like the wind / which is without passport / home am I where I sleep / and where men have a tongue / I love and I live.'[3]

Examples are abundant. The sociologists speak about our world as a village; they describe the revolutions of traffic and communications, the ever-increasing pace at which cultures and continents approach each other. Commerce knows no barriers. The family of man sees the Coca-Cola advertisements on his Philips TV from his Pedersen chair in all six continents. The world looks like a gigantic transistor radio: one little knob suffices to travel across the oceans. On the little screen in our living room, the nations of the earth penetrate the quiet of our evenings.

1. *The Communist Manifesto*, Bantam Classics SC125, pp. 13–14.
2. A *Technocological Era*, Margaret Mead, Seabury Press, New York, p. 16.
3. Amajo Delepo, quoted in *Drum*, July 1962.

But again, let us not be deceived. The peoples of the earth on our little TV screen are not smiling at us. There is a terrifying symbolism in the fact that while what goes on on TV may happen in our rooms, we cannot really get into their midst. The shrinking of our world is *objective*, but is not necessarily communicative. A world in which distances are relativised is not, by definition, a world in which we meet. When we see the dogs of our white fellows jump at negroes in Alabama, we can see and hear them in our rooms; we may shout at them, blow a little whistle at them till our children wake up and our families laugh, but the dogs do not hear us. We may be only a night's distance away from Robbins Island, but Mandela and his imprisoned Bantu friends are no freer for that fact.

We are only a few hours away from the Berlin Wall, the bloodsoaked jungle of Vietnam, the constant terror of Sicily, and those distances can be overcome by turning a knob and dialling a number, but these technicological miracles do not work in tearing down hatred, reconciling warring parties or keeping order in Palermo. A shrinking world brings terror closer, but it does not follow that the action-radius of peace and justice grows.

Let me demonstrate that with one example. Two thirds of the people on our planet are hungry. One third have the skill and the means to produce food and decent living conditions for all. Since the world has become smaller, we all know that. Not only do the rich know that hunger is the normal condition of mankind—they see and hear it daily in press, radio and TV—but the hungry also know that we have and keep the resources. That *mutual* knowledge is new. For ages, people died without knowing that somewhere surplus food was destroyed for economic reasons; for ages, people ate without knowing that a few hours away children died of hunger. Now we know. Knowledge has made the world smaller, it has inter-related the nations, but it increases and heightens the tensions between the nations. It is now generally known that the northern hemisphere starves the southern hemisphere by protective tariff regulations, by refusing a price stabilisation for raw materials, and in general by pushing a 19th century liberal *laissez-faire* economy on the world level. This northern policy, which is openly advocated by our nations in UNCTAD and the WTC, is paid for by a high price: in our world each year an estimated four million people die because of hunger. These four million a year form a bloody contribution to the rising hatred of the coloured south towards the white north. In a political re-ordering of the world economy one would stand in fear and trembling if the southern hemisphere were ever to apply the principle of an eye for an eye or a tooth for a tooth. One thing is certain: if the rich countries continue to consider their wealth to be a right, the poor countries will consider their vengeance to be justice. The F.A.O. has spoken last year of a period of 20 years which we have to share our resources or prepare for a world war of the desperate hungry against the complacent well-fed.

I hope my point is clear: a world of inter-related nations is a small world of towering tensions, in which a threat of mass destruction has become a reality in the areas of hunger and remains a potential danger in the north.

What does the community of faith have to say about a younger generation in a world of inter-related nations? It first has to confess to the world that it has miserably failed in using its potential. Here is a community which transcends the nations, which has produced beautiful volumes about absolute listening and absolute speaking, as it is revealed in the man from Nazareth. It proclaims that the world is created by a word, and that this word transcends all we have and know. It proclaims also that man has a history and that all he does is related to the establishment of God's regime on earth, which will be a community such as we only know from our dreams.

In reality, however, the Church has a long history of war, domination and suppression, and understanding has been exchanged for dogmatic quarrels. So the Church has to be very humble in its speaking about our topic.

Allow me to make two remarks in which we humbly confess our faith in terms of our subject.

(a) *Corporate personality.* When we distinguish between the person and the individual, we do so because in the man of Nazareth a very clear concept of personhood is demonstrated. Jesus is no inner-directed man, who has sufficiency in himself. He identifies with the others. In him, we meet all of Israel; he is indeed a corporate personality. In his life, he acts out the longing of his people: without a profound knowledge of Israel's prophetic tradition, Jesus cannot be understood. In his death, he dies with seven quotations from the Torah on his lips. In him, Israel finally fulfils the law. The promise to Abraham takes on flesh.

The secret of the *homo internationalis* is the man who represents his people to the others, and the others to his people. Vicarious service is the hidden well from which he lives.

(b) *Faith, hope and love.* In that strangely profound letter which Rabbi Paul of Tarsus writes to the Christian congregation in Corinth, he speaks about the many gifts the Spirit of Jesus has given to the Church. But, he says, all these things will in time disappear. Only three concepts have eternity in them: faith, hope and love. The Christian will

therefore see these three as the dimensions of the formation of the
homo internationalis.

By faith, he means dependence and confidence. Dependence on God
is the ultimate antidote to arrogance. It recognises human finitude,
and also does not regard the self as the source of inspiration. When
dependence becomes confidence, faith has reached its climax. From
the negative recognition of the insufficiency of the self, it stands for
the person who bows down and worships a personal God who is not
only greater than the self, but who can be trusted to make all things
work for good. No one has absolute faith. We all have to be satisfied
with growing faith, which is all we shall ever know.

Love is the human transcendence which allows us to identify with
others; it is a quality of life which is the ultimate antidote to natural
self-centredness. It recognises the necessity of the other for our own
life, and regards him as the source of our inspiration. In the other, we
meet at least the symbol of God. Love weeps with the weeping, and
rejoices with the rejoicing. In the world of inter-related nations, it
recognises that our well-being is dependent on that of the others.

Hope, finally, is a dimension of love. It gives direction to our identification with others. It reckons with surprise, and knows that the
call of the future is so strong that it can wipe away the tears and give
people a *telos* in life, worth living for.

ALBERT VAN DEN HEUVEL, *The Carberry Lecture*, 1966

1. Discuss the advantages and disadvantages of TV in creating a 'world of
inter-related nations', and say how far you agree with the author's comments.

2. What can be done to relieve the 'towering tensions' of our inter-related world
of rich and poor, well-fed and hungry nations?

3. What difference does the 'perspective of faith' make to a person's attitude to
the problems of our inter-related world?

4. (a) Do you think the elimination of world hunger can or should provide us
with a *telos*, an aim worth living and working for, in international affairs?
(b) Have we in Britain a responsibility, other than enlightened self-interest, to
help (directly or indirectly) the hungry nations? If we have, from what does
this responsibility arise? How should we set about discharging it?

35. How many people?

The population explosion, as it is commonly called, is a weapon on
the side of poverty and hunger. The explosion today is nuclear. It is
world-wide, and most spectacularly affecting the economically backward nations.

The simple facts are sobering. The estimated total population of the
earth when Jesus was born was 150 millions, slowly climbing to that
figure from ten millions in 7000 BC. It doubled in the following six

centuries. It doubled again in eight centuries, reaching 600 millions in 1700. The next doubling took only 150 years, and the next only a hundred. The acceleration continues, and so far invariably faster than the forecasters predict. 2,500 millions in 1950 was 3,000 millions in 1960. The 4,000 millions mark will be reached by 1980, and by the end of the century there will be 6,000 million human beings to be fed, clothed and housed. The trouble is that it is not due to some phenomenal magnification of human fertility which might be expected to vanish as mysteriously as it arose. Man has altered his own situation. He bred families big enough to survive the quick wastages of death. He is still breeding them, and the pace of wastage has slackened. It is obviously beneficial, and it is comparatively cheap, to reduce infant mortality, to contain epidemics, and to increase the expectancy of life. In the last thirty years the expectancy of life in India has doubled. The child born in 1939 had an average chance of living till he was twenty. The child born to-day has an average chance of living till he is forty-two.

A few years ago I visited British Guiana, and spent a fascinating day with the Italian doctor who rid the colony of malaria. He was a first-class scientist, a brilliant improvisor, and a man of profound humanitarian conviction. He observed that the malaria-carrying mosquito common in British Guiana never struck at moving targets. It preferred to attack the sitting or sleeping. So instead of attempting the impossible task of spraying all the water in that vast, hot and excessively damp country, he sprayed buildings. Within three years the scourge was conquered. He showed me his maps and his tables of comparable statistics with well justified pride.

The victory was dramatically thorough. A disease which enervated and prematurely killed was utterly routed. Those who know anything of the ravages of malaria will have no doubt that it was a splendid and praiseworthy achievement. But the direct consequence is that the population of the colony has doubled within ten years. When I was there, seeing the results of the doctor's devoted labour, development plans were being hopefully and carefully prepared within the narrow limits of the budget of a poor country, eked out by slender external aid. There were plans for agricultural improvement, for the establishment of light industries, for school building and better sanitation. All those plans have been successfully carried through. If the population had been stable there would today be work and hope for all. As it is there is more unemployment, more poverty, more hunger, and the grim pressures are exacerbating the racial tensions that threaten to tear the unhappy nation in two.

What has been said of British Guiana could be repeated with infinitesimal variations throughout Asia and the West Indies, and is rapidly becoming true of Africa and Latin America. If the expansion continues to accelerate—and, in the nature of things, it cannot be slowed for a generation, as the children who live longer are already born—will this be a crippling blow to hopes of a richer life for all, or a lethal blow?

Mr Colin Clark, Director of the Agricultural Economics Research Institute at Oxford, is the most noted optimist. He argues that with the efficient use of known techniques, the earth could feed 28,000 million people, which leaves plenty of margin for developing knowledge after the turn of the century. The hard problem is that of the capital development of the poor countries, but this is not a problem that is inevitably insoluble.

We can assume, says Mr Clark, that the rate of population increase in the economically advanced countries will not exceed two per cent per annum. These countries have a rising level of income. They can meet the needs of their own population growth by setting aside five per cent of the total national income, but are capable of making average net savings of ten per cent. The surplus has been used to catch up the backlog of the depression years and of the second world war, but the lost ground has by now been largely covered. It follows that capital will shortly be available on a really extensive scale for investment in the poorer part of the world. In brief—though this is a deduction, and not a statement explicitly made by Mr Clark—we have the means in spite of population increase to conquer world poverty. If we fail, it will be a failure of determination and desire.

Sir Charles G. Darwin, the grandson of the world famous biologist, paints a strikingly different picture. It would not be far from the mark to comment that he would regard Mr Clark's calculations as wishful thinking, as projections which might conceivably happen but which, given the nature of man as we know him, are most unlikely. One of the most universal laws of zoology is the law of increase. When animals are let loose in a new and congenial situation they multiply until there are so many of them that they exhaust the food supply. Then the ever-present operations of natural selection become painfully evident. Man is an animal who obeys these laws. He is slow-breeding, and has taken about ten thousand years to get in sight of the limits, but if he goes on to 10,000 millions by 2050, 20,000 millions by 2100, and 40,000 millions by 2150 he will be jammed hard against them. The FAO conference in Rome in 1954 sounded the clear note of warning. In seven years intensive education and the application of modern techniques raised world food production by eight per cent, which was an unprecedented achievement. In the same seven years world population rose by eleven per cent. We haven't time to prepare for a future emergency. The emergency is now.

This means, Sir Charles would contend, that we must put away foolish dreams of welfare states and affluent societies. Our own century may live in legend as a fleeting golden age. Life will be a struggle for survival. Only a limited fraction of those born can expect to endure through what we now consider to be a normal life-span. Our kindly, easy charitableness will have to be discarded as too costly a luxury. On the other hand, if we do manage, by a discipline never previously known, to limit human numbers, and so to protect mankind from the searching test of the struggle for life, we may so preserve all inferior genetic mutations that the calibre of man will gradually decline. It sounds very much like: 'Heads, I win, tails, you lose.'

Confronted by expert opinions so contradictory, the normal reaction is to add them together and divide by two. As it happens the judgement of the overwhelming majority of those who have wrestled with the problem does come about half way. Most would agree with the findings of the committee set up by the British Association for the Advancement of Science to advise the sponsors of the Freedom from Hunger campaign whether or not their project was practicable. If it were made a first priority, said the report, and driven forward by a determined and concentrated effort, it would be possible by the end of the century to lift above subsistence level the estimated population of six thousand millions. Lord Boyd Orr, working on a longer time scale, estimates that it would be possible within eighty years to multiply eightfold food production, and so to feed a likely population of ten thousand millions—with the same proviso about determined and concentrated effort.

None of these moderate judgements, on which we should be wise to rely, will go beyond the cautious phrase 'it is possible'. All strongly suggest that unless the rate of population growth is greatly slowed by the end of their time limits a tragic decline in living standards is almost certain.

Up to a very few years ago it was widely held that there would be a more or less automatic levelling off. The 'theory of demographic transition' was beautifully neat. Primitive societies were balanced by a high birth-rate and a high death-rate. As the struggle for survival began to ease, birth-rates stayed high but death-rates fell. But the social pressures of industrialized and urbanized society develop a new stability with a low birth-rate and a low death-rate. The comforting theory is in fact a generalization from a comparatively brief period of European history.

Prophecy is dangerous in the comparatively new field of demographic analysis, but it is a fairly safe guess that living standards do not affect fertility potential. The change from 1860 to 1925 was social. Children were economic assets at the beginning of the eighteenth cen-

tury. They started work at six. In a new social situation at the end of
the nineteenth century they were economic liabilities. But as the
general standards rise the things that had to be skimped and saved
for come more easily in reach. There has been a post-war boom in
babies in the Western world, and it shows no sign of slackening. All
the planning based on the confident prediction that the population had
stabilized has proved woefully inaccurate, so that, for example,
throughout the West, as we know only too well in Britain, crash
programmes are being devised to build new schools, recruit more
teachers, and create new universities.

One clear conclusion is that the anticipation of a semi-automatic
stabilization of population is far too complacent. The further logical
deduction is also clear. If we are able in the next forty or eighty years
to lift the needy peoples of the world above the level of subsistence,
and to set them on the way to a modest prosperity, we dare not assume
that the higher living standard will of itself slow down permanently
the rate of population growth. But unless the rate is slowed down, one
brief generation will see the gleam of hope before the swift and bitter
disappointment of a return to poverty.

EDWARD ROGERS, *Living Standards*

1. Is the 'population explosion' a problem we ought to concern ourselves with?
Why?

2. Is it one we can do anything about personally, anyway? If so, what?

3. What role, if any, has Britain in helping to solve the problem? Ought it to
take steps to stop its own population increase? What are its man-power, land
and food production problems?

4. More food or population control or both are three possible ways of meeting
the world's population problem. Which do you favour? by what methods?
What are the moral or philosophical or theological grounds for your decisions?
(That these exist, even if we are not always aware of them, is clear from our
rejection of genocide or infanticide as accepted solutions to the problem.)

Peace with the bomb?

36–8.

Here are three passages discussing the moral and practical issues arising from the possession of nuclear weapons by the U.S.A., the U.S.S.R., and other countries. Read them carefully and then discuss your own viewpoint on these problems, your reasons for holding it, and the relevance or otherwise of Christian belief to the working out of a solution to them.

36. Kennedy and Khrushchev: the confrontation over Cuba

'Dobrynin said that . . . they had done nothing new or extraordinary in Cuba . . . and that he stood by his assurances that all these steps were defensive in nature and did not represent any threat to the United States.'

At the time the Ambassador was speaking, forty-two Soviet medium and intermediate-range ballistic missiles—each one capable of striking the United States with a nuclear warhead twenty or thirty times more powerful than the Hiroshima bomb—were en route to Cuba. Khrushchev and Mikoyan told Bolshakov to relay word that no missile capable of reaching the United States would be placed in Cuba. The message could not have been more precise—or more false.

The President was not lulled by these statements. (The Bolshakov message in fact, reached him after he knew of the missiles' existence.)

Continued Soviet shipments and the belligerent Moscow statement of September 11, however, impelled the President to deliver an even more explicit statement at his news conference. He underlined once again the difference between offensive and defensive capabilities:

'If at any time . . . Cuba should ever become an offensive military base . . . for the Soviet Union, then this country will do whatever must be done to protect its own security and that of its allies.'

On October 9 the President approved a mission over the western end of Cuba. Delayed by bad weather until October 14, the U-2 flew in the early morning hours of that cloudless Sunday high over Western Cuba, moving from south to north. Processed that night, the long rolls of film were scrutinized, analyzed, compared with earlier photos, and reanalyzed; and late that afternoon they spotted in the San Christobal area the first rude beginnings of a Soviet medium-range missile base.

Around 9 a.m. Tuesday morning, October 16, having first received a detailed briefing from top CIA officials, Bundy broke the news to the President as he scanned the morning papers. His pledge to act was unavoidable. He asked Bundy to arrange for two presentations of the evidence that morning—first to the President alone and then to a list of officials.

At 11.45 a.m. the meeting began. Those summoned were the principal members of what would later be called the Executive Committee of the National Security Council, some fourteen or fifteen men who had little in common except the President's desire for their judgement. At this meeting I saw for the first time the crucial photographs. Soviet medium-range ballistic missiles, said Carter, could reach targets eleven hundred nautical miles away. That covered Washington, Dallas, Cape Canaveral, St Louis and all bases and cities in between; and it was estimated that the whole complex of sixteen to twenty-four missiles could be operational in two weeks. The President was sombre but crisp. His first directive was for more photography. . . . We had to be sure—we had to have the most convincing possible evidence—and we had to know what else was taking place throughout the island. Even a gigantic hoax had to be guarded against, someone said. Daily flights were ordered covering all of Cuba.

Even as he went about his other duties, the President meditated not only on what action he would take but why the Soviets had made so drastic a departure from their usual practice. In the course of our meetings several theories were advanced:

Theory 1. Cold War Politics. Khrushchev believed that the American people were too timid to risk nuclear war. This was a probe, a test of America's will to resist. If it succeeded, he could move in a more important place—in West Berlin or with new pressure on our overseas bases—with missiles staring down our throats from Cuba.

Theory 2. Diverting Trap. If the United States did respond, the Allies would be divided, the UN horrified, the Latin Americans more anti-American than ever while Khrushchev moved swiftly in on Berlin.

Theory 3. Cuban Defense. A Soviet satellite in the Western Hemisphere was so valuable to Khrushchev that he could not allow it to fall. (It should be noted that the Soviet Union stuck throughout to this position.)

Theory 4. Bargaining Barter. Khrushchev intended to use these bases in a summit or UN confrontation with Kennedy as effective bargaining power.

Theory 5. Missile Power. The Soviets could no longer benefit from the fiction that the missile gap was in their favour. Providing Cuban bases for their existing medium and intermediate-range ballistic missiles gave them a swift and comparatively inexpensive means of adding sharply to the total number of missiles targeted on the United States, positioned to by-pass most of our missile warning system.

Whichever theory was correct, it was clear that the Soviet move, if successful, would 'materially . . . and politically change the balance of power' in the entire cold war.

At 6.30 p.m. we met again with the President in the Cabinet Room, as we would regularly for the next several weeks. Much misinformation has been written about this series of meetings. One of the remarkable aspects of [them] was a sense of complete equality. We were fifteen individuals on our own representing the President and not different departments. As the week wore on, the tireless work of the aerial photographers gave an even greater sense of urgency to our deliberations. More medium-range ballistic missile sites were discovered, for a total of six. There could be no mistaking the Soviet intention to have them operational much earlier than we had anticipated on Tuesday. The literally miles of film taken of the island now revealed excavations for three intercontinental ballistic missiles as well.

Each of us changed his mind more than once that week on the best course of action to take—not only because new facts and arguments were adduced, but because, in the President's words, 'whatever action we took had so many disadvantages to it and each raised the prospect that it might escalate the Soviet Union into a nuclear war.' What would Khrushchev actually do if we bombed the missile sites—or blockaded the island—or invaded? What would we do in return, and what would his reaction be then? The bulk of our time Tuesday through Friday was spent canvassing all the possible courses as the President had requested, and preparing the back-up material for them. Initially the possibilities seemed to divide into six categories, some of which could be combined:

1. Do nothing.
2. Bring diplomatic pressure and warnings to bear upon the Soviets. The removal of our missile bases in Turkey in exchange for the removal of the Cuban missiles was also listed in our later discussions as a possibility which Khrushchev was likely to suggest if we didn't.
3. Undertake a secret approach to Castro, to warn him that the alternative was his island's downfall and that the Soviets were selling him out.
4. Initiate indirect military action by means of a blockade.
5. Conduct an air strike—pinpointed against the missiles only—with or without advance warning.
6. Launch an invasion.

Choice No. 1 and choice No. 2 were both seriously considered. All the other courses raised so many risks and drawbacks that choice No.

2 had its appeal. All of us came back to it at one discouraged moment or another. But the President had rejected this course from the outset. He was concerned less about the missiles' military implications than with their effect on the global political balance. The Soviet move had been undertaken so swiftly, so secretly and with so much deliberate deception that it represented a provocative change in the delicate status quo.

Various approaches to Castro (choice No. 3) were also considered many times during the week. This course was set aside rather than dropped. The President increasingly felt that the missiles had been placed there by the Soviets, and would have to be removed by the Soviets in response to direct American action. Choice No. 6 had surprisingly few supporters.

Thus our attention soon centred on two alternatives—an air-strike and a blockade—and initially more on the former.

But there were grave difficulties to the air-strike alternative:

1. The 'surgical' strike was merely a hopeful illusion. It could not be accomplished by a few sorties in a few minutes. All or most of these targets would have to be taken out in a massive bombardment. The more we looked at the air strike, the clearer it became that the resultant chaos and political collapse would ultimately necessitate a U.S. invasion. But invasion with all its consequences was still opposed by the President.

2. The problem of advance warning was unsolvable. A sudden air strike at dawn without warning would be 'a Pearl Harbour in reverse, and it would blacken the name of the United States in the pages of history'. But to provide advance warning raised as many difficulties as no warning at all. It would enable the Soviets to conceal the missiles and make their elimination less certain. It would invite Khrushchev to commit himself to bombing us if we carried out our attack, give him time to take the propaganda and diplomatic initiative.

3. The air strike, unlike the blockade, would directly and definitely attack Soviet military might. Not to respond at all would be too great a humiliation for Khrushchev to bear. 'What will the Soviets do in response?' one consultant favoring this course was asked. 'I think they'll knock out our missile bases in Turkey.' 'What do we do then?' 'Under our NATO treaty, we'd be obligated to knock out a base inside the Soviet Union.' 'What will they do then?' 'Why, then we hope everyone will cool down and want to talk.' It seemed rather cool in the conference room as he spoke.

At first there had been very little support of a blockade. It appeared almost irrelevant to the problem of missiles. Moreover, blockade had many of the drawbacks of the air-strike plan. If Soviet ships ignored it, U.S. forces would have to fire the first shot, provoking Soviet action elsewhere. We could not even be certain that the blockade route was open to us. Without obtaining a two-thirds vote in the Organisation of American States—which appeared dubious at best—allies and neutrals as well as adversaries might well regard it as an illegal blockade. But the greatest single drawback to the blockade was time. It offered a prolonged and agonizing approach, uncertain in its effect, indefinite in its duration.

Despite all these disadvantages, the blockade route gained strength on Thursday as other choices faded. It was a more limited, low-key military action than the air strike. It offered Khrushchev the choice of avoiding a direct military clash by keeping his ships away. It could at least be initiated without a shot being fired. It could serve as an unmistakable but not sudden or humiliating warning to Khrushchev of what we expected from him. Its prudence, its avoidance of casualties and its avoidance of attacking Cuban soil would make it more appealing to other nations than an air strike.

On Thursday afternoon subcommittees were set up to plot each of the major courses in detail. Meanwhile, the President was holding a long-scheduled two-hour meeting with Soviet Foreign Minister Gromyko prior to the latter's return to Moscow. Gromyko, seated on the sofa next to the President's rocker, not only failed to mention the offensive weapons, but carried on the deception that there were none. He turned to Cuba, not with apologies, but complaints. He called our restrictions on Allied shipping a blockade against trade and a violation of international law. All this could only lead to great misfortune for mankind, he said, for his government could not sit by and observe this situation idly when aggression was planned. Gromyko then read from his notes:

'As to Soviet assistance to Cuba, I have been instructed to make it clear, . . . that such assistance pursued solely the purpose of contributing to the defense capabilities of Cuba. . . . If it were otherwise, the Soviet Government would never have become involved in rendering such assistance.'

Kennedy gave no sign of tension or anger. But to avoid misleading his adversary, he sent for and read aloud his September warning against offensive missiles in Cuba. Gromyko 'must have wondered why I was reading it,' he said later. 'But he did not respond.'

On Friday morning, October 19, the President called me in. He wanted to act soon, Sunday if possible—and Bob Kennedy was to call him back when we were ready. Our meetings that morning largely repeated the same arguments. The objections to the blockade were listed, then the objections to the air strike. I agreed to write the first rough draft of a blockade speech as a means of focussing on specifics.

But back in my office, the original difficulties with the blockade route stared me in the face: How should we relate it to the missiles? How would it help get them out? What would we do if they became operational? What should we say about our surveillance, about communicating with Khrushchev? I returned to the group late that afternoon with these questions instead of a speech; and as the concrete answers were provided in our discussions, the final shape of the President's policy began to take form. I worked until 3 a.m. on the draft speech. Among the texts I read for background were the speeches of Wilson and Roosevelt declaring World Wars I and II. At 9 a.m. Saturday morning my draft was reviewed, amended and generally approved. The President's helicopter landed on the South Lawn a little after 1.30. After he had read the draft speech, we chatted in a relaxed fashion in his office before the decisive meeting scheduled for 2.30. Our meeting was held once again in the Oval room upstairs. At the conclusion of the presentations there was a brief, awkward silence. It was the most difficult decision any President could make, and only he could make it. Then Gilpatric, who was normally a man of few words in meetings, spoke up. 'Essentially, Mr President,' he said, 'this is a choice between limited action and unlimited action; and most of us think it's better to start with limited action.' The President nodded his agreement. There was disagreement, however, over what our diplomatic stance should be. The remainder of the meeting was occupied with a brief discussion of the speech draft and its timing. The President wanted to speak the next evening, Sunday. Secrecy was crumbling. But the State Department stressed that our ambassadors had to brief Allied and Latin-American leaders. The President agreed to Monday, but stated he would still speak Sunday if the story appeared certain to break. The speech was set for 7 p.m. Monday, October 22.

At 2.30 that Sunday afternoon, October 21, the President met with the NSC once again. He reviewed the State Department's drafts of instructions to embassies and Presidential letters to allies. He reviewed the approaches to the OAS and UN. He asked Navy Chief of Staff Anderson, Jr. to describe plans and procedures for the blockade. Most of that meeting was spent in a page-by-page review of the latest speech draft. He made dozens of changes, large and small. But struck from the speech any hint that the removal of Castro was his true aim. He did not talk of total victory or unconditional surrender, simply of the precisely defined objective of removing a specific provocation. 'It shall be the policy of this nation to regard any nuclear missile launched from Cuba against any nation in the Western Hemisphere as an attack by the Soviet Union on the United States, requiring a full retaliatory response upon the Soviet Union.'

The whole nation knew on Monday that a crisis was at hand—particularly after Salinger's announcement at noon that the President had obtained 7 p.m. network time for a speech of the 'highest national urgency'. Alone back in the Cabinet Room, we reviewed the text once more; and in a few more minutes the most serious speech in his life was on the air:

'Good evening, my fellow citizens:

. . . Within the past week, unmistakable evidence has established the fact that a series of offensive missile sites is now in preparation on [the island of Cuba]. The purpose of these bases can be none other than to provide a nuclear strike capability against the Western Hemisphere. . . . For many years both the Soviet Union and the United States . . . have deployed strategic nuclear weapons with great care, never upsetting the precarious status quo. . . .

But this secret, swift and extraordinary build-up of Communist missiles, . . . this sudden, clandestine decision to station strategic weapons for the first time outside of Soviet soil, is a deliberately provocative and unjustified change in the status quo which cannot be accepted by this country, if our courage and our commitments are ever to be trusted again by either friend or foe.

The 1930's taught us a clear lesson: aggressive conduct, if allowed to go unchecked and unchallenged, ultimately leads to war. This nation is opposed to war. We are also true to our word. Our unswerving objective, therefore, must be to prevent the use of these missiles against this or any other country. . . .'

He went on to outline the initial steps to be taken, emphasizing the word 'initial': quarantine, surveillance of the build-up, action if it continued, . . . OAS and UN action and an appeal to Krushchev and the Cuban people.

'Our goal is not the victory of might, but the vindication of right; not peace at the expense of freedom, but both peace *and* freedom, here in this hemisphere, and, we hope, around the world. God willing, that goal will be achieved.'

The crisis had officially begun. A U.S. resolution was presented to that month's Security Council President, Russia's Valerian Zorin.

The Alliance held. Macmillan phoned his support, Adenauer, Brandt and the people of West Berlin did not flinch or complain. Despite some wavering by Canada, the NATO Council and De Gaulle pledged their backing. But of far greater importance to Kennedy [than Lord Russell's telegram] was the action taken by the twenty members of the OAS in immediately and unanimously adopting a broad authorising resolution.

In the UN, in Washington and in the foreign embassies, support for the U.S. position was surprisingly strong. This was due in part to the shock of Soviet perfidy, and their futile attempts to deny the photographic evidence of attempted nuclear blackmail. It was due in part to world-wide recognition that this was an East-West nuclear confrontation, not a U.S. quarrel with Cuba. It was due in part to the President's choice of a low level of force at the outset and to his forceful but restrained approach. It was due, finally, to the excellent presentations made in the UN by Ambassador Stevenson; let a UN team inspect the sites, he said.

Stevenson: . . . Do you, Ambassador Zorin, deny that the U.S.S.R. has placed and is placing medium—and intermediate—range missiles and sites in Cuba? Yes or no. Don't wait for the translation. Yes or no.
Zorin: I am not in an American courtroom, sir. . . .
Stevenson: You are in the court of world opinion right now!

The 'quarantine' was a new form of reprisal under international law. Its legality, much strengthened by the OAS endorsement, had been carefully worked out. The proclamation stressed that 'force shall not be used except in case of failure or refusal to comply with directions . . . after reasonable efforts have been made to communicate them to the vessel or craft, or in case of self-defense.'

Other issues were discussed in the two Tuesday meetings of the Executive Committee: what to do if a U-2 were shot down, how to keep the Press and Congress informed, preparations at Berlin, preparations to invade. For the first time low-level reconnaissance flights were ordered over Cuba. These pictures showed in remarkable detail more military personnel and weapons than anticipated.

Kennedy told U Thant, in response to the Secretary General's initial appeal, that the blockade could not be suspended, that 'the existing threat was created by the secret introduction of offensive weapons into Cuba, and the answer lies in their removal'.

To us, Khrushchev appeared to have been caught off balance, to be manoeuvering, to be seeking a consensus among the top Kremlin rulers, uncertain whether to admit that the missiles were there. But the eighteen Soviet dry cargo ships still heading towards the quarantine were no joke. Tuesday night, as the ships came on, the tension built. Robert Kennedy was dispatched that night to find out from the Soviet Ambassador whether any instructions had been issued to the Soviet ship captains. He learned nothing. At our Wednesday morning meeting, held just as the quarantine went into effect, some half-dozen Soviet submarines were reported to have joined these ships. In the midst of the same meeting, more news arrived. The Soviet ships nearest Cuba had apparently stopped or altered their course. At dawn Thursday a Soviet tanker was hailed and, on the instructions of the President, passed through the barrier like all nonsuspicious tankers after merely identifying itself. The real problem was not Soviet tankers but the Soviet cargo ships and their submarine escorts. They would have to be stopped Friday, said the President, if U Thant's proposals had not altered their course by then. The Navy was eager to go far out into the ocean to intercept the key Soviet ships. The President insisted that Khrushchev be given all possible time to make and communicate an uncomfortable decision to his ships. In a sharp clash with the Navy, he made certain his will prevailed.

Gradually, rather than dramatically, the good news came in, mixed, in fact, with the 'bad' news recounted above. Sixteen of the eighteen Russian ships, including all five with large hatches, were reported Wednesday to have stopped, and, finally, Thursday and Friday to have turned around. The value of conventional strength in the nuclear age had been underlined as never before. The quarantine, speculated the President later, 'had much more power than we first thought it did because, I think, the Soviet Union was very reluctant to have us stop ships which carried highly secret and sensitive materials'.

Throughout Thursday and Friday the President and Executive Council pondered new ways of stepping up the political, economic and military pressure on the Soviets. The President refused to rush. Preparations for an invasion as well as other military contingencies were still under way. Soviet ships had turned back. Talks were going on at the UN.

The State Department press officer went beyond the White House position by referring reporters to that passage in the President's Monday night speech which had said 'further action will be justified' if work on the missiles continued. This remark immediately touched off headlines that an invasion or air strike was imminent. For the first time, the President lost his temper. This was going to be a prolonged struggle, he argued, requiring caution, patience and as little public pressure on him as possible. But in the next twenty-four hours he was to joke that [the press officer's] error might have had a helpful effect. A new Khrushchev-to-Kennedy letter was received Friday evening, October 26, in essence appearing to contain the germ of a reasonable settlement: inasmuch as his missiles were there only to defend Cuba against invasion, he would withdraw the missiles under UN inspection if the U.S. agreed not to invade. It was with high hopes that the Executive Committee convened Saturday morning, October 27, to draft a reply.

In the course of that meeting our hopes quickly faded. A new Khrushchev letter came in, this time public, making no mention of the private correspondence. The Jupiter missiles in Turkey must be removed in exchange. More bad news followed. A new Soviet ship was reported approaching the quarantine zone. Permanent and expensive installations of nuclear warhead storage bunkers and troop barracks were going ahead rapidly. Then came the worst news: the first shooting and fatality of the crisis, ground fire on two low-flying reconnaissance planes and the downing of a high-flying U-2. That same day, to make matters worse, an American U-2 plane over Alaska had encountered navigational difficulties and flown deep into Soviet territory, bringing up a bevy of Soviet fighters but no fire, before regaining its course.

Everything was in combat readiness on both sides. If the Soviet ship continued coming, if the SAMs continued firing, if the missile crews continued working and if Khrushchev continued insisting on concessions with a gun at our head, then—we all believed—the Soviets must want a war and war would be unavoidable. The President had no intention of destroying the Alliance by backing down, but he thought it all the more imperative that our position be absolutely clear. He decided to treat the latest Khrushchev message as propaganda and to concentrate on the Friday night letter.

Under the President's direction, our group worked all day on draft replies. And the President released the letter publicly as it was being transmitted to Moscow shortly after 8 p.m.

'The first thing that needs to be done . . . is for work to cease on offensive missile bases on Cuba and for all weapon systems in Cuba capable of offensive use to be rendered inoperable, under effective United Nations arrangements. . . .

. . . The key elements of your proposals . . . are as follows:

1. You would agree to remove these weapons systems from Cuba under appropriate United Nations observation and supervision. . . .

2. We, on our part, would agree . . . (a) to remove promptly the quarantine measures now in effect and (b) to give assurances against an invasion of Cuba. . . .

. . . The first ingredient, let me emphasise, . . . is the cessation of work on missile sites in Cuba. . . . The continuation of this threat, or a prolonging of this discussion . . . would surely lead to an intensification of the Cuban crisis and a grave risk to the peace of the world.'

A copy of the letter was delivered to the Soviet Ambassador by Robert Kennedy with a strong verbal message: The point of escalation was at hand; the United States could proceed towards peace and disarmament, or . . . we could take 'strong and overwhelming retaliatory action . . . unless [the President] received immediate notice that the missiles would be withdrawn.' That message was conveyed to Moscow.

Meanwhile the Executive Committee was somewhat heatedly discussing plans for the next step. The downing of our plane could not be ignored. Neither could the approaching ship, or the continuing work on the missile sites, or the Soviet SAMs. We stayed in session all day Saturday, and finally, shortly after 8 p.m., noting rising tempers and irritability, the President recessed the meeting for a one-hour dinner break. Pressure and fatigue, he later noted privately, might have broken the group's steady demeanour in another twenty-four or forty-eight hours. The meeting at 9 p.m. was shorter, cooler and quieter; and with the knowledge that our meeting the next morning at 10 a.m. could be decisive we adjourned for the night.

Upon awakening Sunday morning, October 28, I turned on the news on my bedside radio, as I had each morning during the week. In the course of the 9 a.m. newscast a special bulletin came in from Moscow. It was a new letter from Khrushchev, his fifth since Tuesday, sent publicly in the interests of speed. Kennedy's terms were being accepted. The missiles were being withdrawn. Inspection would be permitted. The confrontation was over.

THEODORE SØRENSEN, *Kennedy*

37. We are all under judgement

The central problems of modern warfare collide directly with two principles that the Church has insisted upon ever since Christians were somehow first dragooned into armies. (This was much later in the history of the Christian Church than most people realise, since even St Augustine strongly maintained that the individual Christian did *not* have the right to kill in self-defense.) The principles are: first, that there must be discrimination between guilty and innocent, between combatant and non-combatant; second, that there must be due proportion between the violence used and the evil to be remedied—in other words a strict limitation of weaponry, not only as regards human beings but also as regards their property and livelihoods. Even the least lettered of Christians knows that to kill the innocent is murder.

As weapons became more and more powerful and less and less controllable a rationale had to be developed to justify the incidental killing of civilians when an arms factory or a rail junction was destroyed. This rationale was the theory of the *double effect*, or *second intention*. The death of men, women and children who lived around the factory or rail junction was not intended, but was a regrettable side effect of a necessary attack on a valid military target. In the Second World War, with obliteration bombing and finally with nuclear bombing, cities became targets, and war became total. The principles of discrimination and due proportion (with proper limitation of violence understood) were erased from the rules of warfare and presumably from the consciences of Christians.

An American Catholic spokesman recently wrote that the traditional Catholic teaching on the just war 'seems to have trapped itself
into an impossible situation in its handling of the concept of the
immunity of non-combatants from direct attack.' He goes on to state
that the origins and 'authoritative character' of this teaching are much
more 'controversial' than is generally known. What is behind this
concern is that a new rationale is needed to justify such a nuclear
deterrent as is now in the possession of the United States. Since churchmen of the early Middle Ages condemned the use of the crossbow
against human beings, no theologians have been called in to pass
judgment on new weapons before they were used. The theologians
became in the matter of warfare 'merchants of abstraction' *par excellence*. They formulated their concepts after the fact and away from
the scene of slaughter—and more often than not, their conclusions
were accommodations related to the pressure of their societies. A
prime example of this accommodation was that the ban on the crossbow (hitherto permitted only against animals) was lifted in the war
against the infidels.

The 'defense' of the United States rests on a nuclear potential that
includes, according to public testimony, nuclear bombs of 10–1 or
more megaton size. Jerome Wiesner and Herbert York, scientific advisers to the United States Government, point out that: A *one-
megaton bomb is already about 50 times bigger than the Bomb that
produced 100,000 deaths at Hiroshima, and 10 megatons is of the
same order of magnitude as the grand total of all high explosives used
in all wars to date.'

This is the actual United States deterrent. The two scientists draw
a conclusion that 'Both sides in the arms race are thus confronted by
the dilemma of steadily increasing military power and steadily decreasing national security. It is our considered professional judgment
that this dilemma has no technical solution.' They advert to the fact
that national security involves moral and human values.

It might be useful to apply some simple logic to the nuclear deterrent. This threat of megadeath deters an opponent only if he is convinced that it will be utilized. Those who have accumulated the
deterring nuclear warheads intend to use them and to participate in
the massive slaughter of the innocent. We all know that to intend an
evil is sinful, so the guilt is already built in.

At this point, we may hear the argument that the threat of use is
not actual, but rather a bluff to prevent attack by the other side. If
this is the case, those who pose the threat of unleashing the deterrent
are involved in a massive lie—also sinful by Christian standards.

The effects of the nuclear deterrent have been assessed in many
ways. Special attention has been given to the problem of fallout, the

poisoning of the atmosphere as a result of testing, and the poisoning of earth and sea through the disposal of atomic wastes. There is another type of fallout—what one would call a moral fallout, that arises from the possession by ostensible Christian communities of such genocidal machines. The American deterrent is pointed at centres of population across the Eurasian heartland, Russia and mainland China. Both of these nations in certain stages in their drive for a controlled and more egalitarian economy have given scant attention to the demands of the individual person. Americans decry the 'ant civilization' of China, where millions are herded into collective farms and enterprises and forced to fit into a pattern of work and productivity.

The message of Christians, with its personal God and personal Saviour, has always glorified the individual human person, irreplaceable, infinitely loved. A Catholic writer has pointed out that 'the great liberation that Christianity has brought to men in every age is to make them realise they are loved.' When circumstances are against the realization that man is loved by His Creator, then the role of Christians is to serve as the reminder through their expression of that love alone which comes only from the mystery of faith. The Russians and Chinese above all, need such reminders of our love. Instead, they learn that there are missiles, rockets and bombs pointed at them, and careening through the sky over them. If they are treated as less than human personalities in the collective farm or factory, they must realise that to the people behind the nuclear weapons, they are no more than insects to be cremated alive by the million. Who can convince the Chinese peasant that we, the Catholics of America, see him as a temple of the Holy Spirit, infinitely precious in the sight of God, another Christ to be lovingly served?

Slavery began to fall apart when the Christian began to receive his former slave (as Philemon was urged by St Paul to take Onesimus) 'as a brother most dear'. The deterrent system will begin to fall apart, and eventually to be dismantled, when Christians, American Christians first, begin to see their so-called enemies in Russia, China, or across whatever border, as 'brothers most dear'.

Meantime, no pressures from the side of nuclear nationalism should move [us] to see the nuclear deterrent, and the 'balance of terror' that it has brought upon the world, as anything but an eroder of the Christian concept of the infinite dignity of man, inhabited by the spirit of God and made in His image. How could such a threat of mass annihilation of God's human and material creation help preserve peace or stability? How can societies vowed to the defense of the rights of the human person preserve those rights by constant, coldly calculated threats to the bodily integrity of millions of innocent human beings?

There are those who suggest that a way out of the armament trap, which, by heaping overkill on overkill, is impoverishing mankind, would be unilateral steps toward disarmament. Those who are aghast at such proposals might remember that *all* morality is unilateral. We cannot wait for the other person to perform a moral act before we perform it or before we veer from a sinful to a moral course. They need perhaps to be reminded that the armament race, especially the nuclear build-up of the United States, was a unilateral action.

The early Christians had a healthy mistrust of political authority, inspired partly by the fact that that authority was clearly wedded to idol-worship and the persecution of dissidents. Later, Christians often came to identify the concerns of Christ's Church with a particular nation-state. In time of war particularly, the nation-state became the ultimate guide for consciences, claiming an allegiance for Caesar that was due to God alone. The rule of thumb for the ordinary Christian came to be that if injustice was not open and clear, he was to give a 'presumption of justice' to his own governmental authority. Certainly in ordinary situations this may be a reasonable stance. In war time, it becomes less reasonable, and often flagrantly opposed to reason, since every state presumes justice to itself.

The human family as a whole, and the national groups into which it is divided, are best served by the responsible man who puts governmental actions to the test of right reason and his moral conscience. A presumption of injustice by the Christian citizen would help keep the nation-state closer to moral norms, especially in war time. To those who fear anarchy in this use of freedom, it can well be argued that no world can be as lawless as the world where leaders can flout the human conscience and break all human and divine laws. The lessons of Nazism and Fascism, systems that grew in the wombs of Europe's oldest civilization, are perhaps too easily forgotten. These systems could not have swallowed up the German and Italian nations nor turned civilian societies into war machines without a presumption of justice on the part of millions of citizens.

The right of the individual to refuse to participate in war and killing is enshrined in the laws of many countries, including the United States. Regrettably, the American Catholic conscientious objector did not receive from churchmen the same protection for the freedom of conscience that was extended by the political authority.

Franz Jagerstatter[1] was troubled to his dying day by the thought that he was sinning in the eyes of the Church by refusing to take the oath of fealty to Hitler or to fight in Hitler's wars. Jagerstatter was born in the same province as the unfortunate Adolf Eichmann, whose defense against the accusation of genocide was that he was merely

1. See passage 17(b).

carrying out orders. Eichmann seems to stand for all the millions of little Eichmanns who tried to slough responsibility off on those above him. Franz Jagerstatter pondered these matters in his heart and wrote of them in commentaries which were preserved by his wife. 'One often hears it said these days: "It's all right for you to do this or that with an untroubled mind; the responsibility for what happened rests with someone else." And in this way, responsibility is passed on from one man to another. No one wants to accept responsibility for anything. Does this mean that when human judgement is finally passed on all the crimes and horrors being committed at this very time one or two individuals must do penance for them all some day?'

The judgement that we all face is the simple one of how we have treated our neighbour. Have we fed him, clothed him, healed him, sheltered him, ransomed him, or have we not? We know from our earliest years that it is not only by the works of mercy that we enter the kingdom of God. And we know that mercy is only love under the aspect of need. We are all under the judgement of love. If all of us, lay and clerical alike, must meet that same judgement, we should look with terror at any human activity which makes it impossible for us to perform the works of mercy. War does just that. In times of old, the works of mercy were merely interrupted for the duration of the hostilities. Modern war literally reverses the works of mercy. Rather than feed the hungry, we scorch the earth from which the hungry are fed; rather than clothe the naked, we raze the plants where clothing is manufactured; rather than shelter the shelterless, we destroy, in minutes, the shelters that man patiently built for himself and his kind; rather than give drink to the thirsty, we bomb reservoirs serving great cities; rather than heal the sick, we kill them in their beds in homes and hospitals; rather than ransom the captive, we make captives of as many of our opponents as possible. This is the face of modern total war, even of 'conventional' war. Nuclear war, by vaporizing the human being so that he is no more than a shadowy outline on a Hiroshima sidewalk, makes all the works of mercy impossible.

In the United States alone, nearly fifty billion dollars annually goes into the bottomless pit of the nuclear deterrent and that loathsome thing known as overkill. These are the resources that the family of man needs for its health, its educational improvement, its dignity. Here again there is a massive obliteration of the works of mercy, as Pope John XXIII and Pope Paul VI have so eloquently pointed out to the world.

Christians are called to be peacemakers, to reconcile man to man, as their Founder reconciled man to God. Now, when we can resort to violence only at the risk of destroying ourselves, we must make a witness, both as individual Christians and as a Church to a loving reconciling community. The time is upon us for a witness against war and for peace.

DOROTHY DAY in *The Catholic Worker*, July/August 1965

38. A diplomat at work

Of all international issues I suppose that disarmament, and in particular nuclear disarmament, is the most frustrating for the negotiator and presents the most difficult moral problems for the Christian. I know the deep sincerity with which divergent views are held in this field. I know how hard it is to find common and solid ground. If I myself can make any contribution, I suppose it is mainly from the standpoint of a negotiator compelled for four years leading up to the partial test ban to deal not with things as we should like them to be, or as we may think they ought to be, but with the hard and stubborn facts as they are. And before expanding, however briefly, on the courses open to us, I will state at once the general conclusion to which I believe the facts point; namely, to quote my Canadian colleague in Geneva, 'that it is better for the nations to set themselves the objective of a disarmament millennium, even though it may take a long time to achieve, than to resign themselves to a nuclear Armageddon, which may also be a long time in coming, but which will be inevitable if the weapons are kept and are not done away with under international control'. And I believe the need for progress to be compellingly urgent.

It is commonplace to say that the possession of nuclear weapons by the United States and the Soviet Union has resulted in a balance of terror which serves to keep the peace. That has indeed been true for a number of years; it is true now; and it has caused Moscow, although not Peking, to say that war between capitalist and communist states is no longer inevitable. But because it has been true for a period, many people dignify this temporary balance into a permanent principle of strategy, of politics and almost of moral duty. . . . Consider for a moment how many of the systems of arms control and arms limitation proposed by governments, or by theorists, rest on this premise. They rest, so many of them, on the contention that it is Utopian to suppose that great powers will ever give up nuclear weapons; that we must learn to live with the bomb and even to like it; and that the bomb is so dangerous as to be really safe. . . .

As a negotiator in the field of disarmament I can only lift my voice, for what it may be worth, against this thesis. . . . The 'balance of terror' is perhaps a misleading term. A better phrase might be 'balance of prudence', because the balance depends on the prudent and responsible behaviour of the leaders of all nuclear states. The whole course of recorded history indicates that to rely forever, or even for long, on the prudent and responsible behaviour of every national leader is to base one's actions on a dangerous illusion. Few periods illustrate this more dramatically than the last fifty years. In the world of today, faced as we are with conflicting ideologies, with racial strife, with population explosions side by side with hunger, with revolutionary and extremist pressures constantly proving too strong for moderate leaders—in such a world to rely indefinitely on the balance of prudence, seems to me about as risky as to build one's house on the slopes of Mount Etna.

It is an open question whether the balance of terror can be expected to be durable. As of today the two nuclear sides have reached a plateau of scientific discovery. The two sides are almost certainly in some sort of balance of destructive power. Each can annihilate the other for all practical purposes totally, but at the cost of being annihilated itself. . . . Yet, at the same time, each side is trying to secure a scientific break-through which will tilt the balance to its advantage. . . . It is in fact, highly risky to place reliance upon the continuation, for an indefinite period, of a technical balance between the two sides. Nor is that all. We cannot even be certain that nuclear weapons will be confined indefinitely to two sides, to NATO and to the Warsaw Pact countries. . . . But both possession and knowledge may spread outside the two alliances. And what will happen then to the balance between the two sides?

If there is any validity in these thoughts, they seem to me to point inescapably to the conclusion that to base our hopes for the future of mankind on faith in a lasting balance of prudence, on the accumulation of more and more horrible weapons, which might credibly be used at any moment, but never are used, is rather like expecting a Sultan to maintain more and more dancing girls to whom he might make love, but never does. This is not common sense, it is not realism, it is wilful acceptance of the extremely improbable. . . . The risk does not disappear if only the United States and the Soviet Union retain nuclear weapons.

There is one course, and one course only, which can protect future generations against nuclear war, and that is *the abandonment of all nuclear weapons by all countries under international control*. The need for international control stems from two factors—the nature of nuclear weapons and the nature of man. Because nuclear weapons can be manufactured in relative, if not complete, secrecy, and used decisively within a few days, if not hours, no measures short of adequate international control can afford protection against surprise attack or against surprise nuclear blackmail. . . .

Second, the political animal of the twentieth century does not trust his neighbour; and he has, unfortunately, good reason to be distrust-

ful. The Church teaches us that evil exists side by side with good, and
this is a truth we can ignore only at our peril. To trust the devil to be
good, is, I believe, bad theology; it is certainly bad politics. Forces of
evil exist within and around every state. To leave the possession and
use of nuclear weapons to forces of evil, or to give free opportunity for
this to happen, is not to fulfil one's duty to one's family, to one's
country, to the Christian community, or indeed to the world community.

What should be understood by the words 'giving free opportunity
to forces of evil to possess or use nuclear weapons'? I do not mean, of
course, that at least at present any country can be forcibly prevented
by others from possessing or using nuclear weapons. Nor do I mean
that every or any country, other than my own country or our Allies,
is or will necessarily be dominated by evil forces. But I do mean that
forces of evil, such as exist in all countries, can gain control more
easily in some countries than in others; and are more prevalent or less
under control under certain ideologies and beliefs or lack of beliefs
than under others. If such forces can with relative impunity gain a
commanding advantage in nuclear weapons they can use them at any
moment, with no notice, to impose their purposes and to destroy
opposition; and we, I believe, should seek to deny that opportunity as
far as possible.

There are two ways in which a country or group of countries can
gain a commanding advantage in nuclear weaponry—apart, of course,
from a scientific breakthrough. The first way is if . . . for example, the
United States and NATO as a whole abandoned nuclear weapons uni-
laterally and unconditionally, leaving the Soviet Union in sole possession of them. The second way is if there should be an international
agreement between nations to limit or abandon production and possession of nuclear weapons, without adequate international control to
ensure observance by all parties, to ensure observance by a nation
acting in bad faith as well as nations acting in good faith. If there
were no adequate international control, the way would be open to
forces of ambition and evil in any country . . . to prepare domination
in secret and to impose it at the time and in the manner of their own
choosing. Adequate international control, adequate international verification, is, in fact, possible. . . . World-wide control of production of
fissile material might, for example, require about 1,500 scientific personnel, with a supporting staff, making perhaps 10,000 altogether for
the whole world. That would be burdensome; but it is something
feasible and it is surely something tolerable. Indeed, it is the great
moral and political strength of the Western position, and I do not
think this should be overlooked, that the United States and Britain
have said they are prepared to accept any degree of international veri-

fication, however rigorous, buttressed by an adequate peace-keeping force, which may be required to secure disarmament. Unhappily this is not so far the case with the Soviet Union.

To work unsparingly for this goal—the abandonment of all nuclear weapons under adequate international control with strengthened international peace-keeping machinery—must surely be the duty both of governments and of individuals. The fact that the goal is difficult to obtain does not lessen the duty. . . .

In working for the goal, we should, I suggest, bear specially in mind four points. We should never despair that it can be reached. . . . We should try to take the utmost advantage of the present scientific balance to make at least partial progress. We should never allow partial measures, such as the partial test ban, to come to be thought of as anything but temporary steps in the right direction, valuable but insufficient. And disarmament and the solution of political problems can and should go hand in hand. . . .

Now perhaps we may look for a moment at the practical line of action. Above all, our policy must be to strive for constructive solutions of the two major road blocks to disarmament, namely, (1) verification and (2) improved peace-keeping machinery, including the provision of international forces, to take the place in the long run of national forces. These road blocks are not obstacles which have been devised by officials or politicians who wish to obstruct progress—they are real problems which present real dilemmas, and they must be recognized as such and faced.

If there is going to be any far-reaching disarmament, it must surely be obvious that those countries who disarm honestly wish to be assured that all other countries are disarming no less. If that is to be so, it is not sufficient to have international observers witnessing the destruction of say a thousand bombers. That has got to be done, and nobody raises any difficulties about it. But it is necessary in addition to be certain that another thousand bombers, perhaps of a more modern type, are not rolling off the production line to replace those destroyed; and that means there must be verification of production and of non-concealment as well as verification of destruction. . . . As you progress further down the road to disarmament, as you enter the stage of radical disarmament where countries have comparatively few weapons left, so verification becomes more and more important. This is specially so in the case of the most destructive weapon of all, namely fissile material which is relatively easy to conceal and where rigorous verification is required.

The position on verification is that the United States and the United Kingdom, and indeed NATO as a whole, accept any degree of verification at any stage. The Soviet government, during the whole process of disarmament, refuse with virtually no exception anything except verification of destruction. They refuse, for whatever reasons, any adequate verification of production, replacement and concealment during the whole process of disarmament, until you reach total disarmament.

As regards peace-making machinery, the dilemma is real and acute. If countries are going to proceed to radical disarmament, they must be sure that when they give up reliance upon national forces, there is some other force or sanction which will replace the security they are giving up.

The West have agreed that if there is to be radical disarmament there must also be improved peace-keeping machinery; improved peace-keeping machinery at the conciliation, arbitration and legal levels, compulsory jurisdiction for the world court, and, at the end of the road, an effective peace-keeping force which can be used against any breach of the disarmament treaty or any form of aggression.

On this issue the Russian position is widely different. The Russians do not agree to compulsory jurisdiction of the world court. They do agree that there should be a peace-keeping force, but they make two stipulations: first, it must be at the disposal of the Security Council, where, of course, the five great Powers, including the Soviet Union, have a veto; and second, they insist that it must have three co-equal commanders in the field, one communist, one western and one non-committed, and that no action can be taken by the force unless all the three partners, the three commanders-in-chief, agree. In fact, they ask for a double veto. . . .

The dilemma centres round the direction and command of the peace-keeping force. Is that direction to be given to the Assembly of the United Nations, where Outer Mongolia and Mauretania, for example, have the same voice as the United States and the Soviet Union, and majorities are volatile? Or is it to be given to the present Security Council, where there is a great-Power veto? And would this, in fact, add to the security of any country, especially of small and medium sized countries? It would mean that any decision that the disarmament treaty has been broken by the Soviet Union could be vetoed by the Soviet Union. It would mean that any decision to use force against any friend of the United States could be vetoed by the United States, and so on with the other four great members. A little thought shows that these two obstacles, verification and peace-keeping machinery, are not fabricated obstacles, but real dilemmas; and the way out remains to be found. There are, of course, other dilemmas. . . . The biggest is that during the process of disarmament both sides are agreed that a balance of present forces should be preserved, and that is a principle difficult to apply. Lastly, disarmament must be world-wide if it is to be radical, and to be world-wide it must include Red China and France.

... We have to remember, particularly in dealing with the Russians, that to them negotiations are very largely a matter of tactical and strategic manoeuvre, conducted according to rules which are foreign to us. We should not forget that on the first four occasions on which the West offered the Soviet Union a partial test ban the Soviet Union rejected it with ignominy, and argued ferociously against it in Geneva and the United Nations as being totally unacceptable. On the fifth occasion a few months later, the Russians accepted the same offer from the heart and said that it was a great step towards peace. The conclusion to be drawn is, of course, that when you are negotiating with Moscow you must never take a Russian 'never' to mean never. And this is a reason for optimism.

... If we are to make progress in face of these difficulties, it is obviously sensible to begin with those steps which are the easiest for both sides to accept. . . . The partial test ban was one such step; and although it is only partial and although France and China are standing out, nonetheless so long as it remains in force we have the atmosphere clean and free of fall-out. This is something that only two or three years ago would have been thought at once momentous and out of reach.

What further steps are open to us? ...

The first is to try to . . . build up in the United Nations the nucleus of a Peace Force. . . . For instance, it would be possible to create now, without waiting for a disarmament treaty, a small headquarters planning staff, a cadre of say sixty officers covering the fields of communication and logistics, and charged also with making a beginning of planning for the contingencies with which the United Nations might be faced. The next stage might be a build up of specialised sections of such a force, sections such as an internationally recruited signals group, and an internationally recruited logistic group to which individual countries might contribute aircraft and other forms of communication.

While this is going on, we should of course have to rely for the present on actual force contingents, placed at the disposal of the United Nations by states, neutral or not, who are willing to do so. The change over to a force of individuals with international loyalties could be introduced gradually; and in parallel the vexed problems of political and strategic control, including that of the veto rights of the great Powers, could also be tackled, of necessity gradually but tackled nonetheless.

We ought to try to convert the partial test ban into a total test ban.

Only a bare minimum of verification is required for that. We ought to try to get a non-dissemination agreement. . . . Then there are the proposals for the observed destruction of at least certain weapons, such as obsolescent bombers; and for the verified cut-off of fissile material. There is a whole gamut of ideas designed to reduce tension, ranging from various versions of the Rapacki plan for central Europe to a system of observation posts on the territory of both East and West, spreading perhaps into the Soviet Union and into the United States. There has also been the question of a non-aggression pact. . . . Beyond that there remains the main goal, the abandonment of all nuclear weapons and most other weapons by all countries under international control and with an international peace-keeping force.

SIR MICHAEL WRIGHT, *The Road to Peace*

The United Nations: the future

39. The forces of conciliation

I work for the United Nations. I have been a consultant to the United Nations Special Fund and I have recently been several times to Africa to discuss with the African Governments their plans for economic development, to discover how the United Nations can help them to formulate their economic programmes and projects and give them practical assistance in carrying them out. My assignment is limited in scope and in area, but I have the exciting feeling of being among the first of the few who work for a new cause. We bring to our task a new motive and a new spirit.

When I arrive in a new country I go first to report to the United Nations Resident Representative. These representatives act for the United Nations Technical Assistance Board and the Special Fund, but they are increasingly recognised as United Nations ambassadors. They are drawn from many different countries. In Ethiopia, for instance, the Resident Representative is a Canadian, in Somalia a Trinidadian, in Uganda an American of French extraction, in Tanganyika an Australian assisted by a New Zealander, in Kenya an African Southern Rhodesian. These men of so many different origins are building up a new international foreign service. Other Ambassadors and High Commissioners are primarily and naturally concerned with the interests of their own countries. But the United Nations Representatives all have the one clear purpose—to give disinterested help to the Governments of the countries to which they are posted. The African Ministers and officials increasingly turn to them for assistance and for advice too. They have no national interest. They are not trying to sell anything. They represent a new departure in world diplomacy.

Before I went to Africa recently I went to talk over my assignment with one of the chief executive officials of the Special Fund, Paul Marc Henry. He is a Frenchman. It struck me as I walked down the corridor after our conversation that it had never occurred to either of us in talking about United Nations work to allow any consideration of national interest to enter our heads. It was unthinkable that either of us should do so. We were concerned only with the interests of the people of East Africa and how the Special Fund could help them. We would have been ashamed to allow any French or British motive to influence us.

Early in 1963 I met General Rikhye of India in New York on his return from Western New Guinea. There he had had to deal with Pakistani troops sent under United Nations auspices to maintain order in the difficult period of transfer of power. Not easy for an Indian General to give directions to Pakistani troops. I asked him how he had got on. 'No difficulty at all,' said General Rikhye. 'We had an awkward job to do together but we were all on United Nations work and the Pakistani Brigadier and I never had the slightest disagreement.' The fact is that any of us who have the privilege to work for the United Nations instinctively and automatically leave our national differences behind, and work with a new will to a new standard of international co-operation.

This new will and new purpose may be the most hopeful thing in the world. We have grown used to the 'balance of terror'. For a long time now it has seemed that the best we could hope for was that the balance would be maintained. The bomb and the balance were becoming the symbols of our security and the guarantee of our survival. It was a miserable prospect—a sort of deification of defeatism.

But now we can have new hope in the independent initiative of the United Nations. Some people speak and dream of world government. Perhaps I do not fully understand what they mean, but the idea does not yet attract me. Somehow world government suggests to me too many civil servants. But the idea of the new independent initiative of world leadership by the Secretary-General backed by the overwhelming opinion of the world and drawing its authority from the General Assembly, the parliament of the world—that is a child already born. We must not expect too much of it too soon. But if we can persuade proud and powerful nations not to starve or smother or strangle it in its infancy, then soon it will grow strong.

The new men who work for the United Nations are not airy idealists. They have to be severely practical. They cannot afford to be perfectionists. Problems are not brought to them until others have failed. Usually they have to make the best of a bad job. Ideal solutions are often far out of reach. In the Congo, in Western New Guinea, in the Yemen, in Cuba, in Malaysia, in the question of the future of the Palestine refugees, for instance, they have no power to achieve all they would wish. But it is motive that matters. Now there is a band of able men constantly searching for an impartial initiative to keep the peace, and, more important still, to find positive remedies for problems which if left will fester into conflict.

Those of us who work for the United Nations have no illusions. We realise that the Secretary-General and those who work with him high on the 38th floor of the United Nations building are human and fallible. No doubt they make mistakes. It would be amazing if they did not. They work under terrific pressure, usually far into the night. They have to turn hurriedly from one crisis to another. They have no large staff of career experts like the Foreign Offices of the great powers. They have no adequate military organisation and no intelligence service. Above all, there is the desperate shortage of money. They are badgered and buffeted and threatened by all and sundry.

At the lesser level of organisation there are grave weaknesses. The necessity for preserving some balance of employment in the Secretariat between the officials of all the member nations, the difficulty of securing adequate liaison and co-operation between all the U.N. agencies, the need to curb the arrogance and self-importance of inexperienced officials and to cut down the red tape in which any official machine delights, the object of giving to the whole ungainly world-wide organisation cohesion and leadership—all these requirements create constant problems.

The extraordinary thing is that the men at the top can stand up to the strain, and that the whole family of United Nations agencies and departments in fact works so well together.

Some thought that no one could fill the great gap left by Dag Hammarskjold. His brilliant analytical brain and clear sense of high purpose and almost superhuman endurance seemed irreplaceable. But now U Thant, so different in temperament and method, has already established himself with dignity and courage in a personal position of great influence and authority.

He can never refuse to see any visiting Foreign Minister or any Head of Mission. He is constantly subject to every world pressure. Always calmly and courteously he listens—and then he has to judge and to decide and to act. He is abused, jostled and harassed. But within the narrow limits of his authority, coolly and carefully and courageously he and his team pursue their steady purpose to the best of their judgement in the international interest.

The organisation he leads has faced great trials. There are much greater tasks ahead. What a tragedy it will be if the organisation is kept so weak that it will be incapable of acting when the greatest tests come, when the United Nations may well be the sole hope of saving mankind.

But now there is at least a new hope, a new idea, a new ideal. The Secretary-General is the personification of that new force. He and his team are the new men. Now when there is an international dispute there are, as ever, the adversaries snarling at each other, seeking to outwit, to weaken, to defeat, to destroy each other. But now in every dispute there is also a new initiative. Now there is the effort of the new men. They apply a new test and pursue a new purpose. They are not influenced by national greed or national pride. They apply the test of international advantage and the tests of the interests of the common people concerned. That is a new thing in the world.

I have always believed that the forces of conciliation are potentially stronger than those of conflict. The trouble is that the forces of hatred and conflict are so often well organised and well led while the forces of conciliation are ill organised or ill led, or not organised or led at all. Now in the United Nations we have a permanent organisation for promoting international understanding and co-operation. It is this new initiative which gives us new hope in a divided world. It is above all motive that matters, and the strength of the Secretary-General is that he and his team bring to every problem the best motive of all, the motive of disinterested service.

The old barons of greed and pride and hatred and racial domination are as strong and proud and confident and well-mounted as ever. But now a new and hitherto unknown champion has entered the lists. He faces immensely powerful opponents, and his company is small. But the heavier the odds and the smaller the army the greater the honour. I for one am proud to ride behind him.

The extent of the dangers is a measure of the need for new efforts and for a new sense of urgency, and for new methods. Increasingly, we must seek solutions not by old national means but by new international action. The dangers should surely intensify a determination to win freedom from racial discrimination and domination, to settle disputes before violence takes over, to make a new assault on the poverty of more than half the world and, for all these purposes, to support and strengthen the authority and the capacity of the United Nations. Few people will dispute that the dangers exist. The question is whether we understand and care enough to act while there is still time, and time is terribly short.

SIR HUGH FOOT, *A Start in Freedom*

1. The writer lays great emphasis on the 'new' dimension given to world politics by the U.N. Secretariat. In what ways does he see this making a quite new contribution to peace? How do these differ from (a) old attempts, and (b) world government?

2. (a) What does the U.N. lack and what are its weaknesses? (b) How could these be overcome?

3. (a) Has Britain, in particular, any *moral* obligation to help 'win freedom from racial discrimination' for others in other countries, or 'settle disputes (in other countries) before violence takes over'? Why? (b) To what extent is the Government justified in using taxpayers' money for 'altruistic' purposes—to further the 'economic development' of other countries and to help 'make an assault on the poverty of half the world'?

4. (a) What *can* Britain do? Are we doing enough? What more could we do? Is our assistance impeded by lack of popular support? How far can the Government go ahead of public opinion? (b) What can *you* do? Are you attracted by a career with the Secretary-General's 'team'? Even if not, what assistance do you think you might give to strengthen the U.N. and its ideals, as outlined in this passage?

2. The claims of Christ

We ask our questions about God and are left face to face with the man Jesus, who in his own personality provides the best clue we shall get to their answer. . . . While the Christian religion continues to haunt men and women with the personality of the Son of Man, each individual will be summoned to state his own faith confronting the tragedy and the claim of that Cross.

It was so often the method of Jesus. . . . Challenged with religious problems, he replies not by a comprehensive formula but a direct demand for personal obedience. We come to him with our complaints. We are made to consider *him*. And we receive our answer to his question : 'And you, who do you say that I am?'

DAVID L. EDWARDS, *God's Cross in our World*

The response of the uncommitted

'We get rid, to begin with, of the idolatrous or iconographic worship of Christ. By this I mean literally that worship which is given to pictures and statues of him, and to finished and unalterable stories about him.' We might take that quotation from Bernard Shaw's *The Prospects of Christianity* (41) as a clue to the study of the material in this section. What he is saying—with some characteristic exaggeration—is that 'orthodoxy', the orthodoxy of stained glass windows and hymns and theological formulae, can be the worst enemy of genuine Christian insight and commitment. The Church is perennially tempted to assume a kind of 'vested interest' in Christ, to suggest that it possesses a monopoly of true belief and right practice; and that can be the surest way not only of distorting its own vision of the truth, but equally of alienating honest inquirers who want to explore the meaning of the Christian faith.

Fortunately the figure of Christ has always been far too potent in its impact to allow this kind of misrepresentation to be more than partially, or temporarily, successful. In an age in which traditional belief and practice are losing their hold nothing is more significant than that many of those who would not think of subscribing to the official tenets of any Church nevertheless bear witness to the inescapable influence which that historical personality continues to exert upon them.

Much of what these writers have to say is too diffuse to be presented in passages for discussion. The five books listed at the beginning of the 'further suggested reading' for this chapter give a few starting points for the study of more extended material of that kind. The poems and prose passages which follow, however, do present in shorter form a few of the varied viewpoints of the 'uncommitted'. Through their insights, even where they seem wrong-headed or unacceptable, we may be helped to make a fresh assessment of our own response.

In studying the extracts, ask yourself in what ways the writer sees the person or teaching of Jesus Christ as relevant to our understanding of man and the 'human situation'. What is each writer trying to say about Christ and ourselves? What do you think were the origins of their ideas? Are they a fair interpretation of the material on which they are based? Do they ring true to your own experience or understanding of life? Where they do not, on what grounds would you criticize them as false or unsatisfactory?

In addition to discussing these and other questions which will arise in considering the extracts, collect from your own reading of contemporary literature

and contribute from your own insight and experience further illustrations of
the way in which the Gospels challenge most sharply the conventional 'image'
of Christ which the Church and society have tended to foster.

40. Still falls the rain

Still falls the Rain—
Dark as the world of man, black as our loss—
Blind as the nineteen hundred and forty nails
Upon the Cross.

Still falls the Rain
With a sound like the pulse of the heart that is changed to the hammer-
   beat
In the Potter's Field, and the sound of the impious feet
On the Tomb:
Still falls the Rain
In the Field of Blood where the small hopes breed and the human brain
Nurtures its greed, that worm with the brow of Cain.

Still falls the Rain
At the feet of the starved Man hung upon the Cross.
Christ that each day, each night, nails there, have mercy on us—
On Dives and on Lazarus:
Under the Rain the sore and the gold are as one.

Still falls the Rain—
Still falls the Blood from the Starved Man's wounded side:
He bears in His Heart all wounds,—those of the light that died,
The last faint spark
In the self-murdered heart, the wounds of the sad uncomprehending
   dark,
The wounds of the baited bear,—
The blind and weeping bear whom the keeper beat
On his helpless flesh . . . the tears of the hunted hare.

Still falls the Rain—
Then—O Ile leape up to my God: who pulles me downe?—
See, see where Christ's blood streames in the firmament:
It flows from the Brow we nailed upon the tree
Deep to the dying, to the thirsting heart
That holds the fires of the world,—dark-smirched with pain
As Caesar's laurel crown.

Then sounds the voice of One who like the heart of man
Was once a child who among beasts has lain—
'Still do I love, still shed my innocent light, my Blood, for thee'.

EDITH SITWELL

41. The prospects of Christianity

I am no more a Christian than Pilate was, or you, gentle reader; and
yet, like Pilate, I greatly prefer Jesus to Annas and Caiaphas; and I
am ready to admit that after contemplating the world and human
nature for nearly sixty years, I see no way out of the world's misery
but the way which would have been found by Christ's will if he had
undertaken the work of a modern practical statesman.

If Jesus could have worked out the practical problems of a Communist constitution, an admitted obligation to deal with crime without revenge or punishment, and a full assumption by humanity of
divine responsibilities, he would have conferred an incalculable benefit
on mankind, because these distinctive demands of his are now turning
out to be good sense and sound economics. Certain ideas and doctrines
are flatly contrary to common practice, common sense, and common
belief, and yet have, in the teeth of dogged incredulity and recalci-
trance, produced an irresistible impression that Christ, though rejected
by his posterity as an unpractical dreamer, and executed by his contemporaries as a dangerous anarchist and blasphemous madman, was
greater than his judges.

I know quite well that this impression of superiority is not produced
on everyone, even those who profess extreme susceptibility to it. There
is a great deal of hearty dislike of Jesus and of contempt for his failure
to save himself and overcome his enemies by personal bravery and
cunning as Mahomet did. But it is quite clear from the New Testament
writers that Jesus at the time of his death believed himself to be the
Christ, a divine personage. It is therefore absurd to criticize his conduct before Pilate as if he were Colonel Roosevelt or Admiral von
Tirpitz or even Mahomet. Whether you accept his belief in his divinity as fully as Simon Peter did, or reject it as a delusion which led him
to submit to torture and sacrifice his life without resistance in the
conviction that he would presently rise again in glory, you are equally
bound to admit that, far from behaving like a coward or a sheep, he
shewed considerable physical fortitude in going through a cruel ordeal
against which he could have defended himself as effectually as he
cleared the money-changers out of the temple. 'Gentle Jesus, meek and
mild' is a snivelling modern invention, with no warrant in the gospels.
St. Matthew would as soon have thought of applying such adjectives
to Judas Maccabeus as to Jesus; and even St. Luke, who makes Jesus

polite and gracious, does not make him meek. The picture of him as an English curate of the farcical comedy type, too meek to fight a police-man, and everybody's butt, may be useful in the nursery to soften children; but that such a figure could ever have become a centre of the world's attention is too absurd for discussion.

It is important therefore that we should clear our minds of the notion that Jesus died, as some of us are in the habit of declaring, for his social and political opinions. He was executed by the Jews for the blasphemy of claiming to be a God; and Pilate, to whom this was a mere piece of superstitious nonsense, let them execute him as the cheapest way of keeping them quiet, on the formal plea that he had committed treason against Rome by saying that he was the King of the Jews. Pilate, to whom the appeal lay, favored him and despised his judges, and was evidently willing enough to be conciliated. But in-stead of denying the charge, Jesus repeated the offence. He knew what he was doing; he had alienated numbers of his own disciples and been stoned in the streets for doing it before. He was not lying : he believed literally what he said. The horror of the High Priest was perfectly natural : he was a Primate confronted with a heterodox street preacher uttering what seemed to him an appalling and impudent blasphemy. The fact that the blasphemy was to Jesus a simple statement of fact, and that it has since been accepted as such by all western nations, does not invalidate the proceedings, nor give us the right to regard Annas and Caiaphas as worse men than the Archbishop of Canterbury and the Head Master of Eton. If Jesus had been indicted in a modern court, he would have been examined by two doctors; found to be obsessed by a delusion; declared incapable of pleading; and sent to an asylum : that is the whole difference. But please note that when a man is charged before a modern tribunal (to take a case that happened the other day) of having asserted and maintained that he was an officer returned from the front to receive the Victoria Cross at the hands of the King, although he was in fact a mechanic, nobody thinks of treat-ing him as afflicted with a delusion. He is punished for false pretences, because his assertion is credible and therefore misleading. Just so, the claim to divinity made by Jesus was to the High Priest, who looked forward to the coming of a Messiah, one that might conceivably have been true, and might therefore have misled the people in a very dangerous way. That was why he treated Jesus as an impostor and a blasphemer where he should have treated him as a madman.

Why on earth did not Jesus defend himself, and make the people rescue him from the High Priest? He was so popular that they were unable to prevent him driving the money-changers out of the temple, or to arrest him for it. When they did arrest him afterwards, they had to do it at night in a garden. He could have argued with them as he had often done in the temple, and justified himself both to the Jewish law and to Caesar. And he had physical force at his command to back up his arguments: all that was needed was a speech to rally his followers; and he was not gagged. The reply of the evangelists would have been that all these inquiries are idle; John would have replied that it was part of the destiny of God to be slain and buried and to rise again, and that to have avoided this destiny would have been to repudiate his Godhead. And that is the only apparent explanation. Whether you believe with the evangelists that Christ could have rescued himself by a miracle, or, as a modern Secularist, point out that he could have defended himself effectually, the fact remains that according to all the narratives he did not do so. He had to die like a god, not to save himself. The consensus on this point is important, because it proves the absolute sincerity of Jesus's declaration that he was a god. No impostor would have accepted such dreadful consequences without an effort to save himself. No impostor would have been nerved to endure them by the conviction that he would rise from the grave and live again after three days. If we accept the story at all, we must believe this, and believe also that his promise to return in glory and establish his kingdom on earth within the lifetime of men then living, was one which he believed that he could, and indeed must, fulfil. Two evangelists declare that in his last agony he despaired, and reproached God for forsaking him. The other two represent him as dying in unshaken conviction and charity with the simple remark that the ordeal was finished. But all four testify that his faith was not deceived, and that he actually rose again after three days. And I think it unreasonable to doubt that all four wrote their narratives in full faith that the other promise would be fulfilled too, and that they themselves might live to witness the Second Coming.

I must now abandon this attitude, and make a serious draft on the reader's attention by facing the question whether we may not throw the gospels into the waste-paper basket, or put them away on the fiction shelf of our libraries. I venture to reply that we shall be, on the contrary, in the position of the man in Bunyan's riddle who found that 'the more he threw away, the more he had.' We get rid, to begin with, of the idolatrous or iconographic worship of Christ. By this I mean literally that worship which is given to pictures and statues of him, and to finished and unalterable stories about him. The test of the prevalence of this is that if you speak or write of Jesus as a real live person, or even as a still active God, such worshippers are more horrified than Don Juan was when the statue stepped from its pedestal and came to supper with him. You may deny the divinity of Jesus; you may doubt whether he ever existed; you may reject Christianity for Judaism, Mahometanism, Shintoism, or Fire Worship; and the icono-

laters, placidly contemptuous, will only classify you as a freethinker
or a heathen. But if you venture to wonder how Christ would have
looked if he had shaved and had his hair cut, or what size in shoes he
took, or whether he swore when he stood on a nail in the carpenter's
shop, or could not button his robe when he was in a hurry, or whether
he laughed over the repartees by which he baffled the priests when they
tried to trap him into sedition and blasphemy, or even if you tell any
part of his story in the vivid terms of modern colloquial slang, you
will produce an extraordinary dismay and horror among the iconolaters. You will have made the picture come out of its frame, the statue
descend from its pedestal, the story become real, with all the incalculable consequences that may flow from this terrifying miracle. It is at
such moments that you realize that the iconolaters have never for a
moment conceived Christ as a real person who meant what he said, as
a fact, as a force like electricity, only needing the invention of a suitable political machinery to be applied to the affairs of mankind with
revolutionary effect.

Thus it is not disbelief that is dangerous in our society: it is belief.
The moment it strikes you (as it may any day) that Christ is not the
lifeless harmless image he has hitherto been to you, but a rallying
centre for revolutionary influences which all established States and
Churches fight, you must look to yourselves; for you have brought
the image to life; and the mob may not be able to bear that horror.

GEORGE BERNARD SHAW, Preface to *Androcles and the Lion*

42. Man in Christ, and Christ in man

In the year 1845 Johann Ulrich Voss sets out to cross the Australian continent
for the first time. He collects around himself a small party of settlers and two
aboriginals, and pushes inland from the coast. The expedition encounters every
kind of obstacle and hardship. At one time the men have to pass through a
waterless desert; at another, torrential rains fall unceasingly and they are
driven to shelter in a cave where they lie up, week after week, sick, almost
dying, waiting for the rain to stop. This is the tragic story of their journey
and its inevitable end.

But the most important thing in this book is not the external world through
which the characters pass. It is the world of their passions and their moments
of insight; and in this world the figure of Voss looms larger and larger until it
assumes more than the normal dimensions of a man. Strange, proud, inscrut-
able, driven on by some daemon within himself, he appears to the people
around him ambiguously as deliverer and destroyer. Only one thing is constant:
each man sees in him the figure of his own destiny.

Everybody looked, and saw a group of several blackfellows assembled
in the middle distance. The light and a feather of low-lying mist made
them appear to be standing in a cloud. Thus elevated, their spare,

elongated bodies, of burnt colours, gave to the scene a primitive purity that silenced most of the whites, and appealed particularly to Voss.

'Good,' he cried. 'Here is an excellent opportunity to satisfy Judd's eternal craving for material evidence.'

'I do not understand,' shouted the exasperated Judd. 'I will give as well as find evidence. I will fire a few shots right into the middle of 'em.'

'Wait, Albert. I will come with you. Dirty blacks,' contributed Turner, the spotless. 'But I must find my gun first.'

'Neither of you will do anything so foolish,' Voss said sharply. 'I will go, and you will wait here. Na, mach, Jackie!' he called to the native boy.

'A lot will come of your hob-nobbin' with the blacks. As always,' Judd panted. 'I cannot dream dreams no longer. Do you not see our deluded skeletons, Mr. Voss?'

'If you are suffering from delusions, it is the result of our unavoidable physical condition,' said the German, rather primly.

'Arrrr,' groaned Judd.

But everyone fell silent, even Judd himself, while the aboriginals, of superior, almost godlike mien, waited upon their cloud, to pass judgment, as it were.

'As our friend Judd is jealous of my attempts to establish understanding and sympathy between the native mind and ourselves,' Voss observed finally, 'I will ask Mr. Palfreyman to go amongst them, and investigate this matter of our stolen property. He, at least, is unprejudiced, and will act politic.'

Somebody sighed. It could have been Palfreyman, who was startled by this sudden exposure of himself. His skin had turned yellow.

'I am certainly unbiased,' he said, and smiled thinly. 'I shall go,' he agreed. 'I only hope that I may acquit myself truly,' he added.

There he halted. Everyone was aware that he, an educated gentleman, no longer had control over the words he was using.

'Excellent,' applauded Voss.

The circumstances to which they were reduced prevented him from wetting his lips. He was confident, however, that by a brilliant accident he had hit upon a means of revealing the true condition of a soul.

'Here,' said Judd, offering Palfreyman his own weapon.

'Will you go armed?' asked Voss, lowering his eyelids.

'No,' said Palfreyman. 'Of course not. Not armed.'

'Will you, at least, take the native?'

'I doubt whether they would understand him.'

'Scarcely,' said Voss. 'But his presence.'

'No. I will go. I will trust to my faith.'

It sounded terribly weak. Voss heard with joy, and looked secretly at the faces of the other men. These, however, were too thin to express anything positive.

Palfreyman, who was certainly very small, in what had once been his cabbage-tree hat, had begun to walk towards the cloudful of blacks, but slowly, but deliberately. As he went forward he was thinking of many disconnected incidents, of a joyful as well as an unhappy nature, of the love that he had denied his sister, of the bland morning in which he had stood holding the horse's bridle and talking to Miss Trevelyan,[1] even of the satisfaction that he and Turner had seemed to share as he shaved the latter's suppurating face. Since it had become obvious that he was dedicated to a given end, his own celibacy could only appear natural. Over the dry earth he went, with his springy, exaggerated strides, and in this strange progress was at peace and in love with his fellows. Both sides were watching him. The aboriginals could have been trees, but the members of the expedition were so contorted by apprehension, longing, love or disgust, they had become human again. All remembered the face of Christ that they had seen at some point in their lives, either in churches or visions, before retreating from what they had not understood, the paradox of man in Christ, and Christ in man. All were obsessed by what could be the last scene for some of them. They could not advance further.

Voss was scourging his leg with a black stick.

Palfreyman walked on.

Harry Robarts would have called out, if his voice had not been frozen.

Then, we are truly damned, Frank Le Mesurier knew, his dreams taking actual shape.

Palfreyman continued to advance.

If his faith had been strong enough, he would have known what to do, but as he was frightened, and now could think of nothing, except, he could honestly say, that he did love all men, he showed the natives the palms of his hands. These, of course, would have been quite empty, but for the fate that was written on them.

The black men looked, fascinated, at the white palms, at the curiously lidded eyes of the intruder. All, including the stranger himself, were gathered together at the core of a mystery.

Then one black man warded off the white mysteries with terrible dignity. He flung down his spear. It stuck in the white man's side, and hung down, quivering. All movements now became awkward. The awkward white man stood with his toes turned in. A second black, of rather prominent muscles, and emotional behaviour, rushed

1. The girl to whom Voss is engaged, and with whom, throughout the expedition, he maintains a mystical kind of communication.

forward with a short spear, or knife, it could have been, and thrust it between the white man's ribs. It was accomplished so easily.

'Ahhhh,' Palfreyman was laughing, because still he did not know what to do.

With his toes turned in.

But clutching the pieces of his life.

'Ah, Lord,' he said, upon his knees. 'if I had been stronger.'

But his voice was bubbling. His blood was aching through a hole which the flies had scented already.

Ah, Lord, Lord, his mind repeated, before tremendous pressure from above compelled him to lay down the last of his weakness. He had failed evidently.

*   *   *

"You know, Judd, Miss Trevelyan was a friend of Mr. Voss.'

'Ah,' smiled the aged,[1] gummy man. 'Voss.'

He looked at the ground, but presently spoke again.

'Voss left his mark on the country,' he said.

'How?' asked Miss Trevelyan, cautiously.

'Well, the trees, of course. He was cutting his initials in the trees. He was a queer beggar, Voss. The blacks talk about him to this day. He is still there—that is the honest opinion of many of them—he is there in the country, and always will be.'

'How?' repeated Miss Trevelyan. Her voice was that of a man. She dared anyone.

Judd was feeling his way with his hands.

'Well, you see, if you live and suffer long enough in a place, you do not leave it altogether. Your spirit is still there.'

'Like a god, in fact,' said Colonel Hebden, but laughed to show his scepticism.

Judd looked up, out of the distance.

'Voss? No. He was never God, though he liked to think that he was. Sometimes, when he forgot, he was a man.'

He hesitated, and fumbled.

'He was more than a man,' Judd continued, with the gratified air of one who had found that for which he had been looking. 'He was a Christian, such as I understand it.'

Miss Trevelyan was holding a handkerchief to her lips, as though her life-blood might gush out.

'Not according to my interpretation of the word,' the Colonel interrupted, remorselessly, 'not by what I have heard.'

'Poor fellow,' sighed old Sanderson, again unhappy. 'He was somewhat twisted. But is dead and gone.'

1. This meeting and conversation takes place some years after the expedition. Judd was the only survivor; his memories are muddled and inaccurate.

Now that he was launched, Judd was determined to pursue his wavering way.

'He would wash the sores of the man. He would sit all night with them when they were sick, and clean up their filth with his own hands. I cried, I tell you, after he was dead. There was none of us could believe it when we saw the spear, hanging from his side, and shaking.'

'The spear?'

Colonel Hebden behaved almost as though he himself were mortally wounded.

'But this is an addition to the story,' protested old Mr. Sanderson, who also was greatly perturbed. 'You did not mention the spear, Judd. You never suggested you were present at the death of Voss, simply that you mutinied, and moved off with those who chose to follow you. If we understood you rightly.'

'It was me who closed his eyes,' said Judd.

In the same instant that the Colonel and Mr. Sanderson looked across at each other, Miss Trevelyan succeeded in drawing a shroud about herself.

Finally, the old grazier put an arm round the convict's shoulders, and said:

'I think you are tired and confused, eh, Judd? Let me take you back to your lodgings.'

'I am tired,' echoed Judd.

Mr. Sanderson was glad to get him away. Colonel Hebden became aware that the woman was still standing at his side, and that he must recognise the fact. So he turned to her awkwardly at last, and said:

'Your saint is canonised.'

'I am content.'

'Do not tell me any longer that you respect the truth.'

'All truths are particoloured Except the greatest truth of all.'

'Your Voss was particoloured. I grant you that. A perfect magpie!'

Miss Trevelyan replied:

'Whether Judd is an impostor, or a madman, or simply a poor creature who has suffered too much, I am convinced that Voss had in him a little of Christ, like other men. If he was composed of evil along with the good, he struggled with that evil. And failed.'

PATRICK WHITE, Voss

43. Life and the Legend

In trying to formulate what I believe I have to begin with what I disbelieve. I disbelieve in progress, the pursuit of happiness, and all the
concomitant notions and projects for creating a society in which
human beings find ever greater contentment by being given in ever
greater abundance the means to satisfy their material and bodily hopes
and desires. The half century in which I have been consciously alive
seems to me to have been quite exceptionally destructive, murderous
and brutal.

I was enchanted when I first read in the 'Pensées' (Pascal being one
of the small, sublime band of fellow-humans to whom one may turn
and say in the deepest humility: 'I agree') about how magistrates and
rulers had to be garbed in their ridiculous ceremonial robes, crowns
and diadems. Otherwise, who would not see through their threadbare
pretensions? I am conscious of having been ruled by buffoons, taught
by idiots, preached at by hypocrites, and preyed upon by charlatans
in the guise of advertisers and other professional persuaders, as well as
verbose demagogues and ideologues of many opinions, all false.

Nor, as far as I am concerned, is there any recompense in the so-
called achievements of science. It is true that in my lifetime more progress has been made in unravelling the composition and mechanism
of the material universe than previously in the whole of recorded time.
The atom has been split; the universe has been discovered, and will
soon be explored. Neither achievement has any bearing on what alone
interests me—which is why life exists, and what is the significance,
if any, of my minute and so transitory part in it. All the world in a
grain of sand; all the universe, too. If I could understand a grain of
sand I should understand everything. Why, then, should going to the
moon and Mars, or spending a holiday along the Milky Way, be expected to advance me further in my quest than going to Manchester
and Liverpool, or spending a holiday in Brighton?

I have seen pictures of huge, ungainly prehistoric monsters who
developed such a weight of protective shell that they sank under its
burden and became extinct. Our civilization likewise is sinking under
the burden of nuclear defence, and may well soon be extinct. As this
fact sinks into the collective consciousness, the resort to drugs, dreams,
fantasies, and other escapist devices, particularly sex, becomes ever
more marked.

Living thus in the twilight of a spent civilization, amidst its ludicrous and frightening shadows, what is there to believe? Curiously
enough, these twilit circumstances provide a setting in which, as it
seems to me, the purpose which lies behind them stands out with particular clarity. As human love only shines in all its splendour when

the last tiny glimmer of desire has been extinguished, so we have to make the world a wilderness to find God. The meaning of the universe lies beyond history as love lies beyond desire. That meaning shines forth in moments of illumination (which come and go so unaccountably; though, I am thankful to say, never quite ceasing—a sound as of music, far, far away, and drowned by other more tumultuous noises, but still to be faintly and fitfully heard) with an inconceivable clarity and luminosity.

Let me express it, as I have often thought of it, in terms of a stage. In the middle is the workaday world where we live our daily lives, earning a living, reading newspapers, exchanging money, recording votes, chattering and eating and desiring. I call this the Café Limbo. On the left of the stage is an area of darkness within which shapes and movements can be faintly discerned, and inconclusive noises heard; sounds and sweet airs which, as on Caliban's Island, give delight and hurt not. I call this Life. The right of the stage is bright with arc-lamps like a television studio. This is where history is unfolded and news is made; this is where we live our public, collective lives, seat and unseat rulers, declare wars and negotiate peace, glow with patriotism and get carried away with revolutionary zeal, enact laws, declaim rhetoric, swear eternal passion and sink into abysses of desolation. I call this the Legend.

Across this triple stage, between Life, the Café Limbo and the Legend, a drama is endlessly presented. Two forces shape the play— the Imagination which belongs to Life, and the Will which belongs to the Legend. Out of the Imagination come love, understanding, goodness, self-abnegation; every true synthesis ever grasped or to be grasped. Out of the Will come lust, hatred, cupidity, adulation, power, oratory; every false antithesis ever propounded or to be propounded. Those who belong exclusively or predominantly to Life are saints, mystics and artists. In extreme cases—Christ, for instance—they have to be killed. (This is superbly explained in the famous Grand Inquisitor passage in *The Brothers Karamazov*, Dostoevsky being, like Pascal, of the small band.) Those who belong exclusively or predominantly to the Legend are power-maniacs, rulers, heroes, demagogues and liberators. In extreme cases—Hitler, for instance—they bring about their own destruction. In Life there is suffering, deprivation and sanity; in the Legend, happiness, abundance and madness.

I see the two forces struggling for mastery in each individual soul; in mine, in all men's; in each collectivity, throughout our earth and throughout the vast universe. One is of darkness and one of light; one wants to drag us down into the dark trough to rut and gorge there, and the other to raise us up into the azure sky, beyond appetite, where love is all-embracing, all-encompassing, and the dark confusion of life sorts itself out, like an orderly, smiling countryside suddenly glimpsed from a high hill. One is the Devil and the other God. I have known both, and I believe in both.

For us Western Europeans the Christian religion has expressed this ancient, and, as I consider, obvious dichotomy in terms of breathtaking simplicity and sublimity. It was not the first word on the subject, nor will it be the last; but it is still our Word. I accept it. I believe, as is written in the New Testament, that if we would save our lives we must lose them; that we cannot live by bread alone; that we must die in the flesh to be reborn in the spirit, and that the flesh lusts contrary to the spirit and the spirit contrary to the flesh; that God cannot see a sparrow fall to the ground without concern, and has counted the hairs of each head, so that all that lives deserves our respect and reverence, and no man can conceivably be more important, of greater significance, or in any way more deserving of consideration than any other.

It is true that these basic propositions of Christianity have got cluttered up with dogma of various kinds which I find often incomprehensible, irrelevant and even repugnant. All the same, I should be proud and happy to be able to call myself a Christian; to dare to measure myself against that immeasurably high standard of human values and human behaviour. In this I take comfort from another saying of Pascal, thrown out like a lifeline to all sceptical minds throughout the ages—that whoever looks for God has found Him.

At its most obscurantist and debased, the Christian position still seems to me preferable to any scientific-materialist one, however cogent and enlightened. The evangelist with his lurid tract calling upon me to repent, for the Day of Judgment is at hand, is a burning and a shining light compared with the eugenist who claims the right to decide in his broiler-house mind which lives should be protracted and which must be put out.

The absurdities of the Kingdom of Heaven, as conceived in the minds of simple believers, are obvious enough—pearly gates, angelic choirs, golden crowns and shining raiment. But what are we to think of the (in Johnson's excellent phrase) sheer unresisting imbecility of the Kingdom of Heaven on Earth, as envisaged and recommended by the most authoritative and powerful voices of our time? The Gross National Product rising for evermore, and its beneficiaries, rich in hire-purchase, stupified with the telly and with sex, comprehensively educated, heaven lying about them in the supermarket, the rainbow ending in the nearest bingo hall, leisure burgeoning out in multitudinous shining aerials rising like dreaming spires into the sky; happiness in as many colours as there are pills. This kingdom, surely, can only be for posterity an unending source of wry derision—always assuming there is to be any posterity. The backdrop, after all, is the mushroom cloud; as the Gadarene herd frisk and frolic they draw ever nearer to the cliff's edge.

I recognise, of course, that this statement of belief is partly governed by the circumstance that I am old, and in at most a decade or so will be dead.

A sense of how extraordinarily happy I have been, and of enormous gratitude to my creator, overwhelms me often. I believe with a passionate, unshakeable conviction that in all circumstances and at all times life is a blessed gift; that the spirit which animates it is one of love, not hate or indifference, of light, not darkness, of creativity, not destruction, of order, not chaos; that, since all life, men, creatures, plants, as well as insensate matter, and all that is known about it, now and henceforth, has been benevolently, not malevolently, conceived, when the eyes see no more and the mind thinks no more, and this hand now writing is inert, whatever lies beyond will similarly be benevolently, not malevolently, conceived. If it is nothing, then for nothingness I offer thanks; if another mode of existence, with this old worn-out husk of a body left behind, like a butterfly extricating itself from its chrysalis, and this floundering, muddled mind, now at best seeing through a glass darkly, given a longer range and a new precision, then for that likewise I offer thanks.

MALCOLM MUGGERIDGE, in *What I Believe*

44. (a) Was he married?

Was he married, did he try
To support as he grew less fond of them
Wife and family?

No,
He never suffered such a blow.

Did he feel pointless, feeble and distrait,
Unwanted by everyone and in the way?

From his cradle he was purposeful,
His bent strong and his mind full.

Did he love people very much
Yet find them die one day?

He did not love in the human way.

Did he ask how long it would go on,
Wonder if death could be counted on for an end?

He did not feel like this,
He had a future of bliss.

Did he feel strong
Pain for being wrong?

He was not wrong, he was right,
He suffered from others', not his own, spite.

But there *is* no suffering like having made a mistake
Because of being of an inferior make.

He was not inferior,
He was superior.

He knew then that power corrupts but some must govern?
His thoughts were different.

Did he lack friends? Worse,
Think it was for his fault, not theirs?

He did not lack friends,
He had disciples he moulded to his ends.

Did he feel over-handicapped sometimes, yet must draw even?
How could he feel like this? He was the King of Heaven.

... find a sudden brightness one day in everything
Because a mood has been conquered, or a sin?

I tell you, he did not sin.

Do only human beings suffer from the irritation
I have mentioned? Learn too that being comical
Does not ameliorate the desperation?

Only human beings feel this,
It *is* because they are so mixed.

All human beings should have a medal,
A god cannot carry it, he is not able.

A god is man's doll, you ass,
He makes him up like this on purpose.

He might have made him up worse.
He often has, in the past.

To choose a god of love, as he did and does,
Is a little move then?

Yes, it is.

A larger one will be when men
Love love and hate hate but do not deify them?

It will be a larger one.

(*b*) The airy Christ

Who is this that comes in grandeur, coming from the
   burning East?
This is he we had not thought of, this is he the airy Christ.

Airy in an airy manner, in an airy parkland walking
Others take him by the hand, lead him, do the talking.

But the form, the airy One, frowns an airy frown
What they say he knows must be, but he looks aloofly down

Looks aloofly at his feet, looks aloofly at his hands,
Knows they must, as prophets say, nailed be to wooden bands,

As he knows the words he sings, that he sings so happily,
Must be changed to working laws, yet sings he ceaselessly.

Those who truly hear the voice, the words, the happy song,
Never shall need working laws to keep from doing wrong.

Deaf men will pretend sometimes they hear the song, the
   words,
And make excuse to sin extremely; this will be absurd.

Heed it not. Whatever foolish men may do the song is cried
For those who hear, and the sweet singer does not care that
   he was crucified.

For he does not wish that men should love him more than
   anything
Because he died; he only wishes they would hear him sing.

                    STEVIE SMITH in *Penguin Modern Poets*

45. The Lord's Prayer

Edwin Muir described himself at this time as 'an anti-Marx socialist,
a man who believes that people are immortal souls and that they
should bring about on this earth a society fit for immortal souls', but
he said he was not sure that he agreed 'that the only hope of the world
lies in the gospel of Christ'. Very soon after this came one of the
turning points of his life, recorded in the diary entry for 1st March,
part of which is given in the *Autobiography* (p. 246) in a modified
form, but which is worth giving in full as originally written:

'Last night going to bed alone (Willa being in Cottage Hospital) I suddenly found myself (as I was taking off my waistcoat) reciting the Lord's Prayer in a loud emphatic voice—a thing I have not done since my teens—with urgency too, and deeply disturbed emotion. As I recited it I grew more composed; my soul, as if it had been empty and needed replenishment, seemed to fill: and every word had a strange fullness of meaning, which astonished and delighted me, and gave me not so much hope as strength. It was late; I had sat up reading; I was sleepy; but as I stood in the middle of the floor half undressed reciting the prayer over and over, the meanings it contained, none of them extraordinary, indeed ordinary as they could be, overcame me with joyful surprise, and made me seem to realise that this petition was always universal, always adequate, and to life as it is, not to a life such as we long for or dream of: and for that reason it seems to sanctify common existence. Everything in it, apart from the Being to which it is addressed, refers to human life, seen realistically, not mystically. It is about the world and society, not about the everlasting destiny of the soul. "Our Father which art in Heaven" means merely "Our Heavenly Father", not our earthly father. "Hallowed be thy name," defines our human relation to him. "Thy kingdom come", means "Thy kingdom come here on earth", so that God's will may be done on earth as in heaven. It means that we should desire that human society might be directed in accordance with the perfect laws of heaven. And "forgive us our debts as we forgive our debtors". Excuse our failings, and our offences against You, as we excuse those who offend against us. "And lead us not into temptation but deliver us from evil: For thine is the kingdom, and the power, and the glory, for ever. Amen."

'I never realised before so clearly the primary importance of "we" and "us" in the prayer: it is collective, for all societies, for all mankind as a great society. "After this manner therefore pray ye." Not "my Father which art in heaven", not "Give me this day my daily bread", not "forgive my debts"; not "Lead me not into temptation"—as Protestantism almost succeeded in persuading us. And this collective form of prayer was the form enjoined by Jesus. It would be called now, in the jargon of the fashionable revolutionaries, political.

'The difference here between "I" and "we" [is] tremendous: there is no end to the conclusions that follow from it. In "we" it is man, or mankind, or the community, or all the communities. that is speaking: it is human life, and therefore society is the formal embodiment of human life. And to pray as "we" is not only to embrace in the prayer all human life, all the aspirations of mankind for the perfect kingdom when God's will shall be done on earth; it is for the individual soul a pledge for all other souls, an act of responsibility, and an act of union which strengthens him from within and at the same time lends him infinite strength from without. Yet how many centuries this prayer has been recited as if it were the multiplication table. If the revolutionaries had any sense they would bring out the implications of this prayer, which contains the whole philosophy of a desirable life in the world. But "Hallowed be thy name" is enough to restrain them, and bring a sneer to their faces.'

From this time on he recognised himself to be a Christian. 'I had a vague sense during these days that Christ was the turning-point of time and the meaning of life to everyone, no matter what his conscious beliefs; to my agnostic friends as well as Christians.'[1]

His experience of the Lord's Prayer early in 1939 was not an isolated one; it was followed by a return to the Bible, especially the Gospels, and eventually by other religious experiences of which he gives only faint hints, but which must have been of great importance to him. It did not lead, however, to the adoption of any dogmatic system of belief. He wrote to Aitken in January 1940: 'I suppose what I mean when I say I have no philosophy is that I have no explanation, none whatever, of Time except as an unofficial part (?) of Eternity—no historical explanation of human life, for the problem of evil seems insoluble to me: I can only accept it as a mystery, and what a mystery is I do not know. All these thoughts have been roused (and clarified a little in my mind) by writing my life: there is very little in the book itself about them. All I can say I have, confronted by these things, is faith, and I think that perhaps my faith is a little too easy, considering the enormity (?) of these things. But faith can produce a sentence like: "I am the resurrection and the life". (It seems to me the most sublime sentence ever uttered, especially the order of the terms, the resurrection preceding the life, as if a real life only began with a resurrection, even in this world—and I believe this.) So that there may be something more in faith than we can account for, a source of energy and reconciliation which philosophy cannot reach.'

About a month later he wrote: '. . . the difficulty with me is that I have the faith, but that I cannot belong to any one Christian community. I believe in God, in the immortality of the soul, and that Christ is the greatest figure who ever appeared in the history of mankind.'

In another letter written about the same time he says: '. . . I am happier than I have been, in spite of the state of the world, for I have had something like a sense of the presence of God, a sense which I have never consciously been aware of before, though I am now fifty-two; it is too new and strange for me to write about it, and so inexperienced

1. Diary entry 1 March 1939.

that I am afraid of writing about it. I have believed for a long time in the immortality of the soul, but this is something different.'

The poem 'the Question'[1] shows that he had attained to a profounder conception than before of the meaning of self-discovery:

> Will you, sometime, who have sought so long and seek
> Still in the slowly darkening hunting ground,
> Catch sight some ordinary month or week
> Of that strange quarry you scarcely thought you sought—
> Yourself, the gatherer gathered, the finder found,
> The buyer who would buy all in bounty bought—
> And perch in pride on the princely hand, at home,
> And there, the long hunt over, rest and roam?

The words 'the finder found' have a double meaning. The seeker finds himself, his innermost self; but also he is found. The finding of the self turns out to be the finding of God, and that to be a being found by God; for once God is known at all he is known as *alive*, active.

PETER BUTTER, *Edwin Muir, Man and Poet*

1. Sent with a letter dated June 1941.

The response of the committed

'Do I have to believe in the divinity of Christ in order to be a Christian?' That is a not uncommon question to be asked when the Christian faith is discussed. In one sense it's a good one, in that it brings out clearly the fact that the question which Jesus himself put to his friends 'Who do you say that I am?' has always been *the* crucial one on which we have to make up our minds if we are going to take Christianity seriously. But in another sense it is a very unfortunate one. For it can easily obscure the real issue by implying that there is one agreed definition of 'divinity' which everybody understands, and that the only question is whether we can *accept* that definition or not.

The collection of quotations contained in this section should make it abundantly clear that to start with that assumption is really to mistake the whole object of the exercise. When you read them, you will see that what the writers are all doing in a great variety of ways is to try to register the impact of that life, and its consequences in history and experience, and to say what it means to them, what they make of it, and how they measure up to the demands which it makes on them.

Our business in studying this section is to try to enter into the experiences which the passages record, and to ask ourselves what light they shed on Jesus Christ, how far they represent convictions which we share, which of their insights are meaningful and relevant to our own lives, what difficulties we find in the various authors' interpretations of Christ's life and message, and why they seem difficult to us. In some cases further questions are appended to the passages themselves.

When we have done that, we can perhaps begin to see whether our answers add up to anything like some of the classical New Testament expressions of belief: 'God was in Christ, reconciling the world to himself', 'The Son of God, who loved me and gave himself for me', 'No one comes to the Father except through me'.

46. 'This Christianity business'

(a)

One evening an Australian sergeant whom I had never met before came to see me. Finally he said, 'My cobbers and I have been talking things over. We got to wondering if maybe there isn't something in this Christianity business after all. My cobbers they—well, they asked me to ask you if you'd be willing to meet with them—and well, sort of lead the discussion.'

I was floored by his request. I wanted to refuse immediately. But the more we talked the more I felt drawn to this man. We were able to communicate with each other effortlessly.

'All right,' I said, smiling, 'I'll try.'

One thing I knew for certain: in a situation as real as a prison camp there was no use discussing abstract philosophical concepts. Yet I could find little in my prewar experience that promised to be meaningful. At one time I had considered becoming a foreign missionary, but gradually turned my back on such a direction, and, in doing so, turned my back on Christianity as well. Its doctrines and practices seemed irrelevant and other-worldly compared to those of my rationalist friends.

The two expressions of Christian doctrine I had encountered left me unimpressed. The first maintained that the Bible had been literally inspired. The Christian life was one of obedience to a set of arbitrary laws which seemed to me negative, restrictive and frustrating. The chief theological emphasis was placed upon the death of Jesus Christ as a sacrifice made to appease a wrathful God.

Such Christians managed to extract the bubbles from the champagne of life, leaving it flat, insipid, and tasteless. I liked the world and life. I liked good companionship and laughter.

The other expression seemed to hold that Christianity was only for nice people who had been brought up in nice homes and gone to nice schools where they had learned to do all the nice things. Heaven for this group was a kind of continuous tea party with thin cucumber sandwiches and smoky-tasting tea served in fine bone china cups. It was all eminently respectable but rather hard on those outside the pale.

From experiences such as these I had reached the conclusion that Jesus was a figure in a fairy story, suitable for children, perhaps, but not for me. The logical place for me to begin now, I reflected, was with the New Testament, as the only record of his life and teaching available.

I had a Bible. It was all I had to draw on when I faced the group next evening in the bamboo grove. I was not a little dismayed to see that there were several dozen of them.

I began by describing my own uncertain state of grace, telling them frankly of my doubts and conflicts. When I asked them straight out if they were willing to go along with me and face up to the basic issues of human existence, they said they were.

They were very kind, those cobbers. When they began to talk they spoke freely of their own inner questioning. They gave their honest views about life on earth, its object and the life hereafter. They were seeking a truth they would be able to apprehend with the heart as well as with the mind. When the meeting ended I knew I could go on.

At each successive gathering the numbers grew. There were new faces, more and more pairs of eyes to look questioningly into mine. I expounded the New Testament in their language, keeping one lesson ahead of them.

Through our readings and our discussions we came to know Jesus. He was one of us. He would understand our problems because they were the sort of problems he had faced himself. Like us, he often had no place to lay his head, no food for his belly, no friends in high places.

He, too, had known bone-weariness from too much toil, the suffering, rejection and disappointments that are part of the fabric of life. Yet he was no killjoy. He would not have scorned the man who took a glass of wine with his friends or a mug of MacEwan's ale, or who smiled approvingly at a pretty girl. The friends he had were like our own and like us.

As we read and talked, he became flesh and blood. We saw him in the full dignity of manhood. He was a man we could understand and admire; the kind of friend we would like to have guarding our left flank; a leader we could follow.

We were fascinated by his humanity. Here was a working man, yet one who was perfectly free, who had not been enslaved by society, economics, law, politics, or religion. Demonic forces had existed then as now. They had sought to destroy him but they had not succeeded.

True, he had been strung up on a cross and tormented with the hell of pain; but he had not broken. The weight of law and of prejudice had borne down on him but failed to crush him. He had remained free and alive, as the resurrection affirmed. What he was, what he did, what he said, all made sense for us. We understood that the love expressed so supremely in Jesus was God's love—the same love we were experiencing for ourselves—the love that is passionate kindness, other-centred rather than self-centred, greater than all the laws of men.

The doctrines we worked out were meaningful to us. We approached God through Jesus the carpenter of Nazareth, the incarnate word.

We arrived at our understanding of God's ways not one by one, but together. In the fellowship of freedom and love we found truth, and with truth a wonderful sense of unity, of harmony, of peace.

As soon as I was able I joined the Australian sergeant's massage team. We visited our charges daily. As we massaged we listened to their woes and worries. When the opportunity came we talked, seeking to impart assurance, encouraging their will to live.

Nearly all of our patients were young. Some of them were dying. Almost daily I was brought face to face with the great problems of human experience. Nearly all of them were only concealments for the Big One: 'How do I face death? Can death be overcome?'

In the light of our new understanding, the Crucifixion was seen as being of the utmost relevance to our situation.

We did not know the complete answer to the problem of suffering. But we could see that God was not indifferent to such suffering.

We stopped complaining about our own. Faith would not save us from it, but it would take us through it. Suffering no longer locked us up in the prison house of self-pity but brought us into what Albert Schweitzer calls the 'fellowship of those who bear the mark of pain'. We looked at the Cross and took strength from the knowledge that it gave us, the knowledge that God was in our midst.

(b)

I was looking forward to a reunion with Dusty. At last I met a courier who had been on the same work detail with him.

'Yes, I knew him,' he said. 'We were sent to Burma to cut a retreat route for the Japs.'

'Where is he now?' I asked.

The man was reluctant to speak. He stammered for a minute or two. Then he replied,

'The last news I had of him wasn't good, he was in trouble.'

'Dusty?'

'He got the Nip warrant officer in charge of his party down on him.'

'What had he done wrong?'

'That was it. He hadn't done anything wrong.' He swallowed hard. 'The Nip hated him because he couldn't break him. You know how he was—a good man if ever there was one. That's why he hated him.'

'What did the Nip do to him?'

'He strung him up to a tree.'

'You mean—'

'Yes. He crucified him.'

I could hardly speak.

'When?'

'About the beginning of August.'

'Just before the Japs—'

'—packed up, yes.'

He turned away. He had said as much as he could bear.

Dusty—the man of deep faith and the warm heart—the man who was incapable of a mean act, even against a brutal tormentor—had been rewarded for his goodness by hatred—his radiant goodness which must have maddened the warrant officer to the point where he went berserk.

He died, like his Master, so far from his homeland, so far from everyone, yet so near to God.

I moved off to a corner of the camp that I might bear my grief alone. The surroundings misted so that nothing was clear any more; there was only the reality of suffering, disappointment, and sorrow.

Then I could see once again the light that had challenged the darkness in the valley of the shadow—the light that had been reflected from gentle faces.

I could see Ian Carruthers, I could see Dodger Green. I could see Dinty Moore restoring my spirits with his quick wit and kindly humour as he performed some menial task.

I could see Dusty Miller kneeling before me with his rag and his basin, telling me with a smile of his plans for the future as he cleaned my ulcers.

ERNEST GORDON, *Through the Valley of the Kwai*

47. (a) The carpenter's son

Meanwhile, not many miles away, a young man is working in a carpenter's shop in the village of Nazareth. Later, maybe, strange legends will circulate about his birth, but for as long as people in the village can remember, he has been no more than the son of Joseph the carpenter. He had been a lively, intelligent schoolboy, worthy, perhaps of a better career, but he has chosen to help his father in the shop. He might have made a Rabbi—he knows enough about the Bible, but somehow he isn't 'interested in religion'. He speaks well enough to have made a political career. His judgements on current affairs are sound and realistic, but he is not, to that extent, 'interested in politics'. Strange, too, that such an attractive, vigorous young man should not have married. He is not unaffected by women, but he just has not married.

He is friendly with everyone, and never makes moral judgements. The religious wish he was a little more strict. There is an obvious goodness about him, but the company he keeps leaves much to be desired. The irreligious wish they could just once get him drunk enough to carry him off to the local brothel, but it only seems as if, in an uncondemning way, he is slightly sorry for them, so that their laughter is a little more strident as they go.

He can be frightening at times—there is a force and a passion below the calm surface. There was that incident with the wealthy money-lender. The man often says that he'll have the young upstart run out of the village, but he has not yet found the right occasion. There was that time that some of the elders had tried to run the local harlot out of the town. They made some jokes about the reason why he stood between her and the men, but finally they had dropped their stones and gone home.

He has plenty of relatives in the village, but he is not very popular with some of them. They have a feeling that he gives himself airs, though there is nothing they can really pin it down to. He is not as loyal to the family as he could be. There are times when it is the clan against the world, and he has an annoying habit of seeing things from the world's point of view. He does not quote the Bible at them, but sometimes simple things that he says have the same sort of disturbing effect.

People sometimes try to get Joseph to open up about whether he is satisfied for his son to be no more than a carpenter, but he will not be drawn. 'He knows what he is doing.' Anyway, most people are glad he has not left. He is quiet and yet the place would somehow seem empty without him. But there is not much danger. He is already thirty, and no education : where could he go?

His mother worships him, and obviously, even yet, she has great hopes for him. She tries to be patient and trust in the will of God, but sometimes she is sure that he is only wasting his time, and she urges him to move. He tells her : 'My time is not yet come.'

(b) Jesus and the challenge of riches

Jesus' attitude towards material comfort and money is not ascetic. He never chooses hardship for hardship's sake, never speaks about 'duty' or 'honesty' or any of those Puritan virtues that make people and nations prosperous and hard. He speaks about joy and love, which presupposes sharing, and the early Christians naturally found themselves sharing all things in common and 'parted them to all, according as any man had need'. The commentators like to refer to this as 'an early experiment in communism, which failed'. Perhaps it was, in the same way that his death was an early experiment in pacifism that failed. Our subsequent experiments in greed and war are presumably the brilliant successes with which they are to be contrasted.

It is easier for a camel to go through the eye of a needle than for a rich man to enter the Kingdom of Heaven because, in this world, we can only be rich at someone else's expense. The rich man is not necessarily an exploiter, but whether he lives frugally and stores up his riches in barns or banks, or dresses in 'purple and fine linen' and 'fares sumptuously every day', he is doing so in the face of other people's poverty and need. He cannot enter into the Kingdom until he recognises the beggar at his gate as a brother, and to do that means giving away his riches. The man who cannot look a beggar in the eye is hiding from Christ. Jesus does not describe the rich man who builds bigger barns as wicked but as a fool. He is blind to the realities of the human situation.

To the rich young man who would 'inherit eternal life', he says :

'Go, sell whatsoever thou hast, and give to the poor, and thou shalt have treasure in heaven : and come, follow me. But his countenance fell at the saying, and he went away sorrowful: for he was one that had great possessions.'

The rich man can keep the commandments. He can meet Jesus, be loved by him. Like Nicodemus, he can put in a good word for Jesus in the highest council of the nation, provide a tomb for his corpse, and spices. But if he would follow Jesus, he must sell all that he has and give to the poor. For Jesus is found with the poor, the hungry and the cold. He hungers in a tent on the borders of Jordan, or a slum street of Liverpool; he shivers under a bridge in Korea, he sleeps on a bench in London. We cannot keep our riches and live with Jesus. We cannot follow Jesus and be indifferent to his suffering in the dirtiest or most ungrateful of his brethren. To have riches while there are hungry and naked outside our doors, albeit a long way outside, is to hide ourselves from our own flesh, and he who is one flesh with them will hide himself from us. He waits for us in the rain, under the bridge, in the prison. It is not by our professions of love for him, by our frequency at communion or our times of prayer, that he will judge us. We will judge ourselves when we say: 'Lord, when saw we thee an hungered, or athirst, or a stranger, or naked, or sick, or in prison, and did not minister unto thee?'

ROGER TENNANT, *Born of a Woman*

48. 'Who is this Jesus?'

All the city said it then; and all the world has said it ever since. One Figure has haunted the thinking and the conscience of mankind. One Figure has split history in two—so that every event is now dated with reference to His coming, either before or after. His influence is still a more dominating thing, His power more to be reckoned with than the power and influence of any Caesar. No man who has once seen Him can ever quite thrust Him out of sight again or evade His urgent challenge. Who is this Jesus?

The Christian religion is first and foremost and essentially a message about God—that the living God, eternal, immortal, invisible, has at one quite definite point broken through into history in an unprecedented way. Once and for all, in an actual life lived out upon this earth, God has spoken, and has given the full and final revelation of Himself. In Jesus, God has come. Who is He, of whom such amazing things are spoken?

They tell us that for the greater part of His life He was a working carpenter. His home was in an obscure provincial village. He was born in a stable, adjoining a roadside inn. Wealth and official position He had none. He wrote no books, He fought no battles, the applause of listening senates was never His to command. His friends were mostly

as poor as Himself, fishermen and peasants. When He left home and
started preaching, His own family tried to dissuade Him, thinking
and actually saying that He was mad. The crowds which at first
gathered inquisitively to listen to His teaching soon dwindled and
vanished away. His own best friends showed signs of doing the same.
'Will ye also go?' He had to ask them; and at the end, they did desert
Him to His fate. He died a felon's death, reviled and execrated, hanging between two thieves. He was buried in a borrowed grave.

But then a strange thing happened. It was rumoured that death
had not finished Him. It was reported that He had been seen alive.
And then, quite suddenly, His disciples appeared in the streets proclaiming that He had risen. They said He had come back to them.
They said they now saw, what formerly had been hidden from them,
that from the first God had been uniquely present in Jesus; that in
that life and death, the unseen had become visible, and the eternal had
become historic, and God had become man.

Was it surprising that the world, hearing all that, laughed it to
scorn? And when from its home of origin in Jerusalem, it began to
circulate more widely, the whole Roman Empire rang with contemptuous laughter.

But the extraordinary thing was this, that neither with laughter nor
with force, not with the massive arguments of her philosophers nor
by the might of her thundering legions, could Rome stop Jesus.

When the first Christians appropriated the word Lord (the same
hallowed name which the Old Testament had reserved for the Hebrew
Jehovah) and dared to use it of this Galilean Carpenter, were they just
dreaming, romancing, yielding to the intoxication of a foolish fancy?
Or was the thing true?

Mrs. Humphrey Ward tells how she once met Walter Pater at
Oxford. She had thrown off the Christian faith; and reckoning on his
sympathy, she expressed the belief that Christ's day was done. He
shook his head, and looked troubled. 'I don't think so. You think it's
all plain. But I can't. There are such mysterious things. Take that saying, "Come unto me, all ye that labour and are heavy laden." How
can you explain that? There is a mystery in it—something supernatural.'

Even the sceptic has stood troubled and ill at ease before this strange
fact of Christ. Here none of his categories seem to fit. His confidence
deserts him. There is mystery in it.

Now if we try to analyse the mystery, we shall find, I think, that it
is threefold—the mystery of a personality, the mystery of a power,
and the mystery of a presence.

When I speak of 'the mystery of a personality', I am thinking of
the startling coalescence of contrarieties that you find in Jesus. He was

the meekest and lowliest of all the sons of men : yet He said that He would come on the clouds of heaven in the glory of God. He was so austere that evil spirits and demons cried out in terror at His coming: yet He was so genial and winsome and approachable that the children loved to play with Him. No-one was ever half so kind or compassionate to sinners : yet no-one ever spoke such red-hot, scorching words about sin. He would not break the bruised reed, and His whole life was love: yet on one occasion He demanded of the Pharisees how they expected to escape the damnation of hell. He was the servant of all, washing the disciples' feet : yet masterfully He strode into the Temple, and the hucksters and traders fell over one another in their mad rush to get away from the fire they saw blazing in His eyes. He saved others : yet at the last, Himself He would not save. There is nothing in history like the union of contrasts that confronts you in the Gospels. The mystery of Jesus is the mystery of a personality.

But it is more. It is *the mystery of a power*. From that far day when He took a deadly cross, and converted it into a glorious throne, that power has marked the centuries. Empires have gone down before Him. Through His influence, great movements of reform have swept the earth. He has been the master-force behind the onward march of men. The one name before which the Anti-God movement of to-day trembles is the name of Jesus of Nazareth. There is no modern Caesarism which can shoulder Christ off the page of history, or break His grip on the souls of men. The mystery of Jesus is the mystery of a power.

But it is still more. It is *the mystery of a presence*. In every age, His own words have been verified anew—'Lo, I am with you always.' This Christ is a present fact, and men know it. For when we read our Gospels, intending to judge and assess and pass our verdict on what meets us there, gradually an extraordinary thing begins to happen : the central Figure steps out from the page and stands before our Conscience, and judges us. This is not using language dishonestly. In fact, the more honest we are in this matter the more vividly do we grow aware that Someone—not a mere fact of history, but Someone alive and present—is meeting us, is refusing to be held at arm's length or thrust aside, is dealing with us as only God could deal. This is not romancing. It is a strictly accurate, unrhetorical account of what actually happens.

What, then, are we to say of Him? Whoever or whatever else He may have been, whatever other name or predicate we may feel impelled to give Him, He was at least *truly and fully man*.

The Jesus of whom the evangelists tell is veritable man if ever there was one. He knew, as we do, what weariness means, and the burden of sheer physical exhaustion. His tears at Lazarus' grave were not forced tears, but the real grief of a sensitive spirit. He felt, as we do, the need for friends: what volumes that poignant question in Gethsemane speaks—'Could ye not watch with Me one hour?' He had to fight temptation, not only in the desert at the beginning, but right to the end of the journey: what he suffered in His body on the cross, and in His mind and spirit through all the despising and rejecting which culminated there, was not make-believe solemn play-acting, but something so terrible that thought recoils before it. Let it suffice for the moment to be able—with the Roman governor who tried His case at the end—to say, 'Behold the Man!'

There is a most moving passage in which the great Russian novelist Turgenev has described how once there came to him, in a kind of vision, a swift and wonderful insight into the meaning of the humanity of Jesus. 'I saw myself, a youth, in a low-pitched wooden church. There stood before me many people, all fair-haired peasant heads. From time to time, they began swaying, falling, rising again, like the ripe ears of wheat when the wind in summer passes over them. All at once a man came up from behind and stood beside me. I did not turn towards him, but I felt that the man was Christ. Emotion, curiosity, awe overmastered me. I made an effort and looked at my neighbour. A face like everyone's, a face like all men's faces. "What sort of Christ is this?" I thought. "Such an ordinary, ordinary man. It cannot be." I turned away, but I had hardly turned my eyes from this ordinary man when I felt again that it was really none other than Christ standing beside me. Only then I realised that just such a face is the face of Christ—a face like all men's faces.'

He is true man, this Jesus. Some men declare unconcernedly, or even truculently, that they do not believe in Christ. But then, some men have no right to believe in Christ, no conceivable possibility of understanding the fact of Christ, because they have not yielded to the challenge of the fact. I invite you to consider five facts, all pointing decisively to the same overwhelming conclusion: 'In Him dwelleth all the fullness of the Godhead bodily.'

The first cardinal fact is *the claim Jesus made for Himself*. Do we realise how astonishing and unprecedented this is? Think of other great religious teachers—Socrates, Buddha, Confucius—and then ask, What was their paramount concern? Not to fix attention upon themselves, but to win acceptance for their message. 'I am nothing,' they seemed to say, 'the truth is everything.' But with Jesus and with Him alone, it is utterly different.

He deliberately places Himself at the very centre of His own message. He does not merely claim to have found the answer to all men's needs: He claims to *be* the answer. 'Come unto Me, all ye who labour, and I will give you rest.' If the language were not so familiar, it would simply stagger us with its audacity. Calmly He arrogates to Himself a position transcending all the wisdom and the splendour of the centuries. 'A greater than Solomon is here.' He declares that at the Day of Judgement the final test will be 'Ye have done it unto *Me*,' 'Ye did it not to *Me*,' 'Before Abraham was, I am!'

What are we to say about all this? Either it is the infatuation of an absurd megalomania, or else it is really true. You have to choose one or the other: there is no third option.

The second decisive fact concerns *His sinlessness*. The fact stands, on the testimony of Christ Himself. Never once is Jesus heard confessing sin. This Man, whose whole life was a constant self-identification with sin, never had to bow in penitence nor plead for cleansing for Himself. That fact surely is startling. And it becomes all the more startling when you consider that it is precisely the saintliest people in the world who have been most conscious of their own sin. In proportion as a soul draws close to God, the more vividly does it realise its own personal unworthiness. That is the universal rule to which all the saints conform. Does Jesus conform to it? Ought we not to find that Jesus, having a unique God-consciousness, had also a unique awareness of sin? Yes, indeed, if He is just the greatest of the saints, we should. But what if we find it the exact reverse: if so far from having a desperate sense of sin, like Paul and à Kempis and Teresa and all the finest souls in history, He alone has none; if He is thus not only different from all sinners, but different also from all saints—then who is He?

The third decisive fact is this: *Jesus does for men what only God could do.* Here I am thinking particularly of the experience of being forgiven. Suppose I do something which I know to be wrong. Suppose that thereupon I 'rationalise' my action, finding palliating circumstances, and justifying myself to my own satisfaction. Is that the end of the matter? In my heart of hearts I know that something else is needed to deal with what has happened and to right the wrong. The barrier that has been raised is not between my higher and my lower self: it is between me and God. In other words, it is God who must forgive—else there is no true forgiveness possible. But now see what happens. This thing which none but God can do—*Jesus does.*

He did it again and again in Galilee. And, mark you, it was not only that He pronounced words of absolution—but it was this, that He actualised God's forgiveness for those poor sinful folk, embodied it. They knew with a sense of amazed, incredible relief that God was at peace with them, and they with God. When the Pharisees, attacking Him, declared 'No-one can forgive sins but God only,' and argued that consequently Jesus must be a usurper and an impostor, their first statement was perfectly correct. Only God can convey forgiveness: that is true. And that is what we have to square with this other unimpeachable fact, that forgiveness is conveyed by Jesus. Only God can break the chain of a man's sinful nature: yet for thousands Christ has broken it. If Christ thus does for us what only God could ever do, who can He be?

The fourth decisive fact is the *universality of Jesus*. How do we propose to account for the unique phenomenon, that Jesus has laid His spell invincibly upon every century and every race and upon all kinds and conditions of men?

Look at the first circle of His friends. Peter and John were, temperamentally, poles asunder: yet in His eyes they both beheld the answer to their dreams. Matthew, the Jewish taxgatherer and Luke the Gentile doctor had nothing whatever in common: yet to draw His portrait for the world to see was to both men the only thing that mattered. Pass in review the unbroken ranks of His friends and followers throughout the ages. Who can this be who can grip and captivate the souls of men so utterly different as Luther the Reformer and Loyala the Jesuit, as Francis the friar and Moody the evangelist, as G. K. Chesterton and General Booth, as Cardinal Newman and David Livingstone? Could any mortal man thus besiege and lay captive the thinking and the worship of the centuries?

The fifth and final fact is the most decisive of all. It is *the divine self-verification of Christ in conscience*. For there is a very wonderful thing which happens: You begin by dealing with a historic Figure as presented in the Gospels, and gradually you become aware that the ultimate reality and heart of things is dealing with you. You begin by looking for the secret of this Master of life who walked the Galilean road, and piercingly you are made to feel that everything that is highest and holiest and divinest in the universe is looking for you. That is the self-verification of Jesus, demanding—as only God can demand—the entire and utter surrender of my soul; and all I know of God—His nature, attributes and ways of working—has come to me through Jesus.

JAMES S. STEWART, The Strong Name

Who is this Jesus? Consider the author's answers to this question, and discuss the points he makes in support of them.

49. 'You did it to me'

Here are three passages with a somewhat similar theme: the first is a prayer, prefaced by two New Testament quotations; the second a story from a novel; the third a passionate plea.

1. Study each passage and try to say what its point and purpose is.

2. How has the impact of Christ's life and death on these three writers affected their attitude to their fellow-men?

3. Discuss how far these presentations of what Christ is (was) and does (did) help to make His life and death more relevant and meaningful to you.

(a) 'Lord, that face haunts me'

'If he does not love the brother whom he has seen, it cannot be that he loves God whom he hath not seen.' (I John 4 : 20).

'And they too will reply, "Lord, when was it that we saw you hungry or thirsty or a stranger or naked or ill or in prison, and did nothing for you?" And he will answer, "I tell you this: anything you did not do for one of these, however humble, you did not do for me."' (Matt. 25 : 44–45).

'Here is this poor face of a man, like an open book,
The book of the miseries and sins of men;

    the book of
             selfishness,
             conceit,
             cowardice;
    the book of
             greed,
             lust,
             abdications,
             compromises.

Here it is like a mournful protest,

    like a cry of revolt,
    but also like a heart-rending call,

For behind this ridiculous, grimacing face,
Behind those uneasy eyes,
Like the clasped hands of one drowned, white on the dark surface of
    the pool,
Is a light,
A flame,
A tragic supplication,
The infinite desire of a soul to live above its mud.

Lord, that face haunts me, it frightens me, it condemns me.
For, with everyone else, I have made it, or allowed it to be made!
And I realize, Lord, that this boy is my brother, and yours.

What have we done with a member of your family?

I fear your judgment, Lord.

It seems to me that at the end of time all the faces of my brothers, and
   especially those of my town, my district, my work, will be lined
   up before me,

And in your merciless light I shall recognize in these faces
   the lines that I have cut,
   the mouth that I have twisted,
   the eyes that I have darkened,
   and those whose light I have extinguished.

They will come, those that I have known
   and those that I have not known,
   those of my time and all those that have followed,
   fashioned by the workshop of the world.

And I shall stand still, terrified, silent.

It is then, O Lord, that you will say to me
   ... it was I. ...

Lord, forgive me for that face which has condemned me,

Lord, thank you for that face which has awakened me.'

MICHAEL QUOIST, *Prayers of Life*

(b) 'Who was it?'

Manolios made an effort and broke the silence:

'When I was a novice at the Monastery,' he said, 'before archon
Patriarcheas came to fetch me and throw me into the world, my
Superior, Father Manasse—good luck to him if he's still alive, God
rest him in the odour of sanctity if he's dead!—told me one day about
an adventure which happened to a monk, one of his friends. I hadn't
thought of it for years, but this evening, God knows why, it's come
back to me and keeps going round in my head. ... Do you want to go
to sleep?' he broke off, because his friends were silent and he could not
make out their faces very well in the darkness.

'God preserve us!' cried Kostandis, as if he had been insulted. 'Why
do you say that to us, Manolios?'

'Never had our minds so wide awake, Manolios,' said Yannakos in
his turn. 'Don't hurt our feelings so. Go on!'

'Well, this monk, my Superior's friend—the great dream of his life
was that God in His mercy would let him go and bow down at the
Holy Sepulchre. He went from village to village, collected alms and,
after several years, when he was already old, he'd managed to put together thirty pounds, just what was needed for the journey. He did
penance, obtained his Superior's permission and set off.

'Hardly had he got outside the Monastery when he saw a man in

rags, pale, sad, bent towards the ground, picking herbs. Hearing the
pilgrim's staff ringing on the stones, the man raised his head.

' "Where are you going, Father?" he asked him.

' "To the Holy Sepulchre, brother, to Jerusalem. I shall go thrice
round the Holy Sepulchre and bow down."

' "How much money have you got?"

' "Thirty pounds."

' "Give me the thirty pounds, I've a wife and children and they're
hungry. Give them to me, gò thrice round me, fall on your knees and
bow down before me; then afterwards go back into your Monastery."

'The monk took the thirty pounds out of his sack, gave the whole
lot to the poor man, went three times round him, fell on his knees and
bowed down before him. Then he returned to the Monastery.'

Manolios bent his head and fell silent. The three companions were
still listening to his words within them; they remained silent. Their
hearts were overwhelmed.

Manolios raised his head again.

'Later,' he said, 'I learned that that monk who left for the Holy
Sepulchre was my Superior himself, Father Manasse; from humility
he was unwilling to tell me. This evening, after so many years, I
understand who the poor man was whom he met as he left the
Monastery.'

Manolios fell silent. His voice was beginning to tremble. His friends
drew nearer to him on the bench. 'Who was it?' they asked, anxiously.

Manolios hesitated a moment. At last, calmly, like a ripe fruit
falling at night in a garden, his word fell:

'Christ.'

The three comrades jumped. As though suddenly there had appeared among them in the darkness, sad, poorly dressed, persecuted by
men, with His feet bleeding from walking, a fugitive, Christ.

NIKOS KAZANTZAKIS, *Christ Recrucified*

(c) We, the crucifiers

Then Pilate delivered him to their will.

And they took Jesus and led Him away to crucify Him.

    And what is crucifixion?

'The cross itself, as used during the reign of Tiberius, consisted of
an upright stake called a *stipes*—which was generally fixed permanently in a cement socket at the place of execution—and a cross beam
called a *patibulum*, a baulk of timber about seven or eight feet long
which the victim was compelled, as part of the punishment, to
shoulder from the prison-store to the waiting upright. A notch, or
some other similar wood-joint, close to the top of this upright, allowed

the cross-beam to be nailed or bolted in position, and about four or five feet from the ground there would be a series of holes to allow the insertion of a peg, called *sedilis excessus*, to support the victim's crotch : this was to prevent the entire weight of the body from slowly dragging the hands and arms from the nails or other fixing.

'After the scourging the victim would be cut down, kicked and dragged to his feet, and, carrying the *patibulum*, would be driven on by blows from the flat of the sword, or goaded with it, to the place of execution.

'And there the victim would be felled to the ground, the *patibulum* would be thrust beneath his neck, his arms gripped and then tied to the cross-beam with cords, and his hands nailed to it with heavy iron nails, square in section. This nailing would be either through the palm or the forward fold of the wrist, and was intended to prevent the hands jerking free during the convulsion which crucifixion produced.

'Then the cross-beam would be dragged across the ground to the *stipes* and hoisted up until it could be secured in the notch. Other cords might be tied around the waist as an added precaution against the convulsions of agony jerking the body even off the nails—in would go the supporting peg—and then, finally, the feet themselves would be nailed, either with one nail driven between the metatarsal bones of the two crossed insteps, or with two nails, one through each heel behind the Achilles tendon.

'And there he remained hanging until he died, anything up to seven, eight, or nine days later.'

Horrible, terrible, awful, dreadful, harrowing, appalling, . . . remember all the words? Sadistic, psychopathic, depraved, perverted, criminal, . . . remember all the names?

So we're not like that *these* days, are we?
So let us describe death by hanging. . . .
So let us describe death by guillotine. . . .
So let us describe death in the electric-chair. . . .
So let us describe death in the gas-chamber. . . .
So let us describe death by firing-squad. . . .
So let us describe any death made legal. Amen.

And then let us shut up, and remember all the other deaths we are so quick with. War or peace? On the cross or at the blinding heart of an atomic explosion? All can be described, and some merely take slightly longer than others.

Take a deep breath on it and wonder it doesn't choke you, this sweet smell of success and corruption, this odour of sanctity and putrefaction, incense and drunken vomit in high places, the new money and old vices. . . . Go on, smell the food let rot to keep the prices up, the

milk gone bad because it isn't sound economic policy to send it where
starving children could drink it, the wheat burned because there's a
surplus everywhere else except where there isn't any bread, the dead
fish thrown back into the sea because there's a glut and they're not
worth the trouble landing, the cabbages ploughed back, the fruit left
mouldering beneath the trees. . . . Smell all the untended wounds in
the world, leprosy, yaws, ulcers—all the other words and names for
the human condition—and smell, carefully, not the anaesthetic we
are sending but the very latest poison-gas we are preparing, not the
tang of steel tempering for surgical instruments but for armour-
piercing shells, not antiseptics and disinfectants and healing oint-
ments but horrors of chemical warfare and synthetic plague . . . and
remember that we'll need more than air-conditioning when we start
using them.

So finish your drink, Jack, and pour yourself another one—and
there, round the next street, the dry earth cracks and powders, and
the men scratch at it with sticks, and the dust rises and settles on the
withered leaves, and the women watch their men silently, and the eyes
of the children are very large and lifeless, no laughter, and the hot
wind swirls in from the next street but one . . . and what are those
birds wheeling high in the tall days of summer? and what of the
winter next week? will the river of rains pour away into the distant
sea as it has always done?

So cut yourself another slice, help yourself to anything you fancy,
undo another button—go on, treat yourself, there's plenty more
where that came from. . . . And, round the next street, on the lower
pavements of hell, the children—their large and lifeless eyes upon us,
their hands urgent for bread, for life, for hope, even for death as a
mercy. . . .

Always the children. . . .

A boy, his ribs stark, his belly swollen, his thin arms brittle as
charred wood, sitting by the dead or dying body of his mother in the
dry grass of Africa—she may be only sleeping, but has little to wake
for. . . .

The eyes of a girl with trachoma, weeping into the futile night of
blindness. . . .

Another with tuberculosis, one of millions, her eyes dull from
weakness, her mouth too slack to hold its spittle. . . .

And other millions elsewhere—a shilling booklet will give you all
the facts: poverty, ignorance, squalor, exploitation, levels of calorific
intake, the incidence of hookworm, cholera, smallpox, malnutrition,
and the statistics for death by starvation and the lack of love . . . the
misery and shadows of a world in want, the slow murder of our
brothers and sisters, the unspectacular death of children.

O God! always the children!

So let's all have another slice or three, Jack, spread it on nice and thick and juicy, and pour us all another drink while you're at it—for there are snack-bars and cafes and restaurants and tea-shops and food-stores and confectioners and bakers and supermarkets and public houses, and we can go on eating and drinking and laying up treasure to our heart's content, can't we? the next street being the next street even though they tell us it's in the same parish when it comes to Births and Deaths . . . And if you turn on the television, or put another half dozen on the record-player and set the switch to *auto-matic play*, well, there'll be no need to bother *too* much about the grain which *could* have made bread being made into booze, will there? Nor about the land which could have grown potatoes being given over to tobacco. . . . No need to hear the whimpering (funny how that word keeps cropping up), no need to let the children squatting naked in the gutter outside put you off your food—go on, draw the curtains, that way you don't have to see them at all.

No, there's no sense knocking yourself out over things you can't do all *that* much about, is there? You get morbid. . . .

So all right, agreed, there's no magnificence when trachoma and tuberculosis dull the eyes (not like Coventry Cathedral when the light pours in through the great Baptistry Window, probably the greatest piece of stained-glass since the Reformation), no music where lepers rot (like the Gregorian Chant for Good Friday, the Solemn Interces-sions and Adoration of the Cross, the section including the dear old *pange lingua*—brings tears to your eyes every time, it's so beautiful), no romance in hookworm and cholera, no beauty in smallpox, no escape from such life except in death—and there's the Son of God dying it, *there*, all the time, in this haunted landscape of the mind.

Father? Forgive us? We know what it is we do.

GEORGE TARGET, *We, the Crucifiers*

50. 'Hast thou considered my servant Job?'

(Now it came to pass on the day when the sons of God came to present themselves before SATAN *that* CHRIST *also came among them. And*

SATAN [*said unto* CHRIST]. *Whence comest thou?*

CHRIST [*answered* SATAN *and said*]. *From going to and fro in the earth, and from walking up and down in it.* [*And*]

SATAN [*said unto* CHRIST]. *Hast thou considered my servant Judas? For there is none like him in the earth, an evil and a faithless man, one that feareth me and turneth away from God.* [*Then*]

CHRIST [*answered* SATAN *and said*]. *Doth Judas fear thee for naught? Hast thou not made a hedge about him, and about his house,*

*and about all that he hath on every side? But draw back thy hand now
and he will renounce thee to thy face.* [And]
   SATAN [*said unto* CHRIST], *Behold, all that he hath is in thy power.*
     [*So* CHRIST *went forth from the presence of* SATAN.]
He descended to the earth. Thirty-three years are but a moment before SATAN *and before* GOD, *and at the end of this moment* CHRIST *ascends again to His own place. He passes on this journey before the presence of the adversary.*)

Satan. You are alone! Where is my son Judas whom I gave into your
    hands?

Christ. He follows me.

Satan. I know what you have done. And the earth rejected you? The
    earth rejected you! All Hell murmurs in astonishment. But where
    is Judas, my son and my joy?

Christ. Even now he is coming.

Satan. Even Heaven, when I reigned there, was not so tedious as this
    waiting. Know, Prince, that I am too proud to show all my aston-
    ishment at your defeat. But now that you are swallowing your last
    humiliation, now that your failure has shut the mouths of the
    angels, I may confess that for a while I feared you. There is a fret-
    fulness in the hearts of men. Many are inconstant, even to me. Alas,
    every man is not a Judas! I knew even from the beginning that you
    would be able, for a season, to win their hearts with your mild elo-
    quence. I feared that you would turn to your own uses this fretful-
    ness that visits them. But my fears were useless. Even Judas, even
    when my power was withdrawn from him, even Judas betrayed
    you. Am I not right in this?

Christ. You are.

Satan. You admitted him into your chosen company. Is it permitted
    to me to ask for how much he betrayed you?

Christ. For thirty pieces of silver.

Satan (*after a pause*). Am I permitted to ask to what rôle he was
    assigned in your company?

Christ. He held its money-bags.

Satan (*dazed*). Does Heaven understand human nature as little as
    that? Surely the greater part of your closest companions stayed
    beside you to the end?

Christ. One stayed beside me.

Satan. I have overestimated my enemy. Learn again, Prince, that if I
    were permitted to return to the earth in my own person, not for
    thirty years, but for thirty hours, I would seal all men to me and
    all the temptations in Heaven's gift could not persuade one to betray
    me. For I build not on intermittent dreams and timid aspirations,
    but on the unshakable passions of greed and lust and self-love. At

last this is made clear: Judas, Judas, all the triumphs of Hell await you. Already above the eternal pavements of black marble the banquet is laid. Listen, how my nations are stirring in new hope and in new joy. Such music has not been lifted above my lakes and my mountains since the day I placed the apple of knowledge between the teeth of Adam.

(Suddenly the thirty pieces of silver are cast upward from the revolted hand of Judas. They hurtle through the skies, flinging their enormous shadows across the stars and continue falling for ever through the vast funnel of space.

Presently Judas rises, the black stains about his throat and the rope of suicide.)

Satan. What have they done to you, my beloved son? What last poor revenge have they attempted upon you? Come to me. Here there is comfort. Here all this violence can be repaired. The futile spite of Heaven cannot reach you here. But why do you not speak to me? My son, my treasure!

(Judas remains with lowered eyes.)

Christ. Speak to him then, my beloved son.

Judas *(still with lowered eyes, softly, to Satan)*. Accursed be thou, from eternity to eternity.

(These two mount upward to their due place and Satan remains to this day, uncomprehending, upon the pavement of Hell.)

THORNTON WILDER, *Hast thou considered my servant Job?*

51. Only love is necessary

That night Father Onuphrius told me of his visit to Mount Athos in 1924, and how afterwards he had entered a small monastery in the forest, of which Father Daniel was the Superior. They had sheltered proscribed persons and had both been sentenced to twenty years imprisonment.

He had not thought of himself. I saw presently that he was praying, with his eyes closed and his chin on his chest. Later, I asked:

'Do you pray for our guards as well? And for the communists?'

'Of course. They're God's children like the rest of us,' he said in his husky, old man's voice.

When he and Father Daniel were both asleep Michael Popp, a doctor, nudged me and whispered:

'It's bad with me. I can't stand it any more.'

'Still jealousy?'

'No—sheer misery. I'd pray with the priests if I could, but I don't believe in God.'

I said that belief was not necessary, only love. Men had worshipped countless divinities, natural forces, idols, gods and then a single, personal God. But if he could not believe in any of this there was still the impersonal God. And here no question of faith arose, since there was nothing to deny: it was a matter of loving or withholding love. It was a question of loving or hating or remaining indifferent. God, to me, was that which forced this choice upon us.

Michael Popp grunted something and turned violently on his side. He told me later that it was on this night that he tried for the first time to love and worship God. After this he never gave up trying.

As for me, it was at about this time that I began to believe I would never see Sabine and our child again. My family and friends seemed even more remote than they had done when I was a prisoner of war; the whole world had shrunk within the confines of this 're-education camp'. Yet I was conscious of a great peace and serenity of spirit, although every day we had to carry the dead out of the camp and bury them in a place which is now covered with grass, so that one cannot even see where their bones lie. I strove with all my strength to love, and to love all men equally, without exception or omission. It was very easy to love Father Onuphrius or Michael Popp; a little less easy in the case of Father Daniel and certain others of my fellow-prisoners; difficult in the case of poor Oaca, and still more difficult in the case of the man who had committed rape and murder. And how love Lieutenant Luca, and the guards who took pleasure in hitting us? It called for months of striving before I could soften my heart to the extent of loving them no less than Father Onuphrius.

We were loading carts with gravel one day when the man at my side sat down for a moment to rest. He was seventy. He had been wealthy and powerful, now he was much diminished, weak and frail.

'You'd better get up,' I said in a low voice, seeing Luca approach, but by now Luca had seen us. He came up bellowing, and thrusting me aside gave the old man a kick in the stomach that caused him to collapse.

'Skrimshanking, eh? Not so keen on work! It was all right when you had people to do it for you! By God, I'll teach you!'

He snatched up the old man's shovel and began furiously beating him with it. The old man cried in a trembling voice, 'You're killing me' and tried to get on his feet but collapsed again. I let go my shovel and crouched on all fours over his body, feeling the skinny bones beneath his clothing. The edge of Luca's shovel caught me on the hip, and then a light blazed in my head as the next one caught me on the back of the skull. 'I'm going to be killed,' I thought. 'God forgive me and forgive us all!'

Luca shouted for the guards and I heard the shovel fall to the ground. I was still conscious; I knew that it was a fine, sunny day.

The old man was motionless beneath me, and blood was pouring down my face.

'Take this man to the cells,' barked Luca.

I stood up, fell and got to my feet again. The old man had fainted and he died soon afterwards without recovering consciousness. I was driven past the carts and the other prisoners under a clear, blue sky scattered with feathery clouds; and I knew that my death did not matter, or my life; there was only God's love and pity, which henceforth would never leave me, and my own love and pity, which was His.

The cell was a concrete box too narrow to sit down in. One could only bend one's knees a little so that they were thrust up against the door, and the position becomes so agonising that it is hard not to cry out. In the end, after hours have passed, one subsides into a state of constant whimpering. The warmth of urine running down one's leg is pleasant for an instant because of the coldness of the box, but then one's trouser-leg seems to freeze. The need to perform other physical functions is even more painful, and when one has given way to it the shame and the stink are hard to endure, but the relieved body has no shame. To pray in such circumstances is not easy, but it is a great and sweet solace if one can do so, and one must try with all one's strength to love more, not less. I had to struggle not to sink below the level of love and fall back into the realm of hatred, anger and revenge; to love Romulus Luca, not for a moment but continuously. I had to drive my soul to do this as one may push a vehicle with locked brakes. It was now that I came to understand Luca, his blindness and narrow hatred, his reactions which were like those of a dog rendered savage by being chained too long, or of a slave put in charge of slaves, with no freedom except to torment them. And then my thoughts went to those, like Onuphrius and Michael Popp, whom it was natural and easy to love. I found that now I loved them differently, now that I had learnt to love Luca; I came back to them as though from a distant place. And it was in that cell, my legs sticky with filth, that I at last came to understand the divinity of Jesus Christ, the most divine of all men, the one who had most deeply and intensely loved, and who had conceived the parable of the lost sheep; the first of a future mankind wherein a mutation of human hearts will in the end cause the Kingdom of God to descend among men. PETRU DUMITRIU, *Incognito*

1. Wherein does 'I' of this passage discern the 'divinity of Jesus Christ' to lie?
2. How does he see this as affecting his own life and his attitude to his fellow-men?
3. What are the experiences which have led him to this insight about the nature of God and the person of Jesus Christ?
4. In what ways, if any, do you see his insights as having relevance for your own life and convictions?

52. The divinity of Christ

We come to the question which Christ addressed to His disciples:
'Whom do you say that I am?'

The World Council of Churches admits to its membership those
Churches which acknowledge Jesus Christ as God and Saviour. The
difficulty for many people today in committing themselves to that
affirmation is that they are not clear about the meaning of the terms.
We have to recognise that the word God has in the minds of many
people acquired so many wrong associations that in affirming the
divinity of Christ they would be making *false* statements.

In considering this question we must be on our guard against the
fallacy of assuming that we already have, apart from Christ, a sufficiently clear and reliable knowledge of God, the world and men, and
that our problem is somehow to fit Christ into this picture. It is quite
the other way round. It is Christ who has given us the conception of
God that is today in debate. It may well be that He, as Professor Donald Baillie has said, is 'the sole way in which the Christian conception
of God becomes credible or even expressible'. In an essay published
more than twenty years ago, Professor Tillich suggested that Christ is
for Christians the centre of history. All history, if it is to have a meaning, must have a central point from which that meaning is derived.
What for Christians gives to human life its ultimate meaning is the
historical appearance of Christ. The deepest meaning of existence has
been revealed in the life of a person. Those who believe that are at
least on the road towards affirming what the Church intends by its
statements about the person of Christ. Christian theology is right in
resisting the humanist attempts to reduce Christ to the human level
and treat Him as representative of human possibilities. In that case
Christ cannot rightly be regarded as the centre of history, but only as
one element in the stream of time, subject to all the arbitrariness and
ambiguities of the historical process.

Another way of putting things is Tillich's insistence that *new
being* appeared in history in Jesus Christ, that in Him a new aeon
dawned in which humanity was lifted to a new level and that this
way of formulating the Christian faith is the one most likely to convey
meaning and light to people today. This is the same affirmation as the
assertion in the Fourth Gospel that grace and truth (reality) came by
Jesus Christ. It is St. Paul's doctrine of 'new creation'. The great key
words of the writings of the New Testament ascribed to St. John—
Life, Light, Love—have for me a meaning, the full depths of which I
can never fully plumb. In Him was *life*. I am the *light* of the world.
God is *love*.

Let us dwell for a moment on the last assertion. I do not think that it is possible to exaggerate the importance of the question whether we may believe that love is among the attributes of the power behind the universe. If we are able to believe that, there is born in us an invincible hope. We have nothing to fear. That there is that love at the heart of things is the central assertion of Christianity. If that love is there, there is no conceivable way in which it could be manifested except in the life of a person. How else could it be possible to declare that God is love? Nothing greater has ever been written about love than the thirteenth chapter of the First Epistle to the Corinthians. I cannot believe that St. Paul wrote that hymn to love out of his own head. He was plainly painting a portrait of One in whom love had found its incarnation. To believe in Christ is for me identical with believing that love is the ultimate meaning of life. It may be that our hesitancies and reluctances about affirmations relating to the person of Christ have their source in part at least in the narrowness of our own vision and the poverty of our own experience of the meaning of love.

The declaration in the prologue of the Fourth Gospel asserts that *grace*, as well as truth, came by Jesus Christ. Grace is not a word that for many people today is rich in meaning. Yet we have only to reflect on what we know of life to be made aware that grace, in the sense of undeserved favour, unmerited goodness is an incontestable reality of our existence, interwoven with the whole texture of human experience.

How often have we encountered grace when we have been surprised in a thousand different ways by unexpected beauty, or when we have experienced the unanticipated, unbelievable kindness of friends. In the ideal home, where love and mutual helpfulness are the rule, we have perpetual disclosures of the mysteries of grace. So also in the rich variety of human associations in which men are united with one another by the bonds of comradeship, loyalty and fidelity, we are surrounded and upheld by a solid structure of grace. What an inexhaustible wealth of grace, again, is embodied in the manifold traditions by which human life is sustained, nourished and enriched: the traditions of law, of learning in all its branches, of various skills, of administration, of art and of religion. In all these spheres we stand on the shoulders of those who have gone before us and enjoy the unearned increment of their labours.

It is none the less true that through the whole of human existence there runs a deep rift. The experiences I have described are accompanied in our lives by those of disruption, frustration, disappointment, conflict, self-destruction, meaninglessness. It is at this other side of the picture that we must look, if we are to understand the new depth of content which Christianity has given to the conception of grace. To understand that meaning we need to face in its full dimensions the problem of evil.

The pitiless cruelty of man to man, in war and in concentration camps, the unspeakable degradation of human nature, the bestiality that no words can compass—these things belong to the real world in which we live.

Over against this there stands in the centre of human history a Cross as the symbol of love which encountered the concentrated force of evil and was victorious over it. That picture has captured men's imagination through the centuries and given to human life depths of meaning that had never before been plumbed. To take but one witness from our own time: Leslie Paul, who before the last war played an active part in the youth movement and who in the war found his way back to Christian faith, says in his book, 'Angry Young Man', which Harold Nicolson begged everyone to read: 'Christ, the mysterious, suffering figure at the heart of Christianity, the God done to death by man, as man constantly does to death his own spirit, now became, for all one's questions about Him, the most moving and frightening symbol in the whole of history.' If that symbol is a disclosure of the meaning of reality, grace is not merely one element in life but embraces the whole of it.

I do not think that we need allow ourselves to be overawed by the seeming incommensurability between the solitary, broken figure on the Cross and the immense sweep of history, the migrations of peoples and the titanic conflicts of armed nations. It was St. Paul's unshakable confidence that the weakness of God is stronger than men. William James, writing from a standpoint outside the Christian faith, says: 'As for me, my bed is made: I am against bigness and greatness in all their forms, and with the invisible molecular moral forces that work from individual to individual, stealing in through the crannies of the world like so many soft rootlets, or like the capillary oozing of water, and yet rending the hardest monuments of man's pride, if you give them time.' At its heart, the problem is the one of which we have already spoken: Can we believe that love is the ultimate meaning of the universe?

Let us turn our thoughts from the evil in the world to the evil in ourselves. Here again the complacency and easy-going optimism of modern man are amazing. If we have caught one glimpse of what love means, our lives must appear to us in retrospect a miserable failure. We have neglected those whom we might have helped. We have failed those who looked to us and trusted us. We have fallen immeasurably short of realizing our true manhood. No fact seems more certain than that from this unhappy state of things we cannot deliver ourselves. It is our individualism, our self-centredness and self-sufficiency that separate us from love. The only hope for us is that a love should reach us from outside, and bring us into the circle of love. We can only love if we have first been loved. Christianity asserts that that emancipating event has taken place.

If that is true, Christ has an infinite significance, both for individual destiny and for the future of the human race. In regard to the first, the ultimate concern of each of us is whether our life has any abiding meaning. The more honestly and deeply I face the realities of human existence, the clearer it becomes to me that we have nothing whatever to hope for in ourselves. When we become alive to that reality, there is no refuge from despair, no truth in which our minds can rest, nothing that can give us back confidence and hope, except the knowledge that there is an undeserved mercy on which we can cast ourselves and an unmerited grace in which we can put our trust. Historically it was this glad assurance that the Cross of Christ brought to men. It has to be held in conjunction and in continual tension with the truth of man's responsibility for the conduct of life, with a wholehearted devotion to the tasks of civilization and with a full participation in the labours by which men endeavour through their science and skill, through their knowledge and industry to make themselves masters of their fate. But in the end of the day, in the last resort, I know nothing to which the mind and heart of man can cling except the belief that there is a love which accepts us just as we are and will do for us more than we can ask or think.

If the principle that governs the world is love, then we may ask with M. Marcel whether it is 'conceivable that a God who offers Himself to our love should range Himself *against* this same love, in order to deny it, to bring it to nothingness'. God, Christ said with what seems unanswerable logic, is not the God of the dead, but of the living.

The decisive issue which confronts mankind today seems plainly to be whether man is to be increasingly subordinated to the technical and impersonal or whether all his astonishing achievements in controlling the world of things are to be made to minister to the growth of a fuller and richer personal life expressing itself in a community of persons. If that is so, it is obviously a question of the first moment whether for the achievement of the latter end we have to rely solely on what we know too well to be our pitifully weak human resources and fitful human purposes, or whether we believe that, in the words of Paul Tillich, 'personality is rooted in the structure of being as being.' If reality in its depths is personal, the one and only way in which it could fully reveal itself as such is in and through a person

who, in a fully personal relation to God and to man, was the incarnation of perfect love and showed what man's life was meant to be.

J. H. OLDHAM, *Life is Commitment*

53. Religionless Christianity

The thing that keeps coming back to me is, what *is* Christianity, and
indeed what *is* Christ, for us to-day? How can Christ become the Lord
even of those with no religion? If religion is no more than a garment
of Christianity then what is a religionless Christianity? How do we
speak of God without religion. How do we speak in a secular fashion of
God? In what way are we in a religionless and secular sense Christians,
not conceiving of ourselves religiously as specially favoured, but as
wholly belonging to the world? Then Christ is no longer an object
of religion, but something quite different, indeed and in truth the Lord
of the world.

I often ask myself why a Christian instinct frequently draws me
more to the religionless than to the religious, by which I mean not
with an intention of evangelising them, but rather, I might almost say,
in 'brotherhood'. While I often shrink with religious people from
speaking of God by name, with people who have no religion I am able
on occasion to speak of God quite openly and as it were naturally.
Religious people speak of God when human perception is (often from
laziness) at an end, or human resources fail: it is in fact always the
Deus ex machina they call to their aid, either for the so-called solving
of insoluble problems or as support in human failure—always, that is
to say, helping out human weakness or on the borders of human existence. Of necessity, that can only go on until men can, by their own
strength, push those borders a little further, so that God becomes
superfluous as a *Deus ex machina*. I have come to be doubtful even
about talking of 'borders of human existence'. Is even death to-day,
since men are scarcely afraid of it any more, and sin, which they
scarcely understand any more, still a genuine borderline? It always
seems to me that in talking thus we are only seeking frantically to
make room for God. I should like to speak of God not on the borders
of life but at its centre, not in weakness but in strength, not, therefore, in man's suffering and death but in his life and prosperity. On
the borders it seems to me better to hold our peace and leave the
problem unsolved. Belief in the Resurrection is not the solution of the
problem of death. The 'beyond' of God is not the beyond of our per-
ceptive faculties. God is the 'beyond' in the midst of our life. The
Church stands not where human powers give out, on the borders, but
in the centre of the village.

Weizacker's book on the world of physics is still keeping me busy. It has brought home to me how wrong it is to use God as a stop-gap for the incompleteness of our knowledge. For the frontiers of knowledge are inevitably being pushed back further and further, which means that you only think of God as a stop-gap. He also is being pushed back further and further, and is in more or less continuous retreat. We should find God in what we do know, not in what we don't; not in outstanding problems, but in those we have already solved. This is true not only for the relation between Christianity and science, but also for wider human problems such as guilt, suffering and death. It is possible nowadays to find answers to these problems which leave God right out of the picture. It just isn't true to say that Christianity alone has the answers. In fact the Christian answers are no more conclusive or compelling than any of the others. Once more, God cannot be used as a stop-gap. We must not wait until we are at the end of our tether: he must be found at the centre of life: in life, and not only in death; in health and vigour, and not only in suffering; in activity, and not only in sin. The ground for this lies in the revelation of God in Christ. Christ is the centre of life, and in no sense did he come to answer our unsolved problems.

When Jesus blessed sinners, they were real sinners, but Jesus did not make every man a sinner first. He called them out of their sin, not into their sin. Of course encounter with Jesus meant the reversal of all human values. So it was in the conversion of St. Paul, though in his case the knowledge of sin preceded his encounter with Jesus. Of course Jesus took to himself the dregs of human society, harlots and publicans, but never them alone, for he sought to take to himself man as such. Never did Jesus throw any doubt on a man's health, vigour or fortune, regarded in themselves, or look upon them as evil fruits. Else why did he heal the sick and restore strength to the weak? Jesus claims for himself and the kingdom of God the whole of human life in all its manifestations.

Our coming of age forces us to a true recognition of our situation vis-à-vis God. God is teaching us that we must live as men who can get along very well without him. The God who is with us is the God who forsakes us (Mark 15 : 34). The God who makes us live in this world without using him as a working hypothesis is the God before whom we are ever standing. Before God and with him we live without God. God allows himself to be edged out of the world and on to the cross. God is weak and powerless in the world, and that is exactly the way, the only way, in which he can be with us and help us. Matthew 8 : 17 makes it crystal clear that it is not by his omnipotence that Christ helps us, but by his weakness and suffering.

This is the decisive difference between Christianity and all religions. Man's religiosity makes him look in his distress to the power of God in the world; he uses God as a *Deus ex machina*. The Bible however directs him to the powerlessness and suffering of God; only a suffering God can help. To this extent we may say that the process we have described by which the world came of age was an abandonment of a false conception of God, and a clearing of the decks for the God of the Bible, who conquers power and space in the world by his weakness. This must be the starting point for our 'world' interpretation.

Jesus asked in Gethsemane, 'Could ye not watch with me one hour?' That is the exact opposite of what the religious man expects from God. Man is challenged to participate in the sufferings of God at the hands of a godless world.

He must therefore plunge himself into the life of a godless world, without attempting to gloss over its ungodliness with a veneer of religion or trying to transfigure it. He must live a 'Worldly' life and so participate in the suffering of God. He *may* live a worldly life as one emancipated from all false religions and obligations. To be a Christian does not mean to be religious in a particular way, to cultivate some particular form of asceticism (as a sinner, a penitent or a saint), but to be a man. It is not some religious act which makes a Christian what he is, but participation in the suffering of God in the life of the world.

This is metanoia. It is not in the first instance bothering about one's own needs, problems, sins, and fears, but allowing oneself to be caught up in the way of Christ, into the Messianic event, and thus fulfilling Isaiah 53. Therefore, 'Believe in the Gospel', or in the words of St. John the Baptist, 'Behold the lamb of God that taketh away the sin of the world'. (By the way, Jeremias has recently suggested that in Aramaic the word for 'lamb' could also mean 'servant'—very appropriate, in view of Isaiah 53). This being caught up into the Messianic suffering of God in Jesus Christ takes a variety of forms in the New Testament. It appears in the call of discipleship, in Jesus' table fellowship with sinners, in conversions in the narrower sense of the word (e.g. Zacchaeus), in the act of the woman who was a sinner (Luke 7), an act which she performed without any specific confession of sin, in the healing of the sick (Matthew 8 : 17, see above), in Jesus' acceptance of the children. The shepherds, like the wise men from the east, stand at the crib, not as converted sinners, but because they were drawn to the crib by the star just as they were. The centurion of Capernaum (who does not make any confession of sin) is held up by Jesus as a model of faith (cf. Jairus). Jesus loves the rich young man. Finally, Joseph of Arimathaea and the women at the tomb. All that is common between them is their participation in the suffering of God in Christ. That is their faith. There is nothing of religious asceticism here. The religious act is always something partial, faith is always something whole, an act involving the whole life. Jesus does not call men to a new religion, but to life. What is the nature of that life, that participation in the powerlessness of God in the world?

DIETRICH BONHOEFFER, *Letters from Prison and other Papers*

The response of His contemporaries

Here are two selections of extracts from the New Testament, 54 and 56, together with an extract from a novel, 55.

54. Friends and followers

The purpose of the first selection of extracts is to illustrate the impression which the things which Jesus said and did made upon the people who met him in his life time, and their reactions to his influence.

(1) Mark 1 : 16–20

And as he was walking by the sea of Galilee he saw Simon and Andrew, Simon's brother, making casts with their nets, for they were fishermen. And Jesus called to them 'Come and join me! I'll teach you how to catch men.' And immediately they dropped their nets and went after him. He went a little further on, and saw James, son of Zebedee, and his brother John who were also in their boat mending their nets; and immediately he called them. And leaving their father Zebedee in the boat with the paid crew, they went after him.

What do you suppose the neighbours said when these men chucked up a nice little fishing business, with a good local connection, and, in the latter case let the old man down as well, in order to go off with this wandering preacher? Probably it wasn't quite as sudden as it sounds (cf. vv. 14–15). But when he did ask them, what do you think made them drop everything and go?

(2) Matthew 5 : 21–2, 27–8, 33–7, 38–9, 43–4

You know what our fathers were told, 'Do not commit murder; anyone who commits murder must be brought to judgement'. But I say to you that anyone who nurses anger against his brother will come under judgement.

You know that they were told, 'Do not commit adultery'. But what I tell you is that anyone who eyes a woman lustfully has committed adultery with her already in his heart.

You know that they were told, 'Do not break your oath', 'Oaths sworn to the Lord must be kept'. But I tell you not to swear at all . . . plain 'Yes' or 'No' is quite enough.

You know that they were told, 'An eye for an eye, and a tooth for a tooth'. But what I tell you is, Don't pay back evil in kind. If a man slaps you on the right cheek, turn and offer him the left as well.

You know that they were told, 'Love your neighbour, hate your enemy'. But what I tell you is, Love your enemies, and pray for those who set upon you.

Imagine what it felt like to hear the sacred tradition, on which the whole religious life of the nation had been based for generations, quietly turned inside-out if not upside down like this by an ordinary layman. What would be a parallel in Church life today?

(3) Luke 7 : 1–10

There was a centurion whose servant, whom he greatly valued, was ill and near to death. He heard about Jesus; so he sent some Jewish elders with the request that he would come and save his servant's life. They approached Jesus and put in an urgent plea : 'He really deserves that you should help him in this way; he is a good friend to our nation, and he actually built a synagogue for us.' Jesus went with them; but when he was already quite near the house the centurion sent some of his friends with this message : 'Don't put yourself out, Sir; it's not for me to have you under my roof; just say the word, and my servant will be cured. For I too know what authority means, both as a subordinate, and in command. . . .'

Note particularly the centurion's remark in v.8. 'I *too* am a man who knows what authority means, both as a subordinate and in command.' What had he noticed in Jesus which prompted this comment?

(4) Luke 19 : 1–10

He entered Jericho and made his way through the town. There was a man there whose name was Zacchaeus; he was superintendent of taxes, and he had done very well out of it. He was eager to see what sort of man this Jesus was, but being a little man he couldn't get a look at him for the crowd. So he ran on ahead and climbed a sycamore tree from which to see him, because he was going to pass it. And when he reached the spot Jesus looked up and said, 'Zacchaeus, hurry up and come down; I want to stay with you today.' He climbed down as fast as he could and welcomed him with delight. Everybody began to murmur in disapproval. 'Fancy going to stay with a spiv like that,' they said. Zacchaeus stood his ground, and said to the Lord, 'Look, Sir, I'll give half my possessions to the poor; and if I've cheated anyone, I will repay four times over.'

What made Zacchaeus suddenly take this quixotic decision? What sort of reception do you think he got when he went round repaying fourfold? What do you think happened to him and his business?

(5) Mark 10 : 35–40

James and John, the sons of Zebedee, approached him and said, 'Master we want you to grant us a request.' 'What is it that you want?' he asked. They answered, 'Promise us the right to hold the positions of honour, one on your right, and the other on your left.' Jesus said to them, 'You don't know what you are asking. Can you drink the cup that I have to drink, or undergo the baptism that I have to face?' 'Certainly we can,' they answered. And Jesus said to them, 'Very well, you shall drink my cup and share my baptism; but sitting on my right hand and my left hand is not a favour that is in my power to bestow.'

'Master we want you to promise us whatever we ask.' What was wrong with this request? (cf. Matthew 7 : 7–8). 'Can you drink the cup that I have got to drink?' When, a few days later, they were handed a cup with the words, 'Drink this; this is the Cup of the Covenant sealed in my blood', do you think they remembered their confident reply, and began to wonder what they had let themselves in for?

(6) Matthew 26 : 14–16, and Matthew 27 : 3–4

Then one of the twelve, the man called Judas Iscariot, went off to the chief priests and said to them, 'What are you prepared to pay me for betraying him to you?' And they agreed to give him thirty pieces of silver. And from that moment he began to look out for a good opportunity to betray him.

When Judas the traitor realized that Jesus had been condemned he was over-come with remorse and returned the money to the chief priests and elders. 'I have done a dreadful thing,' he said. 'I have brought an innocent man to his death.' But they only said, 'What concern of ours is that? That's your business.'

How do you explain the treachery of Judas? Does ch.27, v.3 throw any light on his motive? Had he not meant, or expected, Jesus to be condemned? What had he hoped to achieve by bringing the conflict with the authorities to a head? Do you think he had ever really under-stood or loved Jesus? It is just possible that the Greek should be trans-lated 'I have made a terrible mistake.'

F. A. COCKIN

55. A television interview with Pilate

Number Two camera came in for a close-up. I looked steadily into the lens and forced myself to relax.

'Early yesterday morning something happened at the tomb of Jesus Davidson. Just exactly what has been difficult to determine, but there was a disturbance of some kind and the Jewish Army guard was badly rattled. The immediate result of this disturbance—whatever it was—has been a widespread and persistent rumour that the dead man is somehow alive again. . . . Anyone who witnessed Friday's execution and the subsequent burial of Davidson's body will find this hard to believe. But there is no doubt that something very strange is going on. We were privileged to obtain a filmed interview with the Governor-General. . . .'

'Lord Pilate,' I said, 'would you care to make a comment on this new crisis?'

He responded immediately to the title. Relaxed and smiling, he radiated confidence. 'Certainly, Mr Tennel. But it's not a crisis, you know. Nothing like one. Everything is under control.'

'That's good to know, sir. But there is this rumour about Jesus Davidson. . . .'

He came down quickly on that. 'Davidson's dead. Dead and buried. I can see no point in discussing him now.'

But I was not to be warned off quite so easily. 'The rumour is, sir, that he's alive again.'

His smile altered subtly, becoming of amused tolerance. 'Alive again? Oh, come now, Mr Tennel, really you know....'

'Still alive then, put it that way.'

He leaned forward, clasping his hands on the table, his face suddenly grave. 'Mr Tennel, he was executed by soldiers of the Tenth Legion. They're not amateurs, you know. When they kill a man, he's dead and stays dead.'

'I quite agree. On the other hand, the rumour is very persistent.'

'But of course,'—and back came the smile, dead on schedule—'this is Jerusalem, my dear chap. We thrive on rumour here. But when you've lived here as long as I have you'll not worry your head about bazaar gossip.'

I nodded encouragingly. Not that he needed encouraging.

'And what is your view of the incident at the tomb this morning, sir?'

Predictably he raised his eyebrows. 'I'm afraid I don't quite follow you, Mr Tennel.'

'The earthquake and so on.'

'Oh, that.' There was the smile again, tinted now with polite disinterest. 'I believe there was a slight tremor just before dawn. It's the season for them, of course.'

'They say it was quite a big one.'

'Do they indeed? I didn't feel it myself.'

'Sleeping the sleep of the just, I'm sure, sir.'

It was the first prick of the knife and he didn't like it. His eyes were wary. I hoped Greg [the camera-man] had him in close-up.

'Er—quite so,' he said, and his voice was far from happy.

I decided to press a little harder. 'Still, it was big enough to burst open the tomb, I believe.'

'Oh really? How very unpleasant.'

It was beautifully done, with exactly the right inflection. I switched. 'Would you care to comment on the behaviour of the guard?'

He shrugged. 'It was unfortunate. Not our chaps, of course. Jewish Army. Good lads, all of them. But a little—well, inexperienced.'

I said, 'You mean they panicked?'

'Shall we say there was some confusion?'

'Lord Pilate, why was it necessary to mount guard over a dead man?'

'I'm afraid the answer is rather complicated. A matter of religion largely.'

'Oh?'

He nodded. 'Jewish religion.'

'But how does religion come into it? I thought Jesus Davidson was a political prisoner, executed for high treason?'

'Indeed he was. He claimed to be the king of the Jews. That was his big mistake. It made him a direct threat to the security of the State. I gave him all the help I could. Bent over backwards to give him a chance to clear himself. But it was no use. In the end I had no choice but to sign the execution order.'

Watching him leaning forward, gazing earnestly into the camera, I saw him as he saw himself—the conscientious, human administrator struggling, in a difficult situation, to give every man a fair hearing and dispense justice with mercy. And then I looked at his eyes and the splendid image blurred.

I said, 'And the religious angle, sir?'

'Well, he claimed to be not only a king but also—well—God.'

'I see.'

'Very embarrassing for everyone concerned. Especially His Grace the High Priest.'

'Lord Caiaphas?'

He nodded. 'A very distasteful business for him, as you will appreciate.'

So that's how it was, I thought. The Church versus the State. Caiaphas holding a pistol to Pilate's head and young Davidson done to death to save the Roman's face.

'You say he claimed to be God?'

'Yes,' Pilate said, and smiled. 'Hence the guard.'

'I'm sorry to be stupid, but why, "hence the guard"?'

'It's fairly obvious, surely? The High Priest insisted on it. You see, Mr Tennel, killing a man is one thing; killing God is something else again. You've no guarantee that he will stay dead. So you must guard his tomb.'

'And come down hard on rumours of a resurrection?'

'Exactly.' He was smiling broadly now, man to man and no nonsense.

'Sir,' I said quietly, controlling the disgust in my voice, 'what did you think of Jesus Davidson?'

The smile disappeared abruptly. 'I was sorry for him,' he said. 'Good material, but unbalanced.'

'You think he was insane?'

He shook his head. 'I wouldn't go so far as to say that. But there was something strange about him—a sort of fatalism—a remoteness. He made no attempt to defend himself, you see. I tried to get him to understand the seriousness of the position, but he seemed oddly unconcerned. Just stood there and looked at me and said nothing.'

'I expect he was afraid.'

'No, he wasn't afraid. It would have been easier if he had been. More normal, anyway. But he wasn't. Just tired and—and remote. As if he had already come to the end of his journey and the trial and execution were unimportant details—the mechanics of closing the door and lying down to sleep. When he looked at me I had the curious feeling that he was sorry.'

'For what he had done?'

'No,' he said miserably. 'For me.'

'It was quite absurd,' he said, and his voice which until now had been deep was suddenly just a little shrill. 'He didn't seem to realize that he was completely in my power. That I had only to speak and he was a dead man.' He leaned forward, his face drawn and pale. 'I had no choice, Mr Tennel. I did everything I could for him.'

This was the real man at last, without the actor's mask; the bewildered boy inside the public image.

'It's not an easy thing to condemn a man to death,' he said heavily.

Especially when he's young, I thought, and you know he's innocent.

'The good of the State must come first, Mr Tennel. Whatever the cost. I hope people will realise how dangerous the situation was. Without firm action we might well have been in serious trouble by now.'

'So now everything's back to normal.'

'Oh yes,' he said, relaxing.

'There is this rumour, sir, all the same.'

'Rumours are not important, Mr Tennel. Only facts. And the fact is that Davidson is dead.'

'You think we've heard the last of him?'

'I do.' He did his best to sound confident, but I was satisfied that his words would convince nobody.

'Well, thank you, Lord Pilate. You've been most helpful.'

He looked over my shoulder at the camera and assumed his vice-regal expression—bland authority based on an understanding of the common man. 'It's been a pleasure, Mr Tennel.'

I took my cue and turned to Number One camera. 'That's the Governor General's view of the situation. Everything is normal. There is no cause for alarm. Davidson is dead and the crisis over. These are reassuring words and everyone here would like to believe them. But the fact remains that Davidson's body has disappeared. The tomb, so carefully sealed and guarded, is empty. . . .'

STUART JACKMAN, *The Davidson Affair*

Look up the passages in the Gospels (Matthew, 27 : 1, 2, 11–26; Mark, 15 : 1–15; Luke, 23 : 1–25; John, 18 : 29–19 : 16) where Pilate's interviews with Jesus are recorded, and compare your impression of these with that conveyed in the passage given above. Is the latter a fair transcription? What qualities in Jesus do you think really made an impression on Pilate, and why? How do you account for Jesus' attitude during the interviews? Why the silence (and before Herod too—Luke, 23 : 7–11) and his refusal to defend or explain himself?

56. The first Christian community

The purpose of this second group of New Testament extracts is to illustrate a rather different type of impression made by the life and death of Jesus upon the first Christian community. While it is of course true that the Synoptic Gospels were themselves compiled from a post-Resurrection point of view, this second group of passages represents a rather more developed stage of reflection on the significance of the events which the Gospels record.

(1) Why is it that the Gospels devote what would appear to be a disproportionate amount of space to the story of the Passion? (Work this out by reference to the text.) These chapters record the ignominious failure of the mission of Jesus to his nation, and the shameful behaviour of most of his followers under the impact of that disaster. Why did they record this in such detail?

(2) Consider side by side Mark 14 : 66–71 and Acts 4 : 13–20:

Mark 14: 66–71. Peter was downstairs in the hall. One of the maidservants of the High Priest came by, and seeing Peter warming himself looked closely at him; 'Why,' she said, 'you too were there with this man from Nazareth, this Jesus.' But he denied it. 'I know nothing,' he said. 'I don't understand what you are talking about.' Then he slipped out into the porch. The maid saw him there again, and began to say to the bystanders, 'He *is* one of them.' And again he denied it.

Again a little later, the bystanders said to Peter, 'Surely you are one of that gang; you must be, you're a Galileean.' At that he broke out into curses, and swore, 'I don't even know this man you're speaking of.'

Acts 4: 13–20. Now as they observed the boldness of Peter and John, and noted that they were untrained laymen, they were astonished; and then they recognised that they were men who had been companions of Jesus. . . .

(v. 18). So they called them in again, and ordered them flatly to abstain from any further speaking and preaching in the name of Jesus. And Peter and John answered them back: 'If the question you're raising is whether it is right in the sight of God for us to listen to you rather than to God, you can answer that one for yourselves. For we can't help telling what we've seen and heard.'

(and you can hear them add, 'and put that in your pipe and smoke it' !) How do you account for the change in Peter's behaviour?

(3) Consider side by side Acts 9 : 1–2 and Gal. 2 : 20:

Acts 9: 1–2. But Saul, still breathing murderous threats against the disciples of the Lord, went to the High Priest and applied for written orders to the synagogues in Damascus, authorising him to arrest anyone he found, man or woman, following the new way, and bring them back to Jerusalem.

Gal. 2 : 20. I have been crucified with Christ. The life that I now live is not my own, but the life which Christ lives in me. My present bodily life is a life of trusting in the Son of God who loved me and gave his life for me.

Again, how do you account for the change?

(4) Gal. 3 : 26, 28; Col. 3 : 9–11 :

Gal. 3 : 26, 28. Through faith you are all sons of God in union with Christ Jesus. There is no such thing as Jew and Greek, slave and freeman, male and female; for you are all one person in Christ Jesus.

Col. 3 : 9–11. You have discarded the old nature with its characteristic ways of behaving, and have put on the new nature, which is constantly being renewed in the likeness of its Creator and brought to know God. There is no question here of Jew or Greek, circumcized or uncircumcized, barbarian, Scythian, free-man or slave; Christ is all and in all.

As a boy Paul would have been taught the prayer said by every devout Jew : 'God I thank thee that I was born not a Gentile but a Jew : not a slave but a freeman : not a woman but a man.' Here he is deliberately *unlearning* that prayer. And he says that it is '*in Christ*' that he has come to see this new truth about human relationships. What do you think he means by this?

(5) John 1 : 1–14 :

The Word (purpose : reason) existed in the beginning, in the mind of God, sharing the very nature of God; the Word was with God in the beginning. It was through this agency that all things were created; apart from that no single thing was created. All that came to be alive was alive with the life of the Word, and that life was the light of men. The light shines on in the dark, and the darkness has never mastered it. . . .

(v. 14). So the Word was embodied in a human life, and came to dwell among us; and we beheld his glory.

It is almost impossible to decide on the right translation of the Greek, for there is no single equivalent word for Logos. It is not even certain whether we should say 'he' or 'it'. But clearly what John is doing is to rewrite the Creation story (cf. Gen. 1 : 1–3). His readers, if they were Jews, would be familiar with the idea that it was through his 'word' that God created ('And God *said*, "Let there be light" '); if they were Greek they would be familiar with the idea of Creative 'reason'. The two ideas fuse here since 'speech' is the externalization of inner 'reason' or 'purpose', which makes it communicable.

But John adds the wholly new idea that in the human life of Jesus the true nature of this creative word has been embodied; this life is seen to be the purpose of creation—what it was meant to attain to as its goal.

Is it possible to interpret evolutionary theory in a way which reflects this line of thought?

F. A. COCKIN

The household of God

The study of the Church is probably the subject which we approach with less enthusiasm than almost any other aspect of the Christian faith presented in this book. The second section 'What's wrong with the Church?' we might well tackle with more gusto; for nothing is easier than to point to the obvious shortcomings which we can discern either in the local set-up as we know it in parish or congregation, or on the wider scale as we think of some of the glaring failures of the Church throughout the course of Christian history.

But before we embark on that fairly straightforward exercise it is worth asking ourselves the question: How do we know what are the things in the life of the Church which *deserve* criticism? From where do we derive our picture of what the Church *ought to be—and isn't*?

And that may well open up a range of pretty far-reaching questions which call for some attention. Some of these will require investigation in the light of what the New Testament has to say. For example: is a Church necessary at all? Did Jesus mean to establish a continuing institution to carry on his work? What evidence have we of the aims and experiments of those who stood nearest to his original ministry and believed themselves to be implementing his intention? What did they mean by the kind of phrases they used: 'The household of faith', 'the pillar and ground of the truth,' 'a fellowship (community) of the Holy Spirit'? Have we, over the centuries, just lost sight of these basic characteristics; or do they still, though often overlaid with lumber and distortions, act as a leaven in Church life today?

The passages that follow, in addition to giving some further pointers to the answering of these questions, take the discussion further and pose additional questions. The first, 57, defines three main characteristics exemplified by the historical Churches; of the remaining four passages, 58 and 59 try to pinpoint the fundamental function of the Christian community, and 60 and 61 to show how the fulfilling of this function and the continuing life of that community depend primarily not on its members but on the presence of the Holy Spirit. Do you agree that these are the marks of what the Church should be? Has anything important been omitted? What bearing has all this on the division of the Churches and the steps being taken towards unity?

57. What is the Church?

If we agree that the Church on earth is the visible body of those whom God has called into the fellowship of His Son, we have to ask—where is that body to be found? We know where it was on the day of Pentecost. It was there in Jerusalem. But where is it today? By what signs or works can a body rightly claim today to be the Church of God? We are all agreed that the Church is constituted by God's atoning acts in Christ Jesus—His incarnation, life, death, resurrection, ascension, His session at God's right hand and the gift of the Spirit. But how are we of the subsequent generations made participants in that atonement? What is the manner of our ingrafting into Christ? That is the real question with which we have to deal.

I think that there are three main answers to these questions, and these answers are embodied in great Christian communions which claim to be the Church.

The first answer is, briefly, that we are incorporated in Christ by hearing and believing the Gospel. The second is that we are incorporated by sacramental participation in the life of the historically continuous Church. The third is that we are incorporated by receiving and abiding in the Holy Spirit.

The moment one has stated these three positions in this bald way, it is at once apparent that they are far from being mutually exclusive, that very few Christians would deny the truth of any of them and that there is an infinite variety of combinations of and approximations to these three positions. Nevertheless I think that we can best approach our problem by isolating these three positions. Classical Protestantism, especially in its Lutheran form, of course ascribes an immense value to the sacraments. But the major emphasis is on faith, and faith comes by hearing, and therefore the pulpit dominates the rest of the ecclesiastical furniture. It also knows and speaks of the work of the Holy Spirit, but does so with reserve. It is shy of enthusiasm, and is reluctant to give a large place to the claims of 'spiritual experience'. Catholicism honours preaching and acknowledges the necessity of faith, but it finds the centre of religious life rather in the sacrament than in the sermon. It acknowledges a real operation of the Holy Spirit sanctifying the believer, but gives the decisive place rather to the continuous sacramental order of the Church. The third type—for which it is difficult to find a single inclusive name—acknowledges and values preaching and the sacraments, but judges them by their experienced effects, and is not interested in the question of historical continuity. All these three answers to the question can obviously make effective appeal to Scripture in support of the truth for which they contend.

LESSLIE NEWBIGIN, *The Household of God*

58. The Church, the Body of Christ

Where would you expect to find the body of Christ, and what would you expect to find it doing?

For the greater part of His life, Jesus lived as a working man; He was apprenticed in a joiner's yard and, it may be inferred, became on Joseph's death the breadwinner for a household of at least eight persons. For the greater part of His life, the body of Christ was exercised in the common processes of industry. Do you think He was out to make a fortune in those years? Do you think slipshod work came out of that shop—badly mortised joints or flaws filled in with putty? Do you think that his apprentices were overworked or underpaid? Do you think that He treated them as impersonal 'hands'? The Church is called to be the Body of Christ in industry. The term 'Church worker' is apt to call up a picture of the Sunday-school teacher or the collector for Foreign Missions, and no one who knows the Church from the inside will slight their important services; but there is a kind of Church worker for whom our age even more urgently calls, and on whom the life and example of Christ set more immediately the seal of discipleship—the man who, to the glory of God and for the good of his fellows, does honest work of the everyday sort; the man who, in the context of that work, is being delivered, reach after reach, from the deep egotism of human nature . . .; the man behind the counter, or at the loom, or in the manager's office, or on the University bench or rostrum, who sees his daily life, and lives it, not as a drudgery, still less as a fight for his own advantage, but as a devotion, a thing offered, his contribution to God's plan of building a wholesome communal life upon the earth. These are the lives which all along have kept society sane and sweet, or rather—alas for human nature!—have kept it from lapsing altogether into savagery; these are Christ's Church on one great and permanent level of its manifold life; these are members of the Body of the Carpenter of Nazareth.

A. C. CRAIG, in *A Diary of Readings*

59. The Church is people

The Church cannot be contained in buildings or confined to institutions. It is something both simpler and more mysterious, more indefinite and yet more comprehensible to men, it is the Body of Christ, the whole body of his people. It is God who builds the Church and its stones are men and women. The action of God in creating the Church is as mysterious and as basic to the Faith and as much an article of faith as his action in the Creation of the world and in the coming of

Jesus Christ. And the nature and purpose of the Church cannot be different from God's purpose in the Creation and Incarnation. Just as the Bible declares that this mess of a world, with all the cruelty and injustice that the Old Testament knew so well, is created by God and sings his praise; just as he comes to us in one who was born of a woman, was tempted in all points like as we are, and died as a criminal on a Cross and is yet the King of Glory, risen and ascended: so the Church is made up of ordinary men and women, yet is, by God's action, his Son's Body on earth, living his life, doing his will, knowing his glory. And, as his body, it is here in the world to be the instrument of God's purpose for the world.

Buildings, clergy, theological colleges and social responsibility with, as the other side of the coin, social respectability are all things that we take for granted for the Church. We cannot conceive of the Church existing without them. If we did not have to raise money to build new buildings and to maintain old ones, if we did not have to train and maintain the clergy and undertake social service in our own country and elsewhere, what would members of the Church do? What did the early Church do when it did not have to trouble about these things? It converted the Roman Empire.

Of course, we need these things in some form. An organization cannot exist without some kind of structure. The Church, no less than the family, needs some kind of institution. But it can be of the flimsiest. The Church—and the family—can do without a building. The Church —and the family—can live in tents: can be on the move. The Church —and the family—can exist without its official leaders. A family still exists when the parents are dead. The Church—and the family—can be outcast and outlawed. The only thing without which the Church— and the family—cannot survive is a way of life, a bond of affection, expressed in custom, tradition and ceremony, which for the Church comes from the life that Jesus lived with men. But, though it needs some structure, the Church, like the family, is not primarily an institution. It is essentially people living a life together: the people of God living the life of Christ.

This conception of the Church is the only one in evidence in the first three centuries of its history. It is to be seen also in the way in which its enemies and outsiders generally refer to the Church—as 'these men' (Acts 5:35), 'unlearned and ignorant men' (Acts 4:13), 'any of this way, whether they were men or women' (Acts 9:2), 'Christians' (Acts 11:26). They use names that apply to people and not to institutions.

We see this also in the way in which they spoke of themselves— 'they that believed', the New Israel, those whom God was building into his new house for the world. If they had thought of themselves as a company apart from and unconcerned with other men they would more easily have adopted the language of an institution. But they did not so regard themselves. They knew that they belonged to the ordering of a new world. They believed that all men belonged, in the purpose of God, to this new order and therefore to their company, because Jesus was Lord of all and had died for all and had broken down the walls of partition. This conviction of belonging to the one body to which all people must belong, even as rebels, was the spring of their mission and the reason why they were persecuted.

We in the countries of the west have never known a Church like this. It is good for us to remember that this was what the Church was like in the beginning and is in essence. By the providence of God its picture is enshrined for us for ever in the New Testament: to remind us that however necessary institutional structures may be, the Church is not primarily an institution but people, by the grace of God, living the life that is in Christ.

RALPH MORTON and MARK GIBBS, *God's Frozen People*

60. 'Where two or three are gathered together . . .'

Some years ago a little company of Russian peasants met for worship, knowing full well that their gathering was illegal, and that if they were discovered they would be haled before the dread tribunal and would be liable to incur the ruthless penalty of the law. While their worship was proceeding, suddenly the door was flung open, and there entered an agent of the secret police, followed by a body of his men. 'Take these people's names,' he commanded; and the names were written down, thirty of them. They were warned to wait their summons, and then the agent turned to go. But one old man in the little group stopped him at the door and said, 'There is one name you have not got.' The officer looked at him in surprise. 'I assure you that you are mistaken,' he retorted; 'I have them all!' 'Believe me,' said the old peasant, 'there is one name you have not got.' 'Well, we'll prove it,' exclaimed the agent impatiently; 'we'll count again!' And they did—verified every name they had taken, and recounted the number. There were thirty. 'You see?' cried the official of police. 'I have them all, every one. I told you I had!' But still the peasant persisted. 'There is one name you have not got.' 'Who is it, then?' demanded the other. 'Speak out—who is it?' 'The Lord Jesus Christ,' was the answer. 'He is here!' 'Ah,' sneered the officer, 'that is a different matter.' These pestilential Christians, wasting his precious time with their trumped-up story, a senseless, maudlin sham! But that old peasant was right.

Jesus, in point of fact, was there. 'Where two or three are gathered together in My name, there am I in the midst.' And it is the Holy Ghost alone who does that.

JAMES S. STEWART, *The Strong Name*

61. The Spirit

To the unenlightened eye the career of Jesus of Nazareth is something belonging to the remote past, long, long ago buried beneath the advancing avalanche of events, and becoming remoter every year. Before the arrival of the Industrial Revolution, before the Reformation, before the Renaissance, before the Middle Ages and the Dark Ages, at the very beginning of the history of the Roman Empire, in a culture, a climate of opinion, a society utterly distant and utterly different from ours, this career took place. To a modern semi-educated reader of the popular press even events that happened as recently as a century ago seem unreal and remote, part of a confused jumble of dates and events which he classes as Ancient History, and regards as wholly irrelevant to life today; how inconceivably shadowy and unreal must events which took place in A.D. 30 seem to him. Yet through the power of the Holy Spirit these almost immeasurably distant events become present and effective for us. The Holy Spirit is the Spirit of the perennially present God, who because he is life-giving Spirit overcomes the limitations of time and matter.

A celebrated French satirical writer of the last century wrote a short story in which he imagined Pontius Pilate at the very end of his life being asked by a friend whether he could remember anything of a Galileean peasant called Jesus whom he had met when he was Governor of Judaea. 'What did you say was the name?' the old man answers: 'Jesus?—no I don't recall the man at all.'

Nineteen centuries of Christian history have at least shown that we cannot, like the imaginary Pilate, completely ignore Jesus. But the story may serve to remind us that it is possible to take a variety of views of the significance of that life which differ widely from that which lies at the heart of Christian faith.

To the ordinary man it probably remains something vaguely sentimental and noble about which he learnt in Sunday School, but which has never had any real bearing on his adult life. To the psychologist the story of the Cross is perhaps a projection into the form of sacred legend of a fundamental need of the human mind for some solution of the problem of guilt. To the anthropologist it could be interesting as an instance of man's capacity to weave such sacred legends into the fabric of his culture or civilization; but that would not of course make it true: it would only be a relic of a pre-scientific stage, and as such obsolete and negligible. To the Marxist the Cross is one of the more notable illustrations of the power of a ruling class to use its political and economic strength to suppress the claims of the oppressed.

What is it which causes men to see in the story of the Crucifixion none of these things, but instead to regard this shameful and embarrassing event as in fact 'God commending his own love to us'? The answer which the New Testament gives is that we see this truth because 'we have the witness of the Spirit'. When we have that we see not only what God was doing in this act, but what he continually does. The Spirit makes the life of Christ contemporary, compelling us to see in an event, so apparently trivial that Pilate could have forgotten all about it, something of universal significance, relevant to every single human being. The primary activity of the Spirit is 'Illumination'. Through him alone can Christianity become 'of infinite personal concern' for us.

R. P. C. H A N S O N, God, Creator, Saviour, Spirit (adapted)

What's wrong with the Church?

The passages in this section should provide their own questions and ample material for discussion. It is worth bearing in mind the more general question, 'What criteria are the authors using to criticize the Church?' If they are not merely expressing personal prejudices, what more objective basis do their criticisms rest upon? They represent many different Church traditions—Monica Furlong is an Anglican, Ralph Morton a Presbyterian, Mark Gibbs, 'Stewart' and Stephen Verney are Anglicans, Christopher Driver and Stuart Jackman are Congregationalists, and Michael Novak a Roman Catholic. Remember that each is criticizing the Church *from the inside*.

62. With love to the Church

The Church stands to witness to the truth, even when the truth brings it no personal advantage. Where is the recognition—a recognition desperately needed in contemporary life—that 'good publicity' represents as wrong a distortion of the truth as the other kind?

The only publicity Christians are allowed is the kind that comes from love and goodness being practised out of deep conviction.

The fruits of the spirit—the hallmarks of a man who has committed himself to being a Christian—are love, joy, peace, longsuffering, gentleness, goodness, faith, meekness, temperance. It follows from this—to anyone who knows the world of publicity—that Christians who live in obedience are almost never going to make the headlines, become television personalities, or have a good public image, because to do these things it is necessary to permit a tampering with the truth of one's own personality.

What if we busy ourselves instead with the proper preoccupation of Christians—the love of God and the love of our neighbour? Much of the time we shall be ridiculed, or (much more painfully) ignored as being outside the circle of people who matter, and outside the arena where the important work goes on. But whether we are truly out of the arena depends upon ourselves, upon whether we are equipped with the knowledge, the insight and the love to say anything relevant to the condition of the world. It is part of our conviction that truth makes itself heard. That the words of a Bonhoeffer, smuggled out of a Nazi prison, hacked out of his own conflict and agony, can reach and change a whole generation of Christians. That the words of a Fr.

Huddleston or an Archbishop de Blank, obstinately proclaiming love and equality in Christ, can reach the conscience of the world without the help, initially, of a vast publicity machine. The Church, of all institutions, must believe in the simplicity of love and truth and their ability to make their way against all obstacles, even against the obstacles of death and destruction. This is our gospel.

If we cannot live by love and forgiveness then the Christian is mistaken in thinking that the life of Christ was a revelation of God, and individuals like myself are mistaken in supposing that when they received a personal revelation of love and forgiveness they were experiencing God.

But I am not disillusioned to the point of believing that I was deluded, nor that the Church's central teaching has been wrong all these years. I believe, on the contrary, that on that afternoon fourteen years ago,[1] I saw reality more clearly than I had seen it before or since. I believe that the Church at its best has called men back time and again from the unrealities of power, of hate, of lies, of cruelty, of fame, of wealth, and reminded them that love is the way, the truth, and the life.

How can it achieve this once more? The most urgent of her priorities should be a turning outwards, away from the petty quarrels and worries which trouble her parishes and her assemblies, to look upon the world with joy and hope and pity and love. 'So God loved the world', the priest rattles off in the Communion service, 'that he gave his only-begotten Son. . . .' God loved the world, but Christians seem unable to offer it anything but criticism and contempt.

It was no accident that it was Bonhoeffer who explored the relevance of Christianity to a godless society. Deprived of his freedom and the right to work as a pastor, separated from friends and fellow-believers, confronted daily by brutality and himself the victim of it, it was not surprising that for him the old answers, even the old questions, made no sense. For the Christian in such circumstances the questions become very simple. What did Christ's death on the cross mean? Did he really triumph over evil or did evil triumph over him? Was there, is there a resurrection? Is it true that if we commit ourselves to love the gates of hell shall not prevail against us? Or is the life of a man a futile, meaningless, painful struggle in which the ruthless and the violent win every time?

The pain of the Christian vocation can be such that we do not often feel like asking these questions, and would much rather retreat into administration, respectability, good works, elaborate piety, or stern morality. But our contemporaries quite properly expect answers and are contemptuous of our attempts at escape. If we have lost our revela-

1. When the author was converted.

tion about love and meaning, then we are of no use to the world at all.
But if we can rediscover it, then we are at one with Christ, at one with
the Suffering Servant, in building up the old wastes, raising up the
former desolations, repairing the waste cities, the desolations of many
generations. Like the Suffering Servant we shall be permitted to bind
up the broken-hearted, to proclaim liberty to the captives and the
opening of the prison to them that are bound, to proclaim the acceptable year of the Lord.[1]

MONICA FURLONG, With Love to the Church

63. God's frozen people

The present life of the Church is not a full life. The members of the
Church as they participate in the life of the Church do not do so fully
as persons. In so far as the Church accepts them into its life and
activities it, as it were, expects them to leave part of their lives outside. And the part that is left outside is the part that is most worrying
—their life of business and politics. In the life of the Church they
participate not as full people but as those who perform certain functions. It is by their usefulness to the Church that they are valued.
They are office-bearers, or teachers in the Sunday School, or members
of the choir, or, at the very bottom, attenders or poor attenders. This
way of speech indicates how narrow is the common conception of the
life of the Church.

Another way of saying it is to say that the life of the Church is not
adult, for what is excluded are the concerns of adult life. There has
been, since the Second World War, a considerable widening of the
range of topics that can be discussed in Church organizations. But the
conviction that controversial topics should not be discussed is still
strong, and even stronger is the idea that the two topics that have no
place in the life of the Church are work and politics. But these, together with sex, are the main concerns of adult life. The Church is
certainly aware of sex, and in the main still deals with it by a conventional silence. Its treatment of work and politics has been that of unawareness. Men and women are, however, concerned in their daily
lives mainly with questions arising out of their jobs and with questions of their relationship with their neighbours, near and far. The
exclusion of industry and politics from the daily life of the Church is
the main reason why men and women engaged in these spheres are
the groups most conspicuous for their absence from the Church today.

So the life of the congregation is not a responsible life. It is not
training and exercising its members in Christian responsibility. Responsibility resides in making decisions and taking action. This is some-

1. Isaiah 61 : 1-2.

thing that a congregation is not accustomed to do except in some carefully regulated ecclesiastical affairs. Its duty is to attend, to listen, to be instructed. Today the Church begins to see that this is not enough. Opportunities are sought for the members of the congregation to ask questions, to study, to discuss. Such opportunities are limited and apt to be poorly supported. This is because they are purposeless. They are not expected to result in decision and action. Discussion must cover all points of view. It must be impartial. But decision is never impartial and action is only possible along one line at a time. Discussion can range from China to Peru and maintain the high-minded impartiality of the irresponsible. Responsibility involves the necessity of choosing one line of action, of committing oneself to it, of taking one's stand alongside other people. The life of the congregation does not train people to do this. Indeed it prevents people from doing this by suggesting that to have a Christian standpoint is enough and that the political duty of a Christian is confined to criticizing other people and, above all, questioning their motives.

It is, of course, not the place of the Church to make decisions on matters on which its members are not informed, nor to take action on all issues. It is its duty to see that its members are being trained and accustomed to making their own Christian decisions and taking their own actions in their own public and private lives. This it is not doing.

A great number of men feel that they cannot honestly be a 'proper Christian' at work and keep their jobs. They must keep their jobs— if only for the sake of their wives and families. So they assume that they just can't be 'proper' Christians; and since hypocrisy is, thank God, one of the most disliked attitudes among men today, they feel it much better not to pretend to be particularly Christian about their daily work. They would rather just be considered 'decent types' and leave it at that. To be a 'Christian', a 'religious type', would mean either becoming a hopelessly pious Bible-puncher, or pretending to some kind of 100 per cent perfectionism *which they know they can't achieve* as salesmen, as bus drivers, or even as school teachers.

Very many men and women in jobs won't consciously relate their faith to their jobs because they don't feel they're 'good enough'. This is a quite damnable and false idea of Christian perfectionism. A Christian is not a 100 per cent perfect human being, he is a sinner saved by the grace of God. He is not being pious or hypocritical if he tries to relate his loyalty to his Lord to his daily work: he is simply doing his plain duty. His sins of omission in trying to run his work and his religion in two separate compartments would be much more serious than anything else. Maybe he will make a mess of things, maybe sometimes he will let down his Lord by not protesting about some abuse or 'fiddle', maybe sometimes he will make a fool of himself and his

Church by protesting too much—but none of this will matter compared with the fact that he is at least struggling, with God's help, to live a consistent Christian life.

It was excellent to see that this point was a main feature of the Laity meetings of the World Council of Churches at New Delhi in November 1961. Miss Mollie Batten, principal of William Temple College, Rugby, said: 'Rarely will the choice be between good and evil. It will be a decision between alternatives, both of which are partly good and partly evil.' And she added, 'in so far as it is for the layman to make a decision and to act upon it, in so far as they make mistakes . . . God will accept their recognition of this, forgive them and give them power to try again. This is our faith.'

She also remarked: 'There will be many occasions on which the layman has to make up his mind whether, in the particular circumstances with which he is confronted, the time has come to make the crucial stand, or to wait and fight another day. I think we have to learn from Jesus Christ that there are many occasions on which the right thing to do is to wait, in order to remain in the situation.'

In brief: the Christian in his daily life has to learn the art of *responsible compromise* (a word which needs to be rescued from its derogatory connotations). It is fair to say that a Christian ought never to compromise with an easy conscience—that he ought always to watch what he is doing, to be *uneasy* about a decline in business standards, to remind himself that God may call him to make a fool of himself in the eyes of the world. Yet it would be a poor thing if, for instance, all Christians in West Africa avoided the legal profession because of their scruples, or if all church-people avoided city government contracts in the States or city police work in Britain.

Each personal crisis demands a different prayerful solution. God may ask one man to resign and another to comply, and neither will be completely happy about his actions.

Penry Jones, writing about his work for ABC Television in the March 1963 *Christian Comment*, gave an excellent example of the kind of job which Christians must not be afraid to undertake. He wrote: 'The religious TV producer is a man of divided loyalties. He is responsible both to the churches and to the world of television. . . . He stands in the Church, but he must at the same time have enough imagination, sympathy and respect to stand for the non-churchman. This is his frontier, and he betrays his trust rather than serves it if he sacrifices too much to the wishes and opinions of his masters—be they in television or be they in the churches.'

Clearly, a life of responsible (as distinct from unconscious) compromise is a dangerous one. But here, perhaps, is some of the zest of the Christian life which we have lost with our safe platitudes and pietism. Certainly it is of the first importance that young people should sometimes pick the ethically tough jobs, and feel that this is their Christian duty. If only the institutional Church would recognise this, and find ways to support the young politician, or shopkeeper, or assembly supervisor, instead of wishing all the time that he would go into what are (quite erroneously) considered the ethically 'pure' jobs of teaching or the ministry. (For teachers and ministers, quietly and rather shamefacedly, spend a great deal of their time too 'compromising'—we hope responsibly).

In the last twenty years, there have been a good many Christians in 'grey' jobs, in the Armed Services for instance, or in the resistance movement in Germany, or in the revolution in Communist China, or in the mental hospital service in Britain, who have not seen the perfect answer, and who have indeed known that the 'greys' are part of the very texture of modern life. God is gracious enough to give to his servants some assurance that they can persevere through the fogs of life; but the fogs do not always disperse after a few hours. It is this kind of reality which the Church should teach us to face, and it is this kind of life that we should be taught to pray about and to relate to the Sacraments.

RALPH MORTON and MARK GIBBS, *God's Frozen People*

64. The Church's business

By courtesy of *New Christian*

'At least we have given them a new Communion Service'

1. What is this cartoon saying?   2. Do you agree with the criticism?

3. What *should* be the Church's concerns? Put them in order of importance.

4. What do you think the Church *can* do about (*a*) economic affairs? (*b*) industrial problems?

65. Decency is no longer enough

Decency is no longer enough. Since the turn of the century, we have
lived through a revolution in men's understanding of the motive forces
behind human personality. Since Freud, whole generations have
grown up which rightly perceive that there is more to their own and
other people's behaviour than can be described solely in the old categories of right and wrong, sin and virtue; and their perception has
created a whole new range of intellectual disciplines, together with
new or revised techniques of social service and manipulation. It is not
only the Free Churches which, with rare exceptions, have quailed
from the task of assimilating all this into their understanding. The
Church as a whole fell short, resenting the 'irreligion' of Freud as it
resented the 'irreligion' of Darwin, and declining to criticize its concepts of sin and conscience, and the pastoral techniques which had
grown out of these concepts.

Some of us have in our experience some atrocious instances of
judgements passed by Dissenting clergy on people exhibiting symptoms of mental stress, and we are not confident that, even now, Free
Church ministerial colleges equip men to take their place as pastors in
a community where other professionally trained people are perform-
ing a similar or complementary function. Personally, I would never
take any sort of problem to a clergyman unless I knew him very well
first, simply because it is impossible to rely on finding the objectivity
and elementary competence that the social sciences have given thousands of men and women outside the churches.

Certainly, no Christian would wish to say that 'sin' (for instance)
is an outmoded concept, even though the word's debasement by
theological illiterates has made it a difficult term for the popular imagination to grasp. But equally, Christians who work professionally in
the field of mental disorder and family breakdown, however anxious
they may be to find an accommodation between the Christian and the
Freudian way of looking, find that the simple black-and-white categories which flow from Sunday School and pulpit are hard to work
out and impossible to apply in this setting. Rather, they have to be
unlearnt before professional progress can be made. When this has
been done, they find themselves returning from the non-judgemental
society of their weekday colleagues to seek the refreshment of worship
among people still locked in the old dispensation—sincere indeed, but
not by modern standards sensitive. Collectively and individually,
modern Dissenting communities are very often, when one gets to know
them, kind and generous both within and without the fellowship.

Rarely do they also give the impression of being relaxed and understanding. They are not the sort of places to which one could confi-
dently recommend a discharged prisoner, or a neurotic, or a divorcee.
Often there is an indefinable feeling of social . . . tension, which shies
away from self-knowledge and emotional release, and hopes to erase
from the inward feelings, or at least from the outward behaviour, all
the drives which pile up for their possessors power, fortunes, prison
sentences, illegitimate children. Clearly this is most obvious in the
nay-saying, lunatic fringe of Nonconformity, where Moral Law Defence Associations are formed. . . . As yet, no great body of opinion
has arisen in the Free Churches to tell the lunatic fringe plainly that
its doctrines are false and its pretensions intolerable. And only here
and there can one discern signs that the churches are starting to catch
up on the social skills of the last half century.

CHRISTOPHER DRIVER, *A Future for the Free Churches?*

66. Suitable for redevelopment

We are not here, after all, to fill empty pews with holy gimmicks. We
are not here to restore the ancient parish church and keep the merry
bells aringing in the steeple and the merry kettle aboiling on the gas-
ring of the Women's Guild. We are here to share God with the world.
Our enemy is the power of death in the minds of the people, not the
ravages of the death-watch beetle in the beams of the church.

Any redevelopment we may plan must primarily be designed not to
bring the people in but to send us out. Out into the world where
people live and work—the factories, the offices, the shops, the bus
queues, the lunch counters, the expresso-bars, the town council meetings, the PTA socials—with something to say and the conviction
necessary to say it well.

In an average congregation what percentage will volunteer to:
—take part in a visiting campaign on a new estate
—deliver leaflets advertising Easter services
—teach in Sunday School
—sing in the choir
—do anything extra at all?

A very small percentage indeed. (I know, I know. They're busy.
They haven't the time. They're not gifted that way. They're shy, inarticulate, just plain scared.)

But in the same congregation what percentage:
—go out each day to work in the world
—go shopping
—talk every day to people outside the church family

—read the newspapers, watch the television

—discuss what they have read and seen with other people?

Practically one hundred per cent.

So the sending out bit is easy. We go out already. The channels are open (as they have always been), the points of contact established. All that is needed is the willingness to speak, and the knowledge to back up the willingness, and the love to enable us to listen before we speak.

If we spent our faith listening to our neighbours instead of trying to make them come and listen to us on a Sunday. If we invested our faith in the translating of the Incarnation, the Crucifixion and the Resurrection into meaningful terms for our twentieth century society instead of in the heart-breaking struggle to raise enough money to install a new heating system and still have a modest balance to give to foreign missions. If we beat the (two-edged) sword of our respectability into the ploughshare of concern, and the spear of our distaste for the world into the pruning-hook of love for our neighbours. If we loved one another on the Christian denominational miserable-go-round enough to agree together to stop it and get off. If we stopped waiting patiently for the Lord and began impatiently following him. If the parson lost his senses and the people came to theirs. . . .¹

If we believed in the Incarnation, would we be content with Christmas cards and lights on the tree in December, and 'I'm all right, Jack' in January when the bills come rolling in?

If we believed in the Sermon on the Mount on Sunday, would our slogan through the rest of the week still be 'Business is business'?

If we believed in the Crucifixion, would we continually hammer home the nails and thrust in the spear in a degrading struggle to keep up with the Joneses (agnostic, humanist, Anglican, Methodist, Congregational and all)?

If we believed in the Resurrection, would we still be afraid to see our church die that another might be born?

If we believed in the reality of the Holy Spirit, would we still be haunted by the ghost of yesterday (the full pew, the thriving Band of Hope, the sinners weeping tears of gratitude)?

If we believed in the actuality of the Kingdom of God, what existing pattern of church life and worship could contain or give expression to the life of the Kingdom within us?

If we believed in the love of God, would we perhaps understand the meaning of mission?

If we understood the meaning of mission, would we discover the means of unity?

'If anyone wishes to be a follower of mine, he must leave self behind; he must take up his cross and come with me. Whoever cares for his own safety is lost; but if a man will let himself be lost for my sake, he will find his true self.'

If we believed that. . . .[1]

STUART JACKMAN, *This Desirable Property*

1. What might happen in and to the Church then? Try answering the questions posed by the author too.

67. The open Church

There are four chief weaknesses which many in the Church have contracted: an uncritical use of abstractions; the loss of honesty and candor; an undue admiration for uniformity, with a lack of esteem for diversity; and a blindness to the spiritual values promoted in the secular world.

1. An addiction to abstractions generates a world of concepts which often cannot be fully verified in the world. Those who are the victims of these abstractions never come to understand the world in which they live. Catholics often seem to speak in abstractions which have no referents, or referents so different from what their language seems to say, that outsiders must believe that they are speaking in riddles. Once one learns the habit of translation, it is easy to understand the jargon; but the need for such a habit brings upon Catholics the accusation of 'doublethink'. Three examples come to mind: that the Church is sinless, essentially never changes, possesses the whole truth.

'The Church,' Catholics will say, 'is sinless and indefectible'; but they will admit that ecclesiastics and laymen are sinners, and that even the just 'sin seven times daily'. What, then, is this 'Church' that is sinless? It exists nowhere but in the abstracting mind. *Under a certain aspect*, namely, the life of God which it shares, the Church is sinless. But the Church is concrete. The Church in which God lives is Pope Paul, the seventy-nine living cardinals, the bishop of Diocese X, the crotchety monsignor at Our Lady of Good Hope, the curate at Sacred Heart, the weary sisters of the parish convent, the mother of too many children and the mother of too few, the corrupt politician at the communion rail, the divorced man who hasn't been to church for twenty-seven years, the girl whom everybody thinks is an angel but who, terrified, has fled into an illicit love from which she can't escape. It is real, not mythical.

The second manifestation of the vice of abstractions which corrupts the Catholic mind is the phrase in essentials the Church never changes'. It is difficult to find an 'essential' that has not 'changed' in the Church. The language of 'essences' is misleading; everything in the Church is life and growth. The Church has grown organically and with consistency. The point of view of 'essences' does so little justice to the reality of the Church. It is curious that there should be such an impassioned devotion to the superficial appearances of changelessness, and such a lack of devotion to the deep organic development which is the Church's greatest glory. An acorn is different from an oak, and a man of sixty from a boy of sixteen; it is the glory of acorn and boy to have changed rather than to have been changeless. 'Essence' and 'substantially the same' are comforting words in a world of flux. They have the appearance of logical solidity and clarity; but they are false to history. The Catholic spirit is adaptable to nearly all cultures, places, times; changeability, not changelessness, has surely been the chief characteristic of its long life. The Church truly belongs to Italy, to Ireland, to Africa, to India. The Church *becomes* Italian, Irish, African, Indian. It retains its identity as Catholic by a certain almost inarticulate self-consciousness. But this sense of identity is not like a firmly held definition of its essence any more than an old man remembers his identity as the boy of many years ago by means of a definition of himself. The sense of identity is not a logical concept but a psychological one. When a living thing ceases to change, it ceases developing toward its own full identity.

A third manifestation of the vice of abstractions is the sentence 'The Catholic Church possesses the whole truth.' It was perfectly evident at the [Vatican] Council that bishops and cardinals disagreed with one another, even on important points. Who, then, in the Church, *in the concrete*, possesses the whole truth? As soon as we take up the language of concrete persons, the pretentiousness of the claim is embarrassing. 'The Church possesses the whole truth' is only a misleading way of saying that the Holy Spirit, the Spirit of Truth, vivifies the Church as it struggles in history, and gives it enough light to answer to its needs.

In short, the abstract concept of a perfect Church, full of truth, never changing, does not exist in the concrete world of history. In the concrete world, God lives and acts in the Church through limited and stiff-necked men, with His unchanging graciousness. God is perfect, full of truth, never changing, but the band of His servants is not.

2. The greatest difficulty of the layman in the Church is the dishonesty in which he is constantly forced to live. Definitions and notions are constantly preventing him from being honest. This dishonesty begins in school or in catechism classes, where he memorizes definitions that he does not wholly accept, since often he does not understand them. But correct answers win good marks; and if he asks the teacher unsettling questions he is labelled rebellious or impertinent. Again, the sermons he hears are often irrelevant and unreflective. But even here he cannot correct the priest or raise questions; he must

tolerate an untruthful situation. The presence of the Church in the world is sometimes so absurd in the light of ordinary common sense that one despairs of ever getting the clergy—who alone can change it —to see the absurdity. Day after day in life in the world, one encounters fallen-away Catholics, non-Catholics affronted by the external life of the Church, and laymen increasingly disturbed by the half-truths and misleading characteristics of ordinary Catholic life.

Criticize Catholic life, the clergy, or events at the Vatican Council, and one hears : 'This sort of thing can't do our side any good. How can a man who calls himself a Catholic write things like that?' Again, the Pope is treated as something more than a man, more even than Christ's humble vicar; it would be virtually impossible for a Catholic writer to criticize him respectfully, directly, and frankly, as he might criticize the president of his own country, without causing the most acute discomfort to many clerics and other laymen. Can we really believe it healthy to preserve the Pope from open criticism? For such criticism would be a constant spur toward the best possible fulfilment of his ministry. Criticism is not idle or in vain; it is the daily bread of normal men, and a great help to them.

The wave of relief which swept the Catholic world as the first session of the Council unfolded, and as the honest, critical reports about its proceedings appeared in print, was because honesty had at last returned to the Church. Now one could disagree, challenge, demand evidence for assertions. One could now grab hold of one's own conscience, and try to understand one's personal vocation, commitments, and beliefs. Moreover, it seems conceivable that within a generation the air will be so cleared that one will be able to speak one's honest mind about marriage, sex, and childbearing. For there is almost no honesty upon these questions at the moment, nor is much possible yet, given the formation and sensitivities of many.

It is difficult to think of a single belief, practice, or aspect of the Church in which educated laymen have not long had more comments to make than they dare to take the initiative to make. It is one of the ironies of our time that, while the clergy are concerned to protect the faith of the ordinary people from too much truth at once, educated laymen seem to be protecting the clergy from still more truth. It is an exciting but precarious time for everyone.

3. In the open Church, recovery from the disease of abstractions and return to the principle of honest speech are the first two orders of business. A third is related to them : respect for diversity. To what extent can a man be his own kind of Catholic? The problem is not that of minimizing Catholic doctrine, but rather that of penetrating it and assimilating it in countless individual ways.

The problem has always existed, but we have not always noticed it.

Catholics already live in great diversity. Catholics in Los Angeles have a different style of faith from Catholics in Chicago; and these differ from those of Boston. Catholics sometimes differ more from other Catholics, in their idea of God, fidelity, and grace, than one group of Protestants differs from another. Sometimes a Catholic and a Protestant can be closer to each other in actual religious belief than either is to his own co-religionists.

For faith takes root in persons, in personal ways, rather than in sects, systems, or abstract propositions. The diversity of spirits mirrors the infinity of God. Creed, system, and community cannot mask the fact that each person has his own perception, sensitivity, and experience. It is a common experience of laymen in the news to recognize that the God spoken of by Father X is not the God of Father Y, and that the image of Christ given by Father Z is almost the reverse of that of Father Q. No doubt many Catholics have the experience of listening to another Catholic speak about his faith, and saying to himself: 'That's not my faith at all!'

Catholics have not noticed this diversity because their preference for abstractions leads all to repeat the same words, without reflecting on the fact that each penetrates the meaning differently. When it becomes possible for more Catholics to feel responsible for the depth and solidity of their own faith, then the diversity of Catholic people, which has always been operative, will be publicly apparent. For individuals then will not be afraid to speak of insights peculiar to themselves, or of personal objections to points they have never understood. Diversity will return to the Church when honesty returns. In a living Church, moreover, diversity is at least as admirable and breathtaking an ideal as uniformity. Nor does diversity destroy unity. All Catholics are united in fidelity to the drive to understand. All love the same Christ, receive the same baptism and the same eucharist, respect the same ministers of the Word.

4. The fourth order of business for the open Church is secularization. For the Church at present is ecclesiastical, clerical, special, precious; it has little in common with the world. If it wishes to sanctify present history, it will have to be secularized in its mode of speech, habits of thought, ways of acting. This does not mean it should cease to judge the world or cease to retain its independence of spirit: quite the contrary. The secular world needs and desires prophetic, honest guidance; it despises pretense, sycophancy, or infidelity to self. Moreover, if the secular world now despises the Church, it is because the Church does *not* seem to speak with an independent voice. Too often, the voice of the Church sounds like the voice of the world—the world of the eighteenth or nineteenth century. It is now many generations since the world itself abandoned that style. The changelessness of the

Church does not appear to be due to fidelity to Christ; it seems rather like a decayed imitation of the world, as if the Church only becomes secularized fifty years or so behind the times.

The backwardness of the Church until Pope John and the Council was tragic, because the Gospels make excellent sense to many in the world in which we live. Many men believe in God in their hearts, even though they are loath to articulate their faith, because they so despise the organized religions they observe. If, for a moment, one imagines oneself not a Catholic, it is very difficult to see how one could ever find one's way into the faith. Imagine looking around : building fund campaigns; Masses on television; billboards about the family that prays together; a public obsession with sexual morality; a legalistic morality; the lack of creativity; the public lack of candor; the defensiveness; the bored faces of ministers at the altar; the listlessness of the people; the misleadingly expressed doctrines; the censoring of books. How could one ever believe that this religion was that of the Christ of the Gospels?

Many of the deepest revelations about God (at least, what He is *not*) and about men have been discovered by non-believers, who reflect on man's history, rather than by religious men. The freedom of speech at the Second Vatican Council, its independence from heads of state, the inspiration of many of its finest speeches came from ideas generated in the secular world. The inspiration and evangelical ideas of the ecumenical movement grew up, under the Holy Spirit, outside the Catholic Church, and for many years met strong resistance from the Catholic Church. The role of laymen in the Church has become important largely because of universal education, an ideal championed not by Catholics but by 'freethinkers'. Thus, in many ways, the Second Vatican Council revealed the Church's indebtedness to modern secular society.

In the open society of our century—the society founded on the concrete rights of persons, rather than on abstract ideas—the Church can live under conditions highly favorable to her inner necessities. No previous form of life was so well adapted to manifesting the message of the Gospel : the freedom of the act of faith, the free community of believers, the service of believers to their neighbors. Moreover, the open society has much to gain from an open Church. The open society needs sources of independent moral insight, and prophetic witness to religious reality. There is already too much conformity, standardization, and spiritual mediocrity in the open society. It will admire the independent, prophetic voice, if that voice is relevant and offers reasons; if it offers insight rather than trying to enforce its own conceptions. That voice will be respected even by those who remain, personally, unconvinced. The open society is, at its best and in principle, a community of reasonable discourse. It has its own rules and style of presentation. When these rules and styles are learned, they will not be found to inhibit, but rather to enhance, the message of the Gospels.

Both the open society and the open Church draw their force from the same source: the unrestricted drive to understand, and the quest for insight. Insight has two moments: one, the moment of intuition; the other, the moment of reflective judgment as to whether the intuition meets the claims of the facts. Thus, discourse both in the open society and in the open Church has two moments: one, the moment of trying to bring others to see as one oneself sees; the other, the moment of presenting the evidence to support one's own vision. Without the first moment, argument is obscure and blind. Without the second, it is groundless. Communication among men requires both moments.

That is why an open Church has an important role to play in an open society. It brings into such a society living interiorly according to the deepest laws of the human spirit: fidelity to understanding, humble charity, affirmation. The lives of such persons are, moreover, the best evidence for religious claims. Besides, the devotion of religious men to the drive to understand pushes the members of an open society even further in their own quest for understanding. Suppose there is a God? Suppose my hunger to understand and my drive for love are, in fact, the clearest signs of His presence in the world? To the open society, the open Church brings a new range of vision, a new depth of understanding. Catholic faith is committed to this world, not to a platonic other world; though it does not try to make itself believe that understanding and love end with death. It is in pursuit of the drive to understand that both open society and open Church find their separate identity and their complementarity. The Second Vatican Council has furthered the vision of an open Church in an open society, as a new achievement of men in their pilgrimage through history.

MICHAEL NOVAK, *The Open Church*

The renewal of the Church

One of the commonest questions posed by Christians and non-Christians alike is 'Why doesn't the Church *do* something about . . .?' This section gives a few glimpses of the Church in action today, and suggests some of the conditions under which this action will be fruitful. Perhaps it may point to what is lacking in places where the local Church appears complacent or moribund (cf. Section B). What about your own local situation? Can you see how new life could be infused into it, by learning from some of these other experiments?

The passages exemplify how the Church is facing the challenge of the human situation in various parts of the world. They are not the only examples which might have been chosen. See if you can find other situations where the Church is active in interesting or unusual ways. You might scan the press for as many examples as possible of valuable work undertaken by the Churches, locally, nationally or internationally. Or you might undertake some study in depth into a particular activity or institution within the Church and work it up into a 'project', with full commentary and illustrations. The fortnightly journal *New Christian* or the Education Department of the British Council of Churches would be possible sources of suggestions for such a project on the Church at work in the world. As an illustration of what the editorial board of *New Christian*, for example, consider to be matters of concern to Christians today here is the table of contents for their issue of 27 July 1967: 'A Leadership Problem' (on the report of the Committee on the Age of Majority); 'No Paper Solution' (on Rhodesia); 'Period Piece' (on Archbishop Fisher's pamphlet about Unity); 'Time to Consult' (on the Public Accounts Committee and Bristol Siddeley); 'Methodists Meet'; 'Ecclesiastical Titles'; 'Persons and Politics'; 'News Flashes'; 'Hooked on Heroin'; 'Amateurs on the Bench'; 'Unfreezing the Laity'; 'Hierarchy or Anarchy—Authority in the Church'; 'Advising the Unmarried'; 'R.C.'s Ecumenical Venture'; 'The "Mission de France"'; 'Church Investments'; Books, Cinema, Visual Arts, Science.

68. Prologue: living springs

A few miles from Assisi, in the valley of Spoleto, there is one of the most beautiful sights in Italy: the Springs of Clitumnus. The Clitumnus is a small, peaceful river, which waters the flat plain at the foot of the hills, and then winds its way southward, till it merges into the Tiber. There is nothing special about it but the Springs. In pagan days this was a sacred spot, for springs were mysterious, and were revered for their religious significance. . . .

Coming nearer we see a chain of pools, lying under trees. . . . Moment by moment fresh water keeps bubbling up from each pool and flowing away to form the river. . . . All, large and small, are always being renewed. But the strange thing about them is this: even the smallest cannot be stopped. Quietly they go on all the time; if anyone were to try to fill them up with earth and stones they would quietly go round another way and create a fresh pool of equally clear living water. Where have they come from—for they appear to spring straight out of the bare earth? Looking up to the range of rocky barren hills we realize that this water must have come down from the heights through thousands of unseen hidden channels, to converge at this spot, where these tiny rills come out into the light of day.

It is no wonder that the ancients regarded this as a sacred place: for it is a wonderful experience to see fresh clean water continually bubbling up out of the dry ground, under a hot sun. It reminds us of the 'river of the water of life', 'bright as crystal', flowing from the throne of God, and of the tree of life, whose leaves are 'for the healing of the nations' (Rev. 22 : 1–2). It reminds us, too, that although there are many seasons of dryness and darkness in the history of the Church, although Christian people have sometimes been on the verge of despair, yet when they least expected it, fresh springs arose in the desert....

Some of them may be very small and apparently insignificant; but whether small or great they are born of the Spirit of God, and they cannot be stopped. Within themselves they bear the promise of renewal for the Church and for the world....

Who would have dreamt, for instance, that the little group of students at Oxford who gathered round the Wesley brothers and tried to reform their own lives, amidst mockery and ridicule, would become part of the great Revival which swept the country and was the beginning of a new era? Or that the Church in France, which seemed beaten to the very ground during the Revolution, would rise again in power? Or that the Church in Germany in the 1930s would rise to such a daring resistance to the pagan government, and emerge from this trial stronger than before? Calvin has said that 'the story of the Church is the story of many resurrections!' Though at the present moment there is no sign of a general 'resurrection' in the Church in Western Europe, there are signs of new life which show that here and there the Church is being renewed from within by 'living' springs.

In every case, this 'new life' emerges from a praying group: whether it is called a 'community' or a 'company' or a 'team'. In other words the 'living water' comes from Christ himself, where two or three meet in his name—and where, as in the first community of Jerusalem, they remain steadfastly together in faith and fellowship, in sacramental life and in prayer. For 'renewal' always comes when we return to the source, to Jesus Christ himself. But all through the course of the history of the Christian Church, this return to the source means going into 'the desert'. It is there, in solitude and silence, that the voice of

God is heard; it is there that the river of prayer is born, that prayer which is the life-blood of the Church.

OLIVE WYON, Living Springs

69. Dream come true

When Charles de Foucauld was killed in the Sahara in 1916 his life appeared to his contemporaries as a strange mixture of heroism and religious eccentricity; considered now, half a century later, the life of this ex-playboy, ex-officer, ex-monk seems altogether odd, very much a period piece and utterly irrelevant to modern life. Yet he has left behind him a legacy that is very relevant to this second half of the twentieth century.

Charles Eugene Vicomte de Foucauld was born in Strasbourg in 1858. Orphaned at an early age, he was brought up by his grandfather, a retired officer, and predictably enough was educated for the army; he just scraped in. As a young officer his loose living proved too much even for the army; he was placed on the retired list at a very early age, though he was allowed to return to help subdue a rebellion in Algeria. He then applied for leave for the purpose of undertaking exploration and when refused resigned on the spot. His subsequent journey into the interior of Morocco, at that time a dangerous and unknown land, was very successful and his book on the subject earned him a gold medal from the French geographical society. Partly as a result of his experiences he returned to his religion and then, with the help of Abbé Huvelin, the priest of whom von Hugel wrote that he was 'the greatest manifestation of the spirit of sheer holiness', de Foucauld decided to become a Trappist monk; he wanted, he said, the hardest and the poorest life that he could find. Seven years experience of the life convinced him that it was not hard enough nor poor enough and he left his monastery to act as handyman to a convent in Nazareth, living in great poverty in a hut in the garden. Then once more he felt the call of the desert, was ordained and set off for the Sahara to live as a hermit. He saw the hermit life as a form of missionary work, and imagined the Sahara dotted with little hermitages whence the Christian message should radiate by the example of a poor, self-denying life. No-one ever came to join him, he never made any converts, though he managed to help some of the troops in the French garrison at Beni-Abbes where he first settled.

In 1906 he moved to Tamanrasset, right in the heart of the Sahara, a thousand miles from Algiers; there he set out to live a strict contemplative life combined with charitable work, endeavouring to show in his life the love of God for man, carrying out the maxim he had made his own, 'to proclaim the Gospel by my life'. He studied the

Tuareg language, wrote down their poems, compiled a dictionary, taught them to grow vegetables. He made no direct effort at preaching the Gospel; that was to come later, after he had prepared the ground. And there in his hermitage, on 1 December, 1916, he met his death at the hands of a raiding band of Senussi, possibly because he was suspected of being a French intelligence agent. And that, when the first biography of de Foucauld was published, seemed to all intents and purposes the end of the story.

Recent events in Africa, and more especially in Algeria, seem to have made of Charles de Foucauld more of a period piece than ever, but in his case, as always, we have to disregard the purely circumstantial elements in his life and concentrate on what is of general application. De Foucauld's importance for us comes from two principles which emerge very clearly from his life.

He wrote a good deal about missionary method, though he did not call it that, in the little book which he produced as a guide for the association of prayer he had started. Taking as his inspiration the Gospel text about not inviting friends or relations to a dinner, but the poor, the sick and the blind, he goes on, 'we shall thus direct our efforts towards the conversion of those who are spiritually the poorest, the most crippled, the blindest . . . the most abandoned souls, those who are most sick, the sheep that are indeed lost'. It was this concern of de Foucauld's to live a fully Christian life among 'the most abandoned' peoples, preaching the Gospel by example, which has been seen as the principal lesson of his life. His vocation was one of presence, to be among these people, to belong to them. To belong fully requires love. De Foucauld loved the Tuareg. It can be seen in his trying to teach them some elements of agriculture, his knitting lessons for the women, even in his dictionary of their language and the collection of their poems; both these were not so much tools for future missionaries as evidence of his love for the Tuareg. He could not be their brother unless he shared with them on a basis of friendship, of love, and so he sought to know them intimately, for knowledge is the root of friendship.

De Foucauld said that he wanted to proclaim the Gospel by his life, by spreading abroad the charity of Christ. He bore witness also to the poverty of Christ by living among the Tuareg in poverty like their own.

The great missionary problem of today is one of communication; it is the difficulty of the insertion of the Gospel message into a culture that is vastly different from that in which the Gospel has been, so to say, acclimatised for many centuries past. And it is here that de Foucauld has something to say to us and offer us; not a cut and dried method, not a practical solution, but a way of life that is applicable under all conditions and circumstances. It was this same message that was understood by Father Perrin, for example, working at the Isère-Arc dam [cf. no. 5(a)] and among the deportees in Germany during the war.

De Foucauld tried the conventional monastic life for seven years and left it because it was not hard enough or poor enough for his ideal. In after years he drew up no less than three schemes for founding some sort of brotherhood which reflected his ideas. No-one ever came to join him and all his schemes were fruitless; it was only after his death that men and women sought to follow his inspiration and adopted a way of life founded on the principles that he had indicated.

Thus in the early thirties the 'Petits Frères' and the 'Petites Soeurs' began at El-Abiodh in Algeria and in the south of France a quasi-monastic life which, after the dispersion caused by the war, and as a result of this experience, evolved into the form in which it is known today, combining the two elements prominent in de Foucauld's period in the Sahara—his hermit life with silence, prayer and solitude and his ever present desire to share the lives of those among whom he worked. So the Brothers and Sisters, in combining these two elements, endeavour to live a contemplative life among the unchristianised or dechristianised masses anywhere in the world. And thus they are to be found in the Sahara, of course, but also in Leeds, in a native village in India, in Lima, in a mining town in Belgium, in an oil refinery in Iran.

They live under the three vows of poverty, chastity and obedience, bearing witness by these means, a witness of presence. But it is through their poverty especially that they bear witness and share the lives of those among whom they live. They own no buildings but rent a few rooms, a worker's cottage; they go out to work and if they are unemployed they are dependent on whatever form of social assistance is available. Despite the often casuistically defined poverty of members of the well-known religious orders the fact remains that some orders are wealthy and powerful corporations in the Church; in joining them a man or woman knows that, except for gross misbehaviour, by professing poverty they will be secure for life. The insecurity of the Brothers' and Sisters' lives is the best witness to the genuineness of their poverty.

And so de Foucauld's dream has come true. The desert, a symbol of the absence of religion in a materialistic age, is dotted with little hermitages, providing a religious presence and a witness, after his example, but possibly under conditions that he could never have imagined.

LANCELOT SHEPPARD in *New Christian*, December 1966

70. Fire in Coventry

Twelve chairs round a fire on a winter evening. Filling three of them, clergymen. Sitting on the edge of the other nine, lay men and women. On opening our little booklets of 'study notes', we found that we were advised to spend our first evening 'getting to know one another'.

'These notes are intended as sign posts, not tram-lines ! They suggest the direction in which groups might care to explore, they are not meant to restrict the direction of the Spirit.' 'Aim at a free and easy conversation, with all taking part. Clergy and laity are all learners and explorers. The one leader of the group is the Holy Spirit.'

We had arrived from three different parishes, and this meant we were strangers to each other. In some cases, we disapproved of the other parish's churchmanship. In the country, we started with that deep prejudice which every village has about its neighbour. But this was not all. Some members of the group were executive types, and some were working class. Some were old, and some were members of the youth club. Most difficult of all, some were clergy ! We had all arrived rather tense, and shy, and expecting that we should have to talk about our Christian faith, which to most English people is embarrassing.

But on that first evening, no one mentioned God, and no one spoke of Jesus Christ. We went round the circle and each one spoke about themselves. They gave their Christian name and surname, and told us if they were married and had children. We learned about their past history, their jobs, their hobbies and interests. By the end we had become twelve real people to each other, and we were all marvelling at the range of personality and experience gathered round that fireside. A retired Air Force officer, a man with a beard who ran a laundry, a girl from a factory, a young farmer, an accountant, a farmer's wife, an engineer, a school mistress, the mother of a family. These were our nine laity, and with them were not just three anonymous clergymen, but three living men, also with Christian names and families, one of whom had served in India, another in the West Indies, and the third had been disguised as a Cretan peasant in the resistance movement.

We had begun to know one another. But something even more significant had happened. After listening in that friendly circle to eleven people talking about themselves, we had experienced a deep sense of the presence of God. If His name had been mentioned, I do not believe we should have experienced His presence. We had first to relax, and know one another, before we could together know Him.

From this beginning, the group launched out on the second evening to discuss 'What is the Church in my parish really for?' This got everyone talking, and when we had all given our rather idealistic views of what the Church ought to be like, we were faced with the next question, 'But is it in fact like that?'

Then came the criticisms. 'Sermons boring, and too long . . . psalms impossible to sing . . . parsons out of touch . . . people think only of money. . . .' And after the criticisms, a growing humility; an understanding of the other man's difficulty; and the discovery that what is really wrong with the church is me.

What sort of a Church would my church be.

If everyone in the Church was just like me?

And after the humility, the real thing which made these groups so exciting: the deep, rich, growing sense of Christian fellowship.

As the year went on, a few of us went round visiting the groups, to try and gather some general impression of what was happening. What was the Spirit saying to the Churches? One thing came back to us from every single group without exception: the astonishing and extraordinary experience of fellowship. It was unlike anything we had known before. Barriers had gone between parishes, between old and young, rich and poor, 'High' and 'Low'; above all between clergy and laity. We were really meeting each other, and coming to know ourselves as a team, who must do the work of God together.

The laity had come to see, with a shock, that they were the *front line soldiers of the Church*. They, not the clergy, were the representatives of Christ who were actually present in the factories, shops, offices, schools and homes of the country. If Christ's compassion was to get into those situations, then they, the laity, must be the channels through which it would come. If Christ's truth was to be spoken, then they must speak it.

Suddenly they felt rather weak at the knees. How could they, selfish, proud, lustful, ill-tempered creatures, be the channels of Christ's compassion? How could they speak His truth, which they did not understand? And so it began to pour out—the utter, bewildered ignorance of the laity about the Christian faith, those elementary questions they had always been ashamed to ask, those doubts they had fought against and never dared to express. And in face of their honest questions, an honest answer from the clergy:

'We, too, understand very little about the Christian faith; we are like children paddling on the edge of an ocean. We, too, doubt. But perhaps through our doubting and our wrestling, and because God really does open the door when men beat desperately and continuously upon it, we have got a little further in understanding, and this we can share with you.'

So there began to emerge a new clergy-laity pattern. The laity, seeing themselves as front line soldiers of the Church, needed the clergy as never before: they needed teaching, so that they could speak Christ's truth; they needed the Sacraments, so that they could know Christ's forgiveness and love, and pass it on to others. The clergy began to see their job in new terms, first and foremost as men of prayer supporting these active-service soldiers and then as trainers and teachers of an eager laity, standing beside them in their doubts, understanding sympathetically the problems of their working lives, exploring and learning with them the meaning of love and prayer.

But in describing these groups, I must not give the impression that they were a 'success'. They went much, much deeper than that. Alongside the exhilarating experience of fellowship, there went in every case a feeling of frustration. One group summed it up like this:

'We feel like the first Christians after Easter and before Pentecost.' What did they mean by that?

First, they had passed through a shaking of the foundations. One priest I know was physically in tears after a group meeting, because he had come to see how shallow had been his whole ministry up to that moment. One lay-woman (there may well have been others) gave up the meetings, because she dared not face the new truth which was springing up at her.

Secondly they had experienced the joy of Christ in the midst, and the sense of forgiveness one towards another. But they felt something was missing. It was all very well sitting cosily round the fire, but they didn't want to become a pious clique. There was a great work to be done, but what exactly *was* that work? And how should they discover the power to carry it through?

So the groups, one by one, were driven to prayer. Not the sort of prayer which is often described like this in the parish magazine, 'After the Vicar had thanked the ladies who had so kindly provided the tea, he closed with prayer'. But prayer that arose out of the group because they had a hearty desire to pray. Some groups learnt to pray *extempore*, each member expressing in simple words whatever was in his mind. Some learnt to wait upon God in silence. Some learnt to bring their prayers to the focal point of the Holy Communion.

This was the second word which God seemed to be saying to us. If the first had been 'love one another', the second was 'pray'. Every group reached the first point, but many dried up because they failed to reach the second. What the Spirit seemed to be saying to the Churches was this:

'I want companies of Christians who will love one another as Jesus loved them, and who will recognise their need for God, and put themselves together at His disposal.'

Love, humility, prayer. Where these came together the groups began exploding. The first to explode was in a remote country district, where two of the vicars concerned were old, and the third had a groggy heart. This was the last place in the world where you might have expected religious revival. Surely it would come where the clergy could give dynamic leadership? But no, it came out of this situation of love, humility and prayer. The lay people in this group were so excited by what was happening that they summoned a public meeting. When the meeting took place these lay men and women spoke simply about their rediscovery of the Christian faith, and those who had come to listen were moved by their words.

A few weeks later, another group followed suit. They called a public meeting, spoke from the platform and answered questions. A young farmer, with no sort of theological training, was answering difficult questions graciously, and with an astonishing insight. After the meeting, some one who had been there said to me, 'I know now how fishermen from Galilee were able to confound the Jewish Sanhedrin.' (The Sanhedrin was the council of religious leaders by whom Peter and John were examined shortly after the day of Pentecost. Peter spoke to them 'filled with the Holy Spirit'. And we read that 'as they observed the boldness of Peter and John, and noted that they were untrained laymen, they began to wonder.')[1]

STEPHEN VERNEY, *Fire in Coventry*

71. Nicky's story

(Continued from part 1, number 9)

'I turned eighteen in July, 1958. That month the Dragons from the Red Hook projects killed one of our boys. We were going down on the subway to get one of them. That's gang law: if one Mau Mau dies, one Dragon dies. We were walking down Edward Street on our way to the subway station when we saw a police car stopped and a whole bunch of Chaplains hanging around. The Chaplains are the Nigger gang in Fort Greene.

'It looked like action so we went over. The Chaplains were all standing around two guys I had never seen, one had a bugle and the other was a real skinny guy. Then somebody brought an American flag and the police car drove away. All it was, the two guys wanted to hold a street meeting.

'As soon as the flag came the skinny guy got up on a chair, opened up a book, and this is what he read out of it:

For God so loved the world that He gave His only begotten Son, that whosoever believeth in Him should not perish.

' "Now," the preacher said, "I'm going to talk to you about 'whosoever'. 'Whosoever' means Negroes and Puerto Ricans, and especially

1. Acts 4:13 (New English Bible).

it means gang members. Do you know that when they crucified Jesus they crucified gang members, too? One on each side of Him. . . ."

'I'd had enough. I said, "Come on you guys, we got business."

'Not one of them moved. It was the first time they didn't follow me. Then I got scared and I called that preacher every filthy name I knew. He paid no attention, just kept on talking, a long time.

'And the next thing you knew the President of the Chaplains flopped down on his knees, right on Edward Street, and started crying. The Vice-President and two War Lords got down beside him and they cried. One thing I couldn't stand was crying. I was glad when the Chaplains left. I figured we would go too.

'But then this preacher comes up to Israel—he was President of the Mau Maus—and starts shaking his hand. I figured he was trying to bust us up and I went up and shoved the preacher. Israel stared at me like he'd never seen me before.

'So that preacher heads for me. "Nicky," he says, "I love you".

'No one in my life ever told me that. I didn't know what to do. "You come near me preacher," I said, "I'll kill you!" And I meant it. Well, Israel and the preacher talked some more, but at last he left and I thought it was over. Only we never went after the Dragons.

'But later this preacher came back and he talked about this big meeting for gangs they were going to have up in Manhattan, and how we should come. "We'd like to come, Preach," says Israel, "but how we going to get through Chink town?" "I'll send a bus for you," says the preacher. So then Israel said we'll come.

' "Well," I said, "not me". I felt like I'd rather die than go to that meeting. But when the gang went it turned out I was with them. I was scared not to be with the gang. I figured I would fix his little prayer-meeting for him. When we got there there were three rows of seats right down front roped off for us. That surprised me some. The preacher said he'd save us seats but I never figured he'd do it.

'A lady was playing the organ and I got the guys stamping and shouting for action. Then a little girl came out on the stage and began to sing. I whistled at her and everyone laughed. It was all going my way and I was feeling good.

'Finally the preacher came out and he said, "Before the message tonight we're going to take up a collection."

'Well I figured I saw his angle. I'd been wondering all along what was in this for him. Now I saw he was a money-grabber like everyone else.

' "We're going to ask the gang members themselves to take it up," he says. "They'll bring the money around behind this curtain and up onto the stage."

'I figured he didn't have any good sense: anyone could see there was a door back there!

' "May I have six volunteers?" he says.

'Man, I was on my feet in a second. I pointed out five of my boys and we piled down there quick. Here was my chance to make him look silly. He gave us cardboard cartons. I wanted to get started right away but he made us stand there while he reeled off a long blessing. I tried not to laugh.

'Well, we worked that whole area. If I didn't like what someone put in, I just stood there till he gave some more. They all knew Nicky. Then we met down behind the curtain.

'There was a door. It was wide open. I could see street lights and I heard a water truck spraying the street. Back in the arena some of them were laughing. They knew what we were pulling. My boys were watching me, waiting the word to cut out.

'And I just stood there. I didn't know what it was; I had a funny feeling. Suddenly I knew what it was: the preacher trusted me. That never happened in my life before; and I just stood there, my boys watching me.

'Inside I could hear they were giving him a hard time. They were shouting and stamping and he having to stand there and face them, trusting me.

' "All right, you guys," I said. "We're going up on that stage."

'They looked at me like I wasn't right in my head, but they never argued. I was that kind of guy that the kids didn't argue with. We went up the stairs and you never heard a place get quiet so fast. We gave him the cartons. "Here's your money, Preacher," I said.

'He just took the money, not surprised or anything, like he knew all the time I'd bring it.

'Well, I went back to my seat and I was thinking harder than I ever thought before. He started talking and it was all about the Holy Spirit. The preacher said the Holy Spirit could get inside people and make them clean. He said it didn't matter what they'd done, the Holy Spirit could make them start new, like babies.

'Suddenly I wanted that so bad I couldn't stand it. It was as if I was seeing myself for the first time. All the filth and the foulness like pictures in front of my eyes.

' "You can be different!" he said. "Your life can be changed!"

'I wanted that, I needed that, but I knew it couldn't happen to me. The preacher told us to come forward to be changed but I knew it was no use for me.

'Then Israel told us all to get up. "I'm President," he said, "and this whole gang is going up there!"

'I was the first one at the rail. I kneeled down and said the first prayer of my life and this was it: "Dear God, I'm the dirtiest sinner in New York. I don't think You want me. If You do want me, You can have me. As bad as I was before, I want to be that good for Jesus."

'Later the preacher gave me a Bible and then I went home wondering if the Holy Ghost was really inside me, and how I would know. The first thing that happened, when I went in my room and shut the door I didn't feel scared. I felt like I had company in the room—not God or anyone like that, but the way I'd feel if my mother came back.

'The next day everyone was staring because word had gone around that Nicky had religion. But another thing happened that made me know it was real. Little kids would always run when they saw me, but on that day two little boys stared at me a minute and then they came right up to me. They wanted me to measure and see which one of them was taller—nothing important. Only I put my arms around them because I knew then I was different, even if it didn't show except to kids.'

DAVID WILKERSON, The Cross and the Switchblade

72. Shelter for the homeless

Today [December 1 1966] a new national campaign for the homeless called Shelter is launched. Five major national bodies in the housing association movement are co-operating to publicise the emergency situation that exists within the housing problem, and to carry out a rescue operation at some of the worst spots. The bodies taking part are the Housing Societies' Charitable Trust, Christian Action, Housing the Homeless Central Fund, the British Churches Housing Trust and the Catholic Housing Aid Society.

Research carried out by the new group, assisted by the Ministry of Housing and Local Government, reveal statistics calculated to depress anyone who believes that he lives in a society in an advanced state of civilisation. Last New Year's day saw 12,411 people in hostels for the homeless, and on another day during the year 4,000 children were in care of the State because of unsatisfactory home conditions or simply because they did not have a home. A government White Paper published during 1965 revealed that 'three million families in Britain today are living either in slums, near slums or in grossly overcrowded conditions'.

Shelter has set itself to raise a large sum of money—it is hoped by 1970 to raise a million pounds every year and to publicise the extent of the housing crisis. The bodies to be assisted will then co-operate with the local housing authority in tackling the local situation. Bruce Kenrick, the chairman of the ecumenical group organising Shelter, is already well known for his work in Notting Hill, and other leaders include Quakers, Anglicans, a Presbyterian, a Roman Catholic priest, and a Scottish Episcopalian.

The plight of the people they are seeking to help was clearly described in the 1965 White Paper which said 'we are faced with an ever-growing shortage of accommodation within the means of poorer families . . . shortage falls heaviest on those least able to pay a high price for their homes. The families in really bad housing conditions—in the slums, overcrowded, in multiple occupation—are, in general, families who can only afford to rent and who in most cases cannot afford to pay an economic rent'. As an initial strategy the money raised will be channelled into seven housing associations working in the four cities with the most severe problems—London, Glasgow, Birmingham, and Liverpool. During the 1961 census it was revealed that these cities had the greatest numbers of wards overcrowded by more than 30 per cent. Glasgow has approximately 100,000 unfit dwellings, Liverpool 73,733, Greater London 50,440, and Birmingham 41,000.

The ecumenical nature of the Trust is a welcome indication of the way in which the churches can work together. At the least it will do much to show that the various churches can meet for more than theological deliberation and it is a matter for rejoicing that they should have been drawn together at this level of social concern. The housing problem is a scandal considering the years that the problem has existed. Not only is housing a fundamental human need but poor domestic conditions are also the source of many other social problems. Education has suffered because of lack of an atmosphere conducive to study. The ranks of prostitutes have been swollen by the misery engendered in cramped conditions. A major factor in the growing colour problem is inadequate housing. These and other human problems are encountered by the local housing associations in the valuable work they are doing.

Shelter claims that more can be done with £1 of gift income than by almost any other charity. Through mortgages raised and by loans and improvement grants each £1 will do the work of £6. Bruce Kenrick has said: 'By pouring large sums of money into a few carefully-chosen black spots we intend to show what dramatic results in terms of relieving human need can be achieved if everybody unites to deal with the emergency'. After this initial attack it is hoped to spread the expenditure more widely in future years.

In wishing them well in this excellent venture it is to be hoped that sight will never be lost of the necessity for influence to be brought to bear on the politicians to tackle the situation at root level. The lesson of the Victorian era was that the treatment of the symptoms of social diseases commended itself to establishment figures, in and out of the Church, much more than vigorous political action. A more fundamental approach would have been to influence governments to deal with the situation.

No doubt to-day's Labour government is aware of the situation. But it is still pouring vast sums of money into maintaining a world posture which would be better used meeting basic social needs at home. The task therefore is one of influencing its selection of priorities. The trustees of Shelter are too experienced to fall into the same trap as the Victorians and it is hoped that they show clearly how much can be done when these priorities are carefully selected.

'Shelter for the Homeless', *New Christian*, December 1966

73. The Iona community

There were Columban monks and missionaries in Iona for nearly six hundred years. During the later Middle Ages they were constantly harried or devastated by Viking raiders from Scandinavia. Then came the Roman period when there were Benedictine monks at the Abbey, and the Augustinian Rule at the Nunnery. When the Reformation came to Scotland all the monasteries were suppressed in 1561. So the last monks disappeared, and gradually the monastic buildings fell into ruin.

The restoration of the abbey in Iona began about 1900. Now the rest of the monastic buildings, including the Cloisters and the Chapel of St. Michael, have been restored by the Iona Community, with the help of gifts from people all over the world.

From time immemorial Iona has been a holy place; it was a centre of pilgrimage, an 'isle of saints' and the burial-place of kings. One looks across white sands and blue-green water to mountain peaks on other islands and on the mainland. On the seaward side one looks out across the Atlantic, knowing that the nearest land is the coast of Labrador. Iona may be small, but its outlook is vast.

The modern community came into being in 1938. It arose out of a time of great distress in Glasgow and the district. Their leader was the Rev. George MacLeod of Govan. Eight men—four parsons and four laymen—decided to go to Iona as a committed group to rebuild the monastery there. Many people thought they were mad. 'What on earth are these young men after? Are they "going over to Rome"? What does it all mean?' But George MacLeod knew what he was doing, and so did the young men who joined him. On Iona a life of corporate and personal devotion had been lived for a long time, with no artificial distinctions between the sacred and the secular. The ruins of the Roman monastery were a mute reminder of the days of the medieval unity, and called them to find a new unity in the universal

Church of our own day. The Reformation period reminded them of their personal vocation, which they now intended to renew in the spirit of their predecessors on that island. 'The object of going there was to learn, in a true community life, how the Church should live and work in the world today'.

The Iona community has been described by its own members as 'a modern movement, anchored to the ancient Faith : seeking to preserve the eternal elements in our Reformation principles and also seeking to reassert those Catholic (i.e. universal) elements in our faith that will alone be adequate for that united world which, through the trials of the present time, is even now being brought to birth'.

This community is not residential, save in the summer months when as many members as possible live and work there together. For them all, the island is their 'home' as well as the place where they are trained in the life and spirit of the community. The community has a threefold Rule which concerns prayer and Bible reading, the use of time and the use of money. This is a determined effort at self-discipline in order to bring the whole of life under obedience to God, and thus to be set free for his service.

Membership is open both to ministers and laymen, and also to men belonging to all churches. The majority of the members are in the ministry of the Church. They work in Scotland and in other countries, as well as overseas in missionary and social work and in education. In 1962 there were about 150 full members. Wherever possible the members meet for a day once a month, and go to Iona every summer. Those abroad try to arrange meetings of the same kind in their own region.

As the years have passed the aim has widened. It is concerned with nothing less than *wholeness*: with the whole of life and with the whole Church. In a broadcast talk, Dr N. Micklem said: 'This Iona Movement is all of a piece: the rebuilding of the old ruins, the coupling of intellectual work with manual, the bringing of the common loaves to Church, the fishing nets round the Holy Table (at another centre), the direct prayer, the insistence that politics and craftsmanship and economics and drama and home religion are not to be separated, the holy indignation that the Church has become to some considerable extent a coterie out of touch with life, a "Sunday affair", a self-contained bit of the national life.'

Thus the Iona Community is profoundly concerned with the present and its needs and demands. It also looks forward to the future. The symbolic statue in the cloisters at Iona, the *Descent of the Spirit*, is prophetic. In the words of George MacLeod: 'If a new reformation be upon us, how are we to put ourselves in the way of recognising the new descent of the Spirit as it comes? The only

way is to get the new answers for our obedience to God at those points
where He is really speaking to us. This is how we must move towards
our A.D. 2000. Only so can we be put into the way of the Descent of
the Spirit for our time'.

OLIVE WYON, *Living Springs*

74. The Enchanters

The Enchanters were one of the most feared gangs in New York City,
and their empire spread through lower Manhattan, the Bronx, and
Brooklyn, and over the river to New Jersey. They were strongest of all
in East Harlem, and they symbolised East Harlem's plight. Their
members were frustrated by the colour of their skin and their lack of
education and work; they believed that the battle with society was
futile, that they were bound to lose; and so they tried to escape life's
emptiness in the harsh world of the gang. They broke into local stores,
they took wild joyrides in stolen cars, they engaged other gangs in
battles which cleared the streets as if by magic while a hundred young
men fought with switchblades and pistols and zip-guns and clubs and
knives.

Their local meeting place was a candy store run by *La Vieja*—the
Old Lady. There, on 100th Street, the leaders smoked endless cigar-
ettes, listened to the jukebox, and planned the next attack on the
Dragons or the Latin Gents. Sometimes the Enchanters talked with La
Vieja's godson, the likeable thirty-year-old Ramon Diaz who belonged
to the Parish church across the street.

For over ten years some of the Enchanters had watched that church
develop. They had seen it get involved in what for them was real life—
the hard world of racketeers and addicts and police. They had seen its
striking triumphs; they had seen its dismal failures; and failures meant
as much to them as any triumph did, for it proved the fact that the
church not only worked but, above all, that it *cared*. It cared enough
to keep on standing by the 'hopeless' addict. It cared enough to keep
on helping hundreds who never joined its ranks. It cared enough to
visit a jailed Enchanter and to write him month after month, year
after year, so that instead of falling apart, as do most men in for
'twenty years or life', he learned a trade, discovered the Gospel, and
became himself a man who cared.

From behind stacked cigarette cartons in the store window they had
watched local people like themselves slowly change, so now they saw
the church's caring expressed not just by its college-bred immigrants
but by those who had grown up in East Harlem, by those who had
once been frustrated and afraid, by those who were now a strong, live
community which seemed to know what life was for.

'Say, Ramon', Boppo's voice was strained, and Ramon Diaz looked up inquiringly from the back of the store where he was opening a crate. Boppo Cruz, in grey leather jacket and jeans, was standing with six other Enchanters, all of whom looked strangely grave. 'Say, Ramon. There's something we gotta say.' Ramon put his hammer down, picked his way between cartons and crates, and then looked with interest at the burly leader of the gang.

'You come to take me away?' he asked with a smile. The Enchanters remained serious.

'Ramon,' said Boppo. 'It's this way. . . .' He ran a black hand through his crinkly hair. 'We kinda need some help. You see . . . We wanna go social.'

There was a heavy pause while Ramon frowned unbelievingly.

'*Social?*' he asked. 'Did you say "social"?' Perhaps he was remembering the time when these Enchanters fired volley after volley at the Dragons from a hallway down the street; or perhaps he was recalling the day when two of the gang were shot and two more stabbed outside his own church door.

'That's it,' said Boppo, and all the others nodded. 'Social.'

Ramon's broad smile came back; but he was unconvinced. He knew the district and the gang too well.

'Go 'way,' he said good-humouredly, turning to get back to his work. 'You guys don't mean it.'

But Boppo and his men were adamant. They made Ramon sit down while they told him they wanted to give up stealing and street fights and narcotics; and they wanted the Parish to help them go straight.

Ramon put them off. He had a great love for people, and a deep, clear trust in God, but this was enough to try the strongest faith. He knew that scores of hardened criminals had found help from the church. He knew that each week more than twelve new addicts were helped to some extent by the church. But that the leaders of the legendary Enchanters should now stand, as it were, knocking on the church's door . . . this just could not happen.

Yet finally, when the gang had persisted for a week, Ramon summoned up the faith to say, 'Well, I'll go see Norm'. Norm Eddy was as doubtful as Ramon. And 100th Street Church Council was more doubtful still. Nor was this surprising; for however much the church believed that it would accept all who came to its door, must there not be a limit in the case of a gang whose history was deeply stained with crime and violence and blood?

But when the vote was taken, the church doors were not shut; and a few evenings later thirty-two Enchanters were packed into the small church hall and were working out with Ramon Diaz the basis for a strong, non-warring gang.

Within weeks they had a code as demanding as that of a fighting gang; they had given up their famous name and were calling themselves the Conservatives; and they had taken the crucial step of giving up all their guns. Now they had no arsenal. They were powerless to fight. They had taken a momentous step of faith.

And at once there came a challenge from the Dragons. The battle was to be the next night. This was the time of real decision. Some of them had sold their guns; some had thrown them into the river; some had buried them, just in case. All that day and the following morning and afternoon, Ramon Diaz talked with the members of the gang individually and in tense groups at the back of *La Vieja's* store. Most, including Boppo their leader, stood by their decision. But a few went down to the basement where the guns had been buried, and when the Dragons reached the corner of 100th Street, they were met by a hail of bullets which whined down among them from a housing project roof. All but one of the attackers were arrested within minutes, for the police had been notified; two of those in the rooftop ambush were sentenced to five years in jail, and the rest were left wondering if there were any real alternative to war.

'It's not easy,' said Norm Eddy, looking round the congregation which included twelve Conservatives, 'when a gang comes into the neighbourhood with their pieces, you want to fight back, and yet something tells you it's wrong. But you're afraid of being called a punk. It needs courage to go beyond that. It needs a special kind of courage—the courage to stand up for God. And if you do that, maybe people will call you a punk for six months, but then finally they'll turn to you and look up to you. But it will be hard.'

It was certainly hard. Some church members insisted that the gang had betrayed their trust; they wondered if they should in fact be barred from the church hall. But after a few days' uncertainty the gang had become more determined than before. They urged Ramon Diaz to help them with their plans, they persisted relentlessly in seeking Eddy's aid, and they stopped other members of the Parish on the street and earnestly argued their case. The world was no longer 'knocking on the church's door'. Now it was hammering hard.

And it prevailed. With the help of Ramon and Norm Eddy they worked hard to get a place of their own where they could make the incredibly complex transition from a fighting gang to a strong, creative club. They spent months earning money to rent their own clubroom, and what they raised was matched by friends of the Parish who wanted to give their help; until one autumn day, on Upper First Avenue, passers-by stopped to stare at the result.

Outside a store-front between the Veteran Bar and a plumbing store, each of the thirty members was taking turns to climb a rickety ladder, dip his hand in a tin of silver paint, and then press on the store's big black signboard. Soon the whole length of the board was covered with shining silver prints, symbols of a radically new way of life, a way that could end finger-printing for good. Boppo Cruz stood back to survey the result, unconsciously stroking the knife scar by his eye; then he led the other members into the clubroom, and the door swung to behind them.

For some, that storefront base became the source of a full and rounded life, with its self-imposed discipline, its rugged recreation pro-gramme, its community service, and its opportunities for education and for finding jobs through Ramon Diaz who now worked full time for the club.

For a few, this rounded life meant more than jobs, recreation and service; it meant the Christian community : it meant God.

BRUCE KENRICK, *Come out the Wilderness*

75. Planning the ecumenical parish

In October, 1965, the Corby Development Corporation gave details of plans which proposed the development of the southern area to accom-modate a further 35,000 people. In February 1966, the Corby Council of Churches published a report, expressing the desire that the area be designated as one for ecumenical experiment.

We began work with the conviction that the churches could no longer afford—either in money, manpower, or on grounds of scandal —to act independently in newly developing areas. Just as industry and secular government want to deal with 'The Church' and not with many churches so we believe that people making a new life in a new area want to face one call and not many. Our basic assumption has therefore been that we must make suggestions for a single Christian congregation with one main centre, sponsored by several (we would hope all) of the major denominations.

It rapidly became obvious to us that this was not possible unless, for the sake of the experiment, we were all prepared to lay aside some of our most strongly held denominational convictions and accept the validity of each others' claims to be part of the Church. This we have done as the only alternative to saying either, that the task was im-possible or, that it could produce so little by way of positive suggestion as to be valueless.

Christians must be sensitive to the pressures of God and of the world, and we are convinced that expression cannot be given to the new insights into the Church and its mission unless it acts ecumeni-cally.

Fundamental convictions

We believe that for this experiment to be carried through certain convictions need to be accepted by all who participate.

1. We believe that within her own obvious community the Church must accept certain disciplines for the good ordering of her life and work. These disciplines relate to belief, membership, and ministry, and must be accepted from the inception of the scheme, together with certain convictions about the mission of the Church. We believe that for the experiment it would be essential to agree on a form of commitment which clergy and laity must accept as a basis for action.

2. We believe those taking part in this experiment must do so as an act of faith, in the conviction that within one fellowship, by the exercise of mutual forbearance and charity they may be led in the unity of the Spirit, to learn what is God's will in the matters of difference between them.

3. We believe the mission of the Church is to make real and credible the Gospel of our Lord Jesus Christ through and within her life and witness as an obvious community within society, and through her involvement within society. The Church exists to serve men where they are, as they are, and serves them best by meeting them at the point of their real need. Within the Gospel men come to see their own and their neighbour's worth. The mission of the Church is to face the tensions of love and to interpret the reality of God's grace within the community in which it is set. Men are made for community and they need each other to be fully themselves. The Church should not do on its own that which it can do with the community.

The Christian team

4. To begin the experiment, the team would be composed of two ordained men of different traditions to give opportunity for dialogue. However, it would be valuable to include one or more laymen coming early on the scene with full time secular jobs who could share the responsibility of leadership and help to counterbalance the assumptions of the traditional approach to the work of the parish. We believe there are laymen with an understanding of this approach to the mission of the Church who would be pleased to move into the area in order to join in the formation of the congregation.

5. One or more of the ordained members of the team might also be in secular employment. This would have the following advantages:

   (a) The assumption that the ministry of word and sacraments is essentially a full-time professional occupation would be counteracted.

(b) The financial situation would be eased.

(c) A certain freedom from traditional patterns of ministry would be possible.

(d) The identification of the minister with society would be intensified and the risk of preoccupation with 'religious' activities reduced.

(e) Housing accommodation could be obtained in the same way as for others coming into the area.

Membership

6. Members in good standing with the participating churches who move into the area would be admitted as full members of the congregation. Committed Christians from non-participating churches would be admitted at the discretion of the Christian team, in consultation with the Sponsoring Body.

7. New members of the congregation would be admitted by a form of initiation. This would consist of baptism by immersion or affusion (if not already administered); a public profession of faith in Christ as Lord and Saviour; the laying on of hands by the Anglican Bishop and team members with a prayer for the gift of the Holy Spirit; and participation in the Holy Communion. Preparation for membership should be given over an extended period and include participation in practical projects related to the congregation's life and mission as the people of God.

8. We recognise that participation by those who practise Believer's Baptism in an experiment of this nature, alongside members of other communions, necessarily involves anomalies, but we believe it calls for mutual forbearance and charity. Within the congregation there must be liberty for christian parents to ask for either baptism or the dedication of their children. On the other hand, all children have the right to Christian nurture and instruction which the congregation would seek to provide. We welcome these challenges to our present practice and believe that under the Spirit of God the tensions would be creative.

Worship

9. The central act of worship should be a weekly Eucharist which would include the preaching of the Word. Full communion among the members of the congregation is essential to be consistent with the spirit of the experiment. We would, therefore, ask for full mutual recognition of all ordained ministers within the limits of the experiment as being the necessary expression of the one mission in the area.

10. We considered the possibility of separate celebrations of the

Eucharist by the different traditions within the experiment but felt bound to reject it because (a) it would divide the congregation during that period of early growth, when unity is essential, and (b) if the habit took root it could prove difficult to terminate.

11. We believe that the sacramental life of the congregation is not confined to its receiving the ministry of the 'Word and Sacraments' but is expressed in the congregation itself being the 'Body' which is 'broken' in its common life in the service of men. The sacramental life of the congregation will be shown as each member seeks to make the ordinary round of daily life a means by which God's presence is felt, and God's Spirit works in the world.

12. A regular, perhaps quarterly meeting of the full members of the congregation is essential. This would give tangible expression to the conviction that ministry and mission are to be shared by the whole people of God. Here the congregation would seek to discover by prayer, Bible study, and discussion, under the Lordship of Christ and by the leading of the Holy Spirit, God's will for them as a distinctive community within the total community.

Mission

13. In new areas where society has little or no shape and initial relationships between individuals and groups are still being formed, it is important that the Church develop naturally with and within the community. It is, then, not simply set over against the society but demonstrating in it, inevitably, the fullness and many-sidedness of its members' response to the Gospel. The resulting 'Christian action' emerging from the life of a church truly involved in its local society is mission.

14. Where the Church is thus continually involved in the life of the local society it must inevitably lose something of its identity and may in certain situations become anonymous. This already happens, e.g. where a church is involved in 'open' youth clubs. This anonymity will be the measure of her identification with her neighbour, that is the society of which she is an integral part. Christ is not taken to the 'unchurched' local community. He is already there. The Church must demonstrate both that this is fact and in what ways it is fact.

15. As part of the community the Church has to think with the whole community about their common needs and to share in community action towards meeting those needs. Though distinct, the Church is fundamentally one with the community in which it is set and must act responsibly and on an equal basis with all other members of the community. Instead of paternalism the Church must aim at identification and involvement even to the point of sacrifice.

16. In planning the mission to a new area we believe that it is of fundamental importance to begin with a team ministry, for it is only in community that the truth about men can be realised and demonstrated. Such a team would be in fact a small community which, through its own inner relationships and by its relationships with the large community of which it is a part, would enable its several members to work out their role within the community.

17. With the help of other Christians in the community, the team would begin to develop a pattern of 'church life' which would be structured to meet the needs of their total community situation. Worship, study, and teaching would all find their place in the life of the emerging congregation. However, the Christian frontier between the Church and her neighbours in the community is to be found at the point where the neighbour lives and not at the point where the Church as a separate community exists.

18. An essential task of the congregation would be to help the community to self awareness, and with it to develop necessary activity. Whatever is done to demonstrate the involvement of the congregation in the community (visiting, study groups, action surveys, etc.,) must express the fundamental conviction that the Church does not do on its own that which it can do with the community.

Premises

19. We believe that the permanent buildings should be a visible expression of the relation of the Church to the community. In consultation with the development authority we should aim at one set of premises to accommodate the activities of the congregation as well as youth facilities, welfare clinics and the varied requirements of a community centre. (Such a complex is becoming known as a 'communicare' centre.)

Conclusion

20. We believe that in any new area of development freedom and courage are demanded to experiment in the sphere of both church structures and mission. This will enable differing traditions to cooperate in such a way that the emerging congregation can develop its own ethos within the disciplines and fellowship of the whole Church. The congregation will then have its own structure of discipline and life within the community in which it is set, so that by its involvement and identification with that community it may manifest the presence of Christ at every level.

NORTHAMPTONSHIRE ECUMENICAL STUDY GROUP,
Planning the Ecumenical Parish

76. The children of the sun

Now I want to show you a man. He is small like all Neapolitans. His body is tight, stringy and compact. His feet are small, his hands too; but these are horny and rough like a workman's. He has jug ears and a mop of curly hair. He is thirty-five years old and his name is Mario Borrelli. Of all the men I have ever met, this one is most a man. He is also a priest; but the long soutane and big platter-like hat match oddly with his crooked larrikin face. He was the son of a labourer in the slums of Naples. He was one of ten children who lived, as I had seen the others living, in the crowded, insanitary conditions of the back-street tenements.

When the war began he was a clerical student. When the war ended, he was a priest, one of the hundreds one sees every day walking in the streets in dusty black, preaching his Sunday sermons to the pitiful congregations of the poor, sitting in the dark, smelly confessional for the weekly litany of sins, shuffling the dying through their grateful exit from the world, baptising the children who were born so hopelessly into it. This was the bad time in Naples, when the city lay prostrate in the inertia of defeat. This was the time when the word of God was a hideous mockery—to the humble who had been twice betrayed, to the mighty who were preparing themselves for a new betrayal. How could you preach the Sermon on the Mount to the starving and disillusioned poor? Small wonder that young priests despaired and old ones settled themselves back into the apathy of formalism, which is the despair of the aged. The demoralisation of the children, the homelessness, the despair, was evident even to the tourist.

In 1950 Mario Borelli began his work. 'I was bitter. I knew that I could not remain a priest; unless I did something worthy of a priest. I could not stand at the altar and hold the body of God in my hands while the bodies of his children slept in the alleys and under the barrows in the Mercato. For the men and women it is bad enough, but for the children it is a nightmare!'

One day, towards the beginning of 1950, Mario Borrelli presented himself for an interview with his ecclesiastical superior, Cardinal Ascalesi, Archbishop of Naples and Primate of the Mezzogiorno. He was twenty-eight, then, remember, a youngster with the oil of his anointing hardly dry on his nervous fingers. Ascalesi was an old man, wise in the world and in the Church, burdened with the manifold distresses of his people, with political intrigues.

He listened, patiently, while Borelli made his request. It was an odd one in any language. He wanted to take off his soutane. He wanted to go out and live in the streets with the scugnizzi.[1] He wanted to understand their lives, their psychology, to make himself their friend, one day, perhaps, to bring them to live with him and teach them to live decently. 'Ever since I entered the seminary I have been taught that a priest must make himself *alter Christus*—another Christ. It is written in the gospels that Christ ate and drank with thieves and street women. How can a priest be wrong if he does the same? How can he be another Christ if he refuses to go down to those who have no shepherd?'

Ascalesi was moved. With more men like this one he might have succeeded in reforming the Church of the South, but now it was late in the day and he was growing old. He shook his head.

'Your Excellency does not understand. How can he, when he does not see? These are children, the little ones of Christ! They sleep on the gratings and the beds of prostitutes. They pimp and steal and lend themselves to murder and violence. They live like animals in the forest, friendless and alone. And Your Excellency tells me to forget them. For what? For those who have faith already? No! If the Church refuses this work, it is not the Church of God!'

Old and grey and terrible, the Cardinal sat in his high-backed chair and looked down at the small, boyish fellow who challenged him. White-faced and trembling, Borrelli waited. If to be a priest of Christ meant to desert the children of Christ, then, he felt, he did not want to be a priest. It seemed an age before the old man spoke again.

'To redeem the children is one thing. To take them off the streets and give them a home—this I can approve. But the other—to live with them on the streets, to become in a sense a partner in their misdeeds— this I cannot understand. Why do you want to do it?'

'Your Excellency, you must understand something of what the life of the streets does to these children. You must know that to be a scugnizzo is to have a man's soul in the body of a child. It is to have suffered in that body the rape of innocence, the pain of hunger, the bleak, desert cold of the city. To be a scugnizzo is to live without love, to trust no one, because the one you trust will snatch the bread from your mouth or the cigarettes from your pocket. To be a scugnizzo is to know that every woman is a whore, and every man a thief, that every policeman is a sadist and every priest a liar. If I went among them as I am now, they would laugh at me or spit in my face. I should never come within a hand's reach of them. Believe me! I was born in the bassi.[2] I know!'

Cardinal Ascalesi pondered. Once in a lifetime, if he is fortunate, twice, if he is singularly blessed, a bishop finds among his clergy a

1. The urchins of Naples.   2. The slums of Naples.

man so marked by God that to turn him away would be like turning away Christ himself.

'I need time to consider this matter. Come back to see me in ten days. Meantime, pray for me, my son. Pray for both of us.'

Mario Borrelli walked out puzzled and unsatisfied. He was too young to know how deeply he had touched the heart of Ascalesi. How could he understand what went on in the back streets? The problem was to make him understand.

Mario Borelli went home and prayed. That night, as he lay wakeful in his narrow bed, the idea came to him. An hour later, he was drinking coffee and talking excitedly with a photographer from a Neapolitan daily. The project they framed was shatteringly simple. In the ten days and nights that were left, Borrelli and the photographer would walk the city together. They would photograph what they saw —the homeless waifs sleeping in the streets, the urchin packs cooking the food over fires in the alleys, the nightly interrogations in the questura.

Ten days later, Mario Borrelli stood before the old man and watched him poring over the glossy prints spread out on the desk. The Cardinal's face was haggard as he scanned the devastating evidence before him. When he spoke his voice was strong with conviction.

'Even had you not shown me these, I should have given you permission for your work. Now that I have seen them, I am doubly sure that it is a good work. But . . . but I am still sure that this work is full of danger—spiritual danger—for the man who undertakes it.'

Borrelli nodded.

'I consider it wise that you should have a companion. He should be a friend as well as a counsellor. I shall relieve him of his present appointment and attach him to you. David goes out to fight Goliath in the streets of Naples. As well that he should have a Jonathan to comfort him.'

Borrelli's tight face broke into an urchin grin. He began to tell the Cardinal of his friend, Spada, young like himself, a priest of the diocese of Naples. His heart was full of love for children, and when the urchins came one day to the house they hoped to have, they would have much need of love and fatherly care.

A few days later the scugnizzi of the Piazza Mercato turned a speculative eye on a new arrival. He was working his way up from the direction of the waterfront, picking up cigarette butts as he came. He wore a filthy shirt, patched in many places. His trouserlegs were ragged and hung down over a pair of odd shoes, cracked and broken at the seams. His hands were stained with grease and tobacco. His face was grimy and unshaven and he wore a greasy peaked cap on the back of his head. At the corner he stopped, took out a half smoked cigarette and lit it. He smoked slowly, legs crossed, bright eyes darting this way and that appraising the trade.

The boys studied him carefully, noting the broken nose and the tight mouth and the insolent tilt of the head. A guappo this one— cocky, tough, dangerous possibly. They hadn't seen him before. They saw how he held his cigarette, how he blew the smoke out of the corner of his mouth, how he spat into the puddle, how he cleaned his nose, how he scratched his thighs and armpits like a man accustomed to lice in his clothes. No doubt about it, he was one of the boys. Now it was time to make contact.

A weedy youth detached himself from one of the groups of loungers. He spoke out of the corner of his mouth in the slurred and sing-song dialect of Naples.

'I haven't seen you before.'

'Naples is a big town. I haven't seen you either.'

The accent was right, the words are right. You can't fake the dialect of the street. The fellow was a guappo all right. You couldn't rattle him.

'You in business?'

'Sort of.'

'Go any contacts?'

'Enough for me.'

'What sort of contacts?'

Borrelli fished in his pocket and brought out, in succession. a packet of American cigarettes, a cheap ring, a dollar bill and a grimy address book with a few scrawled names and telephone numbers. Contraband, theft or receiving, a few girls. It was enough for one man.

'Ever been in gaol?'

'Not yet. But I need a change of air.'

The police had been on the tracks of this fellow, so he was moving his camp. The youth fished in his pocket and brought out his own cigarettes.

'Here, have one of these.'

'Thanks.'

'What's your name?'

'Mario.'

'Mine's Carlucciello. I run things round here. Like to meet some of the boys?'

'Sure.'

Mario Borrelli had become a scugnizzo.

Now there began for him a life that was a grotesque parody of normal human existence. The gang in the Piazza had accepted him. He must make his just contribution to their harsh life. So the moralist became an associate of thieves. Borrelli kept watch and whistled the

warning signals. He ate the bread that was bought with money stolen
from Church poor boxes. He peddled the cigarettes that were smuggled through the customs. The priest became a beggar. He stood with
the boys outside the tourist agencies whining for cigarettes. He carried
bags and jostled for tips. He opened car doors and was jostled and
pushed by the fine gentry who were affronted by his filth. When midnight came, he squatted with the scugnizzi over a fire of twigs and
warmed his scraps of food and talked with them in the argot of the
streets. He slept huddled against them for warmth, under the stairways or in the corners of the courtyard.

For four months he lived this life, and the marks of it are on him
still. What I learned about him was told to me by the boys who had
shared his life and the love he poured out on them even in the tormented existence of the streets.

He is quick to anger when anyone makes a slighting remark about
the poor, or the shabby trades of Naples. He speaks with a Christ-like
gentleness about the girls in the poor back rooms. His fiery indignation pours out on those who profit from this commerce in flesh and
misery. But it was not until I probed deeper that I touched the real
wound. As a Catholic priest, Borrelli believes and preaches that the
end can never justify the means. One day, I put it to him bluntly:

'You are a priest. How did you square your conscience with your
actions as a scugnizzo?'

'I was committed, I could not turn back. I could only make my own
judgment and commit it to the mercy of God. Even so there were
many moments when I was a scugnizzo and not a priest.'

He would always be haunted by those moments when he was a man
and not a priest. Perhaps it is the Almighty's way of saving the best
of his servants from the ruinous sin of pride. I don't know. But I do
know that God will judge Mario Borrelli a lot less harshly than he
judges himself.

Mario Borrelli had two things in his mind when he went down into
the dark kingdom of the urchins: understanding and leadership.
Without understanding, he could not lead. Unless he led, he could not
hope to survive the climatic moment when he revealed himself as a
priest and offered the scugnizzi a home and a hope. When he spoke
of the scugnizzi, his eyes would light up and his voice, too.

'To understand these children, my friend, you must first understand
what it means to be a Neapolitan. We are not Italians. We are a different people. We are a mixture of many, and yet we are one. We are
boastful like the Spaniards, subtle like the Etruscans, greedy like the
Bourbons. Like the Arabs, we have need of God. We are arrogant, we
are humble. We are grasping, we are generous. We are simple, yet
devious. We are languid and we are passionate. We are changeable as

the sea, but there is one thing about us that never changes. We have need of love as a fish has need of water, as a bird has need of air.

'Now my friend, let me tell you the first thing I learned about the scugnizzi. Every one of them had left home because there was no longer any love for him. Consider a moment how it happens. In this family there are too many children and too little bread. The mother has so many cares that her love dries up as her milk does. There are quarrels and angry scenes, unendurable to the child, who is again cheated of love. Here there is misery so great that the child must work to bring in a few hundred lire. To his employer he is cheap labour. To his family, he is a breadwinner. None spares a thought for his starved little heart which dries out and withers like a walnut. So, one day, the child leaves home where there is no love and joins the other loveless in the streets of the city.'

'And does he find love there?'

'Sometimes, yes. The scugnizzi know how to be kind to one another, at least to members of their own band. But, you see, it is never enough. The human heart is a bottomless well and these are cupfuls poured into it only to be soaked up by the arid earth.

'I will show you how a scugnizzo is made. The foundation of his normal life is destroyed. He must build another for himself. He becomes vain and boastful, because there is no love to affirm his real value as a son of a family, as a son of God. He becomes cunning, because there is no love to protect him from the malice of others. There is only himself, the animal. He cheats and lies because honesty would make him the prey of those who have no love in their heart. His body becomes stunted as you have seen, while his mind spreads itself in rank and twisted growth like a weed on a dunghill. Sometimes the burden of life becomes too much for him and he commits suicide.

'When I went on the streets, I was a man. More than this, I was a priest with years of discipline and study behind me. But I tell you, truly, even I was affected by this naked, loveless existence. I knew my hatred was wrong. I knew I had to control it or fall into grievous sin. But the children? How could they understand? Cheated of love and faith, what was left to them but the luxury of hate?'

Watching them at night huddled over their little fire, their skinny bodies shivering with cold, their pinched faces intent on a card game or the tally of the day's takings, he saw that the first things he must give them were food and shelter. He must make a place to which they would return willingly, because it was better than anything they could find in the streets. He must give them security with freedom and food without a price ticket. On the street they had found friendship and a small store of love. This he must not destroy but preserve, adding to it his own love and the abundant gentleness of his friend

Spada, who was tramping the streets every day looking for a vacant place to house them. Later, he must get medical treatment for them. Later still—much later—he must try to educate them. How do you teach a child that the vices which have fed him and kept him alive are suddenly evil? How do you restore the ravaged innocence to which thieving and lying and prostitution and perversion have become a commonplace?

The next day Spada had good news for him. He had found a place—it was an abandoned church. It was filled with dirt and rubbish, but, as Spada said, it had a roof and stout walls. Cardinal Ascalesi was prepared to turn it over as shelter for the boys. Borrelli's eyes shone. Spada grinned at his friend's enthusiasm. Then he presented him with a sobering thought.

'We bring the boys here—good. We give them sleeping room, food and medicine—better still. But how do we keep them fed?'

Mario Borrelli's mouth split into a grin. Not for nothing had he been a scugnizzo! There were more ways of killing a cat than by stuffing it with red peppers! There were a dozen flea markets in Naples where you could sell old clothes and scrap iron. Don't worry! He had learnt a lot about the little 'combinations' by which the urchins lived. He would clean them up and turn them into honest traffic. Spada smiled. When did Mario expect to bring the boys in? Borrelli's face clouded. He was still afraid of that menacing moment of revelation. Italy is the most violently anti-clerical country in Europe. When he informed the scugnizzi that he was a priest, they would not believe him. If he appeared among them in his soutane, they would not believe he was the same man. It would be another trick, and they would edge away from him in fear and distrust. Hence the need of a photographer. He must go round with his camera and take pictures of the boys, and of Borrelli too sharing their activities and their food and their sleeping places. He would give the prints to Borrelli who would use them as exhibits when he faced the critical court of the scugnizzi to establish his faith and good will.

It took the best part of a week, because the scugnizzi were always on the move. But, finally, the pictures were ready. Once more Borrelli slipped away. He conferred with Spada and went with him to the old church to see that everything was ready. What he saw pleased him. There was a row of old sacks filled with sweet new straw. Every sack had a grey blanket, thin and threadbare. There was a rough table and one chair. There was a small pile of firewood. Best of all there was a gunnysack full of macaroni and a can of tomato paste. There were cook pots and a pile of rusty tin dishes and a few forks and spoons that had seen better days. It wasn't much, but it was a beginning. The stable was ready for the Christ-children of the bassi. Borrelli's shoulders shook. Spada led him across to the altar. Together they knelt on the sanctuary steps and prayed.

It was late at night when Mario Borrelli went back to the scugnizzi. He had chosen this time because it was the worst time of all in the life of the urchin. He knew how they felt, wretched, isolated, lost. He had felt so, himself. He had dressed himself in his priestly black. In his breast pocket was the small sheaf of photographs, the proof of his good faith. He walked slowly, praying a little, fearing much. A life's work depended on the outcome of the next ten minutes.

He turned into a narrow lane. It was a cul-de-sac. At the end of it, just settling themselves for sleep, were the boys of his band. When they saw that he was a priest, they cowered back, like small frightened animals. He took off his hat and stood looking down at them. He grinned, cheerfully, and asked them in dialect:

'Don't you remember me? Mario?'

They stared at him with dumb hostility. He took a torch out of his pocket and shone it on his stubbly face.

'Look! You know me, don't you? You, Carlucciello? You, Tonino? You, Mozzo?'

They stared and stared at one another in disbelief. Carlucciello lounged over to him and stared insolently into his eyes.

'You look like Mario, sure. But you're not. Why don't you get back to your convent?'

Borrelli grinned and fished in his pockets for the bunch of photographs. He fanned them out and handed them to Carluciello.

'First I want to show you that I really am Mario. Go on! Take a look at those.'

Carluciello took the torch and then, squatting, shone it on the photographs while the others crowded round. Borrelli talked.

'You remember now, don't you? That's the one where Nino was sick and he was sleeping in my arms all night. You know me, don't you, Nino? I got the medicines for you, didn't I?'

The small wasted child looked up at him.

'It's Mario all right. How would he know all these things, if he was someone else?'

Carlucciello stood up again. His eyes were hostile.

'All right, Mario, what's the game? Yesterday you were one of us, today, you're a black crow. What's the story?'

'The story comes later, Carlucciello. I'm a priest, sure. Why and how I'll tell you later. Right now I've come to tell you that I found a place for us—it's not much, but there are beds and blankets and a fire and food. Nino's sick. If he stays on the streets, he'll die. I'd like you to come and have a look. If it doesn't please you, you can leave. It's your place, not mine.'

Carluccielo's dark face was twisted in anger. He had trusted this fellow like a brother and now he turned out to be a dirty priest. Carefully, he filled his mouth with spittle then voided it full in the face of Mario Borrelli. Then he laughed. The other boys watched in tense amazement. These were the leaders. Of the two Mario was closer to them, but not this way, not in this hated garb of authority. They watched to see what he would do.

Carefully Borrelli wiped the spittle from his face. Still holding the prints in his hand, he squatted down against the wall, heedless of the mud and filth that soiled his black cassock. When he spoke, his voice was quiet and controlled.

'If you'd done that to me yesterday, Carlucciello, I'd have broken your nose and you know it. I could still do it. You know that, too. But I've let you have your fun. Now sit down here and listen. If you don't like what I say, you can go away. But you've got to listen. Is that fair or isn't it?'

The boys nodded. This was Mario all right. That was the way he used to talk. What he said, he did. They squatted beside him. Borrelli took Nino in his arms and cradled him against his breast in the old way. After a moment Carlucciello squatted again, but a little apart. He was too wise to be taken in by shabby tricks like this one. Borrelli said, simply:

'I know what you're thinking: that I want to take you into an orphanage where they close the gates and send you to school and let you out to walk in a crocodile on Sundays. I couldn't do that even if I wanted to. This place I've got isn't much but it keeps the rain out. There's straw for you to sleep on and a blanket apiece. There's wood for a fire and enough food to give you a good meal. You can stay there the night and leave in the morning. If you like it, you can come back again, any time, for a feed and a bed. It's better than the street, isn't it?'

The boys nodded, silently.

'I'm going there now. You can follow me or stay here, just as you want. The only thing is, I'm carrying Nino. I'm going to try to get a doctor and medicine for him. That's all. From here on, it's up to you.'

Abruptly he stood up, hoisted Nino on to his shoulders and carried him pick-a-back down the dark alley. He did not look back. He plodded onwards, head down, arms behind his back supporting the puny child. It was not until he reached the Via San Gennaro that he dared to look behind. The boys were a dozen yards away, padding along his tracks. A long, long way behind, but still following, was the skinny stooping figure of Carlucciello. His heart leapt. His mouth split into a grin and he started to whistle the jaunty little tune of the 'Duckling and the Poppy-flower'.

The Pied Piper of Naples was bringing his children home.

The first thing that strikes the visitor to the House of the Urchins is its poverty. Here are two young men keeping 110 homeless boys and ten paid helpers for less than a dollar a day each. Try it yourself and see if you like the taste of it—a dollar a day for food, clothing, housing, light, water, gas, electricity and medical services, to say nothing of education, textbooks and all the thousand contingencies of a charitable organisation.

The place is clean and the boys are clean, in a rough and ready sort of way. The building is centuries old. The plaster cracks off and the tufa walls shed a fine grey dust that settles on everything. The boys play in an unpaved courtyard between the high walls of crumbling tenements. Yet they are happy. They are free to walk out at any time. They stay because they want to stay, because they have found a warmth and a love stronger even than the call of the streets. They are proud of themselves and of their house, and this pride is the more striking for the poverty in which it flourishes.

It is little, you say, pitifully little after five years' heartbreak and sacrifice. True. But when you think of the ruinous beginning and the rank indifference of the gentry of Naples, it is a very great thing indeed.

The first bunch of uneasy urchins who came to the Materdei for food and straw beds, left the following morning. Mario Borrelli made no move to stop them. He gave them breakfast, stuffed a few cigarettes in their tattered pockets and told them the place would be open all night and all day for any who cared to come. He told them something else, too. If any of them were picked up by the police, the others were to bring him a message and he would bail out the offender.

The next night they were back again, with a few more tattered recruits. The cook pot was bubbling and the warm blankets were inviting. While they ate, Borrelli played them music on his battered accordion. There were no prayers, no lectures, only a warm diffusion of love and companionship. Borrelli is an impatient man, but the urchin life had taught him that the leaven of goodness works very, very slowly.

So they came and went and when they learnt that there was no compulsion, no hidden trickery, they stayed a little longer.

One night, after the food and the music, Borrelli squatted on the floor and laid down his proposition. He had done what he promised to do. Right? He had given them food and shelter without questions and without price tickets. Right?

Right! The boys nodded agreement.

Fine! Now this was his idea. Why not work together? Why not make a home here and organise their own trade?

'What sort of trade?' Carlucciello asked the question.

'What do you do now? You steal old clothes or car batteries or spare parts or carpenters' tools. Then you sell them in the flea market. Check?'

'Check.'

'You do the same thing now. Only you make it legal. You earn the same money as you do now, probably better, because you won't be in trouble with the police. You see?'

Carlucciello nodded.

'It sounds fine so far. But if it doesn't work out, we call it off, eh? We can quit whenever we like?'

'Whenever you like.'

'D'accorde!' said Carlucciello, briskly. 'It's a deal. When do we start?'

'Tomorrow,' grinned Mario Borrelli.

At one stroke, Borrelli had brought off a number of critical operations. He had turned the Materdei from a soup kitchen into a home. He had turned the first scugnizzi from rogues into independent traders. He had established a small source of income for their upkeep. He had enabled the older ones like Carlucciello to qualify for work cards as street vendors or as collaborators of a charitable institution. He had something to show to Cardinal Ascalesi and the civil authorities when he asked for assistance to consolidate and develop the work.

The atmosphere of the Casa is a free and easy one. This liberal attitude is deliberately cultivated in the Casa and is specially important to the boys themselves. The first and most important thing in the minds of Borrelli and Spada is to give the boys a home. All else is secondary. If they feel themselves secure and free at the same time, they will settle down and re-educate themselves. They will act on their own responsibility to preserve their home and the principles on which it is founded.

When I saw the gentle care which the older ones lavished on the youngsters, I believed that Borrelli and Spada were right. Their methods were sound. Their success was obvious.

MORRIS WEST, *The Children of the Sun*

77. Epilogue: bearers of the seed of unity

Many of these communities or groups are small and scattered, and to the eyes of many they may seem insignificant; yet they are 'bearers of the seed of unity'. They are an integral element in the life of the Church universal.

Do they foreshadow a great religious awakening? Or are they destined to form a faithful 'remnant' which will stand firm in a time of terrible testing? We cannot tell. But some points are very clear. In whatever part of the Church these new movements take shape, they are all deeply concerned about the following six points.

1. They are deeply concerned about *the state of their own Church*. They see much that is lacking in it, they are oppressed by its conventionality, its mediocrity, its ultra-conservatism, its unwillingness to change, and its indifference to the needs of the contemporary world. They see that the great need is for *repentance*, beginning with themselves.

2. They are aware that 'the Church exists by *mission* as fire exists by burning', and they are all making real efforts to spread the Christian message, through their lives and by their words.

3. They are profoundly concerned about *Christian Unity*. It is a striking fact that whenever this new life appears both in Protestant and Catholic communities and fellowships, men and women find each other in Christ and begin to pray and work as never before for the extension of this spirit of unity.

4. They all put prayer in the centre. Without God they can do nothing. They restore in their own lives the right relation between prayer and action; for they know that the Church as a whole is languishing for lack of prayer. Prayer for them is first of all *worship*: turning away from themselves to worship the Father in spirit and in truth; and after that, intercession for all mankind—'this thy family' —for which Christ died.

5. They all know the need for, and the value of, *solitude and silence*. They believe that 'society depends for its existence on the inviolable solitude of its members' and that this is not 'just a receipt for hermits, but that it has a bearing on the whole future of man'.[1] This explains why so many of them speak of their longing for 'the desert'.

6. Above all they stand for *single-mindedness*: that is for holiness —for the life that is absolutely given to God for him to use as he wills.

They challenge us all to live more truly as members of the ONE, HOLY, CATHOLIC CHURCH: that is, in unity, holiness, mission—and the three are one. For God is speaking to us, here and now.

OLIVE WYON, *Living Springs*

1. Thomas Merton, *Thoughts in Solitude* (Burns and Oates), pp. 12, 13.

God and nature

Controversy has raged for over a hundred years around the Christian doctrine of creation and the theory of evolution. Some see the two views as irreconcilable; others consider that evolutionary explanations have done away with the need for belief in a Creator-God; others again hold that the two views answer different questions, or complement each other from different standpoints. Passages 78, 79 (a), and 81 in this section take up the third of these three positions; 79 (b) is written by a humanist from the second position; while 80 is not concerned with the theory of evolution at all, but discusses the Cosmological Argument for the existence of God as Creator. Many may find this passage too technical to be helpful or even intelligible. However, the importance of the question will, I hope, justify its inclusion for the more philosophically minded, even if others pass it by. In any case it may also serve as a reminder that the most serious problems of human existence are unlikely to be the most easily resolved.

It is important first of all to try to understand fully what each writer is saying (e.g. what are the similarities and differences between 79 (a) and (b)?) Only then will it be time to question the validity of the arguments and to evaluate their worth and cogency.

Man has been perennially challenged to make sense of the mystery of existence. These passages represent some of the answers to that challenge. What is yours? Does it do justice to the infinite variety of created being? For example, the writer of 80 (who is not a Christian) says that the Cosmological Argument 'expresses something of permanent human importance'. What is the 'something important'? Do you think that what he calls 'ontological anxiety' is sufficient ground for the emergence, in every age and society, of 'the idea of God'?

In what sense does 'the idea of God' 'explain' the mystery of existence? What are the dangers of using it as an 'explanation'? (Compare 79 (a) and (b) with passage 53, pp. 228–231.) What, if anything, can take its place? Is any substitute really adequate to account for the rationally intelligible pattern of the evolutionary process? Does it make sense to explain higher forms of life solely in terms of lower? How does 'purpose' originate from a 'non-purposive' source? How can what is meaningful be explained by what in itself has no meaning?

78. God-Creator

I remember Robin Collingwood, in one of his more exasperated moments, turning on me with the remark: 'The trouble with you

Christians is that you have turned God into a *tame* God.' The thrust
went home; and I have never forgotten it. For much religious speaking and writing does convey that lamentable impression. To hear
some pious folk you would think that God was not much more than a
glorified version of the dear vicar, and the universe he created about
as exciting as a parochial bazaar. Well, that of course is a mere parody.
If we are going to conceive of God at all, we have got to conceive of
him in terms which take into reckoning the sum total of all that we
know of created life, the nebulae and the atom, astronomical space
and a snow crystal, the flowers in an Alpine meadow and the war in
Vietnam, the B Minor Mass and Belsen, Martin Luther King and
Stalin, the fact that there are moments when you and I have some
faint glimpse of a quality of life which far surpasses anything we
have ever attained—*and* the fact that for large spaces of our life we
don't in the least want to attain that quality.

He has got to account for the sum total of existence. That is what
we mean when we speak of him as Creator. 'Who sitteth on the circle
of the earth, and the inhabitants thereof are as grasshoppers.' 'I am
Alpha and Omega, the beginning and the end.'

Can we make sense of this idea of creation? Well, when you look
at the whole of life, natural and human, when you take into account
the infinite range and complexity, the depth and the height of human
knowledge and aspiration and heroism and tragedy—unless of course
you've let all your values get so devalued that you can't see any depth
or height—what explanation are you to give of it? Is it just a pattern
in atomic physics, or the result of an infinitely remote cosmic explosion? To me at least it seems more rational, more congruous with the
demands of the evidence, to think of it as the creation of intelligence,
of a consciousness, a purpose, which must at least include within
itself that which we recognise as the distinctive character of our own
consciousness and purposiveness.

Incomprehensible? Unimaginable? Yes, but that is just precisely
what Christian faith, *any* genuine religious faith, has always insisted
on as the truth about God. It is just this idea that he is comprehensible
—something we can put in our pocket—that's the mischief.

He is Creator—shall we rather say *creative*. Creation is not a single
event in time, as the Genesis story might seem to suggest. It is a continuous act. The whole of life is sustained in being by this unceasing
activity of mind and purpose.

F. A. COCKIN, *Christianity in Common Speech*

79. (*a*) The seamless robe

The Universe is a seamless robe, and the Bible knows nothing of the
natural and the supernatural, material and spiritual, sacred and
secular, or any other of the artificial distinctions we try to make in
order to push God out of at least one little corner of the world and
make it safe for ourselves. The Bible offers no arguments in favour of
a 'supernatural being' or 'spiritual values', or any other scheme for
putting God in his place. We cannot talk about God as if he were
waiting outside the door until we have decided what to do with him.
He is already here and to talk about him as if he were absent is, if not
blasphemous, at least impertinent. If the sergeant-major sends for
him, it is not wise for the new recruit to begin a philosophical discussion about whether there are such things as sergeant-majors. He had
better come at the double—or else! This is how the Prophets, Jesus,
the Christian, are aware of God.

> 'The Lion has roared,
>   who will not fear?
> The Lord God has spoken,
>   who can but prophesy?'

It is God who moves the breath in and out of my lungs every
moment, God who feeds and clothes me, who supports the ground
under my feet, pushes me along in my motor-car. It is the hand of
God underneath when I lie down on my bed. God does not speak to
us apart from our senses, our history, our science, our family, our
work and play, but in, through, and by them. It is this understanding,
this awareness, that makes the life of Israel and of the Christian different from the lives of other nations and other people. When St
Teresa of Lisieux thanks God for sending snow on her birthday, it is
not egotism, nor ignorance of meteorology, but understanding. The
movement of the Universe is the vibration of God's voice, and if he
were to shut his mouth it would cease to be. This is one way to look
at the world. The other equally logical, equally unprovable way is the
atheist's view. There is no other way. We are frightened of atheism,
so we try to give God a suitable place, to mention him on certain ceremonial occasions, to find time for prayer among our other duties, to
have a Department of Religion among the many activities of man.
But that is not Christianity. As soon as we speak of 'The need for
religion', 'spiritual values', 'ideals', 'the supernatural order', we are
back with Adam hiding among the trees.

ROGER TENNANT, *Born of a Woman*

(b) The evolutionary frame

The knowledge explosion of the last hundred years since Darwin is giving us a new vision of our human destiny—of the world, of man, and of man's place and role in the world. It is an evolutionary and comprehensive vision, showing us all reality as a self-transforming process. It is a monistic vision, showing us all reality as a unitary and continuous process, with no dualistic split between soul and body, between matter and mind, between life and not-life, no cleavage between natural and supernatural; it reveals that all phenomena, from worms to women, from radiation to religion, are natural.

It will inevitably lead to a new general organization of thought and belief, and to the development, after centuries of ideological fragmentation, of a new and comprehensive idea-system. The Middle Ages had a comprehensive vision and a comprehensive idea-system, and so does Marxist Communism today; but neither was founded on comprehensive knowledge. The present is the first period in history when man has begun to have a comprehensive knowledge of stars and atoms, of chemical molecules and geological strata, of plants and animals, of physiology and psychology, of human origins and human history. The knowledge is highly incomplete; new and surprising discoveries are being made every year and will continue to be made for centuries to come. But it is comprehensive, in the sense of covering every aspect of reality, the whole field of human experience.

Its upshot is clear. Man is not merely the latest dominant type produced by evolution, but its sole active agent on earth. His destiny is to be responsible for the whole future of the evolutionary process on this planet. Whatever he does, he will affect that process. His duty is to try to understand it and the mechanisms of its working, and at the same time direct and steer it in the right direction and along the best possible course.

JULIAN S. HUXLEY, *Essays of a Humanist*

80. God and cosmos

Many apologists have trained their spotlights upon the design and order of nature or upon natural beauty as requiring belief in a divine Author.

St Thomas's Third Way begins with an empirical premiss. 'We observe in our environment how things are born and die away.' What does St Thomas think follows from that? Things that come into being and go out of being again can be said to 'happen' to exist. With any one of them you choose, it always makes sense to say, 'It *might* not have existed at all.' As a recent translator of Aquinas so well puts it, these things are all 'might-not-have-beens'. The core of the argument is this. Not everything, says St Thomas, could have been a might-not-have-been. Otherwise at some time nothing whatever would have existed. But if this has been so, nothing would exist today. (An utter, universal 'gap' in existence would be irrevocable.) We are compelled, then, to say that *something* must exist 'necessarily' (not just *happen* to exist). And that being is God. God is no mere contingent item of nature; for every item in nature hovers between being and non-being. But the non-being of God is unthinkable.

St Thomas's Third Way uses the concepts of 'contingency' and 'necessity'. The contingent is what happens to exist, but need not have existed: necessary being is being that *has* to exist, that cannot *not* exist. The argument states that if there are contingent beings, there must be a necessary being. The one is correlative to the other, like 'front' and 'back', 'up' and 'down', 'convex' and 'concave'. The fact of a contingent world implies the fact of a necessary being whose world it is, and whose permanence stands behind the world's mutability.

The first difficulty about this version arises from the fact that 'necessary' and 'contingent', when used as correlatives, are words normally at home in speaking not of things or beings, but of propositions; a 'necessary' proposition being one that cannot be denied without contradiction, whereas a contingent one can. If we wish to keep this logical use of 'necessary' and 'contingent', we could rephrase the Argument in this way: 'The proposition "God exists" is necessary.' That is, it would be contradictory to deny God's existence. But Hume very properly objected to this that one may deny the existence of any thing or person whatever and never involve oneself in logical contradiction, although sometimes, of course, in falsity. To get a contradiction in such a sentence, one would have to include in the *concept* of whatever being one was considering the idea of its existence. Only then would the denial of its existence contradict what had already been said. Before 'existence' *could* be part of the concept of any being, it would have to be looked on as a characteristic or attribute of that being— like its colour or size or personality. But there are good logical reasons for saying that 'existence' is *not* a word that stands for a characteristic, that it cannot stand as part of the minimum description of any being. Once all the describing is complete, one may then add, 'And there is such a being'; or, 'It doesn't exist really.' But to say this is not to go on listing new characteristics: it is to do something quite different.

To sum this up: if the Argument demands a regress from beings whose non-existence is conceivable to a being whose non-existence is inconceivable, then it fails. There can be no such regress, for its terminus would be not only infinitely remote but also logically impossible.

The arguments[1] we have looked at are of very dubious validity, and yet their very persistence over the centuries, their deep psychological appeal to many of us, compel one to realize that they also express something of permanent human importance, whatever it is.

What is expressed seems to me to have two principal facets—the expression of *wonderment* and the expression of *anxiety*, both directed to highly general features of our experience. In the first case the Argument embodies the experience of wonder at the fact of there being a world at all: it is a movement of thought away from taking the world for granted; a shifting of attention from the nature, function, and uses of things to the simple but remarkable fact of their existence.

From another point of view the Argument expresses what can be called (solemnly) 'ontological anxiety', the anxiety inseparable from our situation as finite beings, vulnerable to all kinds of accidents and ailments, vulnerable above all to death: beings whose aspirations and yearning very often exceed their capacity to satisfy them. We may imagine a mode of being that is instead stable and invulnerable, where there is 'world enough and time' to accomplish our aims. The Argument indeed believes it can do more and can show that one being does really possess all these blessings and can bestow them on us. But it is here that we part company with its reasoning.

Paul Tillich's analysis of the Argument is wholly in accord with the tenor of this discussion. To him, the Cosmological Argument expresses our lack of self-sufficiency, but fails to prove that there exists a God who is all-sufficient and underivative. To talk of 'necessary existence' reminds us dramatically of *our* finitude and dependence; does not prove that any being *does* exist necessarily. 'The arguments for the existence of God neither are arguments nor are they proof of the existence of God. They are expressions of the *question* of God which is implied in human finitude.'

We are entirely right to feel that the Kantian, Humean, and linguistic critiques of the Argument leave something important unsaid. But what they do not adequately deal with are not *logical* issues but those deep non-intellectual elements of wonderment and anxiety that seek expression in all of the many variant forms of cosmological reasoning. By themselves, however, they cannot repair the logical defects. In a world that no God had made, we could still wonder at the fact of its existence and ours. There might very well be less to wonder at than

1. i.e. St Thomas's Three Ways and other variations of the Cosmological Argument.

in the theist's world: but *this* fact would not be changed. In a godless world too, we should be perfectly able to experience ontological anxiety; but there is no sure path of inference from the presence of anxiety to the necessary existence of a comforter.

RONALD W. HEPBURN, *Christianity and Paradox*

81. Would God have made a world like this?

Would God have made a world like this? Well, I think we may say that if anyone thought it up, it must have been God; we could never have done it. Fred Hoyle's lectures on the Nature of the Universe, given on the B.B.C. three years ago, did more than anything else in recent years to bring home to popular imagination the astonishing picture of the world as astronomy reveals it. He says, 'It is my view that man's unguided imagination could never have chanced upon such a structure as I have put before you in these talks. No literary genius could have invented a story one hundredth part as fantastic as the sober facts which have been unearthed by astronomical science'. And again, 'Here we are in this wholly fantastic universe with scarcely a clue as to whether our existence has any real significance'.

It seems to me that the main point where Hoyle is wrong is in even expecting that mathematics, physics, and astronomy should give any clue to meaning and purpose. It is rather like trying to understand the meaning of a Beethoven quartet by analysing the physical vibrations of which it is made up. You can only know what it means by hearing it. The scientist is bound to leave out of account the fact of himself as the enquiring mind, and the fact of himself as the Lover of Knowledge with an artist's eye, and maybe a mystic's heart. But he too is part of the world, and in one sense more mysterious than all the rest put together....

I do not believe that you can find the true God just by looking at the universe, and asking, 'What is behind it?' But I do say, that if you refuse to consider the possibility of its being made by God for a good purpose, you have a pretty fair problem on your hands. As I said at the beginning, the universe is here, and among other things it has produced us. It contains among other things reasonable beings like you and me (at least let us suppose that we are reasonable), beings capable of love and unselfish sacrifice, capable of appreciating beauty and creating it, and finding everywhere beauty and order. In fact, the very difficulties of disorder, suffering and evil are difficulties for us only because there is something in us which can stand, as it were, apart from them and say they ought not to be. The problem of evil is only a problem because of the existence of good. The problem of disorder is only a problem when we know what order is. And it seems to me that the agnostic gets away with it too easily. He delights in pointing out the difficulties of believing in God, and stops short of giving any other explanation of the existence of goodness, including beauty and truth. I always find it incredible that Shakespeare and Gandhi, not to mention other great examples, have come about by chance; I always find it incredible that order and beauty and heroism came about by accident, and that the mindless movings of innumerable electrons and the rest going on for long enough could, in fact, produce among other things beings who could know them and criticise the electrons and each other. Nor does the magic word of evolution, as understood either by Herbert Spencer or Julian Huxley, explain it.

I am therefore ready to welcome an account of God the Creator which shows that we ourselves are made for a purpose which is greater than ourselves. I shall not expect to understand the whole of the plan; but I shall try to understand as much of it as I can, and to fit in with what I can understand.

We are entitled, as a preliminary, to call the bluff of mathematical hypnotism—I mean the hypnotic effect of large numbers. After all, numbers are a human device, and you can do almost anything with them. They say there are as many molecules in a teaspoonful of water as there are teaspoonsful in the Atlantic Ocean. What a horrid thought! But I can drink the teaspoonful just as easily as if I did not know it. The notion of infinity is very hypnotic. But it is only a mathematical device; it has a perfectly clear meaning to the mathematician, and he does not let it get him down. There is an infinite number of prime numbers, horrid thought—but that does not make two times three equals six any more difficult to cope with.

I need not refuse to see pattern and purpose when they are under my nose, because I cannot see at all what is over the horizon.

And we need not be sentimental about the so-called wastefulness of nature. Waste is a human conception, which applies only when the supply is limited. A little ship 'uses' less of the ocean to float it than the Queen Elizabeth does, but you do not say the little ship is more wasteful. It is no tragedy that the codfish mother produces two million eggs, of which on an average only two will grow to maturity. (I say two, because I suppose one has to be a codfish father; the rest are eaten by other fishes and do their bit.) Nor need we be afraid because we are told there may be rational life on other worlds. Why not, indeed? God's way with this world is all we know, and all we need to know. . . .

I do not find that the Christian answer deals with all my questions; I do find that it deals with more of them than any other does, and that it sets the others in a light where they can be coped with practically, if not completely understood. . . .

'God created the heavens and the earth.'

How he created it, and still creates, we may learn in great part from science, and we are still learning. But science alone, as Hoyle and many others agree, cannot give us a clue to the purpose, if any. How much further can we get if we pursue the clue which Israel so surprisingly was given? . . .

At first there is only the raw material of a world. 'The earth was without form and void; and darkness was upon the face of the deep. And the Spirit of God moved upon the face of the waters.' Herbert Spencer called this an incoherent, indefinite homogeneity, a world in which there are no distinctions.

The rest of the process is the introduction of distinctions and of new and ever richer forms of pattern. The beginning of pattern and new order into what is there already is not less creative than creation out of nothing. If you do not see this you confine God the Creator to one action in the indefinitely far past, and attribute all the really interesting things that happened afterwards to chance or the working of unalterable law. . . .

God said, 'Let there be light, and there was light. . . . And God divided light from the darkness.' Here is the first permanent distinction. Do we get much further if we say that God divided the protons from the electrons?

By the work of the second day, 'Let there be a firmament in the midst of the waters', Genesis means the division between the water in the clouds above the sky, and the water of the sea and springs; it is followed on the third day by the distinction between the three states of matter, without which nothing more interesting can appear. It is the condition of combined permanence and change. In the narrow range between too hot and too cold, too runny and too still, things begin to happen. (How dull the sun and moon are compared with the earth ! One is far too hot for anything to stay put, and the other too cold for anything to alter.)

But the really interesting part begins with the creation of living things. Here is a kind of new creation. Created being must co-operate with the Creator. It is 'Let the earth bring forth', 'Let the waters bring forth'. It can no longer be done by merely thinking or by a bare word, or by manipulation of what is there already. Living beings *can* only be created by being allowed to grow, and their distinctive excellencies *can* only be developed by being allowed to grow in a world where other living beings are. There is here something preparatory for the freedom of response which we certainly find higher up, and God must sanction, maintain, and even delight in the adventures of his creatures in solving the problems which the conditions of their life set to them.

A mountain reaching up into the sky is a thing of beauty and delight; and we can in our moments of vision see something of the beauty and catch something of the delight. The same mountain, clothed at its foot with jungle, and that jungle full of wild life, each thing living in its own way and bringing forth after its kind is more delightful and beautiful. And since every increase of knowledge and sympathy increases the beauty and delight, I believe that an infinite knowledge and sympathy must delight in it too; for God can see not only the multitudinous things in every present instant, but the past and future of their species. He loved them into being, and he must delight in them. He need not grieve because they are creatures of an hour; they are meant to be like that, and do not grieve at it themselves. They were not, are, and will not be. Birth, reproduction and death are all part of the pattern.

Now see, on the edge of the jungle there is a human village. The picture is enriched again, as much as when the jungle clothed the mountain. And if you came to know that village intimately you would find in it things the jungle could not show. You would find the women and children, learning to control their environment and themselves, looking before and after, learning by experience; decorating their houses and themselves, growing flowers for pleasure, wrestling with problems of conduct and beginning to ask the questions 'Why?' and 'How?' Alas, you would find something else which you could not find before, people knowing the right and doing the wrong, hatred, malice and deliberate untruthfulness.

Leave that for a moment. Sin apart, what should we see? Reasonable being exercising 'dominion over the fish of the sea, and over the fowl of the air, and over every living thing that moveth upon the face of the earth', and exercising that dominion in line with the purposes of God; sharing in the work of creation as gardeners and artists do, seeing, loving and enjoying the world, and beautifying and enriching it by their presence. Take one example. When there were eyes to see, the beauties of perspective were created; the mountain viewed from this point or from that is other than the mountain merely thought by God. Its lower slopes are worked into little fields, enriched by human labour, human love and the legends of the people. It is climbed upon, built upon, perhaps prayed upon.

The infinite, trusting love of God has called this into being. He has done it by loving and trusting, letting men grow, and giving them their world to love and work in. He wins them to it for he cannot force them, and all that went before was necessary for this, besides being good in itself. The constant framework of the physical was necessary if they were to learn responsibility, and the boundless prodigality of nature in and around them was necessary if they were to experiment and learn by failure and success.

But the love which is in creation is not yet satisfied. We have seen that for the animals mortality is not a tragedy, nor for their creator. But with man it is different. To be made in the image of God means to be capable of intercourse with him, to pass beyond the creation to the creator, from the many to the One, from the particular to the universal. It means to seek the real beyond appearances, to be unsatisfied with anything short of perfection, to have a hunger for the infinite. It means to understand and to respond to an unconditional obligation, and to strive after an ideal which can never be realised in time. This creation of a finite being with a capacity for the infinite is the greatest creative miracle of all. This least of all could be done by the exercise of a mere *fiat*, of compulsive power. Here only loving invitation could serve. Nothing but the Word of God, addressed to his own heart and mind, mediated indeed in nature and love of man to man, communicated through the shared experiences of religious worship, but speaking also in the innermost privacy of the soul; nothing but the Word of God inviting men to love him more than these, and to lose even life for his sake, could make the creature capable of eternity.

If there was delight in the singing together of the morning stars, in the intricate play of the cosmic pattern; if there was more delight in the grace and subtle devices of animals and plants, and yet more delight in man, conscious of nature and of his part in her life; who can measure the joy that there must be when all this reaches its climax, and one human soul returns to share the joy of its creator for all eternity? And only the saint, who has an inkling of that joy, can guess the pathos, when one soul, to whom so much is offered, is content with less.

In fact they all went wrong. If you look at the world you cannot deny it, and if you look ever so far back into the past you will never come to a time when there were men who were unspoilt. . . . The Bible says that the essence of the error was self will, self will expressing itself in pride which took to itself what was God's prerogative, and tried to be equal with him. In fact they wanted to live for self-chosen ends instead of by his direction.

They were made by and for love, and so necessarily the condition of their life was co-operation, where no one lived to himself, but everyone affected everyone else. . . .

I think, as a matter of fact, that things began to go wrong before there were any men at all. The risks of freedom reach right down into the animal creation. Whole species missed their way because they specialised too soon. Some went in for defence, and covered themselves with armour, and became incapable of growth. Some went in for attack and developed jaws and teeth at the expense of brain space. Some went in for size, and got bigger and bigger till they died of very bigness. Some took the easy way, and became parasitic, like the horrid rhizocephala. . . .

Some species were so comfortable that they refused to grow up, like the axolotl. That interesting fish lives in the lakes round Mexico City, where the water is always warm, and there is plenty of food. It was always supposed to be just a fish, till some specimens were taken away in a tank to Paris, and there in colder water, and introduced to strange food, they suddenly transformed themselves in the next generation, and turned out all the time to have been the larvae of salamanders. At home in the warm water, they did not trouble to grow up, and had learnt even how to reproduce their kind while still remaining infants. I sometimes seem to see axolotl-like forms facing me in the pew.

T. R. MILFORD, *Foolishness to the Greeks*

God and morality

In the face of much scepticism about moral values and a tendency to relegate morality to the level of convention, the Christian is committed to a belief in the ultimate seriousness of morality, however much he may share other men's difficulty and puzzlement in making actual moral decisions. He holds that goodness exemplified, say, in the character of a person (supremely, he would say, in the person of Jesus Christ) is recognizably as different from evil as chalk from cheese, and that there is a crucial difference between matters of taste and questions of moral value.[1] Such beliefs are not exclusively held by Christians, of course, but where they disagree with agnostics who might share the above convictions is in seeing a connection between these and a belief in God.

The passages that follow make an attempt to explore some of the issues concerning this connection. After the introduction, 82, passages 83 and 84 both tackle the same central problem of the basis of moral judgements, 83 at the relatively straightforward level of the ordinary thinking man, 84 at the more complex level of the professional philosopher. Some will find the challenge of the latter enticing and bracing, but some will find it altogether too complicated. It is suggested that the former read 83 first and then go on to tackle 84 in detail (along the lines indicated at the end), while the latter spend their time solely on 83.

The remaining passages, 85-8, take up the question of Judgement, which for the Christian is inescapably bound up with the *ultimate* seriousness of morality. Heaven and Hell reflect what Christians have to say about this ethical evaluation, and each writer in his own way tries to illuminate the two concepts—in particular, what they are not. Between them they raise a number of questions which deserve very careful consideration:

(i) Does it *really* matter what sort of people we are, how we behave, how we use our gifts and opportunities, how we treat others? If not, what are the implications of believing that it does not? How much is lost by discarding the concept of Heaven and Hell? If these things do really matter, in what way do they matter, how is their importance brought home to us? (See, for example, in passage 85, the phrase 'the truth of final consequences'. What does this truth assert?)

(ii) What bearing has the problem of Free Will and Determinism on the question of the Judgement of God? What are your views on the former and on what are they based?

(iii) Does it help our understanding of the problem if, instead of talking about The Last Judgement, we talk about the Last Court of Appeal? Do we recognize that in other spheres of experience there is a standard of judgement other than merely human valuation? For example, scientists, historians, and artists, when they speak of their integrity being at stake, imply that their work is judged by something else than other people's opinion; to deny this is 'damnation' (see Charles Williams's novel *Descent into Hell*).

1. For a fuller exposition of this conviction see no. 20, The Dilemma of Morality.

(iv) Do you believe in 'Heaven' and/or 'Hell'? On what grounds do you accept or reject belief in them? How do you conceive of them? What are the difficulties? Discuss the attempts made in these passages to clarify the concepts. Which do you find helpful and which unhelpful? What, in particular, is passage 87 trying to tell us?

82. God as the source of moral order

The purpose of this introductory passage is simply to remind ourselves of some of the Biblical evidence for the conviction which is central to the Hebrew-Christian tradition that the basis of the right ordering of man's life and of his relation to his fellows is to be found in the 'righteous' will of God, the knowledge and acceptance of which constitute man's true well-being. (Cf. for a simple statement of this Deut. 6: 1–9, 10: 12–13, 30: 15–20.)

This section makes no attempt to work out in detail the development of this conviction from its early rudimentary form, in which (as in Deut.) the reward of obedience to God's will is represented as national security and prosperity, to the higher levels of spiritual insight. The passages are selected to illustrate certain distinctive notes in the conception of God's 'righteousness'.

So far as the *Old Testament* is concerned they are chosen mainly from the great eighth century prophets, Amos, Hosea, Isaiah, Micah. Their distinctive achievement was to transform the conception of a 'national' God whose business is to watch over his chosen people into the conception of a God whose ethical demand sets a standard of conduct and relationships which is ultimately seen to be 'universal' in its application to humanity as a whole.

(1) God's will for man is essentially *social*. It demands justice and fair dealing.

   Amos 5: 10–15. Micah 3: 1–5: Isaiah 1: 21–23.

(2) It repudiates 'religious observance', orthodoxy and conformity, as a substitute for (1).

   Isaiah 1: 10–17, 58: 1–11. (a later passage but clearly influenced by 8th cent.) Micah 6: 6–8. Hosea 6: 6.

(3) It takes account of *national* as well as personal standards and includes all nations under its judgements.

   Amos 1: 3–3.2 The sting of the passage is in 3: 1–2. You can get the sense of the whole passage if you think of a British statesman making a sweeping criticism of the iniquities of Russia, China, U.S.A., South Africa, France and then turning at the end to lash the internal rottenness and hypocrisy of Britain.

It is worth noting that none of these men are 'professionals', priests or theologians. They are ordinary laymen of widely differing backgrounds. Amos is a peasant farmer with a countryman's scorn of urban luxury. Isaiah is a man of high standing who can speak on equal terms to nobles and the King.

Their ethical insights spring from direct observation of what they see around them in the corruption of their society, and from their inherent sense that these things are an offence against what they know to be God's standards.

New Testament

It does not take any profound study of the gospels to realise how unmistakably the teaching of Jesus picks up and reinforces many of the same ethical insights.

(1) There is the same insistence on the fact that it is the way in which men behave to their fellow-men that is the basis of God's judgement.

Matt 20 : 1–16. The labourers in the vineyard. Matt. 25 : 31–46. The parable of 'the great surprise'. Luke 16 : 19–31. Dives and Lazarus.

(2) There is the same repudiation of religious performance as a substitute for justice and mercy.

Matt. 5 : 23–24. 23 : 23–28. cf. Matt. 12 : 1–14. Luke 13 : 10–17. His constant protests against the official attitude to the Sabbath.

(3) There is the same refusal to recognise any claim to national privilege.

Matt. 8 : 5–13 (note vv. 11–12). The Centurion. Luke 10 : 25–37. The good Samaritan.

The point at which the teaching of Jesus diverges significantly from that of the prophets is this : Their emphasis falls mainly on the inevitability of God's judgement upon the wrong-doing of their nation, though at the same time they look forward to a moment when God will intervene to right these wrongs and bring in an era of righteousness.

Jesus starts with a different assumption, a revised time-table, as you might say. Cf. Mark 1 : 14–15. 'Jesus came into Galilee proclaiming the good news of God in these words : 'Time's up ! The reign of God is on your doorstep. Make a fresh start and believe the good news'. His whole understanding of human life is dominated by the conviction that *here and now* it is possible for men to see and enter into a new 'dimension' of living, a dimension in which 'God reigns', his sovereignty is acknowledged, and his will is done (cf. the Lord's Prayer). It does indeed involve a radical break with the past. *Metanoeite* (repent) means 'Change your whole outlook, make a fresh start'; and he is under no illusions as to the difficulty and the cost of doing this. Not the least part of the difficulty consists in getting rid of mistaken views of God's nature and what he really desires as man's response to his will. But once that is seen and accepted, morality ceases to be a painful struggle to earn God's approval by keeping rules, and becomes a free response to a love which takes us as we are and makes us what we were meant to be.

F. A. COCKIN

83. The basis of moral judgements

We have to deal with a number of separate questions of general principles. We may distinguish the following:

1. Does morality derive from God's will or from man's judgement?
2. Is morality static or revisable?
3. Is it best embodied in rules or ideals?
4. Does it bear mainly on actions, or on motives and dispositions?
5. How much liberty of interpretation rests with particular cultural groups or individuals?

. . . All Christians will presumably accept, in some form, the view that morality is an expression of the will of God for mankind; and that the divine will was uniquely embodied in the life and teaching of Jesus Christ. There is thus bound to be a conflict between Christians and every kind of agnostic or atheist humanist as regards the formal definition of morality. However this conflict need not necessarily extend to the *content* of morality—though of course it often does so. Christians believe in a God who is personal and loving and who wills for each man and woman the most enduring and complete happiness of which they are capable. But many humanists also take as their fundamental axiom the promotion of human happiness; and it may happen that their ideal of human happiness coincides more or less closely with the Christian one. In such cases there will be a considerable measure of agreement on the qualities of character and the conditions of human life that should be sought, even where there is acute disagreement as to the best means of promoting them. To take the obvious instance, many humanists would agree that a contented and stable marriage is a most desirable condition even though they disown the Church's theology and also reject its insistence that marriage is a union for life.

However the first question posed above is linked with the others. Thus humanists are apt to claim that the Christians' reliance on divine authority prevents them from considering moral issues with proper sympathy and detachment, and inclines them to give restrictive and repressive answers to questions (2) and (5). . . . There are at least two forces inclining Christians to a conservative approach; on the one hand, their reliance on the Bible and on the example of Jesus

Christ in particular; and on the other the acceptance, by important Christian communities, of the theory of Natural Law.

The appeal of the Bible

Intelligent Christian opinion no longer regards the Bible, or even the New Testament, as a text-book from which one can extract authoritative rulings which automatically decide contemporary problems. . . . Older fashions of thought no doubt survive among Christians, but we are inclined to think they are overstressed by humanists, who not unnaturally desire to point out the weakest features of the faith they are opposing. Nevertheless, the Christian reliance on the New Testament operates as a restraining force, whether one regards it as a source of stability or as a brake on progress. . . . When all allowances are made it is hard to escape the conclusion that Christ laid down *some* positive and definite rulings for his followers. It is well known that St Paul, in I Corinthians, regards the pronouncements of Jesus, where available, as literally applicable and as the final court of appeal; and it should be remembered that this letter is a valuable historical document which can be dated with some precision and which is of earlier date than the gospels.

Despite all this, there is an impressive body of Christian tradition which has long been prepared to stress the relative liberty of the Christian calling and the necessity of re-interpreting Christ's teaching to meet changing situations. St Gregory of Nyssa and St Augustine, at the end of the fourth century, were already arguing for the view that God makes different demands on different human generations; indeed this view had been expressed even earlier by Christians, in order to justify their abandoning restrictive or crude moral rules found in the Old Testament. There is, therefore, nothing strictly new in the contention that Christian discipleship can be identified in each generation by its temper and attitude rather than by its adherence to a fixed moral code. Nevertheless, within this general pattern of thought it is perfectly possible to argue that certain moral rules acquire a position in which it is inconceivable that they should be justifiably abandoned. We cannot imagine any circumstances in which it would be right to tolerate all forms of homicide. . . .

The theory of Natural Law

There is a second factor which has impelled large sections of the Church to regard moral rules as fixed and unalterable, namely the theory of Natural Law. This theory is not confined to Christians today; a version of it, though much reduced in content, has been persuasively restated by Prof. H. A. L. Hart.[1] Nor did it originate with

1. *The Concept of Law* (Oxford, Clarendon Press, 1961).

Christianity but was worked out by Stoic philosophers, and was stated in all its essentials by Cicero *c.* 55 B.C.:

'True law is right reason in agreement with Nature; it is of universal application, unchanged and everlasting; it summons to duty by its commands, and averts from wrongdoing by its prohibitions. . . . There will not be different laws at Rome and at Athens, or different laws now and in the future, but one eternal and unchangeable law will be valid for all nations and for all times, and there will be one master and one ruler, that is, God, over us all, for He is the author of this law, its promulgator and its enforcing judge.'[1]

The law which this theory envisages is something that has imperative or prescriptive force, telling us how we ought to act; it is thus clearly distinguishable from the 'laws of nature' as the scientist of today conceives them, which are indicative statements telling us how things actually do behave. . . . So far as the theory is denied or restricted we are left with alternative systems of morality, one of which, in the Christian view, rests on a divine revelation made through Christ to the Church. Christians may and should commend such a morality to non-Christians; they are entitled to argue that all men should adopt it; but they are not entitled to claim (as they could if the Natural Law theory held good) that all men have a duty to obey it.

We have to ask, therefore: What, if any, is the content of the Natural Law? The barest possible minimum that has sometimes been suggested is the principle that good should be done and evil avoided. But this is vacuous principle that can hardly be denied without absurdity. On the other hand, modern anthropology, by revealing the extraordinary diversity of custom obtaining in different cultures, has made it extremely difficult to point to any considerable body of moral rules as commanding universal agreement.[2]. . . The most that can easily be claimed is that all moral systems recognise certain basic features of the human situation and claim to regulate certain areas of human life; but the method of regulation varies widely in different cultures. This variation does not of course imply that all such methods are equally good; it is quite legitimate to argue that some sets of rules are better than others. But it does tend to discount the view that God made known a definite set of moral requirements to all men everywhere. . . .

Three Christian positions examined

POSITION I. The extreme conservative position, which has been most

1. *De Republica*, III. xxii. 33, as translated in D'Entreves, *Natural Law*, pp. 20–1.
2. This point was already made by Locke in denying 'Innate Practical Principles'; see *Human Understanding*, I. iii. 9–13.

fully worked out in the Christian developments of the Natural Law theory, regards moral rules as possessing permanent and absolute validity, so that the morality of a particular act is ultimately determined by whether or not it falls under the relevant rule. . . .

We find this position untenable for a variety of reasons. Our discussion of Natural Law has already suggested that permanent and absolute validity can only be claimed for a small number of exceedingly general principles which no reasonable man would dispute. The main principles of our working morality cannot be regarded in this light; since, first, moral rules can conflict, and in any such case one of the conflicting rules must be set aside; and secondly, it proves in practice very difficult to lay down absolute moral principles in precise terms so as to be morally acceptable without committing the fallacy of circular definition. Thus the principle that (e.g.) stealing is always wrong, is only helpful if there is some reasonably objective criterion of what constitutes stealing; it becomes circular if there is a tacit convention not to call an act 'stealing' unless we already agree that it is wrong.

Besides these technical objections to the extreme conservative position, we have a more important reservation, though admittedly one which is less easy to substantiate. We judge that in their traditional form the moral systems based on the concept of Natural Law cannot be sufficiently harmonized either with the best moral sense of our own day or with the teaching of Jesus as we have come to understand it. We are now much more ready to recognise moral goodness among people who live by very different moral codes from our own. . . . In doing so we think we can appeal to our Lord's example. This suggests that moral goodness is not to be identified with adherence to a particular code, even if that code be the best one, to the extent that the traditional moral systems imply. Indeed, quite alien moral codes may foster distinctive forms of virtue which are worthy of respect and are not to be dismissed simply as moral errors committed in good faith; and we are entitled to say this without in the least implying that the choice of codes is a matter of indifference, or one on which no rational argument is possible. . . .

POSITION II. The position which commends itself to a majority of our group, might be described as a modified conservative position. This would give considerably more weight to motives in evaluating moral action, though without adopting the radical thesis that motive is the only significant criterion or that love is the only significant motive. It would seek to define the position of moral rules by saying that even if moral rules are not theoretically perfect, or exactly indicative of God's will at the deepest level, yet in many cases they provide the best guidance we have, so that for practical purposes it is rational to treat them as absolute. This policy involves no dishonesty or lack of realism; it simply endorses the verdict of Aristotle that morality can never be an exact science.

This verdict has been widely approved and has even impressed itself on common speech; to say that something is 'morally' or 'practically' certain is to say that it is almost certain, and in this way, 'practically' has come to be used as a synonym for 'almost'.

Developing this line of thought, it is possible to make motive and character the primary subject of moral judgement, while also giving great weight to the value of a sound moral code as an indispensable framework within which good motives and dispositions will be encouraged. However, all actual codes contain elements of greater or lesser importance; and we could suggest that some moral rules are of such weight that no code could justifiably omit them. Consequently

(a) It may be held that certain rules are for all practical purposes universally valid, so that it is never morally justifiable to break them; . . . or

(b) It may be held that even if such rules do not completely coincide with the rights and wrongs of each case taken in isolation, yet they do prescribe what is normally good for our society. In this case we may have a duty to uphold the rule even at some sacrifice of personal liberty.

POSITION III. The third position, which finds some support among our group, may be described as a modification of the liberal view. It has been outlined by one of our members in the following terms :

Moral rules only express the collective choices of different human individuals and societies, some of them Christian, but most not, over the centuries. They have evolved, and are evolving. They are relative rather than immutable, though some are naturally less mutable than others. They are essentially educative devices though they may be valuable in, as it were, the post-graduate period by their provision of a concrete familiar body of doctrine against which human beings involved in difficult situations can test their own incomplete knowledge, mixed motives and unreliable emotions.

On this view, moral rules, regarded as 'educative devices', are to be treated with respect but in no case as the final court of appeal. The mature individual at least is free to set aside the rule, after due consideration, and decide a case in accordance with his own judgement of the best interests of the parties involved, and of society. The rightness or otherwise of the act will on this view depend partly on whether his judgement is sound, and partly on the integrity of his motives; though these two criteria are not always clearly distinguished. It may be noted that even fairly radical moralists are willing to retain moral rules in some such advisory capacity. It is after all fairly obvious that they are the only device which is simple and concrete enough to be useful to children and to many ordinary people. But writers of this school often suggest that they themselves and many of their readers have attained the necessary moral maturity to reinterpret the rules and on occasion to set them aside.

... We may perhaps [take] the case of truth-telling. It might be said that the good of society requires that lies be avoided, and that we consequently teach children to tell the truth, the whole truth and nothing but the truth; at a more mature age, they will still fulfil their duty to society if they are usually truthful; but this allows them to set aside the rule on occasions when accuracy would be pedantic, or a disclosure unkind, or an untruth clearly advisable despite the general presumption against it....

Some such position is attractive to some members of our group. To state it in a form which Christian judgement can accept, however, requires a fairly careful consideration of two of its main features, namely the use of motives as a criterion, and the assumption that the liberty claimed is compatible with a responsible attitude to society at large.

BRITISH COUNCIL OF CHURCHES COMMITTEE
on *Sex and Morality*

84. Duty and God's will: a symposium

(*a*)

Morality [according to the view *criticized* by this writer—Ed.] is an affair of being commanded to behave in certain ways by some person who has a right to issue such commands; and, once this premise is granted, it is said with some reason that only God has such a right. Morality must be based on religion, and a morality not so based, or one based on the wrong religion, lacks all validity.

It is this premise, that being moral consists in obedience to commands, that I deny. Suppose that I have satisfied myself that God has commanded me to do this or that thing, it still makes *sense* for me to ask whether or not I *ought* to do it. God, let us say, is an omnipotent, omniscient creator of the universe. Such a creator might have evil intentions and might command me to do wrong; and if that were the case, though it would be imprudent to disobey, it would not be wrong. We must judge for ourselves whether the Bible is the inspired word of a just and benevolent God or a curious amalgam of profound wisdom and gross superstition. To judge this is to make a moral decision, so that in the end, so far from morality being based on religion, religion is based on morality. A man might decide to put his conscience wholly into the hands of a priest or a Church, to make no moral decisions of his own but always to do what the priest tells him. Even he, though he makes but one moral decision in his life, must make and continually renew that one. Those who accept the authority of a priest or a Church on what to do are, in accepting that authority, deciding for themselves.

To deny that morality need or can have an external non-moral basis on which to stand is by no means to deny that it can have an internal basis, in the sense of one or a few moral beliefs that are fundamental to the other beliefs of the system. A man's views on gambling or sex or business ethics may form a coherent system in which some views are held *because* certain other views are held. Utilitarianism is an example of such a system in which all moral rules are to be judged by their tendency to promote human happiness. A moral system of this kind is like a system of geometry in which some propositions appear as axioms, others as theorems owing their place in the system to their derivability from the axioms. To move towards this goal is to begin to think seriously about morals.

In any system of morality we can distinguish between its content and its form. By its 'content' I mean the actual commands and prohibitions it contains, the characteristics it lists as virtues and as vices; by its 'form' I mean the sort of propositions it contains and the ways in which these are thought of as connected with each other. The basic distinction here is between a teleological morality in which moral rules are considered to be subordinate to ends, to be rules *for* achieving ends and consequently to be judged by their tendency to promote those ends, and a deontological system in which moral rules are thought of as absolute, as categorical imperatives in no way depending for their validity on the good or bad consequences of obedience, and in which moral goodness is thought to lie in conformity to these rules for their own sake.

How there can be these two radically different ways of looking at morality, can best be understood if we consider the way in which we learn what it is to be moral. For a man's morality is a set of habits of choice, of characteristic responses to his environment, in particular to his social environment, the people among whom he lives; and habits are learnt in childhood. Growing up morally is learning to cope with the world into which we find ourselves pitched, and especially to cope with our relations with other human beings.

I shall concentrate on a few points that seem to me to bear directly on the issue between the religious morality of law and the secular morality of purpose. Piaget made a detailed study of the attitudes of children of different ages to the game of marbles, and he found three distinct stages. A very small child handles the marbles and throws them about as his humour takes him; there are no rules governing his actions, no question of anything being done right or wrong. Towards the end of this stage he will, to some extent, be playing according to rules; for he will imitate older children who are playing a rule-governed game. But the child himself is not conscious of obeying rules; he has not yet grasped the concept of a 'rule', of what a rule *is*. We may call this the pre-moral attitude to rules.

The second type of attitude is exhibited by children from five to nine. During this stage, says Piaget, 'the rules are regarded as sacred and inviolable, emanating from adults and lasting for ever. Every suggested alteration in the rules strikes the child as a transgression.' Piaget calls this attitude to rules 'heteronomous' to mark the fact that the children regard the rules as coming, as indeed they do, from outside, as being imposed on them by others. We might also call this the 'deontological stage', to mark the fact that the rules are not questioned; they just *are* the rules of marbles, and that's that. At this stage the child has the concept of a rule, he knows what a rule is; but he has not yet asked what a rule is *for*. He does not question the authority of the rules.

Finally, at the third stage, the child begins to learn what the rules are for, what the point of having any rules is, and why it is better to have this rule rather than that. 'The rule,' says Piaget, 'is now looked upon as a law due to mutual consent, which you must respect if you want to be loyal, but which it is permissible to alter on condition of enlisting the general opinion on your side.' He calls this type of attitude 'autonomous' to mark the fact that the children now regard themselves, collectively, as the authors of the rules. This is not to say that they falsely suppose themselves to have invented them; but they are the authors in the sense of being the final authorities; what tradition gave them they can change. We might also call this stage 'teleological' to mark the fact that the rules are no longer regarded as sacred, as worthy of obedience simply because they are what they are: but as serving a purpose, as rules for playing a game that they want to play. Rules there must certainly be; and in one sense they are sacred enough. Every player must abide by them; he cannot pick and choose. But in another sense there is nothing sacred about them; they are, and are known to be, a *mere* device, to be moulded and adapted in the light of the purpose which they are understood by all the players to serve.

I want now to compare the religious with the secular attitude towards the moral system which, in its content, both Christians and Humanists accept. It needs little reflection to see that deontology and heteronomy are strongly marked features of all religious moralities.

First for deontology. For some Christians the fundamental sin is dis-obedience to God. It is not the nature of the act of murder or of perjury that makes it wrong; it is the fact that such acts are transgressions of God's commands. On the other hand, good acts are not good in them-selves, good in their own nature, but good only *as* acts of obedience to God. 'I give no alms only to satisfy the hunger of my brother, but to accomplish the will and command of my God; I draw not my purse for his sake that demands it, but his that enjoined it' (Sir Thomas Browne). Here charity itself is held to be good *only because* God has told us to be charitable. It is difficult not to see in this a reflection of the small child's attitude towards his parents and the other authorities from whom he learns what it is right to do. In the first instance little Tommy learns that it is wrong to pull his sister's hair, not because it hurts her, but because Mummy forbids it.

The idea of heteronomy is also strongly marked in Christian mor-ality. 'Not as I will, but as thou wilt.' The demand made by Christ-ianity is the total surrender of the will. If we dare to ask why, the only answer is 'Have faith'; and faith is an essentially heteronomous idea; for it is not a reasoned trust in someone in whom we have good grounds for reposing trust; it is blind faith.

The postulation of a god as the author of the moral law solves no more problems in ethics than the postulation of a god as first cause solves problems in metaphysics. Nor need we base morality, as I have done, on the metaphysical conception of Man as a rational, social animal, though we shall do so if we care to maintain the link with the old meaning of the word 'humanist'. To me some systematic view of the whole of my experience, some metaphysic, is essential, and this conception of the nature of Man makes more sense of my experience than any other I know. Inquiries into the nature of Man are relevant in two ways; first, because I have to live as a man among men, sec-ondly, because all men are to some degree alike and some of my limita-tions are common to us all. It is only in so far as men are alike that we can even begin to lay down rules as to how they should (all) behave. Morality consists largely, if not quite wholly, in the attempt to realize these common elements in our nature in a coherent way, and we have found that this cannot be done without adopting moral rules and codes of law. Humanism does not imply the rejection of all moral rules, but it does imply the rejection of a deontological attitude to-wards them. Even Piaget's older children could not have played marbles without rules; but they treated them as adaptable, as subservient to the purpose of playing a game, which is what they wanted to do. They treated the rules as a wise man treats his motor car, not as an object of veneration but as a convenience. This, I suggest, is how we, as adults, should regard moral rules. They must retain a certain inflexibility, since, in our casual contacts, it is important that people should be reliable, should conform so closely to a publicly agreed code that, even if we do not know them as individuals, we know what to expect of them.

But, though morality in this sense is necessary, it is not all. Rules belong to the superficial periphery of life. Like the multiplication table and other thought-saving dodges, they exist to free us for more important activities. It is beyond the power of any man to regulate all his dealings with all the people with whom he comes in casual contact by love; for love requires a depth of understanding that cannot be achieved except in close intimacy. Rules have no place in marriage or in friendship. This does not mean that a man must keep his word in business but may break promises made to his wife or to a friend; it is rather that the notion of keeping a promise made to a wife or friend from a sense of duty is utterly out of place, utterly foreign to the spirit of their mutual relationship. For what the sense of duty requires of us is always the commission or omission of specific acts.

That friends should be loyal to one another I take for granted; but we cannot set out a list of acts that they should avoid as disloyal with the sort of precision (itself none too great) with which we could list the things a man should not do in business. However large we make the book of rules, its complexity cannot reach to that of a close personal relationship. Here what matters is not the commission or omission of specific acts but the spirit of the relationship as a whole. A personal relationship does indeed consist of specific acts; the spirit that exists between husband and wife or between friends is nothing over and above the specific things they do together. But each specific act, like each brush-stroke in a picture or each note in a symphony, is good or bad only as it affects the quality of the relationship as a whole. The life of love is, like a work of art, not a means to an end, but an end in itself. For this reason in all close human relationships there should be a flexibility in our attitude to rules characteristic of the expert artist, craftsman or games player. Our chief consideration should be, not to conform to any code of rules, but simply how we can produce the best results; that we should so act that we can say in retrospect, not 'I did right', but 'I did what befitted the pattern of life I have set myself as a goal'.

I should like to end by descending to the relatively specific, and to consider as an example one moral rule, the prohibition of adultery. By 'adultery' I understand the act of sexual intercourse with someone other than one's spouse. It is expressly forbidden in the Bible, absolutely and without regard to circumstances; until very recently it was almost the only ground for civil divorce. A marriage is supposed to be a life-long union. It could be entirely devoid of love—some married couples have not spoken to each other for years, communicating by means of a blackboard; yet no grounds for divorce existed. Or the husband might insist on sexual intercourse with his wife against her will and yet commit no sin. But let him once go out, get drunk, and have a prostitute and the whole scene changes. He has sinned; his wife has a legal remedy and, in the eyes of many who are not Christians but have been brought up in a vaguely Christian tradition, he has now done a serious wrong. This is a rule-and-act morality according to which what is wrong is a specific act; and it is wrong in all circumstances even, for example, if the wife is devoid of jealousy or so devoid of love that she would rather have her husband lie in any bed but hers. If we look at this rule against adultery from a teleological standpoint it must appear wholly different. A humanist may, of course, reject the whole conception of monogamy; but if, like myself, he retains it, he will do so only because he believes that the life-long union of a man and a woman in the intimacy of marriage is a supreme form of love. If someone who holds this view still thinks adultery is wrong, he will do so because it appears to him to be an act of disloyalty, an act likely to break the union which he values. Two consequences follow from this. The first is that if a marriage is, for whatever reason, devoid of love, there is now no union to break; so neither adultery nor any other act can break it. The second is that since adultery is now held to be wrong, not in itself, but only *as* an act of disloyalty, it will not *be* wrong when it is *not* an act of disloyalty. An adultery committed with the full knowledge and consent of the spouse will not be wrong at all. A so-called 'platonic' friendship, even too assiduous an attendance at the local pub or sewing-circle, anything that tends to weaken the bonds of love between the partners will be far more damaging to the marriage and consequently far more deeply immoral. Just *what* specific acts are immoral must, on this view, depend on the particular circumstances and the particular people concerned. Christians also insist on the uniqueness of individual people; but since law is, of its nature, general, this insistence seems wholly incompatible with the morality of law to which they are also committed.

P. H. NOWELL-SMITH, in *Christian Ethics and Contemporary Philosophy*

(b)

Nowell-Smith carefully distinguishes between the form and the content of religious morality. The content, however, he regards as not specifically religious, being the property of humanists also. What he objects to is the formal aspect of Christian behaviour, and by that he means primarily its reliance on rules. And this view of the matter I find extraordinary. It is not that I wish to question his views on the place of rules in the good life: by the time that he has had time for his accustomed qualifications, the sharp edge of his distinction between rule and end is considerably blunted, and the result is one which a Christian would not wish to challenge. No: what is extraordinary is what Nowell-Smith believes Christians to believe. For if there ever was a religion which challenged the morality of rules, it is Christianity. Right from the beginning, Christ preached that the 'rules' of the Jewish law were not enough: 'Except your righteousness shall exceed the righteousness of the scribes and Pharisees, ye shall in no case enter into the kingdom of heaven.' It is the character of Christian morality to do more than any rule could demand, in a spirit of love and service. 'The wind bloweth where it listeth: so is every one that is born of the Spirit.' Could Nowell-Smith demand a looser texture than that? The Gospel has confronted and confounded Roman rules, Nordic rules, Shinto rules, Confucian rules, and not least Greek rules; and the common charge against Christians among responsible Eastern conservatives today is that by breaking down rules they produce anarchy and pave the way to communism—a charge more disconcerting, because better grounded, than Nowell-Smith's. Certainly the basic Christian texts are as hostile to mere rules as Nowell-Smith himself. If Christian behaviour has impressed him otherwise, it is not because it is Christian, but because it is not Christian enough.

There is, of course, a place for rules in Christian behaviour. 'Think not I am come to destroy the law, or the prophets: I am not come to destroy, but to fulfil.' 'The law was our schoolmaster to bring us unto Christ, that we might be justified by faith.' These represent the law as a stage on the journey and not as a destination. And this is exactly what Nowell-Smith wants. He understands the part played by rules in the education of children; he merely protests that they should not continue to play the same part in adult life. Paul's analogy of the schoolmaster should surely suit him admirably.

In the more intimate and affectionate relations such as marriage and friendship, one does not stop behind with the rules; and this is the reason why these relations are so much more central than those which require of us only justice. But even here, and elsewhere much more, sitting loose to the rules can be a perilous adventure for the unprepared; it so often means not rising above them, but sinking below them. We are constantly pricked by desire or enraged by opposition; and the best thing we can do is to sit on ourselves till we come round. To that end rules are a great stand-by, and they are most serviceable when most inflexible; otherwise we shall make exceptions in our own favour. If Nowell-Smith has never felt like that, he is to be congratulated, but he is not in a position to speak to the multitude. Nowell-Smith proposes to treat rules as a wise man treats his car, 'not as an object of veneration but as a convenience'. 'Convenience' is an under-statement resulting from his underplaying of evil (one *can* do without a car); but substitute 'necessary second best' and there is nothing to distinguish him from a Gospel Christian. I hope he will not be dis-appointed. Nowell-Smith supports the specifically Christian and reli-gious element in Christian morality against the Pharisee, the Roman, and the modern rationalist pagan. On the subject of rules orthodox Christianity is, from Nowell-Smith's point of view, on the side of the angels.

There are, however, other matters on which Nowell-Smith dissents from 'religious' morality. The first is his subordination of deontology to teleology. On this I shall only observe that he assumes that atten-tion to duty means attention to rules. Against it I should urge that attention to duty can never be attention to rules only, because what is in question, whenever one does one's duty, is what one ought to do in a particular case, and every particular case is a meeting-place of rules at least potentially in conflict. For duty, as for Nowell-Smith's alterna-tive, 'coping with the world in a manner satisfactory to ourselves', rules are in the category of ways and means. Duty is not the end-product of a Christian life, any more than it is for Nowell-Smith.

By heteronomy Nowell-Smith means the determination of the will by reference to some external authority. It is clear that this does happen in the nursery, and also that the answer 'Because I tell you' may be unreasonably perpetuated beyond its proper age-limit. The authority which he is concerned to challenge is the will of God. ('Not as I will, but as thou wilt', he quotes with disparagement—forgetting not only the divine compassion of it but also the agonizing effort of a human decision.) There are many other authorities which he might have challenged, especially the political mass-movements which have been in the past most effectively withstood by men who appealed to the will of God. However, it is the most liberating authority which most disturbs him, so let us follow where he leads.

To appeal to the will of God, then, even against tyrants, is to submit oneself *and not to decide*. If that assertion is mistaken, the whole argument breaks down. I propose to argue that this view of the matter is both untenable and bad theology. The first qualm induced in the reader is set in motion by Nowell-Smith himself. He observes that 'those who accept the authority of a priest or a church on what they are to do, are, in accepting that authority, deciding for themselves'. This is surely true, and it shows that authority and deciding are not incompatible. And if it is true of a priest or a church, *a fortiori* it is true of the decision to follow God's will. It might be replied that it is a decision, but a decision to end decisions; but Nowell-Smith sees that this account will not do. He realizes that the decision has constantly to be reaffirmed. His objection must therefore be either to the content of the decision, or to the reasons for the decision. But he has already conceded that the content is common ground between himself and his opponents. It must be the reasons for the decision which he finds fault with. But, supposing he were right on this issue, it would still be wrong to confuse it with the quite different issue, whether doing the will of God entails the total obliteration of decision.

The objection which Nowell-Smith takes to the will of God as a *reason* for moral action is that it is not a reason. It is not even based on 'a reasoned trust in someone in whom we have good grounds for reposing trust'; it is 'blind faith'. And one effect of this attitude is to cut away all the good social reasons even for such of our actions as the will of God also commends to us, substituting for them the sole requirement of 'the right relation to God'.

Nowell-Smith quotes Sir Thomas Browne as saying: 'I give no alms only to satisfy the hunger of my brother, but to accomplish the will and command of my God: I draw not my purse for his sake that demands it, but his that enjoined it.' He interprets this to mean that 'charity itself is held to be good *only because* God has enjoined us to be charitable'. He has certainly misinterpreted Browne by displacing the word 'only': he has made it appear that in Browne's view reference to the will of God *excludes* reference to the man's hunger, whereas all Browne said was that the expressed will of God is a further reason for relieving it. The man's hunger is one of the things the will of God is about. Love of God and love of neighbour are presented as complementary and collateral, but not as cause and consequence. Text for text, it would actually be possible to argue the other way round. 'If a man loveth not the brother whom he hath seen, how shall he love the God whom he hath not seen?' 'Blessed are the pure in heart, for they shall see God'—not vice versa. The Christian God cannot be loved by high-minded, self-centred people, and this is why Jesus kept up the barrage against the Pharisees. In doing what we can for others, we are *ipso facto* doing it for God; God is not so other than others, that we can serve them without serving him. It is the will of God that we should love our neighbour *because he is our neighbour*; only so do we do it for his greater glory.

Thus Christian heteronomy is always qualified. Obedience to the will of God is never pure and simple. If we sometimes think the will of God commands us to do to others what does not befit children of God, we can be sure we have got it wrong. The tradition of the Church warns us to be on our guard against diabolical simulations of the will of God; and if it is wholly heteronomous there is no way of telling the one from the other. So far from disagreeing with Nowell-Smith on this point, I entirely endorse him.

Nowell-Smith, in his conclusion, discusses a practical moral problem; and it is right that anyone joining issue with him should do the same. Nowell-Smith takes as his special case the moral rule prohibiting adultery. It is in fact a trump card. Adultery is the only kind of activity with specific and overt characteristics which the Sermon on the Mount condemns without exception or qualification. And he attacks the rule, *qua* rule, as he attacks rules in general, on the ground that 'just *what* specific acts are immoral must depend on the particular circumstances and the particular people concerned'. Now we have argued that Christianity is not a religion of rules. But here it would seem that we have as bleak and categorical a rule as ever existed.

Nowell-Smith proposes to look at the rule against adultery from a 'teleological standpoint', as opposed to the 'rule-and-act' morality of the traditionalists. Nowell-Smith's teleological morality condemns adultery, because he thinks highly of loyalty as a principle of action and accepts 'life-long union in the intimacy of marriage' as 'a supreme form of love'. Now this means that adultery is to be avoided only because it conduces to the breakdown of loyalties. In that case, where adultery is consented to by the other party, or where there is no love left in the partnership, the rule against it no longer applies.

The question for a Christian who has offered the defence that Christianity is not a religion of rules is how he can avoid Nowell-Smith's conclusion; or, if he insists on unqualified condemnation of adultery, how he can avoid Nowell-Smith's premise, i.e. that Christianity *is* a religion of rules.

1. The first oddity in the argument is the tie-up between 'teleology' and 'loyalty'. Loyalty in itself is not in any sense a matter of consequences. *In so far* as they are done from loyalty actions are not motivated by consequences at all.

2. The second oddity in the argument is the extremely subjective interpretation of 'loyalty'. It is read off as 'feeling loyal', and not as 'having loyalties'. But it is a part of the morals of loyalty that one *has* loyalties whether one *feels* loyal or not—and the overruling of disloyal feelings is not a reversion to the morality of rules. Loyalty is mainly a matter of status and certainly not only a matter of contract. Even if neither party feels like observing it, they owe it to their families, their neighbours, their country, and themselves to work themselves back into wanting to observe it. An overt breach such as adultery makes the task harder. And if we are talking about consequences, it is necessary to consider the effect of adultery by consent on unilateral adultery, which stands condemned as cheating on Nowell-Smith's own formula. Human nature being what it is, i.e. rather more

fascinated by wickedness than Nowell-Smith thinks it is, it is to be suspected that the effect would be considerable.

3. It begins to be apparent that loyalties are nearly as exacting as rules; but they have the great advantage of being owed to persons and not to principles. If Nowell-Smith takes his stand on loyalties, he may have to go farther than he intends. And he makes it quite clear that he does want to stand on loyalties. He thinks it a good thing that there should be loyalties (and therefore no adultery) even if he sees nothing wrong about adultery in the absence of loyalties. But loyalties don't just happen : they have to be sustained by example and environment. They are hardly encouraged by a mutual agreement that they need not be observed.

4. It is now clear why adultery has no place in the Christian life. The Christian *agape* is a liberal and flexible kind of loyalty, not restricted to the demands of justice, willing to take the initiative in reconciliation, and centred, not on society, but on people's relation with each other. If this attitude is displayed by the parties to a marriage, adultery will be inconceivable. This is not the result of external rules (the breach of which is only too easily conceivable), but the internal and necessary expression of a way of life. And if it be asked why, then, the prohibition? the answer is that the way of life is practised by men who in its despite sometimes relapse into unsanctified imaginings; and then it is surely appropriate that they should be snapped out of them by a stiff injunction. The injunction, however, is not the reason for their loyalties, but merely the measure of their failure. If that is what Nowell-Smith finds distasteful in the New Testament, in view of his evident concern about loyalties, I cannot see why.

5. Nowell-Smith uses no other test than that of loyalties to distinguish humanist believers in monogamy like himself from other humanists who reject monogamy; and the critic is entitled to explore the implications of his criterion. If it is taken seriously, it is not consistent with adultery by mutual consent : loyalty is shown by what people do, and even if they agree to do what is disloyal, it is disloyal all the same.

I agree, of course, that adultery is not the only offence against married loyalties; I agree even that some unstigmatized offences may well be deadlier. And I do not believe that the ordinary ban on adultery is simply a taboo or arbitrary rule. But it does not follow that it is merely 'one of a set of recipes' 'for the achievement of an end'—even though it is admitted to be a good recipe and the end the generally laudable end of maximum and integral satisfaction.

A. BOYCE GIBSON, ibid.

(c)

I do not want so much to controvert Professor Nowell-Smith's thesis as to complement it. Most of what he says is true, and needs to be far more widely known by Christians than at present. My aim, as a Christian, is, rather, to make some further points about the Christian understanding of man and morality, so as to show that Professor Nowell-Smith's thesis, instead of being against Christian morality, is essentially consonant with it.

Professor Nowell-Smith criticizes the rule-bound character of many religious codes. Quite rightly. But Christ and St. Paul made the same criticisms long before. The very slogan that Professor Nowell-Smith chooses to fight under—'the Sabbath was made for man, not man for the Sabbath'—was first uttered by Christ. Christ it was who, holding the same high ideal of monogamy as that put forward by Professor Nowell-Smith, nevertheless refused to condemn the woman taken in adultery. Christ is much harder than Professor Nowell-Smith on the conventional morality of the conventionally religious; St. Paul is more concerned with the Law, but from the multiplicity of his utterances, one thing at least is clear : he is not a deontologist in Professor Nowell-Smith's sense. 'The letter killeth, the Spirit maketh alive.' Christian morality is as much concerned to controvert what he is trying to controvert as he himself is. For it is a sad truth that most professing Christians are in fact practising Pharisees, all Christ's own teaching to the contrary notwithstanding. Moreover, not everything Christ said would meet with Professor Nowell-Smith's approval : 'Except your righteousness exceed the righteousness of the Pharisees, ye shall in no wise enter into the Kingdom of Heaven.'

The Old Testament is not simply a set of commandments and laws, though Judaism became largely just this : its primary theme is the growing sense of the inexorability of God, a greater and greater awareness of a reality other than oneself, making for good. The peculiar tone of religious morality stems from this sense of the objectivity of values. Just as my believing something does not make it true, so my choosing something does not make it good : and just as I find myself under a relentless pressure to discover what the truth is, so equally I feel an unremitting urge to seek out and perform whatever it is that I ought to do. The Christian differs from the humanist not only in believing in God, but in disbelieving in man. The Christian holds that men are always imperfect : that though their aspirations may be infinite, their achievements are always limited. Being the mere mortal clay that we are, we never do have and never shall have Holy Wills. Although each of us is autonomous in the sense that only he can make up his own mind, it does not follow from a man's having made a decision, that he has made it rightly. And our decisions not only may be wrong, but quite often are. Autonomy for the humanist is a standard of adult behaviour which most men do, or can, attain: the Christian does not believe that men can attain an adequate standard. To the end of our lives we remain something of the child in moral matters. The Christian does not regard 'child-like' as a pejorative word. 'Unless ye turn and become as little children, ye can in no wise enter into the kingdom of heaven'. By comparison with the ideal of autonomy, we are none of us fully adult. We need the Moral Law, St. Paul can be roughly rendered, because we are not adult enough to take our own decisions correctly. But when, and if, we come to a full knowledge of God's love, then we shall be emancipated from the shackles of the Law, and shall be able to enter into the full freedom of the Christian who takes all his decisions for himself, and being filled with the spirit of love takes them all correctly. St. Paul sometimes talks of complete emancipation coming at a man's conversion to Christianity; but occasionally speaks as if even converted Christians see through a glass darkly, and only in the next world face to face. I think the latter view is right.

Often the father lets the child go its own way, and learn by its mistakes, but sometimes he lays down a ruling, the reason for which is beyond the comprehension of the child, but which the child is nevertheless required to obey. To me it seems obvious that one's attitude to an omniscient and loving being should be the same. The Christian, just turned twenty-one, is enjoined to follow the Christian teaching on, say, to take the most unpopular example, sexual morality in the same spirit of blind obedience as that in which, at an earlier stage, he followed his mother's injunctions about washing behind the ears. It is not, as Professor Nowell-Smith suggests, the arbitrary edict of a capricious being, but rather the wise instructions of an infinitely far-sighted one. Many men come in the end to believe with Professor Nowell-Smith that monogamy is the best and happiest form of life; and not a few will testify that chastity supports and supplements monogamy. But few adolescents really believe them, nor every adult; even among the middle-aged there are some who are tempted to break up their marriages, and will regret it if they do. The Christian code is clear and firm on this point. Of course it is not enough, as Professor Nowell-Smith points out, to secure the happiness of a marriage; nor would it be necessary to lay it down at all if we were all the time fully apprised of the pattern of life we wished to live and the means required to secure its realization. But for men such as we actually are, often inconsiderate, often lustful, often impatient, the seventh commandment is a helpful instruction.

The basic objection Professor Nowell-Smith has to Old Testament morality is the element of blind obedience. The Christian is prepared to do things for no other reason than that God tells him to do them. This objection can be largely met by a consideration of a disposition Professor Nowell-Smith does approve of, loyalty. For, though I cannot set out a precise list of acts that constitute loyalty or disloyalty, it seems to me to be the essence of loyalty that one trusts the person one is loyal to *beyond* the limits of one's own knowledge. I show my loyalty to someone when I do a thing which he wants me to do and which I would *not* have done on my own account, when I believe in him and accept his judgment without being able to justify it in the particular case under consideration. To believe one's friend when one can see for oneself that what he says is true is not to show any loyalty towards him; one would do that much for anyone. Loyalty, like faith, is an essentially heteronomous idea. It involves being ready to say 'Not as I will, but as thou wilt'. Churchill showed his faith in, and loyalty to, Roosevelt when in 1940 he made a sacrificial sale of Courtauld's American assets to the United States Government. It was certainly not something he would have done if he had been acting according to his own judgment nor something for which he could see any justification at the time of the request. Some degree of loyalty, faith, obedience, trust, is a necessary virtue for non-omniscient, finite, fallible beings, such as we ourselves are, if we are to have any relations with other beings, and are not to be utterly autarkic and sufficient in ourselves. Secondly, the obedience demanded of a Christian, although blind in the particular instance, is not without a general justification. The Christian is told to be chaste, to be long-suffering, not to impute bad motives to other people, irrespective of whether he can see how these characteristics fit into a desirable pattern of life, or are justified in any other way. But his obedience and loyalty to God are themselves justified by his belief that God loves him. Much has to be taken on trust, so much that some people's faith in God is severely strained. But the obedience demanded of the Christian is not utterly blind. Faith is not arbitrary. Although we are told not to expect God to justify his ways to us to our own satisfaction, we have a fair token of his general good will towards us in his willingness to undergo the agonies of death upon the cross. The non-Christian will reject that this actually happened, but that does not affect the *logic* of the Christian's position. The Christian's loyalty, although complete and unswerving, is not groundless or arbitrary. He has his reasons for believing in God and in God's goodness towards us.

The great merit of rules and commands is that they are fairly precise. I know how to keep the rules and obey commands long before I am able to carry out the agapeistical policy of loving God and doing what I like, and whereas there may be many disputes about what the best pattern of life is, or wherein the greatest good of the community lies, there is little room for dispute on whether one has committed adultery or whether one has broken the speed limit. And therefore we make use of rules, in spite of all their many disadvantages noted by Professor Nowell-Smith. There are dangers in making use of rules. What was intended to be a signpost can become a straitjacket, and men are all too ready to regard the observance of rules as a sufficient condition, instead of merely a necessary condition, of trying to live according to a certain ideal in common with other men. Many churchmen have been deplorably rule-bound. What gives Professor Nowell-Smith's paper its point is that what he is attacking corresponds so often with the actual practice of Christians; but not the practice of Christ nor the teaching of the Christian Church. Christians are, however, a good deal readier to recognize the necessity of having rules than Professor Nowell-Smith would be himself. This is because Christians take a very much lower view of themselves than do humanists. The Christian differs from the humanist, therefore, in having a much livelier sense of the difficulty of leading the good life or of coming to the knowledge of the truth. He differs also from some humanists at least, and all sceptics, in having an overpowering conviction that, incompetent though he is, there is a truth to be discovered and a good life to be lived; and these for him are based on his belief in God, and therefore are an absolute 'must'.

J. R. LUCAS, ibid.

Try to separate the different strands of the argument and to evaluate the worth and cogency of the three writers' treatment of each of them.

Imagine you are the fourth participant in the symposium and write your own contribution to the discussion.

85. The judgement of God: Hell?

J. S. Mill justly remarked that compared with the doctrine of endless torment any other objection to Christianity sinks into insignificance. In the past all Christians believed in hell on principle and enjoyed describing it in terms as grisly and crude as those employed by many Roman Catholics today. When enough people realized that, whatever the fate of those who repudiate God, a doctrine which implies that the Creator is less good than the creature must be false, then that doctrine had to be abandoned. Not without hesitations and quibbles, however, for the price of the abandonment was heavy. Rome is not yet prepared to pay it. Faithful to her view of revelation, she constantly and consistently preaches what she has received. In whatever imagery it is clothed, the existence of hell is still taught as part of the Faith without accepting which no Catholic can see God—a god whom, if he believed what he was told, no one in his senses would wish to see. Nor, apart from some pitiful efforts here and there to minimize the number of the lost, has she tried to dilute its significance. Dr. Arendzen, in *The Teaching of the Catholic Church* (1952), tells his readers, 'if all that was ever written, or painted, or carved expressive of the tortures of hell could be brought before us at a glance, it would certainly fall immeasurably short of the truth.' A book published in 1964 with the Southwark imprimatur and intended for Roman Catholic children in grammar schools, speaks of the physical fires of hell and the wicked writhing in envy and remorse for all eternity. Here credulity and superstition are combined.

We should, however, appreciate both the far-reaching implications of any rejection of orthodoxy, and admire the staunchness with which Rome has insisted on the annihilating effect of sin. Further, we must frankly face the fact that parodoxically those from all creeds most conscious of the love of God are frequently the very people who have held firmly to the doctrine of everlasting suffering. The explanation must surely be that it is a perversion of a truth, the truth, to use Von Hugel's term, of final consequences. Men can and do lose God by unrepentant rejection of him as he speaks with the voice of conscience. It is precisely because these great lovers of God saw the dreadfulness of this self-chosen negation and loss so clearly, that making use of current imaginative and conceptual expressions, they perverted it into an everlasting state of positive suffering.

MAGDALEN GOFFIN, *Superstition and Credulity*

86. The judgement of God: Heaven

We will begin by listing a few principles.

1. To hope for heaven has nothing particularly selfish about it. No one ever thought he could keep heaven to himself.

2. Heaven is not a cash payment for walking with God; it's where the road goes.

3. Heaven isn't an optional extra; our belief is nonsense without it.

4. Our reason for believing it isn't that nature points to it, but that it leads us to itself.

I should like to develop the last point a bit. Heaven is nothing that created nature produces; it is a new creation. Two consequences follow from this. The first is, that we have no interest in trying to isolate a piece of us called soul, which tends to outlive the body's collapse. Our immortality is the new gift of God, not the survival of our old nature, whether in whole or in part. It was pagan Greeks who talked about immortal soul, and with reason; for (to put it shortly) they thought the human spirit was a piece of godhead, able to guarantee immortal being to itself. The religion of the Bible teaches no such doctrine. God alone can give us a future. It is better, then, to talk about the resurrection of man than about the immortality of the soul. Belief in resurrection is belief not in ourselves, but in God who raises us. It is in fact the acid test, whether we believe in God or not. A God who raises the dead is a real power; he is not just a fanciful name for the order of nature, whether physical or moral. A God so identified with the natural order that he adds nothing to it is difficult to distinguish from the world he rules, or from the laws which govern it.

Now to take the second consequence. If the heavenly state is not something nature produces, but something God bestows, our ideas of heaven are bound to be ideas of a relation to God. Not that the heavenly state can simply consist of a relation to God; the citizens of heaven must have some way of being which is proper to them, some nature which God gives them; only we do not happen to know what it is.

It is silly to say, 'How marvellous to be in heaven! Our shirts will be whiter than the latest detergent can wash them, and we shall have no need to switch on the electric light'. It is not silly to say, 'Every now and then, perhaps, I manage to be at the disposal of God's will. How marvellous to be in heaven! I shall live in it all the time.' Nor is it silly to say, 'From time to time I think I catch a glimpse of what God is doing. How marvellous to be in heaven! I shall see his purposes in everything, as clearly as I read my friends' feelings on their faces.' Nor is it silly to say, 'Every now and then I see a bit of what God has put into the people round me. How marvellous to be in heaven! I shall see it all.' Nor is it silly to say, 'I acknowledge Christ by faith, and bless him in words for being very God and very man. How marvellous to be in heaven! I shall be familiar with the man in whom the Godhead is.'

If you consider the marvels I have mentioned, you will notice three things that are true of them all. First, they are joys of which we have a foretaste in this life; and so we know what we are talking about when we mention them. Second, they are joys which arise from a more perfect relation with realities—with God and with the children of God. Third, they are joys which might be actualized (for anything we know) under a variety of conditions, or states of being. Our faith in heaven is a confidence in the pattern of perfect relations; as for the state of being, we can leave it to God.

It is often said that heaven is the presence of God. There is nothing wrong with the formula, so long as it is taken to mean that the presence of God is what makes heaven heavenly; it is nonsense if it means that the presence of God defines a region or even a condition in which the blessed dead find themselves. And where is heaven? When I was a lad it was still supposed to be an insoluble problem. If heaven is completely non-spatial, then (we used to say) the heavenly life must be a featureless sea of feeling, a shapeless ecstasy; or anyhow nothing you could fairly call the resurrection-state of man. Whereas if heaven has any force of spatial dimension, then it falls somewhere in the field of space; a telescope might record it, an astronaut might reach it. And so heaven is pulled back into the perishable universe.

A pretty puzzle, and I was amazed to hear it solemnly restated the other day by a professor of philosophy; for I had supposed that Einstein had shown it up once for all as a piece of nonsense. According to his unanswerable reasoning, space is not an infinite pre-existent field or area in which bits of matter float about. Space is a web of interactions between material energies which form a system by thus interacting. Unless the beings or energies of which heaven is composed are of a sort to interact physically with the energies in our physical world, heaven can be as dimensional as it likes, without ever getting pulled into our spatial field, or having any possible contact with us of any physical kind. There may well be contacts which are not physical at all between earthly minds and heavenly minds, but that's another story.

Think what we may of heavenly dimensions, heaven is a sphere of created being, where God bestows his presence. And this he does at least in three ways: by a more visible providence, making the whole order of things the evident expression of an infinite goodness; by a more abundant grace, making the minds of his people transparent to his thought and their hearts to his love; by an incarnate presence with them in the glorified man, Jesus Christ.

Christ in glory is the heart of heaven, and it is difficult to see how those Christians who leave the life to come an open question can be Christians at all. If Christ is not now in glory, then this is a Christless world and God is a Christless God and we are Christless men.

Nothing is plainer in the faith of the New Testament than the ties attaching Christians to a living Christ. Because he is beyond the death we still have to face, our union with him is union with an achieved immortality. By dying, Christ not only made a supremely generous sacrifice, both overcoming enmity, and reconciling sinners to God; he also took the decisive step into that better state of being which lies beyond death. Sinners die into death, but Christ, strong in the power of God, dies into better life.

This annexing of an earthly fellowship to the heavenly state was begun when Christ, risen from death to glory, visited his surviving friends. Nothing like it ever has happened, or can happen—that the heart of heavenly being should visit earth, to leave on earthly senses the stamp of heavenly substance. No thoughtful Christian can allow the Resurrection to be placed in one category with any other class of events, any more than he can allow God to be placed in one category with any class of beings.

It is our business to state the Christian belief, as well as to examine the grounds for it. We turn to the other branch of our duty and ask a critical question. Why should anyone believe in the life to come?

The old-fashioned answer was, 'Because God has promised it'. If you asked how and where, they turned you up Bible texts. God had written the book, God could not lie. It is difficult for us to recapture so submissive an attitude to the written word. I would like to keep the formula, nevertheless: God has promised it, even though the fact is not sufficiently shown by citing chapter and verse. I should want to say that God's promise is a rope of several strands. If we untwist the rope, and take the strands separately, then very likely no one of them seems sufficient to take the weight. But they belong together, and there is no reason why they should not be allowed the mutual support they naturally offer one another. They are not five promises but one.

First there is the promise which lies in the very nature of man. Since the promise is God's promise, it depends on man's being the creature of God; it is not a promise atheists could read. But allowing that the creator has control over his works, we ask what he means by bringing up a creature capable of immortal hope; capable besides of drawing on the source of everlasting renewal by a personal and voluntary attachment to his creator. Does not the maker show his hand? Is there not an implicit promise of immortalization in the nature of such a creature as this?

The weakness of the promise lies in its inarticulate character; it lies buried in the facts, we have to spell it out by our own reasoning effort, and we are too familiar with the suspicion that a counter reason can be found to every reason. But though this strand would not bear the weight alone, it contributes greatly to the strength of the cord. The more striking and positive promises might appear irrational and isolated by themselves. It is otherwise if we can see them to lie in the line of a purpose which our very creation suggests.

The second strand we may take to be the teaching of Christ. It is not merely that so divine a teacher made his own a hope of future life which had begun to dawn in Israel. It is that he wagered his existence on it; that he accepted an early and a violent death as the gate of a kingdom in which he was appointed to rule the people of God.

The third strand is the evidence for the fulfilment of his hope; that is, of the resurrection. His body was not found, his friends could pay it no cult, his enemies could not use it in disproof of the gospel. And by visitations of his presence which they could not disbelieve, he convinced his disciples of a miracle which laid the cornerstone of heaven.

The fourth strand is the possibility which Christians find of relation to a living Christ.

The fifth is the orientation of such religious life as God's grace gives us, or as our co-operation allows. If it is real to us, how can the end be unreal to which it tends, and from which it derives its meaning? It would be possible to distinguish further strands in the rope of promise, but at least the five we have named are vital; vital not only to the strength of the whole cord, but also to one another. The Gospel-facts would not convince, if they were not real in our present experience. Present experience would not convince us even when overlaid upon the Gospel facts, if it found no foundation in the nature of man as a created being.

AUSTIN FARRER, *Saving Belief*

87. The judgement of God: The radiance of the King

When Clarence (a white man) went to Africa in the King's service, one glimpse of the King of Kings in the glittering dusty durbar was enough to convince him that it was only in His service that he would find peace.

But before he could do anything he had to disentangle himself from the twining embrace of his debts, the coils of a corrupt justice and the contempt of his fellow white men.

Then came the gruelling trek to the savage south—through the forest, tormented by the hidden power of the undergrowth, the soporific languor of exotic jungle scents and the frustration of innumerable false trails.

When Clarence reached Aziana there were still mountainous problems to be overcome before he could achieve his ambition. But at last the King arrived, and Clarence's opportunity of a meeting had come.

'The more Clarence looked at the king, the more he realised what courage, what audacity would be needed to go up to him.

'And it was not just his nakedness, it was not just his vileness which prevented Clarence from going up to him; it was something else—many other things. It was the fragility—the fragility as well as the great strength of the king—the same adorable fragility, the same formidable strength that Clarence had observed on the esplanade; the same smile, too, the same far-off smile which, like the look in his eyes, could be taken for disdain, and which really seemed to float round his lips rather than be an actual part of them. And probably his garments, too—the immaculate whiteness of the mantle, the gold of the twisted rope tied like a heavy turban round his head; so many other things, too, so many other things that would have taken a lifetime to enumerate. . . . But above all, so much purity, so much blazing purity. All these prevented Clarence from going up to him.

' "Those are the things I am losing for ever . . . " said Clarence.

'And he had the feeling that all was lost. But had he not already lost everything? He had the measure of his own unworthiness. He would remain for ever chained to the South, chained to everything he had so thoughtlessly abandoned himself to. Oh ! if only he could have his life again ! But can one ever go back and start again? Can one ever wipe out what has been? His solitude seemed to him so heavy, it burdened him with such a great weight of sorrow that his heart seemed about to break.

' "And yet. . . . My good-will . . ." he thought. "It's not true that I was lacking in good-will. I was weak, no one has ever been as weak as I am; and at nights, I was like a lustful beast. Yet, I did not enjoy my weakness, I did not love the beast that was inside me; I should have liked to throw off that weakness, and I should have liked not to be that beast. No, it's not true that I was lacking in good-will."

'But of what use was this good-will? Clarence was about to curse it, curse it for its failure to help him. And the tears sprang to his eyes.

'But at that moment the king turned his head, turned it imperceptibly, and his glance fell upon Clarence. That look was neither cold, nor hostile. That look. . . . Did it not seem to call to him?

' "Alas, lord, I have only my good-will," murmured Clarence, "and it is very weak ! But you cannot accept it. My good-will condemns me : there is no virtue in it."

'Still the king did not turn his eyes away. And his eyes. . . . In spite of everything, his eyes seemed to be calling. . . . Then, suddenly, Clarence went up to him.

'He went forward and he had no garment upon his nakedness. But the thought did not enter his head that he ought first of all to have put his boubou on; the king was looking at him, and nothing, nothing had any more meaning beside that look. It was so luminous a look, one in which there was so much sweetness that hope, a foolish hope, woke in Clarence's heart. Yes, hope now strove with fear within him, and hope was growing stronger than fear. And though the sense of his impurity seemed to be holding him back, at the same time Clarence was going forward. He went on with stumbling steps; he stumbled as he trod on the rich carpet; every moment it seemed to him as if his legs or the ground beneath him were going to disappear. But he kept moving forward, forward all the time, and his legs did not betray him, nor did the ground open up under him. And that look. . . . That look still did not turn away from him. "My lord ! My lord !" Clarence kept whispering, "is it true that you are calling me? Is it true that the odour which is upon me does not offend you and does not make you turn away in horror?"

'And because that look still calmly rested upon him, because the call was still going out to him, he was pierced as if by a tongue of fire.

' "Yes, no one is as base as I, as naked as I," he thought. "And you, lord, you are willing to rest your eyes upon me! " Or was it because of his very nakedness? "Because of your very nakedness! " the look seemed to say. "That terrifying void that is within you and which opens to receive me; your hunger which calls to my hunger; your very baseness which did not exist until I gave it leave; and the great shame you feel. . . ."

'When he had come before the king, when he stood in the great radiance of the king, still ravaged by the tongue of fire, but alive still, and living only through the touch of that fire, Clarence fell upon his knees, for it seemed to him that he was finally at the end of his seeking, and at the end of all seekings.

'But presumably he had still not come quite near enough; probably he was still too timid, for the king opened his arms to him. And as he opened his arms his mantle fell away from him, and revealed his slender adolescent torso. On this torso, in the midnight of this slender body there appeared—at the centre, but not quite at the centre . . . a little to the right—there appeared a faint beating that was making the flesh tremble. It was this beating, this faintly-beating pulse which was calling! It was this fire that sent its tongue of flame into his limbs, and this radiance that blazed upon him. It was this love that enveloped him.

' "Did you not know that I was waiting for you?" asked the king.

'And Clarence placed his lips upon the faint and yet tremendous beating of that heart. Then the king slowly closed his arms around him, and his great mantle swept about him, and enveloped him for ever.'

CAMARA LAYE, *The Radiance of the King*

88. The judgement of God: The weight of glory

I turn next to the idea of glory. There is no getting away from the fact that this idea is very prominent in the New Testament and in early Christian writings. Glory suggests two ideas to me, of which one seems wicked and the other ridiculous. Either glory means to me fame, or it means luminosity. As for the first, since to be famous means to be better known than other people, the desire for fame appears to me as a competitive passion and therefore of hell rather than heaven. As for the second, who wishes to become a kind of living electric light bulb?

When I began to look into this matter I was shocked to find such different Christians as Milton, Johnson and Thomas Aquinas taking heavenly glory quite frankly in the sense of fame or good report. But not fame conferred by our fellow creatures—fame with God, approval or (I might say) 'appreciation' by God. And then, when I had thought it over, I saw that this view was scriptural; nothing can eliminate from the parable the divine *accolade*, 'Well done, thou good and faithful servant'. With that, a good deal of what I had been thinking all my life fell down like a house of cards. I suddenly remembered that no one can enter heaven except as a child; and nothing is so obvious in a child—not in a conceited child, but in a good child—as its great and undisguised pleasure in being praised, the specific pleasure of the inferior: the pleasure of a beast before men, a child before his father, a pupil before his teacher, a creature before its Creator. I can imagine someone saying that he dislikes my idea of heaven as a place where we are patted on the back. But proud misunderstanding is behind that dislike. In the end that Face which is the delight or the terror of the universe must be turned upon each of us either with one expression or the other, either conferring glory inexpressible or inflicting shame that can never be cured or disguised. It is written that we shall 'stand before' Him, shall appear, shall be inspected. The promise of glory is the promise, almost incredible and only possible by the work of Christ, that some of us, that any of us who really chooses, shall actually survive that examination, shall find approval, shall please God. To please God, to be loved by God, not merely pitied, but delighted in as an artist delights in his work or a father in a son—it seems impossible, a weight or burden of glory which our thoughts can hardly sustain. But so it is.

The sense that in this universe we are treated as strangers, the longing to be acknowledged, to meet with some response, to bridge some chasm that yawns between us and reality, is part of our inconsolable secret. And surely, from this point of view, the promise of glory, in the sense described, becomes highly relevant to our deep desire. For glory means good report with God, acceptance by God, response, acknowledgment, and welcome into the heart of things. The door on which we have been knocking all our lives will open at last.

Perhaps it seems rather crude to describe glory as the fact of being 'noticed' by God. But this is almost the language of the New Testament. St Paul promises to those who love God, not as we should expect, that they will know Him, but that they will be known by Him (I Cor. 8: 3). It is a strange promise. Does not God know all things at all times? But it is dreadfully re-echoed in another passage of the New Testament. There we are warned that it may happen to any one of us to appear at last before the face of God and hear only the appalling words: 'I never knew you. Depart from me.' In some sense, as dark to the intellect as it is unendurable to the feelings, we can be both banished from the presence of Him who is present everywhere and erased from the knowledge of Him who knows all. We can be left utterly and absolutely *outside*—repelled, exiled, estranged, finally and unspeakably ignored. On the other hand, we can be called in, welcomed, received, acknowledged. We walk every day on the razor edge between these two incredible possibilities.

And this brings me to the other sense of glory—glory as brightness, splendour, luminosity. We are to shine as the sun, we are to be given the Morning Star. I think I begin to see what it means. In one way, of course, God has given us the Morning Star already: you can go and enjoy the gift on many fine mornings if you get up early enough. What more, you may ask, do we want? Ah, but we want so much more—something the books on aesthetics take little notice of. But the poets and the mythologies know all about it. We do not want merely to *see* beauty, though, God knows, that is bounty enough. We want something else which can hardly be put into words—to be united with the beauty we see, to pass into it, to receive it into ourselves, to bathe in it, to become part of it. That is why we have peopled air and earth and water with gods and goddesses and nymphs and elves—that, though we cannot, yet these projections can, enjoy in themselves that beauty, grace, and power of which Nature is the image. That is why the poets tell us such lovely falsehoods. They talk as if the west wind could really sweep into a human soul; but it can't. They tell us that 'beauty born of murmuring sound' will pass into a human face; but it won't. Or not yet. For if we take the imagery of Scripture seriously, if we believe that God will one day *give* us the Morning Star and cause us to *put on* the splendour of the sun, then we may surmise that both the ancient myths and the modern poetry, so false as history, may be very near the truth as prophecy. At present we are on the outside of the world, the wrong side of the door. We discern the freshness and purity of the morning, but they do not make us fresh and pure. We cannot mingle with the splendours we see. But all the leaves of the New Testament are rustling with the rumour that it will not always be so. Some day, God willing, we shall get *in*. When human souls have become as perfect in voluntary obedience, as the inanimate creation is in its lifeless obedience, then they will put on its glory, or rather that greater glory of which Nature is only the first sketch. For you must not think that I am putting forward any heathen fancy of being absorbed into Nature. Nature is mortal; we shall outlive her. When all the suns and nebulae have passed away, each one of you will still be alive. Nature is only the image, the symbol; but it is the symbol Scripture invites us to use. We are summoned to pass in through Nature, beyond her, into that splendour which she fitfully reflects.

The whole man is to drink joy from the fountain of joy. In the light of our present specialised and depraved appetites we cannot imagine this *torrens voluptatis*, and I warn everyone most seriously not to try. But it must be mentioned, to drive out thoughts even more misleading —thoughts that what is saved is a mere ghost, or that the risen body lives in numb insensibility. The body was made for the Lord, and these dismal fancies are wide of the mark.

Meanwhile the cross comes before the crown and to-morrow is a Monday morning. A cleft has opened in the pitiless walls of the world, and we are invited to follow our great Captain inside. The following Him is, of course, the essential point. That being so, it may be asked what practical use there is in the speculations which I have been indulging. I can think of at least one such use. It may be possible for each to think too much of his own potential glory hereafter; it is hardly possible for him to think too often or to deeply about that of his neighbour. The load, or weight, or burden of my neighbour's glory should be laid daily on my back, a load so heavy that only humility can carry it, and the backs of the proud will be broken. It is a serious thing to live in a society of possible gods and goddesses, to remember that the dullest and most uninteresting person you can talk to may one day be a creature which, if you saw it now, you would be strongly tempted to worship, or else a horror and a corruption such as you now meet, if at all, only in a nightmare. All day long we are, in some degree, helping each other to one or other of these destinations. It is in the light of these overwhelming possibilities, it is with the awe and the circumspection proper to them, that we should conduct all our dealings with one another, all friendships, all loves, all play, all politics. There are no *ordinary* people. You have never talked to a mere mortal. Nations, cultures, arts, civilisations—these are mortal, and their life is to ours as the life of a gnat. But it is immortals whom we joke with, work with, marry, snub, and exploit—immortal horrors or everlasting splendours. This does not mean that we are to be perpetually solemn. We must play. But our merriment must be of that kind (and it is, in fact, the merriest kind) which exists between people who have, from the outset, taken each other seriously—no flippancy, no superiority, no presumption. And our charity must be a real and costly love, with deep feeling for the sins in spite of which we love the sinner—no mere tolerance, or indulgence which parodies love as flippancy parodies merriment.

C. S. LEWIS, *The Weight of Glory*

God the Father

In the preceding sections we have been taking a look at two of the central beliefs of Christian faith about the nature of God. He is 'Creator', in the sense that everything that exists draws its being from him and is the expression of his originating and sustaining purpose. And he is the source of moral order, because human life is 'made to the specification' of his will, which is for the good of his whole creation.

These two convictions stand out unmistakably in the record of the Old Testament revelation. But when we turn to the New Testament it is equally evident that the emphasis has shifted. The operative word here is not creator or almighty but Father. And beyond any question the distinctive note of Christian experience has been the sense of intimate relationship with a God who, however far beyond our full comprehension, is personal in the sense that we can know, and be known by him, and can cooperate with him in prayer.

It might at first sight seem paradoxical that it should be in this most intimate sphere of faith and experience that some of the greatest difficulties arise today. But on further reflection it is understandable. For it is just at the point at which the emphasis falls on the element of *personalness* in God's nature that the perplexing problem of 'images' arises. It may be possible to think in fairly abstract terms of 'a creative power' or 'a principle of moral order'. It is much less possible to do so when we use the term 'father'. Painting and sculpture, literature and drama all continue to impress on our imagination a personal image. The language of hymns and prayers, and most emphatically of the Bible itself, reinforces the impression; while at the same time the expanding sweep of our ever widening knowledge of astronomical space or of the ages of pre-human history make the conception of 'a personal God in an impersonal universe' more and more a seeming contradiction.

Nor is this the only form in which the difficulty appears. The revelation or God which Jesus proclaimed, which in his own life he embodied, was a revelation of love. This did not indeed supersede or detract from the attributes of majesty and power which had been characteristic of the Old Testament revelation; but it did radically transform their character. And the rest of the New Testament is evidence of the effects which that transformation had produced in the lives of those who had experienced it.

Needless to say the truth of this conviction for which Jesus lived and died has been challenged in every age by the contradiction of so much in human life which appears to make a mockery of the idea of God's loving care. But it is at the present time, with the accumulation of evidence which has piled up over the last fifty years, with the ever more daunting realization of the lives of millions spent in a setting of hate, fear, cruelty, poverty, disease, hopelessness, that men are beginning to ask, in what would seem to be a new mood of angry repudiation, whether this sorry Christian pretence is not just about played out. Whatever may be the power which shapes the pattern of human destiny it cannot be a *loving* omnipotence.

This section will make the attempt to deal with these very real difficulties. Here and now it will be enough to suggest possible lines which may be worth exploring.

1. With regard to the first difficulty it will be useful to consider in some detail the whole question of 'images'. Is it essential to a vital religious faith to be able to *picture* to ourselves the object of our belief and devotion? Is it possible that popular religion has paid too exclusive attention to the 'father' image, and has neglected other images or symbols which undoubtedly form real elements in the New Testament picture of God as a whole—Spirit, Light, Energy (*dunamis*), Truth? Would a closer concentration on these enable some people, who find the 'personal' image a real difficulty, to *identify* experience of God, with which they may be quite familiar, without having given it the traditional name?

2. With regard to the second it may be worth while to examine rather more searchingly the 'Time-Scale' on which our reckoning is being based. 'After two thousand years', the critics say, 'is this all that Christianity can show for itself?' But on the time-scale on which our modern knowledge operates two thousand years is no more than the blink of an eyelid. Do we perhaps need to set our sights for a rather longer range before we conclude that the experiment has failed?

And, most emphatically, we shall need to take a good deal more of the contemporary evidence into our reckoning. The very fact that we are so much more acutely aware of the extent of evil and suffering in human life than many previous generations have been, is in itself evidence of a heightened Christian sensitivity and conscience. And compared with even a century ago the range and effectiveness of the agencies at work for the relief of suffering, and the removal of the causes of it in human ignorance and selfishness, are immensely greater than at any previous period of history.

89–93. What does 'God' mean?

This is perhaps the most difficult and the most puzzling problem facing us today when we try to take seriously the claims of Christianity on our allegiance. Here are some of the questions which must be answered:

1. What impression is made on you by the images used in the Bible in speaking of God? Which, if any, 'ring a bell'?

2. Historically the images of the Bible arose out of the particular experience of a particular people (for example, the dominance in Hebrew thinking of the experience of the Exodus). Can you see any source of new images in the modern world (for example, Peace? Truth? Energy? Psychology?)

3. What elements are there in personal experience, or insights arising from your reading, which you find pointing to a dimension of life unexplained in spatio-temporal terms?

These and other questions are raised in the passages which follow. The authors express the significance of 'God' in various ways, and describe the experiences which have made the concept meaningful to them. Discuss fully the points they make, and then use the passages to help you answer the questions given above.

89. What does 'God' mean? : Image—old and new

This is a time of ferment in new ideas about God and religion. In particular, a number of writers in recent years have spoken of 'Christianity without religion', and of the need to discard familiar images of God. It may startle and puzzle some of us to hear that, if we are to understand Christianity, we must turn away from 'religion' and find our Christianity not in 'religion' but elsewhere.

This should, however, not be too difficult for us to follow. There have been great Christian teachers in the past who have dwelt upon the contrast between the living God on the one hand and our own thoughts about him and pious practices on the other. It is on the first, not on the second that we must build. I recall a saying of F. D. Maurice more than a century ago: 'We have been dosing our people with religion when what they want is not this but the living God.' Then, too, our religion is always filled with the 'images' of God in our minds. These images may come from the Bible, and be essentially true, yet just because they *are* images, like 'Father' or 'King' or 'Shepherd', the feelings and the meanings which we put into them may be very inadequate; and it is these feelings and meanings which make up our 'religion', and God is greater than they. It is the putting of our own feeble little grasp of God, or our own individual picture of God, in place of God himself which is the peril of 'religion'. But there is a peril greater still. Religion (I can now drop the inverted commas) can mean a set of pious attitudes and practices within which we look for God, forgetting that God may *sometimes* be found less amongst them than amongst the things we call non-religious or secular.

To-day, various trends show that attempts are being made to find God not in the realm of religion alone but in the secular; not on the fringe but right in the middle of a secular age. For instance, Edward Wickham, now Bishop of Middleton, in his book *Church and People in an Industrial City* argued that the new scientific and technological organization of society was not to be seen as something apart from God but as something through which God himself is at work challenging us.

We can perhaps get most help from a quotation from Tillich's book *The Shaking of the Foundations*. Tillich is trying to help modern men and women, from whom the old religious language is very remote, to find God *within* rather than *beyond*. He says in effect: 'Do not try to think of a supernatural person outside you or above the world. Think in terms of depth.'

'The name of this infinite and inexhaustible depth and ground of all being is God. The depth is what the word God means. And if that

word has not much meaning for you, translate it, and speak of the
depths of your life, of the source of your being, of your ultimate concern, of what you take seriously without any reservation. Perhaps in
order to do so, you must forget everything traditional that you have
learned about God, perhaps even that word itself. For if you know that
God means depth, you know much about him. You cannot then call
yourself an aetheist or unbeliever. For you cannot think or say : Life
has no depth ! Life is shallow ! . . . He who knows about depth knows
about God.'

I think that quotation has meaning for us. It is an attempt to help
a man who is estranged from ordinary religious talk but may find
God by forgetting all ordinary religious talk, and thinking in depth
about himself and his own meaning. I believe that many of us who
try to commend Christian belief to-day have half-consciously been
saying this in a similar way. I find for instance that in the published
book of the addresses given by me in a mission at Oxford in 1960, I
began with these words : 'I am going to be speaking about God. You
would expect that. But I am not at the outset going to use the word
"God". This is because the word has become conventional, and I am
asking you to think about a reality rather than a word. It is also because I want to suggest that I am talking about what is already going
on inside you, and not about a sort of outside technicality which I
have come to sell to you.' I have never been a disciple of Tillich, or
indeed a close student of him. But perhaps I spoke thus because I was
feeling after a similar idea. Religion can often seem to mean 'a sort of
outside technicality which I have come to sell to you', whereas God
may be found in 'what is already going on inside you'.

It is the theme of the book entitled *Honest to God* by the Bishop of
Woolwich that the image of God not only in popular piety but also in
orthodox theology is outmoded. Humanists and secularists are right to
reject God when he is presented in the current religious image. The
image has, Dr Robinson says, gone through two stages already. The
New Testament writers thought of God as literally 'up there' in a
local heaven. (I am not at all sure that they were as literal-minded as
that.) Then came the change to a less literal and more symbolic view :
the spatial imagery was used, but rather as a scheme of *thought*; God
is 'out there', a supernatural person beyond the created universe. We
have for centuries, says Dr Robinson, thought of God thus : he is
beyond; he comes to us; we go to him; it is not a spatial but a metaphysical 'outsideness' in idea. It is this which is, he thinks rightly,
being rejected by the modern world.

What then? His advice is this. Relinquish the image of God as
Beyond. Cease to think of God as a definable, supernatural person.

Relinquish definitions of God such as 'God is—' or 'God is—'. Begin the other way round. Look into the depths of human existence, and discover deep down the ultimate reality, the ultimate meaning of things. This ultimate reality is personal; it is love. Then we can say that love, the ultimate reality, is God. But, for the Bishop, there is great significance in which way round we put it. He prefers not to start with the name God and apply definitions to him, for that is to cling still to the old religious idea of a supernatural being 'outside', and it is misleading. Rather he would begin with the ultimate reality in depth. That is the point of departure, and that is personal; it is love, it is God. To say this is to reject theism as religiously defined, and to reject the image of God as 'outside'. But if we ask whether this does not really identify God with the world, Dr Robinson would reply that 'transcendence' is truly found in his doctrine. God is the Beyond discovered in the depth of existence.

We need to try our utmost to grasp, and to feel, the idea which is being put to us. If we turn back to the quotation from Tillich we can begin to see whither the argument is going. 'To assert that "God is love" is to believe that in love one comes into touch with the most fundamental reality in the universe, that Being itself ultimately has this character'. This realization comes when we have parted company with the religious descriptions of God and with the quest for God in the realm of religion. Dr Robinson illustrates 'God within the secular' by a quotation from the book of Jeremiah : 'Did not your father eat and drink and do justice and righteousness? Then it was well with him. He judged the cause of the poor and needy; then it was well. Is not this to know me? says the Lord.'

What do we make of this idea ?

Religion is to be, we are told, no longer the frame of a Christian's relation to God. That relation is to be set within the secular. Yet will it not still be a relation to a Beyond? Call it deep down, but it always means a Beyondness. So, I would ask, because that is so, will not religion still be with us: reverence, awe, dependence, adoration, penitence? Will not these be still with us, however secular our Christianity becomes, if indeed the 'ultimate' is real and personal? And will not these call for the old poetic images to express them? Even if the revolution were to happen and the new ideas were to prevail, religion would keep returning to the scene, or rather keep welling up from the deep. It is significant that near the end of the book Dr Robinson allows the old language still to have a place, innocuously, in liturgy, and he seems thus to want both to eat his cake and have it. Banish religion with its stuffy pietism, find God and Christ in the experience of the common life—but will all be prose? Will not 'psalms and hymns and spiritual songs' find their way from *deep down* in the Christianity of depth?

I ask where 'revelation' and 'grace' come in? If there is ultimate reality which is love and personal, does not the initiative come not from us but from thence? That is what we have meant when we have spoken of 'revelation' and of 'grace': God finding us rather than we finding God.

MICHAEL RAMSEY, Image—Old and New

90. What does 'God' mean?: Three in One, and One in Three

The doctrine of the Trinity was not a doctrine arrived at by abstract speculation about the nature of God. It was the result of an attempt to formulate, in so far as it is possible for human language to do that, truths which men were convinced had come home to them as they reflected on facts of experience. It was, one may say, a doctrine arrived at empirically, as the result of observation.

These men were devout and convinced monotheists. For them as for their fathers there was one God, 'beside whom there is none other'. But that God had made himself known to their nation through the agency of his 'Spirit'. That had shown itself through the calling and endowment of particular men for special tasks: kings, national heroes, above all prophets. Such endowment had been selective and, as it were, intermittent. But all along they had sensed that this was only a partial demonstration of the Spirit's nature and power. They had cherished the hope that there would come a day when God would 'pour out his Spirit upon all flesh: your sons and your daughters shall share the prophetic inspiration: your young men shall see visions and your old men shall dream dreams: and even upon slaves and slave-girls in those days will I pour out my spirit, saith the Lord' (Joel 2:28,29). And alongside this they had cherished another hope: that there would come one in whom this possession by the Spirit of God would be no longer intermittent—'the Spirit of the Lord shall *rest* upon him' (Isa. 11:2).

Some of them had been eye-witnesses of a life in which, and as the result of which, they believed that these hopes had been fulfilled. They had noted his authority, the unquestioning claim to know the mind and will of God, the claim to exercise powers over the bodies and souls of men which only God could exercise. And they had noted that the message which he preached, and the welcome which he extended, were clearly not confined to any aristocracy of birth or wealth or education or piety. 'The common people listened to him gladly.'

There had been a black moment when that life had ended in apparent disaster and failure. 'This was the man who, we had trusted, was going to redeem Israel'—and now. . . . And then they had come out on the other side. And that experience of seeing unbelievable victory won out of the jaws of defeat had convinced them once for all that his claim *had* been true. They came forward as men prepared to witness to that faith.

But they found themselves witnessing to something more than that. The Spirit which they had seen in Jesus was now at work in themselves. Now indeed the prophecy of Joel was being fulfilled under their eyes; small shop-keepers and dock-labourers, yes, and slaves, were sharing in this gift.

And there was another discovery, of even greater significance. In the earliest stages the influence of the Spirit had shown itself mainly in the heightening of men's natural powers, physical vigour, intelligence, sometimes artistic ability, or in an access of ecstatic fervour producing 'prophetic' outbursts. In the great eighth-century prophets it had indeed developed on to an infinitely higher plane of moral and spiritual insight. But throughout the Old Testament period the emphasis on transformation of *character*, as the result of the Spirit's influence, plays but a comparatively small part.

Now something different had happened. Because 'Jesus had been glorified', because men had seen in him the true character of the servant of God, the Spirit's power could be, and was being, released in its true form. Now it became possible to see what *Holy* Spirit really meant.

How did they describe and explain what they were finding?

Clearly it was the work of God. No other explanation could account for its transforming effects. But it was, if one can so put it, the work of God with a difference, the difference which had come through the radical modification of their conception of God made by the life, death, and resurrection of their Master. The activity of God, through the Spirit, had been raised to a new degree, given a new richness of meaning and content, not indeed added, but now realised for the first time. The Spirit was seen to be the Spirit of Jesus, not only the Spirit as it had been in Jesus, while he was with them, but the Spirit as it was continuing to be in Jesus, still effective, even more widely effective, in their own lives. It is not easy to be certain exactly how Paul would have distinguished between his two great phrases 'life *in Christ*' and 'life *in the Spirit*'. But that there was a distinction in their minds is indicated by that one closing greeting at the end of 2 Corinthians, 'The grace of the Lord Jesus Christ, and the love of God, and the fellowship of the Holy Spirit'. The very fact that elsewhere 'the grace of the Lord Jesus Christ' is used as an adequate salutation makes the one occasion when 'the fellowship of the Holy Spirit' is added more significant.

Christianity is a monotheistic religion. It believes in one God. It believes that there can only be one God, for the good and sufficient reason, among others, that on no other basis is the conception of a Uni-verse possible. Whatever the doctrine of three Persons in one God may mean, it does *not* mean tritheism.

What the Christian faith does affirm is that the unity of God is not a bare mathematical unity. It is that, in the sense that unity is the opposite of multiplicity. There is only one God. But it is also an organic unity, the nature of which is, so to speak, that it is not uni-cellular. It is a unity subsisting in three '*personae*'. The Latin word *persona* did not mean either 'person' or 'personality' in the sense in which we commonly use these words, as implying a distinct centre of consciousness. It meant originally the status held, or the function discharged, by an individual in the life of the community; and then, by transference, the person holding that status or discharging that function. The nearest equivalent in current usage is the survival of the phrase 'dramatis personae', the roles in a drama, and so the actors taking those roles. When we try to find an exact English equivalent, it is extraordinarily hard to do so. It is true that the words 'aspect' or 'mode' are inadequate. They imply too much a temporary phrase through which the 'person' passes, a partial expression of his full individuality. On the other hand, 'person' is misleading. It suggests too much the idea of 'an individual'. Perhaps the nearest we can get is to say the nature of God is personal, existing and expressing itself in three eternal characters and activities which together constitute the divine being.

Can we translate this into language which, though perhaps not much easier, is at least a little nearer to our ordinary ways of thinking? There is, within the being of God, pure Godhead, God as he is in himself, wholly transcendent. But if this were all that God is, if he were nothing else, there could be no going out from himself in creation: he would remain a bare self-contained and self-sufficient 'Unit'. There is also present within the being of God his Logos, his Word, reason, power of self-communication, the inherent necessity to express himself in act. But this again, by itself, is not sufficient. It is, in itself, only the potentiality, even the necessity, of expression, of communication, but not the action itself. That is the work of the Spirit whose characteristic description is that he 'proceeds', goes out in creation and inspiration, from the Father and the Son.

To quote Dr. Kelly's survey of early Christian doctrine: 'The divine action begins from the Father, proceeds through the Son, and is completed in the Holy Spirit: none of the Persons possesses a separate operation of his own, but one identical energy passes through all three.' (Kelly, *Early Christian Creeds*, Longmans, 1950).

It is commonplace to say that the heart of the Christian Gospel is the affirmation that God is love. That is his nature, his being. The very fact that it is a commonplace means that we seldom stop to reflect on what it implies. Love is by definition a relationship. It cannot be exercised in isolation. If this is what we are meaning when we affirm that that is the essence of God's being, it carries a profoundly important implication. By contrast with the classical view which envisaged God as isolated in the contemplation of his own perfection, the Christian faith maintains that from all eternity there exists within the being of God an internal relationship which alone makes love possible. In our Lord's prayer on the last night of his life he speaks of the love with which God has loved him 'before the foundation of the world' (John 17.24). It looks as though the doctrine of the Trinity was not after all a mere theological puzzle, let alone a mathematical absurdity, but rather the attempt to give some kind of rationale of that which had become, through the revelation in Jesus, the deepest certainty in the faith of his friends.

F. A. COCKIN, *God in Action*

91. What does 'God' mean? : Faith and belief

It may happen to a person that he realizes, with surprise perhaps, that he cannot help believing in God. He may or may not be able to recall some particular experience from which this belief-state appears to have resulted. But at any rate his present condition is that he cannot help believing in God. It is the most precious possession that he has, and far from wishing to give it up, he would wish anyone else to be in a similar condition.

All the same, if the person we are speaking of happens to be a philosopher, it may well seem to him that he is in a very painful dilemma. Surely he ought to have good reasons for this belief of his. But it is very difficult to think of any, and not very difficult to think of pretty strong-looking reasons against it, from the ancient ones which constitute the Problem of Evil to the modern contention that the basic propositions of theism are unfalsifiable and therefore void of content.

I am only concerned with the type of theism whose central concept is the concept of love, the love of God for finite persons and the love of finite persons for God, since this is the only type of theistic religion with which I have any personal aquaintance. The more we consider its implications, the more astonishing it appears. For theism of this type is committed to maintaining that God loves sinners as much as saints, fools as much as wise men. More important still, we have to say that he loves those who do not love him as much as those who do. He loves atheists, agnostics and materialists as much as he loves theists—

as much, in the sense that his love for each of us is without limit. His love is not only universal, but also unconditional. He loves each of them individually, each for his own sake, as an end in himself. He is indeed *Deus Optimus Maximus*, best as well as greatest. For what could conceivably be better than universal and unconditional love?

The philosopher I spoke of finds himself believing in God. He finds he cannot help it, though previously he could. What reasons, if any, could there be for holding this belief? Or rather, what reasons, if any, can he himself find for holding it? For it is not enough that there should in fact *be* good evidence for believing such and such a proposition. If a person is to believe reasonably, he must himself *have* good evidence.

But have we stated the problem correctly? Is there perhaps something inappropriate, out of place, in the suggestion that one should look for 'evidence' in favour of 'the theistic hypothesis'? If believing in God were just a case of believing *that*, of course the demand for evidence would be appropriate. But is it a case of believing *that*? Are we accepting a hypothesis when we believe in God, and has religion much to do with hypotheses at all?

The trouble is that the verb 'to believe' has two distinct functions. It corresponds both to the noun 'faith' and to the noun 'belief'. The philosopher said that he found himself believing in God. But the attitude in which he found himself to be was one of faith, rather than believing 'that'. A person might believe that God exists and that he loves every one of us. Yet such a person might still be completely irreligious. He might have no faith in God at all. He might not love him at all nor even try to, nor trust him at all, nor pray to him, nor adore him. This presumably is the position of the devils mentioned in St James's Epistle: 'Thou believest that there is one God. Thou doest well. The devils also believe, and tremble.'

It is not of course that the man who has faith disbelieves these theistic propositions, or doubts them. It is rather that he does *more* than believe them. He has, or he claims to have, some sort of degree of personal relationship with the Being about whom these propositions are asserted. Faith, I would suggest, is not a propositional attitude at all. It is more like an attitude of loving adherence to a person, or at least to a Being with whom one may have personal relations. It is as if (in the old feudal manner) one had given one's allegiance to someone and accepted him—voluntarily and gladly—as one's lord. It is like an act of homage, but a continuing one, repeated whenever your thoughts turn towards him. We can address him whenever we will, and when we do, it is not like talking to empty air on the off-chance that someone may hear. It is like speaking to someone in whose presence you are.

So if we use the word 'belief', we have to describe the man who has faith ('a believer') as one who believes *in* God, and distinguish between believing 'in' and believing 'that'. The term 'belief in' emphasizes the trust which is an essential part of the faith attitude. It might be argued that one cannot trust someone unless one loves him at least a little. At any rate, it seems clear that 'faith without love' is a contradiction. Whereas 'believing *that* . . . without love' is no contradiction at all, even though the propositions believed are propositions about God.

Yet we should be going too far if we said that faith had no connection whatever with believing 'that'. Beliefs 'that' are usually the precursors of faith. Moreover, beliefs 'that' are among the results of it. Those who have faith in God believe that he will be gracious to them in the future as he has been in the past, that he loves not only themselves but everyone else too, that therefore they should try to love others because he does, and that he will help them to do this if they ask him, and humbly acknowledge the lack of love which is their present condition.

The beliefs 'that' which we have just been considering come *after* the faith attitude, whether as consequence of it or as substitute for it when it has temporarily or permanently lapsed. But there are also beliefs 'that' which precede it and play an important part (normally at least) in bringing it into existence; and other propositional attitudes play an important part in this process too.

In religious literature there is a familiar distinction between 'seeking' God and 'finding' him. 'Seek and ye shall find.' 'Knock and it shall be opened unto you.' God gives his grace to whom he will, and sometimes he gives it to those who do not ask for it. But ordinarily we do not find him unless we seek him, and we may have to seek for a long time.

We can say, I think, that at least in our age and our society, the seeking for God most commonly begins with the acceptance of human testimony, the testimony of religious people; or if not with the acceptance of it, at any rate with the inclination to be interested in it and take it seriously. There is a certain human quality which one can recognize sometimes when one meets with it. We call it 'spirituality' for want of a better name. It is both attractive and puzzling, and sometimes it can be awe-inspiring as well. Certain moral qualities enter into it, especially charity, but perhaps the most impressive feature of it is a certain inward peace or serenity. Spirituality is not at all the same as religiosity, nor can it be said that everyone who asserts the basic propositions of theism is a 'spiritual' person in this sense. But some of those who assert them do possess this strange, impressive and attractive human quality.

The respect which we cannot help having for these persons may well alter our attitude to the theistic propositions themselves. When a person of this spiritual sort asserts them he does so because he has 'faith in' the Being about whom they are asserted. When he makes these strange metaphysical assertions, which in themselves seem incredible or even perhaps devoid of any clear meaning, he makes them because of some personal relationship which he has experienced in his own inner life. If we ask him what kind of experience this is, he may well reply that he cannot describe it in literal language, and that only a person who has 'lived through' it himself at first-hand can know what it is like. But he will add, 'You can have this experience yourself if you sincerely wish to have it. Seek for God yourself, and you will find him. It is true that you could not hope to find him by your own efforts alone. But though you cannot yet believe it, he loves each one of us, and if you sincerely seek for him, he will himself help you to find him.'

There are certain practices which are recommended in religious literature, and we may try them for ourselves. The word 'practices' must be understood literally. What is traditionally called 'seeking for God' is something that we *do*, and may have to continue doing for a long time. But further, and even more important, this doing is an inward doing. It is essential to insist that there is such a thing as 'inward doing'. We engage in such inward doing whenever we voluntarily direct our own private thoughts to one subject rather than another. 'As a man thinketh, so is he.' That is what it comes to. The spiritual practices which seekers for God are recommended to use are applications of this maxim. And it is what a man thinks privately, in his own mind or heart, that matters most, not the thoughts which he expresses overtly to others.

The practices recommended are of at least two kinds. First, there are what may be called meditative practices. Here we voluntarily and privately fix our thoughts on the basic theistic propositions themselves. At this stage it is quite proper to describe these propositions as the contents of 'the theistic hypothesis'; for it *is* to us a hypothesis when we set out upon the activity of seeking. At this stage it is not necessary that we should believe it. All that is required of us is the suspension of disbelief: we should be *interested* in these theistic propositions and willing to take them seriously. What we have to do is to entertain them attentively and repeatedly, to ruminate upon them and to consider what it would be like if they were true. We may assist ourselves by reading some of the parables by which these propositions are illustrated in the Scriptures. To illustrate the proposition 'God loves every one of us' we can ruminate upon the parable of the Prodigal Son, for example. If any words have power, surely the words of the Gospel parable do. If they are ruminated upon, and pictured as far as possible in mental imagery, they have power to change a man's whole life. What our thoughts dwell on matters more than what we believe in the believing 'that' sense. The meditative practices I have described are intended to produce a change in our manner of entertaining the basic propositions of theism. Gradually we come to entertain them in a 'real' manner; we come to 'realize' what their import is.

But these meditative practices are not the only ones which are recommended to those who wish to 'seek for God'. There are also others, equally inward, which are of a more directly devotional kind. There are such forms of speech as prayers, hymns of praise and pious ejaculations. We are recommended not merely to listen to them, or read them, thoughtfully and attentively, but also to use them ourselves. We are to try to pray to God, inwardly, in our own hearts. Consider such words of praise and adoration as the first few lines of the *Te Deum*. 'Te Deum laudamus, Te Dominum confitemur . . . pleni sunt caeli et terra maiestate gloriae tuae.' Try to say them yourself, not just as splendid poetry, but as if you really meant what you say.

How can we possibly carry out such instructions? Surely we could only say such things if we had faith in God already, and a pretty firm faith too? But at present we are no more than 'seekers' and are not even sure that any such Being exists at all. Nevertheless, it can, I think, be done. Sometimes we have to act in this way in order to find out whether a hypothesis is true. It is surely a mistake to suppose, as some do, that resolute and pertinacious action is only possible when we are already in a state of complete conviction. When a man is seeking for God he can act (inwardly) as he thinks a person would who had found him. He can try, voluntarily, to 'assume the role' of such a person. It is a more important capacity than we suppose. It enables one to experiment, as it were, with the possibility of being quite a different sort of person. The reading of imaginative literature has a rather similar function, and these devotional practices we are discussing could be regarded as imaginative exercises.

So far, while we are only seeking, it is proper to speak of the theistic hypothesis and to ask what evidence we have for it. If I am right, the only evidence we have for it at this stage is the evidence of testimony. Such evidence is nothing like conclusive. Perhaps we may think that if the theistic hypothesis were true, the evidence for it *ought* to have been conclusive. There is a story about a celebrated philosopher who was the guest of honour at a dinner of a society of agnostics. One of them asked him, 'What would you say if God himself suddenly appeared among us in this room?' The philosopher replied: 'God,' I should say, 'why did you make the evidence for your existence so inadequate?' This is indeed a problem which may trouble us. Perhaps the solution of it has something to do with the 'uncompellable' character of love. What good would there be in settling this theoretical question, if one had no love at all for the Being whose existence was thus conclusively established? Perhaps God's will or plan was that we should love him; and love cannot be compelled, even if assent can. Love has to be given freely, if given at all. But if God must be sought for at the expense of considerable effort and trouble, and can only be found by those who wish to find him, they will love him when and if they do find him.

The process of seeking may be long. There may be ups and downs in it. It might also be said that the process of seeking never ends. To use a human analogy: suppose you have heard of some very wonderful person and want to meet him. You now have what you wished for; but once you have it, you wish for more. You do not have to seek for *him* any longer, but you still seek for something—to be as well acquainted with him as he will allow you to be.

So much for 'seeking'. But what of 'finding'? The 'finding', I suggest, is just the establishment of the personal relationship of faith *in* God. Now we begin to have experiences of being somehow in personal touch with Someone in whose presence we seem to be, Someone who seems to be giving us a loving welcome now that we are there.

Have we found him? Perhaps it might be more appropriate to say that he has found us. But even so, there is some cognitive factor on our side. The claim to *know* the One and Only Lord of All is so enormous that one shudders at it. Perhaps it might just be allowable to use the word 'acquaintance' by itself. Perhaps we might say that when we come to have faith in God we are 'with' him in a way we were not before. The difficulty about it is that 'being with' is a symmetrical relation. If A is with B, it follows that B is with A. But we wish to say that God has been with us always, whereas we have not always been with him. While we were seeking him we were not as yet with him. Indeed, to be with him was the goal of our search. Still less were we with him before we had even begun to seek for him. But he is with each one of us all the time.

Perhaps we should content ourselves with parables or figurative expressions. 'Knock and it shall be opened unto you.' Well, something *can* happen for which 'it is opened' is an appropriate metaphor. Something can happen for which the return of the Prodigal Son to his home, and the welcome he receives, are appropriate metaphors. It is a matter of experience that it does happen. There is testimony that it does, and each of us can verify that testimony for himself, if he chooses to try. But he can choose not to. There is a door, but we are not compelled to knock at it. There is a way home, but we are not compelled to take it.

I used the empiricist word 'verify' just now. And it is worth while to notice that the empiricist notion of 'try it and see for yourself' is by no means absent from religious literature. 'O taste and see how gracious the Lord is' is an example. A still more striking one can be found in a well-known hymn:

> 'O make but trial of his love,
> Experience will decide.'

'Experience will decide.' This is the voice of British empiricism. If we are to make trial of God's love, we must do it by trying to *accept* his love, gladly and thankfully, instead of just benefiting from it passively as we have hitherto done. It must be a loving confidence, analogous to the confidence we have in a human being whom we love, and not just the confidence we have in a well-supported proposition about a matter of fact.

If theism is the metaphysics of love, it is not very surprising that love should come first in the epistemology of faith. The ordinary religious person, one who is not a philosopher or a theologian, might well say 'I do not very much mind whether it is a case of belief or knowledge or something different from either. All that matters is that one should try to love him who first loved us; and that is good enough for me.' Perhaps it is good enough for anyone.

H. H. PRICE in *Faith and the Philosophers*

92. What does 'God' mean?: To speak in a secular fashion of God

On April 30, 1944, Dietrich Bonhoeffer wrote to one of his friends from his prison cell words that have both tempted and tormented theologians ever since. 'We are proceeding toward a time,' he wrote, 'of no religion at all. . . . How do we speak of God without religion. . . . How do we speak in a secular fashion of God?'

. . . Bonhoeffer drops an invaluable hint about how we should proceed. He reminds us that in the biblical tradition, we do not speak 'about God' at all, either 'in a secular fashion' or in any other. When we use the word GOD in the biblical sense, we are not speaking about but 'naming', and that is an entirely different matter. To name is to point, to confess, to locate something in terms of our history. . . .

It entails our discerning where God is working and then joining his work. Standing in a picket line is a way of speaking. By doing it a Christian speaks of God. He helps alter the word 'God' by changing the society in which it has been trivialized, by moving away from the

context where 'God-talk' usually occurs, and by shedding the stereo-
typed roles in which God's name is usually intoned. . . .

Carl Michalson describes the biblical doctrine of the hiddenness of
God in these terms :

'. . . it is God's way of life to be hidden. He is ex-officio hidden.
Hiddenness is intrinsic to his nature as God. . . . The doctrine of the
hiddenness of God . . . is not a counsel of despair or a concession to
human finitude, but a positive description of God himself which
performs a merciful service. It prevents man both from looking for
God in the wrong place and from esteeming God's role in reality
with less than ultimate seriousness.'

This biblical concept of God's hiddenness stands at the very centre
of the doctrine of God. It is so commanding that Pascal was echoing
its intention when he said, 'Every religion which does not affirm that
God is hidden is not true.' It means that God discloses himself at those
places and in those ways he chooses and not as man would want. And
he always discloses himself as one who is at once different *from* man,
unconditionally *for* man, and entirely *unavailable* for coercion and
manipulation *by* man. . . .

But what part does Jesus of Nazareth play in this hiddenness of
God? If Jesus were a theophany, an 'appearance of God' in the cus-
tomary religious sense, then in Jesus the hiddenness of God would be
abrogated. But this is not the case. God does not 'appear' in Jesus; He
hides himself in the stable of human history. He hides Himself in the
sense that we have just mentioned, showing that He is not anything
like what religions have wanted or expected from their gods. In Jesus
God does not stop from being hidden; rather He meets man as the
unavailable 'other'. He does not 'appear' but shows man that He acts,
in His hiddenness, in human history. . . .

As Bonhoeffer says, in Jesus God is teaching man to get along without Him, to become mature, freed from infantile dependencies, fully
human. Hence the act of God in Jesus offers slim pickings for those in
hope of clues for the erection of some final system. God will not be
used in this way. He will not perpetuate human adolescence, but insists on turning the world over to man as his responsibility. . . .

But where does the transcendent God meet us in the secular city?
Whatever the name we give Him, however we finally respond to Him,
where does he find us? . . .

We meet God in those places in life where we come up against that
which is not pliable and disposable, at those hard edges where we are
both stopped and challenged to move ahead. God meets us as the
transcendent at those aspects of our experience which can never be
transmuted into extensions of ourselves. . . .

We have already suggested that God comes to us today in events of social change, in what theologians have often called history, what we call politics. But events of social change need not mean upheavals and revolutions. The events of everyday life are also events of social change. The smallest unit of society is two, and the relationship between two people never remains the same. God meets us there, too. He meets us not just in the freedom revolution in America but also in a client, a customer, a patient, a co-worker....

Is this so farfetched? Recent discussions of the concept of the covenant in the Old Testament suggest it means that Yahweh was willing to stoop so low as to work in tandem with man, to work on a team, no matter how poorly the human partner was working out. Whether or not this is true, it can certainly be said that in Jesus of Nazareth God did show that He was willing to take man's side of the unfulfilled covenant, to become the junior partner in the asymmetric relationship. It is not demeaning to suggest that the notions of teamwork and partnership need to be explored much more in our conceptualization of God. He who is 'high and lifted up' suggests in the life of Jesus that he is willing to put himself in the position of working within a group, of washing his fellows' feet and of needing someone to carry his cross. What seems at first sight irreverence may be closer to the heart of the self-humbling truth of God than we imagine.

The idea of an I-You partnership between God and man is strongly hinted by the language of Galatians 4. In this passage man is viewed as a son and heir. The emphasis is on *son* as opposed to child, and on *heir* as having assumed responsibility. This implies that the strictly vertical relationship which informs a father's relationship to his minor boy is discarded for the adult partnership which obtains between a grown man and his father.

Perhaps in the secular city God calls man to meet Him first of all as a 'you'. This has far-reaching implications. It suggests that man is not to become fascinated with God himself. Like his relationship to his work partner, man's relationship to God derives from the work they do together. Rather than shutting out the world to delve into each other's depths the way adolescent lovers do, God and man find joy together in doing a common task. Of course this type of relationship will not satisfy the man who is driven by a compulsive interest in 'finding' or 'experiencing' God. Such people are always dissatisfied by the admittedly sparse revelation of Himself which God has made. It is not the kind of revelation which encourages delving. God wants man to be interested not in Him but in his fellow man....

Paul had little patience with the religious questers after the unknown God he ran across in Athens. 'This unknown God,' he said, 'I

declare unto you.' In Jesus of Nazareth, the religious quest is ended
for good and man is freed to serve and love his neighbour.

HARVEY COX, The Secular City

93. What does 'God' mean?: Discernment and commitment

To what kind of situation does religion appeal? What kind of empirical anchorage have theological words?

Let us recall Butler's summary of the chapter [on Immortality] at
the end of Part I of the 'Analogy'. It is, he says there, 'contrary to
experience' to suppose that 'gross bodies' are ourselves. Belief in immortality is thus founded in an awareness that as 'living agents' we
are more than our public behaviour. Here, I suggest, is the discernment without which no distinctive theology will ever be possible; a
'self-awareness' that is more than 'body awareness' and not exhausted
by spatio-temporal 'objects'. Such a discernment lies at the basis of
religion, whose characteristic claim is that there are situations which
are spatio-temporal and more. Without such 'depth', without this
which is 'unseen', no religion will be possible. We cannot usefully
begin theological apologetic without first making plain the distinctive
kind of discernment in which theology is founded.

But more needs to be said about this characteristic situation than has
so far been covered by calling it a 'discernment'; this brings us to the
second memorable theme of the 'Analogy'—a total commitment, appropriate to a 'question of great consequence', a commitment which is
based upon but goes beyond rational considerations which are 'matters
of speculation'; a commitment which sees in a situation all that the
understanding can give us and more. Let us illustrate. A man who can
scarcely swim is walking by a river. A child is in difficulties and
apparently sinking. Even though the chance of effecting a rescue
might be the slightest possible, we should expect the man to jump in
(says Butler) with the same determination as if he were jumping in on
a theoretical background of the highest certainty. 'A man would be
thought in a literal sense distracted who would not [so] act and with
great application.' Why should we think that the man was 'distracted' if he failed to jump in? Because here is a question 'of great
consequence'. The life of a child is something we would die for. Here
is a dominating loyalty linked with a world view, and in particular
with a certain assessment of personality. If, for instance, we took a
different world view—reckoning that the child was only one of millions which nature threw up in an inexorable process of reproduction,
no more than a piece of flotsam—there would then be no question 'of
great consequence' and it would be unreasonable for the man as a poor
swimmer to jump into the river to try to effect a rescue.

Or take another example. We are climbing with someone we love, who slips to fall on a ledge hundreds of feet below. Though we happen to be an indifferent climber, we try to effect a rescue; our whole life is centred to this end. 'I shall make the attempt if it kills me', we would say. 'The probability' may be greatly against our succeeding, but we should be 'thought in a literal sense distracted' if we refused to descend to the ledge because we had not worked out an absolutely convincing theoretical background which would make the attempt cut and dried. The risk we would take is a measure of the 'devotion' which 'inspires' us.

So religion claims (*a*) a fuller discernment, to which we respond with (*b*) a total commitment. Such a commitment without any discernment whatever is bigotry and idolatry; to have the discernment without an appropriate commitment is insincerity and hypocrisy.

Can we find any parallels from ordinary experience to the two-fold characterization of religion as a discernment-commitment? No example will tell the full story. But it is our hope that the examples will make much clearer the kind of empirical situation to which theology appeals, will make clearer to an unbeliever what a religious man is talking about.

A. The first, illustrating what we have called 'religious discernment', are those about which we use phrases that are in certain ways odd, peculiar and unusual. We should say, for instance, of these situations at the point where they provide parallels to religious discernment, that they 'come alive'; that the 'light dawns'; that the 'ice breaks'; that the 'penny drops', and so on.

Let us recall the setting of a High Court—all very impersonal, all very formal, quite lacking in 'depth' and 'vision'. The name of the judge is made as suitably abstract as possible—Mr. Justice Brown. The wigs and scarlet are meant to conceal the fact that Mr. Justice Brown is after all a human being. Nor is the argument of the Court interested in persons. We have, instead, 'the Crown', 'the accused' and 'the prosecution'. Here is a situation as impersonal as may be; a mere façade of human existence. Then, one morning, Mr. Justice Brown enters the Court to see as the 'accused' the closest friend of his undergraduate days. 'Eye meets eye'; astonishment; an odd word is uttered —'Sammy!' The result is (as the papers will tell us next day) that the Court is 'electrified'. An impersonal situation has 'come alive'. Mr. Justice Brown has seen in the 'accused' something he has never seen before, and the accused has seen in the judge of the Queen's Bench Division, something which scarlet and ermine did not express, something which goes far beyond the wigs and the legal language. It is important to see that the significance of words like 'Sammy' is proportionate to their comparative lack of empirical relevance. The situation has not 'come alive' merely by containing an unusually large range of facts; rather, in stretching to include these facts, the situation has taken on 'depth' as well—it has become in a certain way partly elusive. The very lack of observational ties which a nickname like 'Sammy' possesses, enables it all the better to claim a measure of spatio-temporal elusiveness about the situation of which it is appropriately used. 'Sammy', for instance, may have been a word which, for some quite trivial reason, was associated once with Mr. Justice Brown—there may have been some pun on a Sam Browne belt—but it is not used with any observational unpacking in mind, its significance is that it has always belonged to *characteristically personal situations*. Such a word would be in violent contrast to the language used normally in the setting of the High Court, and this violent contrast makes the point (or so I hope) that a characteristically personal situation cannot be contained or expressed in legal language and customs, as it cannot be contained in any 'impersonal' object language. The situation is more than 'what's seen', it has taken on 'depth'; there is something akin to religious 'insight', 'discernment', 'vision'.

For a second example, let us recall the experience we have all had of an argument in relation to which there is no sort of mutual understanding. We say—and significantly—'I might just as well be talking to a brick wall.' The situation is indeed, impersonal. But there is one way of assured success, and this will be found if (as we say) we know the weak points in his armour—and once again notice that his personality is concealed by this impersonal word 'armour'. It may be that he is never, as we should say, 'more himself' than when he is fishing. Nothing so good as a river and fish for evoking 'depth'; fishing is an 'inspiration' to him. Let us suppose then that we are trying to argue the merits of 'equal pay for equal work'. We illustrate it from this angle and from that, but there is no penetration. The head always shakes, and the face looks blank. And then we remember the fishing and we say, 'look here, Jim, what I mean is "equal fishing pay for equal fishing work" ', and he smiles; his face breaks significantly, the penny drops. He says: 'Now I understand perfectly.' Once again it is a word odd to the context which has evoked that characteristically-different situation, which in this case occurs when an argument is grasped, and we 'see' the conclusion in a way which is more than merely 'entertaining' the appropriate proposition.

This discernment can also be illustrated I believe by the use of such diagrams as are commonplace in Gestalt psychology. Let us recall how there could be drawn twelve straight lines which at first sight might look no more than two squares with corners joined. But then there dawns on us 'depth', and we see the twelve straight lines as a 'unity'. The lines indeed represent a cube and this cube may, as is well known, seem to enter into or stand out of the surface on which the lines are drawn. Here again is a characteristically-different situation which dawns on us at some recognizable point. This is the point where twelve straight lines cease to be merely twelve straight lines, when a characteristically-different situation is evoked which needs odd words like 'depth' and 'unity' or mathematically the idea of a 'new dimension', 'volume' besides 'area'.

Let no one condemn the examples I have given on the grounds that they assimilate religion to psychology. The examples are certainly psychological in so far as they appeal to situations which are experienced, but they are *not* psychological in so far as they would reduce religion to what would be called 'subjective experiences'—whatever that phrase may mean. All these characteristically different situations, when they occur, have an *objective* reference and are, as all situations, *subject-object* in structure. When situations 'come alive', or the 'ice breaks', there is objective 'depth' in these situations along with and alongside any subjective changes.

B. We now turn to our second group of examples which illustrate total *commitment*.

We shall first comment on the kind of commitment involved in doing mathematics, something as distinct from religion as that. Thereafter we shall contrast with this kind of commitment the devotion we may give to a pastime, a ship or a person, and finally argue that religious commitment does something to unite the distinctive features of both kinds of loyalty.

No doubt we all remember how we once proved that the three angles of a triangle were 180°. A triangle was drawn; its base produced . . . etc., etc. Here is a typical example of mathematical reasoning, none the less typical for being specially simple. Each step follows indubitably from the one before—*but how do we start?* It might be said: with 'obvious axioms' that no one can doubt. But of course if we said that we would be wrong. The axioms of mathematics are only options, and by now it is notorious that Euclid does not give us the only possible option—what of Lobatchewsky, Bolyai, Reimann, and the rest? In other words, when we claim to prove that the angles of a triangle are 180°, what above all else we are doing is to display the starting point to which we have *committed* ourselves.

This kind of commitment, with these different options, shows itself in correspondingly different axioms, different *posits* in relation to the different geometries. Here, nothing very serious in involved, nothing very violent occurs, when one posit is exchanged for another. There are no placard-bearers in mathematical departments with legends like 'There'll always by a Euclid', or 'Prepare to meet thy Riemann today'. On the other hand, what is true, for example, of a Euclidian triangle,

is true in Oxford and Cambridge, Moscow and New York, Mars and
the moon. No one correct assertion in pure mathematics is ever wrong,
though it may not always be useful; and it may not always be adequate for understanding a particular situation. Here then is a *partial*
commitment extending to the *whole* universe.

Let us now look at something very different. Consider someone devoted (as we would say) to some pastime like cricket. A man's whole
life may centre around it—it is the one subject of his conversation,
his planning, his hopes. So much so that his language becomes coloured by it. Face him with some insoluble problem and he is 'stumped';
violently disturbed over some moral or political situation, he claims
that it's 'not cricket'. Here is his last stronghold; his court of final
appeal. Here indeed is a loyalty involving the whole of a man and
expressible in terms of a key-word or cognate vocabulary.

Again, take a captain's devotion to his ship. So much so that in
some disaster he sinks with it. The ship is his life. Once again, as in
the cricket example, we have a total commitment to what . . . some
thing? . . . no, the ship is personalized—'she'—so that it comes to be
paralleled with our total commitment to someone we love.

Which brings us to agape, love, human affection. Suppose someone
says, 'I am longing to go to Widnes,' and we say 'Why? It isn't that
you like the dirt?' 'No.' 'The smell?' 'No.' 'The cold?' 'No.' We seek
for an explanation but in vain. We say, 'You must be mad.' But then
the penny drops, the light dawns: *'She's there.'* At once the whole
circumstance is illuminated, and we understand how our friend 'sees'
Widnes: and so 'sees' it that its dirt, smell and cold are organized
within a dominating loyalty. What took him there would be the same
kind of feature about love which McTaggart noticed when he remarked that a single smile or a look may dominate our whole existence in its totality. Here is a commitment, a total commitment, with
a strange empirical relevance. Here is a commitment, a final option,
which organizes the whole of a man's life, something associated with
what we call 'insight', something whose anchorage is given when the
penny drops: 'she'.

So we come now to the main point. So far we have seen two kinds of
discernment-commitment—'mathematical' commitment and 'personal'
or 'quasi-personal' commitment. Religious commitment, I suggest,
partakes of both. It combines the total commitment to a pastime, to a
ship, to a person, with the breadth of mathematical commitment. It
combines the 'depth' of personal or quasi-personal loyalty—to a sport,
a boat, a loved one—with the range of mathematical devotion. It is a
commitment suited to the whole job of living—not one just suited to
building houses, or studying inter-planetary motion, or even one
suited to our own families, and no more. There are two ways in which

it resembles the second kind of commitment we mentioned rather more than the first.

1. We say that cricket 'grips' us; the boat 'dominates' us; we 'fall' in love. Note the words: 'grips', 'dominates', 'fall'. Likewise, religious commitment is a response to something 'from outside us'—'Ye have not chosen me, but I have chosen you. . . .' (John 15 : 16.)

2. Here is a commitment which we give up only at the cost of a personal revolution. We saw that we could embrace other mathematical options without any special heart-searching. But what of the cricket fan, the captain, the lover? He will always resist all attempts to break his loyalty. When people comment adversely on someone you love, it is a measure of your love as to how far you will resist the tales told to weaken your affection. But if in the end they succeed, the result is, not that we exchange, without any heart-searching, one sort of 'axiom' for another—there is now a personal revolution, the whole of one's life is altered, our 'vision' ceases. Here is something precisely parallel to religious commitment. If we have not been converted to it, we should certainly have to be converted out of it; converted, as William James would have said, 'to infidelity'; when the world becomes 'flat'—lacking in 'depth', vision and commitment disappear together.

So we see religious commitment as a *total* commitment to the whole universe; something in relation to which argument has only a very odd function; its purpose being to tell such a tale as evokes the 'insight', the 'discernment' from which the commitment follows as a response. Further, religious commitment is something bound up with key words whose logic no doubt resembles that of the words which characterize personal loyalty as well as that of the axioms of mathematics, and somehow combines features of both, being what might be called 'specially resistant' posits, 'final' endpoints of explanation, key-words suited to the whole job of living—'apex' words. In particular the Christian religion focuses such a cosmic commitment on Christ—on Christ as Jesus of Nazareth, born, dead and buried, but also on the risen and ascended Christ.

If our examples have done something to indicate the kind of empirical basis which belongs to religion, what do they tell us about religious language? They suggest, I think, that religious language will be logically odd in at least two ways, which are by no means unrelated, any more than are our two groups of examples.

(i) If religious language has to talk about situations which bear great affinities to those we were discussing in the first group of examples, situations which are perceptual with a difference, perceptual and

more, its language will be object language and more, i.e. object
language which exhibits logical peculiarities, logical impropriety.
Now have we any general guide to this oddness, this impropriety?
Well, does not the way in which distinctively *personal* situations
parallel those which are *characteristically religious*, suggest close
logical kinship between 'I' and 'God'? Both, by the standards of
observational language, are odd in their logical behaviour. Take
'I'. Plainly 'I' is in part tractable in observational language—what
'I' refers to is not something entirely independent of our public
behaviour. On the other hand 'I' can never be exhausted by such
language. So, if we wish to speak of everything which, for each
of us, this 'I' refers to, we shall have to use phrases which—while
beginning with and having some foothold in observational language—are somehow or other qualified to make it plain that their
reference is in part beyond such language as well. The same is true
about 'God'.

The example of the Gestalt diagrams suggests that the oddness of
theological language may arise because of certain mixings of ordinary
words, mixings of what at one time might have been called 'universes
of discourse'. For the Gestalt diagram, by a certain mixing and juxta-
position of ordinary symbols manages to tell a tale which is more than
a linear one, and to justify thereby an odd word like 'unity'.

(ii) Our second group of examples suggests that we may expect religious language to contain significant tautologies, tautologies
whose function is to commend those key words—those ultimates
of explanation—which arise in connection with its character as a
commitment.

Suppose [a man Smith] is called at four and responds 'freely'. Later
in the day we ask 'Why did you get up at four?' The answer might
be: 'Because I wished to get a bus.' 'Why did you wish to get a bus?'
'Because I wished to go fishing.' 'Why did you wish to go fishing?'
'What a question! You know what fishing is for me. Fishing is fishing.
Why did I want to fish? Because I'm I.' An answer of the same 'final'
form might have been given at the start. Fishing is something not to
be questioned: it is something which exerts an authoritative claim
on the person in question. It was in response to this claim—the 'discernment', the 'obligation' that fishing brings with it—that Smith
acted 'freely' when he rose at four. To the tautology which expresses
the claim of the 'object': 'Fishing is fishing', there can be paralleled
that tautology which expresses the subjective response: 'I'm I.' In
[this way], then, if they command key-words, the tautologies of religion will be apt currency for its *commitment*; and such key-words,

when they are from the standpoint of perceptual language 'odd', will also be apt currency for *discernment* as well.

Let us recall how in the loyalty to a ship or a person, to a college, school or nation, we found a parallel to religious commitment. It is then not surprising that this loyalty is sometimes expressed in phrases which like those of theology have their own peculiar logic, e.g. 'My country right or wrong'. If this is taken to be no more than an ethical assertion, it is plainly open to the gravest difficulties. But if it is a way of insisting that loyalty to a nation may be something even greater than one which is expressed in moral words, then it is not obviously silly and certainly not self-contradictory. In other words, 'My country right or wrong', is a way of representing and proclaiming a dominant loyalty to a nation, in which case 'country' for the 'absolute' patriot would have a logical placing very similar to 'God' for the theist. After this I need do no more than recall briefly that parallel to theological 'key-words' are also the axioms of mathematics, reached when questions have pushed us to the 'irreducible posits' of a particular system. These express in tautologies, in necessary propositions, the loyalty, the option of the mathematician, as he posits the particular conventions.

So to some concluding remarks. We should expect religious language to be constructed from object language which has been given appropriately strange qualifications. For example, it is sometimes asked: how can religious people speak of a 'sense' of what is 'unseen'? A word with a perfectly good meaning in perceptual language— 'sense'—is given a qualification of such a kind that the ensuing phrase seems to be bogus, if not self-contradictory. So can parallels to the impropriety of religious language be found in other areas, and if apparent nonsense is repeated in places widely apart, we shall be hesitant before we say that such phrases are entirely devoid of meaning.

We may also expect religious language to centre on 'God' as a key-word, an 'ultimate' of explanation, which becomes the subject of significant tautologies. We all know how the phrase 'God is Love' has been criticized as being a platitude, because it is alleged to say nothing. But may not this be because it has the logical form of a tautology? If so, we misunderstand it if we do not see it as a *significant* tautology labelling a commitment. The logical structure of the phrase 'God is Love' would be something as follows: We should have to tell a story of human devotion until a characteristically religious situation was evoked. We should have to tell the stories of the 'lives of good men' until a point was reached where we did not merely admire the 'goodness', but where, when the characteristic 'discernment' was evoked, we responded with a total commitment. 'Love so amazing, so divine, demands my soul, my life, my all.' It would be in relation to such a situation that the religious man would then posit the word 'God' or the word 'Love'. To say that 'God is Love' is thus to claim that the word 'God' can be given in relation to a total commitment (*alternatively labelled 'Love'*) which can be approached by considering those partial commitments which we normally describe in terms of the word 'love'.

For the religious man 'God' is a key word, an ultimate of explanation expressive of the kind of *commitment* he professes. It is to be talked about in terms of the object-language over which it presides, but only when this object-language is qualified; in which case this qualified object-language becomes also currency for that odd *discernment* with which religious *commitment* will necessarily be associated.

To understand religious language or theology we must first evoke the odd kind of situation to which I have given various parallels above. At the same time we must train ourselves to have a nose for odd language, for 'logical impropriety', and it is possible to do this by concerning ourselves with other examples of odd language which may not in the first instance be religious: poetry is plainly an example; the person who by inclination is more scientific than poetical might well look for the odd words and phrases which his scientific theories will throw up. Such words range from 'absolute space' for Newton, to 'continuous creation' for Hoyle. Words such as these will certainly have an 'odd' logical behaviour compared with those which are contained in the more straightforward generalizations which the theory incorporates, and which can, in a fairly obvious sense, be 'verified'. A useful antidote to the craze for straightforward language might be found in suitable doses of poetry or greater familiarity with the curiously odd words thrown up in scientific theories. There is an important place for odd language; odd language may well have a distinctive significance, and we might even conclude in the end that the odder the language the more it matters to us.

I. T. R A M S E Y, *Religious Language*

94–101. The world of pain and evil

It may well seem that this concluding section needs no introduction. We all know that for many men and women, including some of the finest and most sensitive characters, the thing that makes it hard, if not impossible, to believe in God is the fact that millions of their fellow men are living in a world of hate, fear, cruelty, exploitation, starvation, and disease, which makes talk of a loving God a mere mockery.

The passages included in this section set out the problem bluntly enough; and also present some of the lines on which Christian thinkers have attempted to find an answer which provides at least a clue, if not a final solution. Passages 95–7 tackle the problem from the standpoint of everyday argument; passages 98–100 are written from a more theological/philosophical standpoint, and take the discussion to a deeper and more difficult level.

In studying the evidence it may be worth while to keep one or two leading questions in mind:

1. Are suffering and evil *identical*? Do they both present *the same* challenge to faith? Or do we draw a distinction between them, at least in the sense that there is a real moral difference in our attitude to (*a*) a brutal parent ill-treating a child, or a slum-landlord exploiting his tenants, and (*b*) the effects upon their victims? Which is the real enemy to be fought?

2. Can we say that suffering as such is always evil? Consider the difference between the kind of suffering just described, and the suffering consequent upon a severe operation, or the suffering entailed in an arduous exploit, say climbing Everest. Do they all constitute the same challenge to belief in the goodness of God? Can we say that, on the basis of a true moral evaluation, a world which contained no suffering would be in some ways a poorer world?

94. The world of pain and evil: Prologue: the Christian conviction

In a world in which men can crucify Christ anything wicked or appalling may happen at any time. And we Christians are ready for just that, and just that does not stop us hoping. For there is no situation so chaotic that God cannot from that situation create something that is surpassingly good. He did it at the creation. He did it at the Cross. He is doing it today in our present world.

It is this exciting conviction which makes the Christian able to hold his Bible in one hand and the daily newspaper in the other and allow them to interpret each other, so that the Bible is seen to be even more up-to-date than the newspaper, and the newspaper, while faithfully reflecting some aspects of our world, does not cause us either distaste or panic. For this world we see in the newspapers is the world God loves and in which he is busy at his work of creation, for to redeem is to create. 'In Christ . . . the new has come' (II Corinthians 5 : 17 RSV).

But let us be very clear that we dare not write like this, think like this, or hope to live like this, or attempt to persuade others to hope, unless each one of us has seen 'his own personal situation in all its nakedness and reality,' as Professor J. L. Hromadka says. 'Nobody really understands who Jesus of Nazareth is and what the Gospel is unless he has been shaken in his own self-security and self-righteousness. The light of the Gospel reveals man to a depth such as no philosophy or psychology can do.'

God in the light of the Cross: ourselves in the light of the Cross—that is the point from which we go out in hope to our world.

M. A. C. WARREN

95. The world of pain and evil: What the papers say

Here are a series of newspaper cuttings which exemplify the ills which beset the world we live in.

1. In what sense, if any, do they constitute a 'problem' for a thoughtful person:
   (a) if he is a materialist?
   (b) if he is a non-Christian humanist?
   (c) if he is a Christian?

2. Are some different in kind from others? If so, in what ways? And does this make a difference to your answers to 1?

3. A good deal might be said 'on the other side'. What kind of cuttings would be needed to redress the balance and give a fair picture of the 'human condition'? How do these things fit into your understanding of the meaning of life?

Famine ration for full-grown man—4 oz. of grain a day

We were standing on the bed of a bone-dry reservoir outside a village called Sonia in south Bihar. All round us men, women and children were digging holes 10 ft square and a foot deep and carrying the hard earth in head-baskets to the top of the earth dam.

They were working on a famine relief job designed for them by the Sub-Divisional Officer and were getting 1s. 9d. a hole with which to buy an uncertain daily ration of coarse grain—four ounces for grown-ups and two ounces for children.

The Bihar Chief Minister himself thinks this ration is scandalous and would like to see the rest of India cut its consumption for Bihar's benefit. When I met him earlier here in the State capital, in a vast secretariat put up in 1911 by the British, he said his people needed at least three times as much to sustain life.

Nobody on the famine relief job at Sonia looked gay and I asked the gloomiest of them—a thin young man, pallid with sickness—who he thought was to blame for his present condition. 'Who is to blame except the *Sirkar*—the Government?' he said.

The young man doesn't belong to that army of landless labourers in south Bihar who, without the Government's relief work, would have nothing whatever to keep them alive. He farms seven acres, and in this part of the world that puts him in the top 10 per cent. But when last summer the monsoon failed over Bihar, it killed off the whole of his rice crop and left even the paddy so withered he couldn't feed it to his bullocks. He grew a little maize in the first illusory rains, but in a week or so that will be gone, leaving him no better off than the landless.

There must be thousands more hovering on the brink of the same plight. In these southern districts of Bihar the landscape of crop failure on the small rice fields looks like an enormous dump of tennis courts, all long disused, bare and cracked. And most of them have produced nothing, or next to nothing.

From CYRIL DUNN, Patna, 3 December

Declaration of famine in Bihar

An official declaration of famine in large parts of Bihar not only emphasizes the grave situation created by the prolonged drought but also commits the state government to tasks probably beyond its competence.

By this declaration, the Government has assumed responsibility for feeding nearly 13 million people, a quarter of the state's population, who live in areas that make up a third of Bihar's territory.

The declaration, under what is known as the 'famine code', will not increase the Government's capacity to supply food but may lend more urgency to efforts to relieve scarcity and distress. Under the code's provisions, the Government will have to remit all land revenue and suspend the collection of dues from those to whom it has given agricultural credit.

The problem in Bihar is of staggering dimensions, but it has been so for several months. Neither the state government nor Delhi acted promptly and efficiently, and it is only recently that relief operations have been organized on a proper basis. More than 100,000 volunteers are now engaged in relief work. Several foreign and international organizations, including Unicef and Oxfam, are giving valuable help.

From our correspondent, Calcutta, 19 April

Man speaks of 6-hour ordeal

Mr. Benjamin Coulston, one of the alleged victims in the 'torture' case, told the jury at the Central Criminal Court yesterday of his ordeal which lasted six hours, on the night of January 18 to 19, 1965.

He said he was taken by force to the South Lambeth office of Charles Richardson; he was stripped naked and beaten with iron bars; his gums were torn with a pair of pliers; burning cigars were stubbed out on his arms and legs; an electric fire was held close to his face and body, and blows to his feet removed the skin from his toes.

Finally, he added, he was tied up in a tarpaulin sheet in which two 14lb. weights had been put after Mr. Charles Richardson had said: 'Get rid of him.' He thought he was going to be dumped in the river. While all this was going on his tormentors were drinking, laughing, smoking, and enjoying the fun, he added.

'£30 under pillow'

Mr. Charles Richardson, seven other men and a woman have pleaded

Not Guilty to 22 counts alleging robbery with violence, grievous
bodily harm and demanding money with menaces. Not all the defend-
ants face the same charges.

Mr. Coulston said Mr. Charles Richardson asked him about £600
which he said Mr. Coulston had taken from two of his men in one of
his shops or businesses. 'I told him: "I do not know what you are
talking about" and was hit a couple of times on the head with lumps
of metal or wood.' Then he was further assaulted.

Eventually he was given a new shirt and driven home by Edward
Richardson. Asked if he or his wife intended reporting what had
occurred to the police Mr. Coulston replied: 'I will tell them I fell out
of a car.'

Mr. Sebag Shaw, Q.C., for the Crown—What made you give that
answer?

I knew what these people would do. I was frightened for my wife
and baby. I knew if my wife or I had gone to the police I would not
be on this earth today.

Later he was taken to hospital where he received a visit from Mr.
Charles Richardson's father and his own brother. They said the police
would be visiting him. That led him to run away from the hospital in
his pyjamas with the stitches still in his head. Thirty pounds had been
left under his pillow by Mr. Charles Richardson's father.

The trial was adjourned until today.

Village children go in fear of killer

'Maniac at large' theory

Every boy and girl in this Berkshire village and in the hamlets for six
miles around was escorted to and from school today by police or parents as the search intensified for the killer of the two girls aged nine
who were found dead in a gravel pit near here yesterday.

Similarity between the girls' deaths and that of Yolande Waddington last October has convinced police that a maniac is at large in the
area. They are working desperately to solve the riddle of three deaths
before another child is killed.

The two girls found dead yesterday were Jeannette Wigmore, who
had been stabbed and pushed into a pond, and Jacqueline Williams,
drowned in six inches of water and mud.

Yolande Waddington, aged 17, a children's nurse, was found
stabbed and strangled two miles from the scene of yesterday's murder.

Guard dropped

One villager told me: 'When Yolande was killed we all decided to
keep our children in at night. During the day we kept a very wary eye

on them. But as the long evenings began we dropped our guard and this terrible thing happened. It will be a very long time before we let our children out of our sight again.'

In the village school, where the girls were known as a 'couple of little chatterboxes', prayers were said for them at morning assembly.

In St. Mary's parish church their names remain with those of other children who collected money for the Church of England Children's Society. Jacqueline Williams and her sister, Caroline, raised £1 5s. 2d. and Jeannette Wigmore managed 6s. 8d.

Detective-superintendent W. Marchant of Scotland Yard, who is helping local police, gave details of the killings tonight. Jeannette Wigmore had been stabbed and pushed into a pond; she died from a haemorrhage. Jacqueline Williams was drowned. Police believe that her attacker chased her and then held her face down in 6in. of water and mud until she died.

From C L I V E   B O R R E L L, Beenham, 18 April

Torrey Canyon disaster

Help us to save thousands of birds from a hideous DEATH IN OIL

Newspaper makes new attack on S. African prisons

Allegations by warders and prisoners

The *Rand Daily Mail* today devoted two inside pages to allegations about treatment of prisoners at a gaol at Boksburg, about 20 miles east of Johannesburg. It said that the allegations—by a warder and a head warder at the gaol and by two Africans who served sentences there—were substantiated by sworn affidavits.

The allegations concern electric shock treatment, torture and beatings.

This is the second series of allegations about conditions in some South African prisons published by the *Rand Daily Mail*. Four weeks ago it published three articles by Mr. Harold Strachan, who recently completed a three-year sentence for conspiring to cause explosions. Since then there has been a demand for a judicial inquiry into the country's prisons.

The Johannesburg *Sunday Times* last week published a sworn statement by a head warder alleging serious breaches of prison regulations by warders at the gaol at Boksburg. Today's report in the *Rand Daily Mail* refers to the same prison and also quotes the same head warder.

Legal offence

In an introduction to its two-page report the *Rand Daily Mail* asked: 'What happens behind the walls of South Africa's gaols? Little is known because of the restrictions on publications contained in the Prisons Act of 1959.'

This makes it an offence to publish any information about prisons, knowing it to be false or without taking reasonable steps to verify it.

The *Rand Daily Mail* referred to the articles it published by Mr. Strachan and added: 'Strachan was promptly placed under house arrest—and no word of his experiences can again be published.'

Johannesburg, 30 July

U.S. bombers kill 14 in error

Saigon, April 16.—American aircraft today accidentally bombed their South Vietnam allies for the second time in 24 hours, killing 14 and wounding 25.

Yesterday, 29 Vietnamese soldiers were killed and 70 injured north-west of the central port of Qui Nhon. Today the victims were in a village housing Vietcong defectors near Truc Giang in the Mekong delta.

The Vietcong today overran a small village 40 miles east of Saigon, setting houses on fire and tying six civilians to posts and shooting them through the head. The villagers were to have voted in local elections today.

In Quang Tin province, 350 miles north-east of here, a bus hit a guerrilla mine. Nine passengers were killed and 12 wounded.

REUTER

Police accused of racial brutality

Report urges legislation

Complaints that the police discriminate against coloured immigrants are made in a report by the Campaign Against Racial Discrimination published yesterday. The report says: 'Complaints of brutality or ill treatment by the police occur with disturbing frequency.'

The report makes no pretence to be a survey but is a selection of 43 cases that have been reported to C.A.R.D. in the past nine months. It appears on the eve of publication of the long-awaited Political and Economic Planning report on racial discrimination in Britain, which has made a special survey of discrimination in employment.

In one complaint against police in a northern city, a Jamaican woman immigrant says that she was thrown to the ground by a police officer and fractured her ankle. In another complaint, also against police in the north, another Jamaican immigrant says that he was taken to the rear of a police station 'where I was beaten by about six policemen. As a result I sustained a broken nose and a badly damaged eye'.

In London, a West Indian immigrant claimed that she was held by police while a man with whom she had been arguing was able to strike her on her face and in her stomach. She was later charged with assaulting the police. Her comment to C.A.R.D. afterwards was that she 'would never forget this act of British injustice'.

'I can beat five'

Another complaint against the police comes from a Jamaican who was taken to a West London police station and was questioned about drugs. He claims that he was taken upstairs and a policeman hit him in the stomach and battered him against a window. He says that the policeman told him: 'I can beat five of you coloured men at one time. You black men are yellow—and don't laugh either. Why don't you hit me in the face?'

The report says that 'it is not our contention that all these complainants are blameless in every respect. In two of the cases the complainants were involved in situations which were, to put it at the lowest, suspicious'. Nevertheless, the report says: 'It is not altogether surprising that immigrants do not on the whole regard the police force as a body to whom they can turn with any kind of confidence.'

These are not the first allegations of racial discrimination to be made against the police. Last year the West Indian Standing Conference claimed that the police in London went 'nigger-hunting'; claims that were indignantly denied by the police.

Other cases given in the report claim that there is discrimination in employment, housing and insurance. C.A.R.D. say that they show that further legislation is urgently needed.

By our home affairs correspondent

Orders to shoot in tornado town

Tornadoes swept through America's Middle-West last night, leaving behind 60 dead, 1,500 injured and a trail of destruction.

Hardest hit was the Chicago suburb of Oak Lawn. At least 24 people died there, and the coroner's office said the total could reach 100 when all the wreckage was cleared.

It has been declared a disaster area and the most badly damaged section has been cordoned off to prevent looting.

Sheriff Joseph Woods ordered guards who were posted at every corner to 'shoot looters on sight'.

A supermarket in the suburb was crowded with weekend shoppers when the storm suddenly struck. A dark funnel-shaped 'twister' went on to wreck a restaurant, destroy a caravan camp and then tore through a children's skating rink.

Several victims, laid out in a temporary morgue, were children still wearing their roller skates.

All that remains of the supermarket is a large pile of rubble with some section of wall still standing.

Hundreds of police and firemen with earth-moving equipment are searching for bodies.

Also badly hit was Belvidere, 65 miles north-west of Chicago, where 20 died. The storm struck as children boarded buses after school.

As the black twister approached most of the children turned and ran into the school library and huddled against a wall.

But the wind blew out the windows and injured dozens with shattered glass. Outside, the buses were lifted off the ground and thrown against buildings.

One bus was carried away more than a mile.

CHICAGO, 22 April

New wave of tornadoes sweeps U.S. Midwest

President Johnson has ordered all possible Federal aid for the areas of Missouri, Illinois, Indiana, Iowa and Michigan struck by Friday's tornadoes.

Another wave of tornadoes yesterday ripped into the United States Midwest, already devastated by Friday's winds which killed 52 people and injured 1500.

At least seven people were hurt, one critically, in South-west Missouri. Heavy damage to buildings in the business section of Springfield was reported. At Lake Zurich, Illinois, homes were damaged.

Estimates of damage to Oak Lawn, Belvidere and eight other communities hit by the tornadoes ranged from $20 million to $50 million (£7.1 million to £17.8 million).

Smallpox deaths in Tibet

Many deaths from an outbreak of smallpox in Tibet have been reported by travellers in Lhasa. The deaths were said to be mainly in Keyrong and the adjoining areas close to the Nepal border.

Chinese Red Guards were reported to have been carrying out mass inoculations in an attempt to check the epidemic.

From our correspondent, Katmandu, 21 April

96. The world of pain and evil: What the readers think

(a) Why pain?

Wasps and asps and stinging nettles all remind us that pain is an essential part of the natural order. A burned thumb from grabbing a hot casserole reminds us that pain is part of our early warning system. Yet stomach ache, headache, backache, guts ache, heartache outrage our sense of what is reasonable and proper and we spend millions of pounds a year on drugs trying to escape from pain. It is as if we believed that given enough money medical science could abolish not only disease but pain as well.

Nonsense, isn't it? Whatever protective and preventive medicine discover our flesh will still bleed and bruise and blister, our bones break, our lungs choke. There will still be hurricanes, floods, fires, landslides, earthquakes, which we don't begin to understand how to prevent. There will still be the hazards of the forces we have only partly got under control like electricity and nuclear energy. The possibilities of physical pain are enormously greater than they were in the days of pestilence, famine, and civil war—and these still exist, too.

Many people found a recent television programme on the artist Francis Bacon quite unbearable because of his obsession with pain. Paul Johnson wrote in the *New Statesman* that he stamped off to bed in a rage. It distressed me, too, to the point of having to switch off, and the thought of anyone choosing to live with a Francis Bacon painting of the agonised scream was intolerable.

But then I began to wonder . . . is Francis Bacon perhaps trying to say that since the Cross became stylised, an exercise in Design, instead of a literal representation of the extreme social suffering, we have been shutting our eyes to the reality of pain and taking refuge in squeamishness? Is he trying to remind us that we have stopped asking *why* pain?

Why pain? Primitive peoples find their answer in the work of evil spirits who must be propitiated or enemies who must be slaughtered. Primitive religions explain pain as punishment for disobedience to a jealous and vengeful god. Christians through many centuries believed that pain was a just punishment for sin, and at the same time that it was a means of grace, a passport to bliss in the afterlife; even that, as under the Inquisition, pain to the extent of torture to death at the stake might save the sinner from everlasting torment in hell.

We had better admit that there are survivals of such attitudes into our own time. In *What I Believe*[1] John Wren Lewis reveals that his mother died (just before Dunkirk) 'still believing that a local bargee in the Medway had been literally struck blind for uttering the oath "Gor Blimey"'. The story is often told, apocryphal or not, of the Scottish minister who cried to the boy heard giggling in church 'Ye will not laugh in hell, boy'.

It was the idea that pain and suffering were retribution for wrongdoing even in children that the Victorian rationalist could not stomach. As Bertrand Russell says: 'I find it difficult to think that a child of four or five years old can be sunk in such black depths of iniquity as to deserve the punishment that befalls not a few of the

1. *What I Believe*, a symposium published by George Allen and Unwin.

children who suffer torments in children's hospitals. Again I am told that though the child himself may not have sinned very deeply, he deserves to suffer on account of his parents' wickedness. I can only repeat that if this is the Divine sense of justice it differs from mine, and that I think mine superior.'

Yet still there are people who think that it is a just punishment for fornication that an unmarried mother *and her child* should suffer; even more who believe that flogging is reformative; more still who accept that the sins of the Vietcong should be visited on their children by blasting them with napalm bombs.

In a remarkably penetrating essay in a newly published book, *The World of Children*,[1] Marghanita Laski dates the coming of pity, the desire to spare children—and adults too—from pain, to an inexplicable change of sentiment in the eighteenth century. In spite of the horrors of the industrial revolution, even in spite of the gas chambers of Auschwitz, even in spite of Hiroshima and Vietnam, humanity has grown more sensitive to pain, not only its own, but others. There has been a steady retreat from the belief that it is *right* to inflict pain deliberately. But the more sensitive we grow, the less is pain explicable.

It is not for me to discuss how present-day Christians interpret the Cross of the Atonement—the suffering of the One on behalf of the many—because it seems to me that a man should bear his own pain and not off-load it on Another. But Christians do have the Cross as a point of reference when they think about the meaning of pain.

Where can the rest of us look for answers? Has pain a meaning, a purpose, in the universe? Can it be *used*? Is there any line of research to be followed in the experience of some mothers who, following natural childbirth methods, *use* the birthpangs and are even exhilarated by them? Is there any theologian, philosopher, or scientist who can suggest an answer to my question? *Why pain?*

M A R Y   S T O T T in the *Guardian*, 15 and 23 November 1966

(b) To the Editor, the *Guardian*

Recently I met a small boy who suffers from the condition called 'congenital indifference to pain'. At six weeks he had chewed his tongue nearly through. At four years he broke his ankle and walked on it for a month without discovery. Result—that leg is shorter than the other and he wears a surgical boot. His mother has suffered such anxiety that she has required psychiatric treatment.

Pain therefore is a necessary warning. Once that is allowed the possibility of undeserved and unnecessary pain has to be allowed as well, for it is impossible to imagine a rational universe where fire will

1. *The World of Children*, an illustrated symposium published by Paul Hamlyn.

burn me if I go too close to it, but will not burn me if someone else throws it at me.

When patients ask me 'Why does this happen to me?' I don't of course answer them like this. To say in effect, 'It is likely to happen to anyone, why shouldn't it happen to you?' is not going to help. The reason for pain should be looked for in the future, not in the past. 'What can I let it make of me?' This is easier to say of mental than of physical pain. A broken heart can make the owner more considerate and understanding. It can, of course, make him bitter. This is where I need Christian theology.

I am sorry that Mary Stott thinks that Christians 'unload' their pain on to Christ. The Cross is the proof of God's love for us, and the Resurrection is its vindication. Because we see what God, in Christ, is willing to suffer, we can find the willingness to suffer too. To accept our pain, and let Him make something out of it for ourselves or for somebody else. Again, this is easier to say about mental than about physical pain, but even physical pain can be offered. Of course, it still hurts, which means that the 'answer' isn't the one we were hoping for, but it is the only one I know.

To forestall the criticism I can hear coming let me add that what I have said refers only to our own pain. Other people's pain has to be relieved, not accepted.

Yours sincerely,
'J.B.', M.B., B.S., D.P.H., London

(c) To the Editor, the *Guardian*

Mary Stott rightly says that 'humanity has grown more sensitive to pain, not only its own, but others''. Together with this sensitivity goes a self-protective mechanism; a wish not to know and a sense of outrage when faced with the suffering of another.

The reminder of the dark side of life is too much for us and we are understandably angry at our inability to help. Our anger and our 'switching off' mask the natural fear of our own pain and possible ultimate death in pain. On the good side, this sensitivity leads to the relief of suffering to the greatest extent in our power. On the bad side, when relief seems impossible, the sensitivity can lead to a desire to shut away the suffering person, to form ghettoes of the incurably sick, where our sensitivity (which brings its own pain) is helped by the knowledge that 'they' are somewhere suitable and conveniently out of sight and sound. Compassion means literally 'suffering with'. Perhaps the eventual elimination of continued pain by the active compassion (mental, physical, and spiritual) of others will be a step forward in the evolution of man.

Anon. in pain

(d) To the Editor, the *Guardian*

It is difficult to believe that life, existing so precariously within a tiny depth of atmosphere and within an equally tiny range of temperatures and pressures on a relatively large body which is yet insignificantly small in the inconceivable vastness of space, can be any more than a spontaneous chemical phenomenon of the minutest importance.

If that is accepted it is clear that pain is an evolutionary development essential to prevent life destroying itself. Its beginnings are as simple and as complex as the beginnings of life itself. In fact it is a part of any form of our sort of life in all cases where that life has to compete with its environment.

Why not some other way of guiding self-preservation? Perhaps there *are* other ways. As yet we can only judge what other creatures feel by what we feel ourselves, but it would seem that pain is the usual way. No doubt of all the ways evolution tried this one worked best; or perhaps it was the only one which did work? It could be that one day man will find a better way and build it into *his* further evolution. I wonder how much ill such a good wind would blow? I wonder where that would lead the character of this new creature that would evolve from men?

C. J., Yorkshire

Write your own contribution to this correspondence in the *Guardian*.

97. The world of pain and evil: From death to life

My good friend Tom Rigden who had operated the escape service with me on the Indragiri River, had recently been brought to Chungkai to work on the railroad. One evening Tom came to see me in the Death House. He wanted to tell me he had organized the building of a small hut which I was to have all to myself.

The M.O. [came] with the S.M.O. They stood beside me, [and then] moved away a little, beyond my listening range—or so they thought. But I could hear them.

'He's had the works,' the M.O. [said]. 'Malaria, dysentery, beriberi, plus some queer kind of blood infection we can't identify. Oh, yes, he's also had an appendectomy. And on top of that a bad case of "dip" which left him without the use of his legs.'

'Not exactly in the pink, eh?'

'The only thing left is to let him have a decent end.'

The death sentence had been pronounced on me by experts.

It was a voice other than Reason that replied, 'You could live.

There's a purpose you have to fulfil. You'll become more conscious of it every day that you keep on living. There's a task for you; a responsibility that is yours and only yours.'

'Good enough,' I said to myself. 'I'll get on with it.'

That afternoon I sent word to Tom that I could leave the Death House. In contrast to the Death House, my new home, clean and neatly swept, was fresh with tangy smells of newly-cut bamboo and atap palm. I stretched back gratefully on my rice sacks. I heard a polite cough. A man was standing in the doorway. He was quite naked except for his clean loincloth. What impressed me most was his easy, friendly smile.

'Good evening, sir,' he said in his soft north-of-England voice. 'I've heard you needed a hand. I wondered if you'd care to have me help you.'[1]

I could hear myself saying faintly, 'Thank you, I would. Come in.'

I saw that he had a fine face. There was kindness in it, and a gentle strength.

'You don't know me,' he said, 'but I was posted to your company.'

'What's your name?'

'Miller, sir.'

' "Dusty", eh?'

'Yes sir—'

'Dusty, are you quite sure you want to help me?' It seemed aeons since I had heard anyone volunteer to help a sick man. 'I'm still pretty weak. There's hardly anything I can do for myself.'

'Of course I want to help you,' he replied with such warmth and enthusiasm that there was no doubting his sincerity. 'I'm recovering from an attack of diphtheria. I've a night job in the kitchens, so I can be with you most of the day.'

'That's kind of you. I'll try not to give too much trouble.'

'I'm sure you won't. Here, let me get you settled for the night. I'll fetch some hot water from the cookhouse and give you a proper wash.'

Dusty returned, carrying a steaming bamboo bucket, a basin, and some rags. He then proceeded to refresh me with the first decent wash I'd had in six weeks. It felt good to be clean again !

With one knee on the ground, he was bent over, intent on making me comfortable. He considered carefully before he spoke. There was an air of natural innocence or goodness about him. I did not quite know what to make of him. I was accustomed to companions who were quick of tongue and temper. Why the devil, I thought, is he so pleased to be alive?

I couldn't say how or when, because it happened so slowly, but

---

1. Another soldier, Dinty Moore (a Roman Catholic), also volunteered to help; between them they helped save the writer's life.

gradually sensation returned to my limbs. I started a strict regime.
The time came when I was able to stand on my feet by holding onto
Dusty. One morning I found that with the help of a bamboo staff,
I could propel myself in a clumsy, halting way as far as the door. In a
matter of days I ventured outside.

What I had experienced—namely, the turning to life away from
death—was happening to the camp in general. We were coming
through the valley. There was a movement, a stirring in our midst, a
presence.

Stories of a different kind began to circulate around the camp, stories
of self-sacrifice, heroism, faith and love.

'Do you remember Angus McGillivray?' Dusty asked me late one
afternoon as he made me ready for my wash.

'Yes, I knew him all right. Why?'

'He's dead.'

'Dead? How?'

For a moment Dusty could not speak. I could see that he was feeling
deeply. 'It has to do with Angus' mucker,' he began, 'who became very
ill.'

It was the custom among Argylls for every man to have a mucker—
that is, a pal or friend with whom he shared, or 'mucked in', everything he had.

'It seemed pretty certain to everyone,' Dusty continued, 'that the
mucker's number was up. Certain, that is, to everyone but Angus. He
made up his mind that his mucker shouldn't die. Someone had stolen
his mucker's blanket. Angus gave him his own. Every mealtime
Angus would show up to draw his ration. But he wouldn't eat it. He
would bring it round to give to his friend. Stood over him, he did, and
made him eat it. Going hungry was hard on Angus, mind you, because
he was a big man with a big frame'.

'Perhaps you know the end of the story,' he continued. 'The mucker
got better. Then Angus collapsed. Just slumped down and died.' Dusty
could say no more.

'And what did the docs believe to be the cause?' I asked.

'Starvation,' answered Dusty, 'complicated by exhaustion. He had
mucked in with everything he had—even his life.'

'And all for his friend!'

Dusty sat in stillness. After a while I said 'By some ways of reckoning, what he did might seem foolish.'

'But in other ways,' Dusty returned, 'it makes an awful lot of
sense.'

He bent over my legs and went on cleansing my ulcers. During the
next few days I heard other prisoners discussing Angus' sacrifice. It
had fired the imagination. He had given us a shining example of the

way we ought to live, even if we did not. The examples set by such men shone like beacons. Our regeneration—sparked by conspicuous acts of self-sacrifice—had begun.

It was dawning on us all—officers and 'other ranks' alike—that the law of the jungle is not the law for men. We had seen for ourselves how quickly it could strip us of our humanity and reduce us to levels lower than the beasts.

Death was still with us—no doubt about that. But we were being slowly freed from its destructive grip. We were seeing for ourselves the sharp contrasts between the forces that make for life and those that make for death. Selfishness, hatred, jealousy, and greed were all anti-life. Love, self-sacrifice, mercy, and creative faith, on the other hand, were the essence of life, turning mere existence into living in its truest sense. These were the gifts of God to men.

We began to notice these forces at work around us. When we marched out into the countryside on labor details we saw them in the actions of Christian natives. We were accustomed to being treated by the natives with indifference or contempt. Our plight meant nothing to them—why should it? But we came once to a village where the treatment we received was so different it astonished us. There was mercy in the eyes of those who rushed to the roadside to watch us go by. Before we had reached the end of their settlement they were back laden with cakes, bananas, eggs, medicines, and money which they thrust into our hands. In time we learned that this village had been converted to Christianity by missionaries, and that the Japanese, who found out about their friendly behavior, severely punished them for it.

A key figure in carrying the light of Christianity to these jungle outposts had been an elderly missionary woman who managed to continue her work during the Japanese occupation. When she was forced finally to take to the jungle, she was handed from one group of Christians to another. The Japenese knew of her existence and were never far behind. But although they put a high price on her head, she eluded them.

These brief contacts with the outside world were helpful reminders that a saner, more human way of life still existed. No word had been said. But the message had been given.

Within the camp there were also daily inspirations. The strong and simple faith of Dusty Miller was one of them. It suggested that he had found the answer so many of us sought. Before he went off to work in the kitchens one evening we were having a discussion about the horrifying waste of life at Chungkai.

'Dusty—do you realize that more than twenty men are dying here every day, and most of them are young? When you examine the facts, isn't it hard to see any point in living?'

Dusty got up from the ground where he had been kneeling, moved his basin into a corner out of the way, and looked at me with hurt surprise.

'I'm not sure I follow you. I see a lot of point in living.'

'It's quite simple. All I'm saying is that we may dream about love, truth, beauty, and aspiration for our own amusement, to dull the ache of existence. In fact, it's about all we can do. Actually, they're nothing but froth on the wave.' I was warming to the thrust of my logic. 'Religion and the arts are like a gramophone record we play to drown the cries of pain from the people of the world. Admittedly, they help to numb the sense. But drugs can do that so much better.'

Dusty looked puzzled.

'No, sir, I cannot believe that,' he replied with spirit. 'I don't think there *is* anything accidental about our creation. God knows us. He knows about the sparrow and each hair of our heads. He has a purpose for us.'

I studied him.

'Do you really believe that?' I asked.

'Yes, I do !' he answered with conviction.

'Then why doesn't He do something, instead of sitting quiescently on a great big white throne in the no-place called heaven?'

Dusty considered for a moment. Then he said, 'Maybe He does, maybe He does, but we cannot see everything He is doing now. Maybe our vision isn't very good at this point, "for here we see as in a glass darkly". But we shall see and understand sometime. We have to go on living and hoping, having faith that life is stronger than death. Only God can give life. We have to receive it—and that daily. Here's a verse I've always found to be of help.

> "No one could tell me where my soul might be
> I sought for God, but God eluded me
> I sought my brother out and found all three
> My soul, my God, and all humanity." '

Next day when Dusty returned he said jubilantly, 'I've found it !'

'Found what?' I asked.

'I've found the passage I was looking for—the one that sums up what we were talking about last night. Here—I'll read it to you.' He opened his New Testament and read aloud from the letter of St. John: 'There is no fear in love; but perfect love casteth out fear; because fear hath torment. He that feareth is not made perfect in love. We love him, because he first loved us. If a man say, I love God, and hateth his brother, he is a liar: for he that loveth not his brother whom he hath seen, how can he love God whom he hath not seen? And this commandment have we from him, That he who loveth God love his brother also.'

I lay back on my sleeping platform and let myself dwell on those words. There was truth in them. Both Dusty and Dinty exemplified them. For the first time I understood. Dusty was a Methodist—Dinty a Roman Catholic. Yet in each it was their faith that lent a special grace to their personalities; through them faith expressed a power, a presence, greater than themselves.

I was beginning to see that life was infinitely more complex, and at the same time more wonderful, than I had ever imagined. True, there was hatred. But there was also love. There was death, but there was also life. God had not left us. He was with us, calling us to live the divine life in fellowship.

E R N E S T   G O R D O N, *Through the Valley of the Kwai*

1. What was it that made the writer refuse to give in to the doctors' 'death sentence'? What sort of 'task' and 'responsibility' do you think he was called to undertake?

2. What else besides his own will to live pulled him through?

3. What were the things that made it dawn on the P.O.W.s that 'the law of the jungle' is 'not the law for men'? What *is* the law for men?

4. In Chungkai selfishness, hatred, jealousy, and greed were seen to be 'anti-life'. Do you think that this is what makes these attitudes wrong in everyday life? If not, why are they wrong? Or aren't they?

5. (a) Do you believe that love, truth, beauty and aspiration are 'for our own amusement'? or 'nothing but froth on the wave'?

   (b) Dusty Miller (and Dinty Moore too) didn't think they were these things; they believed they were real and important—linked with their belief in God. What do you think it was that lent support, in the eyes of the writer, to the truth of their belief?

   (c) Do Dusty and Dinty help you to understand that faith in God might be relevant to the problem of pain and evil?

   (d) How do you think one can set about the discovery of 'a power, a presence greater than' oneself? How does the passage suggest one might?

98. The world of pain and evil: 'My God, my God, why hast thou forsaken me?'

The darkest horror of man's sin and the deepest proof of God's Love, this word comes very near the end. For hours Jesus has hung there bound and nailed to the Cross; down below the soldiers have gambled and played with dice; the priests have mocked him, 'He saved others, himself he cannot save'; the thoughtless Bank Holiday crowd have passed on their way, laughing and gossiping.

This is what it has all come to in the end. The Son of God, Friend of Sinners, the greatest Teacher, the Man who spoke as never man spoke before, the Healer of men's souls and bodies, the Lord, the Lover of men has come to this in the end.

And now He is quite alone; and entering into the horror of a great darkness. The sun has gone in; great storm clouds have come rolling

up over the sky; all round is the thick, dark, clammy, breathless heat
which precedes some tremendous storm. The lights of the world are
going out:

Jesus—the Light of the World

Jesus—the Light to lighten the Gentiles

Jesus—Light of Light

Jesus is entering into a thick darkness, 'and all the lights of Heaven
are afraid'. And out of this darkness comes this terrible, heart-rending
cry 'My God, my God, why . . .'.

There are scholars who think this was the *only* word which Jesus
spoke from the Cross. It is indeed the only one recorded by S. Mark
and S. Matthew and anyway it is by far the most important. For here
we come to the very heart of the Gospel.

Think for a moment: why was He hanging there? It was not because of His teachings: it was not because of His miracles: *it was
because He claimed to be God.* He had committed the final, the absolute blasphemy: he had said 'I and the Father are one'. *That* was why
they yelled 'Crucify Him! crucify Him'.

Remember if you or I had been there we would almost certainly
have been on the wrong side. We too should have regarded Him as a
madman. Supposing you heard that a quite outstanding preacher had
come and was preaching, and supposing he was also a faith-healer who
was *actually* curing the sick and the deaf and the blind, would you
not go along to hear him and very likely would you not applaud and
tell your friends that though he was a bit odd and not at all the sort
of person to have to tea, yet he certainly was a very remarkable man?
But supposing he came into church and walked up the aisle and got
up into the pulpit and told you that you had got your religion all
wrong and that he had come to show you what God was *really* like
and that when you had seen Him you had seen the Father—what
then? Would you not condemn him as a lunatic and say that his
cures and his teachings were of the devil?

So it was then: Jesus hangs there convicted of blasphemy, and
either you are watching the death of a lunatic or you are watching the
death of God.

And then, out of the darkness, comes this intolerable cry. Jesus,
whose whole life has been one long unbroken communion with His
Father, now cries 'My God, My God, why hast *Thou* forsaken me?'

He has come to this in the end: to dark despair, to the atheism of
the Son of God.

What does it mean? If we can see only a tiny part of this terrifying
mystery it will light up our faith in the Gospel as nothing else can do.

Jesus feels forsaken: separated from God: He is going down to the
very depth of human experience. First of all he is experiencing the

uttermost of human pain and suffering and this humble, human God is being broken by it. But the physical suffering is small compared with the suffering of his mind: for here on the Cross He has, by His exquisite and perfect sympathy, identified himself with all the sin of all the world. As S. Paul said, 'He was *made* sin on our behalf', and sin always separates a man from God. It is the price of sin, and Jesus is paying it by a black horror of desolation. But, most of all, the suffering we witness on the Cross is spiritual; just because Jesus is genuinely human and just because His love is perfect He is experiencing the worst, the very worst, that can happen to anyone. He has lost the thing which holds a personality together, which makes a a man what he *is*: he has lost faith.

Have you ever seen anyone in this hell? It is stark horror: the man is broken, defeated. His whole personality is disintegrating. He is beyond your power to help; your advice, your sympathy is no use to him now. It's no use telling him to pull himself together. That is the one thing he cannot do. He is beyond all that. He has reached the edge of the edge. He is done for.

And by this cry of utter desolation Jesus shows that he is with that man still; his brother; his friend.

This is the heart of the Gospel: the dying of the Son of God. What Gospel is there in that? There doesn't seem much good news, hope, in the sight of a man dying in the extremity of suffering, engulfed by sin, with his faith wrecked and in utter despair. 'All the suffering of the world is His'. No, there doesn't *seem* much Gospel there. But look again. Who is He? He is a man but He is also God and He has shared all human life to the uttermost limit. There is *no* experience which He has not had and made His own.

This is why *we* need never despair. We may often feel hopeless about ourselves—our sin, failure, stupidity. We may often feel despairing about the world—fear, suspicion, jealousy, war. But God cannot and does not despair of us or of our world because once the Perfect Man took it all on Himself, experienced the uttermost of despair and desolation. Because Christ entered into the depths of despair on our behalf we know that God knows what it is like; and *because of that* He can never despair of us. Because *He* has hope in us we can never despair of ourselves.

Some years ago a young man in serious trouble—bewildered, frightened, despairing—came to me. I said 'If I believe in you and trust you and hope in you, I who have only known you for a very short time, don't you think that God, who knows everything about you and loves you more than I could ever begin to love, don't you think that He trusts you and believes in you too?' 'I hadn't thought of it like that'.

KENNETH M. CAREY

99. The world of pain and evil: Resurrection

The teaching of Jesus is not compatible with the view that human life
ends with physical death. But then human life itself is not compatible
with an end in physical death. Nothing in Jesus' teaching is more
human than this. All human poetry, drama, art cry out against it, and
above them all, human morality utters a piercing shriek. Human life
becomes all but meaningless without the dimension of eternity. And
yet there is no obvious immortality. There is a very plain and obvious
mortality. The very images Jesus has used to reassure us can suddenly
jolt us. If God clothes the flower of the field with more beauty than
Solomon in all his glory, will he not also clothe us, O we of little faith?
And if the flower withers, will not also Solomon in all his glory, and
we without much glory?

The seed grows, the flower blooms, it fades and dies; and it does not
live again. In spring, there is certainly a sort of resurrection, but it is
a very ironical answer to our hopes. It is new grass, different grass,
that reclothes the hills. We cannot comfort the dying blade of grass
with the promise of a resurrection: why should we try to comfort
ourselves just because our chemistry is more complex? From grass to
fish to animals to man, we see increasing complexity, but no essential
distinction. All follow the same cycle of birth, growth, decay, and
death. What justification can we have for dreams of immortality?
Dream we may, but the funeral meets us at the city[1] gate, and no
need to ask for whom the bell tolls.

No biological knowledge, no filling in the links of our slow and
painful evolution, can evince the slightest hope of immortality. That
comes only if we look for a purpose of God through endless ages to
produce as the final end of the process not only 'evolution reaching
the stage of self-consciousness', but evolution reaching the stage of
making a response to its Maker. If the final end of our evolution is
something that can look up and speak to its source, someone who can
say, 'Our Father, which art in Heaven!'; if this is what God has
patiently worked and waited for through a million years, then all
things are different. We have a Father. We are children, we are loved.
We can dream of things prepared for us, and not be accused of mad
presumption. We can expect the end of so much trouble to be something good, something solid and eternal.

It is not a new experience that men are asked to go through when
they are asked to 'seek God, if haply they might feel after him, and
find him'. We have been through the same experience once before.

1. The writer refers here and later in the passage to Jesus' meeting the widow
of Nain and her dead son.

We were a seed in the womb. We came out blind into the world, and were loved, fondled, and fed until a day came when we discerned the outlines of a face above us, and before many months had passed we were able to cry 'Momma, Mother !' There is also a process by which we may learn to cry, with the rest of Christ's brethren, 'Abba, Father !'

Any man who has cried 'Father !', and found his cry answered, he knows not how, yet answered in such a way that he knows that he has a Father—to this man Christ's promises can begin to make sense. Our hope of immortality is based on a personal relationship of love. If I know that God loves me, I know that he will not abandon me, that he has a future for me. If I do not know God, or do not know that he loves me, nothing else can convince me. Attempts to prove the 'immortality of the soul' are self-frustrating, for they are attempts to turn a personal relationship into a mechanical necessity. We may be half persuaded by some clever analogy, some comparison of the caterpillar becoming a butterfly, but it will not stand up to the sight of a corpse and the widow's wails. These analogies may illuminate our faith, but they cannot create it. Only he can create it who creates all things, who said to his friend Lazarus, 'Come forth !'. Only if he is also our friend can we hope that we too shall hear his voice and live unto him, 'for he is not the God of the dead, but of the living'.

ROGER TENNANT, Born of a Woman

100. The world of pain and evil: Evil and the God of love

We have seen so far both what the problem of evil is for the Christian and what some of his responses to it are. These responses may be on the practical level—how to face suffering, how others who are suffering may be helped to face it, how God Himself deals with it through Christ's own sufferings; or they may be theoretical—how Love Almighty can be reconciled with ills unlimited.[1] In the epilogue we have the response of Prayer, in which the Christian tries to share in Christ's identification with the suffering of the world. But just as Prayer finds its practical expression in loving action, so it finds its *raison d'être* in the mind's attempt to understand, so far as finite minds can, how God's purposes of love may be discerned in a world of pain and evil. The passage which follows outlines some of the reasons which Christians have adduced in their attempt to penetrate the mystery of 'Evil and the God of Love'[2] and to demonstrate that the fact of Evil does not show Christianity to be false: 'those who have some degree of Christian faith should not abandon it in face even of this agonizing problem, nor should those who lack Christian faith rule it out on this account as a possibility for themselves.'[3]

The problem of Evil and the God of Love is simply enough stated. The answers to it are exceedingly complex and far-reaching, as is the

1. Cf. Austin Farrer's book *God Almighty and Ills Unlimited*.
2. Cf. John Hick's book of that title.
3. John Hick, op. cit., p. xiii.

case with many other fundamental problems of philosophy, such as the validity of sense-perception, the possibility of knowledge, or the validity of moral judgement. The manifestations of Evil are themselves manifold—natural disasters, physical pain, grief, unmerited suffering, moral evil. Each properly calls for long and detailed examination, and raises in turn a whole series of theological problems—Creation and the Fall, Redemption, Salvation and Judgement, Freewill and Destiny, the Will of God and the Nature of Man. Here we can do no more than indicate a few lines of enquiry which have been pursued in recent years by Christians who have grappled with these issues. Solutions have been attempted along four main lines. Taken together they point to a justification of the ways of God to man which deserves serious consideration. Unlike the simple but more superficial answers of dualism and naturalism they neither cut the Gordian knot, nor ignore it.

The first strand of the solution is found in considering the kind of universe which God has created. The world in which we live is a world of inter-related systems, the higher and lower elements of nature organised into a whole. At each level the elements have their own forms of organisation; as modern physical enquiry has shown us, they are not passive, but active, busy being themselves in their own way. But at the same time they are related to each other, the rhythm of each level of creation fitting in with, or failing to fit in with, the organisation of the whole. Where there is mutual interference, instead of harmony, you have a misfit between the properties of different systems placed in mutual relation; this mutual interference may be called the grand cause of physical evil. 'But if this is the general cause of physical ills, and if God knows it, why does not he remove it? ... What would a physical universe be like, from which all mutual interference of systems was eliminated? It would be no physical universe at all. It would not be like an animal relieved of pain by the extraction of a thorn. It would be like an animal rendered incapable of pain by the removal of its nervous system; that is to say, of its animality. So the physical universe could be delivered from the mutual interference of its constituent systems, only by being deprived of its physicality.'[1] Again, 'Why is it hard for a statesman to impose forms of political or economic order on multitudes? Because the component individuals are busy living their own lives and providing for their households. He must persuade them that their co-operation with the systems imposed will forward rather than frustrate the purposes which as individuals they entertain. In some such fashion we may say that God respects the action or organisation of nature's elements; he does not violate it by the higher levels of organisation

1. Austin Farrer, op. cit., p. 51.

and higher modes of action he superimposes. Now in the political sphere a hundred per cent success for public order or for economic planning is unthinkable, so long as individual freedom is given its rights. So in the natural world a hundred per cent success for animal bodies is unthinkable, if the cellular, chemical and atomic systems of which they are composed are to retain their rights, and go on being themselves in their own way at their own level. When we contemplate the physical creation, we see an unimaginable complex, organised on many planes one above another; atomic, molecular, cellular; vegetable, animal, social. And the marvel of it is that at every level the constituent elements run themselves, and, by their mutual interaction, run the world. God not only makes the world, he makes it make itself; or rather he causes its innumerable constituents to make it.'[1]

The second strand of the solution takes the conception of God's creation a stage further. The world was not created as a perfect place for God's perfect creature, Man, to dwell in. For man is not yet perfected; he is in process of becoming the perfected being whom God purposed. For this reason the world is not a perfected environment, but one in which the hazardous adventure of man's development towards perfection takes place. God's purpose in creation is thus teleological, and the question we must ask of the world is not: 'Is the architecture of the world the most pleasant and convenient possible? The question that we have to ask is rather, Is the kind of world that God might make an environment in which moral beings may be fashioned, through their own free insights and responses, into "children of God"?'[2] The world is 'the scene of a history in which human personality may be formed towards the pattern of Christ; . . . the presence of pleasure and the absence of pain cannot be the supreme and over-riding end for which the world exists; its value is to be judged by its fitness for its primary purpose, the purpose of soul-making.' In this way God acts even as a wise human father would act towards his children when he refuses to provide a purely pleasurable environment, in which there is no hazard or challenge, nor any opportunities for exercising moral integrity, courage, compassion, unselfishness.

The other two strands of the solution are implicit in the first two—namely Free-will and a future life.

Human freedom presupposes some degree of autonomy over against God. This is indeed what our actual situation presents us with—a situation in which God is hidden, veiled by His creation, but know-

1. Austin Farrer, 'Providence and Evil', in *Saving Belief*, pp. 50-1.
2. John Hick, op. cit., p. 293.

able by a free personal response on man's part. This in turn implies
the possibility of moral evil. For if man is to be free, really free, to
choose God, he must also be free to choose the opposite—alienation
from Him. In determining man's freedom God has also determined
the conditions in which moral evil and suffering are possible. Furthermore, if the world is to allow the possibility of disinterested moral
action, there must be the possibility of undeserved or excessive
misery. 'We do not acknowledge a moral call to sacrificial measures
to save a criminal from receiving his just punishment or a patient
from receiving the painful treatment that is to cure him. But men and
women often act in true compassion and massive generosity and self-
giving in the face of unmerited suffering. . . . It seems then that in a
world that is to be the scene of compassionate love and self-giving
for others, suffering must fall upon mankind with something of the
haphazardness and inequity we now experience. It must be apparently unmerited, pointless, and incapable of being morally rational-
ized. For it is precisely the feature of our common human lot that
creates sympathy between man and man and evokes the unselfish
kindness and goodwill which are among the highest values of personal
life. No undeserved need would mean no uncalculating outpouring
to meet that need. . . . The alternative to the present apparently
random incidence of misfortune would be that happiness should be
the predictable result of virtue, and misery the predictable outcome
of wickedness. . . . A world in which the sinner was promptly struck
down by divine vengeance and in which the upright were the immediate recipients of divine reward would be incompatible with that
divine purpose of soul-making that we are supposing to lie behind
the arrangement of our present world.'[1]

The fourth strand is belief in an after-life. This is not only part of
the total organism of Christian belief; it is crucial to the resolution
of our problem. God's purpose, we have said, is that man, as a morally
free agent, should ultimately come to perfection. This purpose is
clearly not fulfilled, even for the best of men, in this world. It is only
in the resurrection-life that this vale of soul-making can find its ultimate justification. We cannot resolve our problem by looking merely
to the past—the constitution of God's created universe and the grant-
ing of freedom to man; we must also look to the consummation of God's
creative purpose in the final blessedness of a life beyond the grave.
This alone makes sense of all that went before. 'It represents the best
gift of God's infinite love for His children— . . . not a reward or a
compensation proportioned to each individual's trials, but an infinite
good that would render worth while *any* finite suffering endured in
the course of attaining to it.'[1] There is a further point. We see the

1. John Hick, op. cit., pp. 370-1.   2. Ibid., p. 377.

perfection of earthly human nature in the man Jesus—the free response of love in the face of the most unmerited suffering of all. 'This is the gospel of Christ's Passion—that God saves us by suffering.'[1] The pledge that this is so was given us on Good Friday; but it was not till Easter Sunday that the pledge was redeemed. It is only with the Resurrection that we see, looking back, the justification of Christ's endurance through suffering and evil, and, looking forward, the promise of our own perfecting. In the risen Christ we can at last glimpse the triumphant fulfilment of God's good purpose and His victory over evil.

ROGER W. YOUNG

101. The world of pain and evil: Epilogue: the response of prayer

Lord, we would pray for others.
Not people in the abstract,
But real people, suffering people—
People with whom You came to dwell,
With whom your Presence is now.

Lord, daily we read about such people.
We would bring them and ourselves before You in prayer.

Last week, Lord, we read in our newspapers
33,000 people were discovered starving to death
In a remote part of one of our States.
They weren't far from help, Lord,
But far enough away,—
They were out of sight and so out of men's mind, our minds.

We pray for these people, Lord.
We pray too, Lord, for the Block Development Officer and others—
Who do not make suffering known—
The administrative machinery that will not move.
We pray for all those who allow
Man to be crippled and to die for want of food.

We pray too Lord, for the affluent nations,
Who give from their bounty to the hungry,
Yet make sure
Their wealth, their affluence,
Will not only continue but increase.
And the poor become poorer,

1. Austin Farrer, *Love Almighty and Ills Unlimited*, p. 172.

The problem of hunger remains unsolved.
We pray for ourselves, Lord,
For in other men's insensitivity
We see ourselves.
We know that outside the gate of our life
Men, women and children suffer but—
We would rather not see.

We pray, Lord, for sensitivity
Amongst B.D.O.s, clerks, M.P.s, Nations,
Ourselves,—
So that—33,000 people, 10,000 people, 100 people,
One person,
Will not suffer, without us knowing—
Without the world caring.

We pray for the sensitivity of Christ
Who became one with suffering men
Who met man's deepest suffering.

Two days ago, Lord, we read in the newspapers—
A 14-year old Negro girl was shot.
Racial violence on Chicago's west side.
Lord, she was an innocent bystander !
We pray for the innocent bystanders of the world
Who are shot down, trodden under, destroyed.

We pray for the Negroes of the United States,
The people of South Africa, Rhodesia, Angola, Mozambique,
Who, at this moment, now, are seeing
Their children destroyed—
Crippled through inferior education,
And trodden under by discriminatory laws,
Innocents dying as surely as if shot by a gun !

We pray for these people, Lord,—
And the innocents in our own part of the world,
Our neighbours,
The people of Vietnam.
Whose lives have become pawns
As callous men and nations
Play their clever game of power politics—
Clever for them, bloody for the rest—
In the name of just causes
And moral uprightness.

Lord, we pray for justice.
Thou art a God of Justice and Righteousness !
Thou hast no patience with moral pretension,
Idle ceremony and pious prayer.
May justice roll down like waters . . .
Righteousness like a mighty stream.

Lord, we have just read that in one of our cities—
Six students committed suicide !
We pray for them, Lord, and their families.
We pray for all students for whom
Education is a matter of life and death.
We pray for parents whose high expectation
Drives young people to cheat, bribe—
Destroy themselves.
We pray, Lord, for our Nation and culture
Where insecurity and loss of face
Lead young people to take their own lives.
Some of us are students, Lord.
We know that those six young lives
Are close to us
In expectations, hopes and fears.
We pray, Lord, for honest expectation,
Loving acceptation.

Lord, we pray for the presence of Christ
Who in the power of His accepting Love,
Releases men to honest demands upon themselves,
Freedom from fear.

Lord, today is a special day for us.
Thou hast called us to serve Thee through this fellowship.
Deep down, O Lord, because we are sinners,
We don't want this fellowship to be very demanding,
An occasional Bible Study—
To show how religious we are.
One or two speakers to listen to, but—
Nothing, O Lord, that will make us think
Deeply,
Get our hands
Dirty !

Lord, when we really look into our hearts
We know this about ourselves.
Help us to see that such an attitude to life

Makes a world where—
33,000 people can starve to death
Without anyone knowing or caring.
A 14-year old can be shot down
On the porch of her own home.
Six students can feel so desolate and lonely
They kill themselves.

Help us to feel deeply and see clearly, Lord.
Save us from ourselves !
Enable us to admit our errors and weakness.
Grant us the grace to change our ways,
The wisdom to choose aright,
Courage and strength to complete our efforts,
Guidance that we may fearlessly and constantly
Serve Thee.

                    A prayer given at an S.C.M. Inaugural Service

References to the passages

The author and publishers gratefully acknowledge permission from copyright owners and publishers to reproduce passages from their copyright works. Although pages are mentioned, a number of the extracts have been shortened and are not quoted in full.

1. ERNEST GORDON, *Through the Valley of the Kwai*, pp. 60–5, Collins Publishers and Bantam Books, 1963.
2. A. S. NEILL, *Summerhill*, chap. 1, Hart Publishing Co., and Victor Gollancz, 1961.
3. CAL MCCRYSTAL, *Sunday Times*, 13 March 1966.
4. ALAN DALE, *New World* 2. *The Message*, pp. 41–2. Oxford University Press, 1966.
5. (a) *Priest and Worker: The Autobiography of Henri Perrin* (tr. Bernard Wall), pp. 171–225, Macmillan, 1965.
   (b) *The Times*, 22–4 June, 1967 (Times Newspapers and the Press Association); *The Observer*, 25 June 1967.
6. DAVID LAWTON, *Guardian*, 7 April 1966.
7. T. S. ELIOT, Chorus III from 'The Rock', *Collected Poems 1909–1962*, Faber and Faber, 1963.
8. GERALD JONES and JOHN PENYCATE, *Sixth Form Opinion*, no. 4, 20 June 1962.
9. DAVID WILKERSON, *The Cross and the Switchblade*, pp. 91–4, Hodder and Stoughton and Spire Books, 1964.
10. GRAHAM GREENE, *The Living Room*, act I, scene ii, William Heinemann, 1953.
11. BILL NAUGHTON, *Alfie*, pp. 147, 161, 110, 34–5, 183, A. D. Peters and Panther Books, 1966.
12. RONALD FLETCHER and CHARLES DAVEY, *Marriage Guidance*, November 1963 and January 1964.
13. (a) GEORGE TARGET, *We, the Crucifiers*, pp. 29–30, Hodder and Stoughton, 1964.
    (b) JOY DAVIDMAN, *Smoke on the Mountain*, pp. 30–1, Hodder and Stoughton, 1955.
14. DAVID WILKERSON, *The Cross and the Switchblade*, pp. 146–9, Hodder and Stoughton and Spire Books, 1964.
15. TREVOR HUDDLESTON, *The Observer*, 24 April 1966.
16. CHAD VARAH, *New Christian*, 4 November 1965.
17. (a) PLATO, *The Republic*, Book II (tr. H. D. P. Lee), Penguin Books, 1955.
    (b) DOROTHY DAY, *The Catholic Worker*, July/August 1965.

18. KIM MALTHE-BRUNN and DIETRICH BONHOEFFER, *Dying We Live*, pp. 76-85 and 191-3, Collins Publishers and Fontana Books, 1958.

19. ALBERT CAMUS, *The Plague* (tr. Stuart Gilbert), pp. 117-37 and 165-71, Hamish Hamilton and Penguin Books, 1960.

20. F. A. COCKIN, *Christianity in Common Speech*, pp. 28-32, Holywell Press, 1950.

21. JAMES BALDWIN, *Nobody Knows my Name*, chap. 4, Michael Joseph.

22. PHILIP BERRIGAN, *The Catholic Worker*, April 1965.

23. JOHN HOWARD GRIFFIN, *Black Like Me*, pp. 24-7 and 51-9. Collins Publishers and Signet Books, 1962.

24. CHARLES HOOPER, *Brief Authority*, pp. 43-51, Collins Publishers, 1960.

25. SOUTH AFRICAN EMBASSY, *South Africa in Fact*, October 1965.

26. ABRAM FISCHER, *The Observer*, 8 May 1966.

27. WILHELM RÖPKE, *Schweizer Monatshefte*, 44th year, no. 2, May 1964.

28. ROY PERROT, *The Observer*, 24 April 1966.

29. E. R. BRAITHWAITE, *To Sir, With Love*, pp. 36-44 and 142-9, Bodley Head, 1959.

30. ELSPETH HUXLEY, *Back Street New Worlds*, pp. 158-63, Chatto and Windus, 1964.

31. JOHANNES HAMEL, *A Christian in East Germany*, pp. 18-28 and 47-9, S.C.M. Press, 1960.

32. PETRU DUMITRIU, *Incognito*, pp. 296-308, Collins Publishers, 1964.

33. (a) *The Observer*, 14 February 1965 and 6 February 1966.
    (b) NICOLE ENTREMONT, *The Catholic Worker*, June 1966.
    (c) LADY ALEXANDRA METCALFE, *The World's Children*, Summer 1966, The Save the Children Fund.

34. ALBERT VAN DEN HEUVEL, The Carberry Lecture, 1966.

35. EDWARD ROGERS, *Living Standards*, pp. 42-50, S.C.M. Press, 1964.

36. THEODORE SØRENSEN, *Kennedy*, pp. 737-92, Hodder and Stoughton and Pan Books, 1966.

37. *The Catholic Worker*, July/August 1965.

38. SIR MICHAEL WRIGHT, *The Road to Peace*, pp. 42-54, S.C.M. Press, 1965.

39. SIR HUGH FOOT, *A Start in Freedom*, pp. 242-6, Hodder and Stoughton, 1964.

40. EDITH SITWELL, *Collected Poems*, Macmillan, 1957.

41. G. B. SHAW, *Androcles and the Lion*, pp. 9-14 and 49-56, Penguin Books, 1946.

42. PATRICK WHITE, *Voss*, pp. 362-5 and 472-4, Eyre and Spottiswoode Publishers, 1957.

43. MALCOLM MUGGERIDGE, *What I Believe*, pp. 139-45, Collins Publishers, 1966.

44. STEVIE SMITH, *Selected Poems*, Longmans, Green, 1962.

45. PETER BUTTER, *Edwin Muir, Man and Poet*, pp. 167-9 and 182-5, Oliver and Boyd, 1966.

46. ERNEST GORDON, *Through the Valley of the Kwai*, pp. 100-7 and 190-2, Collins Publishers and Bantam Books, 1963.

47. ROGER TENNANT, *Born of a Woman*, pp. 4-6, 15-16 and 117-18, S.P.C.K., 1961.

48. JAMES S. STEWART, *The Strong Name*, chaps. vi and vii, T. and T. Clark, 1940.

49. (a) MICHEL QUOIST, *Prayers of Life*, pp. 55–7, Gill and Son, 1963.
(b) NIKOS KAZANTZAKIS, *Christ Recrucified*, pp. 251–3, Faber and Faber, 1962.
(c) GEORGE TARGET, *We, the Crucifiers*, pp. 138–46, Hodder and Stoughton, 1964.

50. THORNTON WILDER, *The Angel that Troubled the Waters*, pp. 91–4, Longmans, Green, 1928.

51. PETRU DUMITRIU, *Incognito*, pp. 379–83, Collins Publishers, 1964.

52. J. H. OLDHAM, *Life is Commitment*, pp. 69–78, S.C.M. Press, 1953.

53. DIETRICH BONHOEFFER, *Letters from Prison and Other Papers* (revised edition, 1967), pp. 152–5, 174–5, 188–9, 196–7, 198–9, S.C.M. Press.

55. STUART JACKMAN, *The Davidson Affair*, pp. 21–33, Faber and Faber, 1966.

57. LESSLIE NEWBIGIN, *The Household of God*, pp. 29–31, S.C.M. Press, 1953.

58. A. C. CRAIG in *A Diary of Readings* (ed. John Baillie), Day 166, Oxford University Press, 1955.

59. RALPH MORTON and MARK GIBBS, *God's Frozen People*, Collins Publishers and Fontana Books, 1964, pp. 106 and 31–2.

60. JAMES S. STEWART, *The Strong Name*, pp. 259–60, T. and T. Clark, 1940.

61. R. P. C. HANSON, *God: Creator, Saviour, Spirit*, pp. 76–82, S.C.M. Press, 1960.

62. MONICA FURLONG, *With Love to the Church*, pp. 81–95, Hodder and Stoughton, 1965.

63. RALPH MORTON and MARK GIBBS, *God's Frozen People*, pp. 118–20 and 68–73, Collins Publishers and Fontana Books, 1964.

64. 'STEWART', *New Christian*, 20 October 1966.

65. CHRISTOPHER DRIVER, *A Future for the Free Churches?*, pp. 60–2, S.C.M. Press, 1962.

66. STUART JACKMAN, *This Desirable Property*, pp. 85–8, Lutterworth Press (Edinburgh House Press), 1964.

67. MICHAEL NOVAK, *The Open Church*, chap. 24. Darton, Longman and Todd, 1964.

68. OLIVE WYON, *Living Springs*, pp. 9–11, S.C.M. Press, 1963.

69. LANCELOT SHEPPARD, *New Christian*, 1 December 1966.

70. STEPHEN VERNEY, *Fire in Coventry*, pp. 23–7, Hodder and Stoughton, 1964.

71. DAVID WILKERSON, *The Cross and the Switchblade*, pp. 91–4, Hodder and Stoughton and Spire Books, 1964.

72. *New Christian*, 1 December 1966.

73. OLIVE WYON, *Living Springs*, pp. 51–4, S.C.M. Press, 1963.

74. BRUCE KENRICK, *Come out the Wilderness*, pp. 184–9, Collins Publishers and Fontana Books, 1965.

75. *Planning the Ecumenical Parish*, Northamptonshire Ecumenical Study Group, 1967.

76. MORRIS WEST, *The Children of the Sun*, pp. 78–123, William Heinemann and Pan Books, 1958.

77. OLIVE WYON, *Living Springs*, pp. 125–6, S.C.M. Press, 1963.

78. F. A. COCKIN, *Christianity in Common Speech*, pp. 12–13, Holywell Press, 1950.

79. (a) ROGER TENNANT, *Born of a Woman*, pp. 20–1, S.P.C.K., 1961.
    (b) JULIAN S. HUXLEY, *Essays of a Humanist*, pp. 120–1, Chatto and Windus, 1964.

80. RONALD W. HEPBURN, *Christianity and Paradox*, pp. 155–9, 171–2, and 184–5, C. A. Watts, 1958.

81. T. R. MILFORD, *Foolishness to the Greeks*, pp. 18–28, S.C.M. Press, 1953.

83. BRITISH COUNCIL OF CHURCHES, *Sex and Morality*, pp. 17–29, S.C.M. Press, 1966.

84. P. H. NOWELL-SMITH, A. BOYCE GIBSON, and J. R. LUCAS, in *Christian Ethics and Contemporary Philosophy* (ed. I. T. Ramsey), chaps. 5 and 6; also *Rationalist Annual*, 1961, and *Journal of Theological Studies*, vol. xxiii, part 1, April 1962.

85. MAGDALEN GOFFIN, *Objections to Roman Catholicism* (ed. Michael de la Bedoyère), pp. 24–5, Penguin Books, 1966.

86. AUSTIN FARRER, *Saving Belief*, pp. 140–9, Hodder and Stoughton, 1964.

87. CAMARA LAYE, *The Radiance of the King*, pp. 281–4, Collins Publishers and Fontana Books, 1966.

88. C. S. LEWIS, *Screwtape Proposes a Toast*, pp. 101–9, Geoffrey Bles and Fontana Books, 1965.

89. MICHAEL RAMSEY, *Image—Old and New*, pp. 3–8, S.P.C.K., 1963.

90. F. A. COCKIN, *God in Action*, pp. 91–102, Penguin Books, 1961.

91. H. H. PRICE, *Faith and the Philosophers* (ed. John Hick), pp. 3–25, Macmillan, 1964.

92. HARVEY COX, *The Secular City*, pp. 241–68, S.C.M. Press, 1965.

93. I. T. RAMSEY, *Religious Language*, pp. 14–48, S.C.M. Press, 1957.

94. M. A. C. WARREN, *Our Response to God: Far and Near*, November–December 1966, p. 52.

96. MARY STOTT et al., *Guardian*, 15 and 23 November 1966.

97. ERNEST GORDON, *Through the Valley of the Kwai*, pp. 73–98, Collins Publishers and Bantam Books, 1963.

99. ROGER TENNANT, *Born of a Woman*, pp. 62–4, S.P.C.K., 1961.

101. THE REVD. VERNON R. WISHART, *Aikya*, vol. xii, no. 9, September 1966.

Further suggested reading

1. Learning from the world

Community or chaos?

GEORGE C. HOMANS, *The Human Group*, Routledge and Kegan Paul, 1951.

W. J. H. SPROTT, *Human Groups*, Penguin, 1958.

REINHOLD NIEBUHR, *The Children of Light and the Children of Darkness*, Nisbet, 1945.

RICHARD TAYLOR, *Christians in an Industrial Society*, S.C.M. Press, 1961.

JUDITH EARNSHAW, 'Teacher Relations Survey', *Sixth Form Opinion*, no. 6, 1963.

BEL KAUFMAN, *Up the Down Staircase*, Barker, 1965.

SALLY TRENCH, *Bury Me in my Boots*, Hodder and Stoughton, 1968.

HARVEY COX, *The Secular City*, S.C.M. Press, 1965.

Personal encounters

MARTIN BUBER, *I and Thou*, T. and T. Clark. 1937.

ERIC FROMM, *The Art of Loving*, George Allen and Unwin, 1957.

STEPHEN COATES, *Loving and Hating*, Hodder and Stoughton, 1965.

BRITISH COUNCIL OF CHURCHES, *Sex and Morality*, S.C.M. Press, 1966.

WILLIAM P. WYLIE, *The Pattern of Love*, Longmans, Green, 1958.

EVELYN MILLIS DUVAL, *Why Wait till Marriage?*, Hodder and Stoughton, 1966.

ELISABETH MONTEFIORE, *Half Angels*, The Faith Press, 1961.

HOWARD ROOT and HUGH MONTEFIORE, *God, Sex and War*, chaps. 2 and 3, Fontana Books, 1963.

Face to face with yourself

C.E.M., *Probe*, no. 2, *Drugs*, Christian Education Movement, June 1967.

RUTH FIRST, *117 Days*, Penguin, 1965.

ARTHUR MILLER, *The Crucible*, Cresset Press, 1956.

C. VIRGIL GHEORGHIU, *The 25th Hour*, Heinemann, 1950.

American or Negro?

HARPER LEE, *To Kill a Mocking Bird*, Popular Library Paperback, 1962.

MARTIN LUTHER KING, *Strength to Love*, Fontana Books, 1969.

RICHARD WRIGHT, *Native Son* and *Black Boy*, Dennis Dobson, 1940 and 1945.

Apartheid

MARTIN JARRETT-KERR, *African Pulse*, Hodder and Stoughton, 1960.
ALBERT LUTHULI, *Let my People Go*, Collins, 1962.
E. L. ADAMS, *Dark Symphony*, Sheed, 1943.
HANNAH STANTON, *Go Well, Stay Well*, Hodder and Stoughton, 1961.

Integrating immigrants?

GOVERNMENT WHITE PAPER, *The Commonwealth Immigration Act*, H.M.S.O., 1962.
—— *Immigration from the Commonwealth*, H.M.S.O., 1965.
RICHARD HOOPER (ed.), *Colour in Britain*, B.B.C. Publications, 1965.
PAUL FOOT, *Immigration and Race Relations in British Politics*, Penguin, 1965.
HENRI TAJFEL and JOHN L. DAWSON (eds.), *Disappointed Guests*, Institute of Race Relations/Oxford University Press, 1965.
C.E.M., *Probe*, no. 3, *Racial Discrimination*, Christian Education Movement, 1967.

Encounters with Communism

ARTHUR KOESTLER et al., *The God that Failed*, Hamish Hamilton, 1950.
DONALD SWANE, *Communist Faith and Christian Faith*, S.C.M. Press, 1965.
BORIS PASTERNAK, *Doctor Zhivago*, Collins/Harvill, 1958 and Penguin.
JOHN GUNTHER, *Inside Russia Today*, Hamish Hamilton, 1962.
ROBERT CONQUEST, *Common Sense about Russia*, Gollancz, 1960.
GUY WINT, *Common Sense about China*, Gollancz, 1960.
W. A. SEWELL, *I Stayed in China*, Allen and Unwin.
THICH NHAT HANH, *Vietnam: The Lotus in the Sea of Fire*, S.C.M. Press, 1967.

Haves and have-nots

C.E.M., *Probe*, no. 1, *Population and Family Planning*, Christian Education Movement, February 1967.
—— *A World in Revolution*, Christian Education Movement, 1968.
ROBERT GARDNER, *A World of Peoples*, B.B.C. Publications, 1965.
RITCHIE CALDER, *Common Sense about a Starving World*, Gollancz, 1962.
BRITISH COUNCIL OF CHURCHES, *World Poverty and British Responsibility*, S.C.M. Press, 1964.
RICHARD M. FAGLEY, *The Population Explosion and Christian Responsibility*, Oxford University Press, 1960.
WORLD COUNCIL OF CHURCHES, *The Development Apocalypse*, Risk Paperback, 1967.
CHRISTIAN AID, *World Divided—by Wealth and Poverty* (Sixth Form Study Outline), Christian Aid, 1968.

Peace with the bomb?

D. M. McKINNON, *God, Sex and War*, chap 1, Fontana Books, 1963.

CONFERENCE ON CHRISTIAN APPROACHES TO DEFENCE AND DISARMAMENT, *Peace is still the Prize*, S.C.M. Press, 1966.
CHRISTOPHER THORNE, *Ideology and Power*, Collier/Macmillan, 1965.

2. The claims of Christ

A. WHO DO YOU SAY THAT I AM?

F. W. DILLISTONE, *The Novelist and the Passion Story*, Collins, 1960.
NAOMI MITCHISON, *Behold Your King*, Frederick Muller, 1957.
WILLIAM FAULKNER, *A Fable*, Chatto and Windus, 1955.
JAMES BALDWIN, *The Fire Next Time*, Michael Joseph, 1963.
PATRICK WHITE, *Riders in the Chariot*, Eyre and Spottiswoode, 1961.
ELIZABETH GEORGE, *The Bronze Bow*, Peacock Books, 1964.
CLIVE SANSOM, *The Witnesses* (in *Poems, 1951*), Penguin, 1951.
FYODOR DOSTOYEVSKY, *The Brothers Karamazov* (Book V, chap. v, 'The Grand Inquisitor').
ALBERT SCHWEITZER, *The Quest for the Historical Jesus*, A. and C. Black, 1963.
RUDOLF BULTMANN, *Jesus and the Word*, Fontana Books, 1958.
JOHN HICK, *Christianity at the Centre*, S.C.M. Press, 1968.
ROBERT SHORT, *The Gospel according to Peanuts*, Fontana Books, 1966.
HOWARD WILLIAMS, *Down to Earth*, S.C.M. Press, 1963.
D. M. BAILLIE, *God was in Christ*, Faber, 1961.
EDWARD K. TALBOT, *Retreat Addresses*, S.P.C.K., 1954.
NILS S. F. FERRE, *Christ and the Christian*, Collins, 1958.

B. THE CHRISTIAN COMMUNITY

CHARLES WILLIAMS, *The Descent of the Dove*, Faber, 1950.
EDWARD WICKHAM, *Church and People in an Industrial Society*, Lutterworth Press, 1957.
VICTOR DE WAAL, *What is the Church?*, S.C.M. Press, 1969.
F. A. COCKIN, *God in Action*, Penguin, 1961.
HAROLD LOUKES, *The Quaker Contribution*, S.C.M. Press, 1965.
PIERRE BERTON, *The Comfortable Pew*, Hodder Paperback, 1966.
ROGER LLOYD, *The Ferment in the Church*, S.C.M. Press, 1964.
WERNER PELZ, *Irreligious Reflections on the Christian Church*, S.C.M. Press, 1959.
BARRY TILL, *Changing Frontiers in the Mission of the Church*, S.P.C.K., 1965.
JOHANNES HAMEL, *A Christian in East Germany*, S.C.M. Press, 1960.
JOHN LAWRENCE, *The Hard Facts of Unity*, S.C.M. Press, 1960.

C. GOD THE FATHER OF ALL THINGS

God and nature

J. B. PHILLIPS, *Your God is too Small*, Epworth Press, 1952.
JAMES PARKES, *Good God*, S.C.M. Press, 1966.
HELMUT THIELICKE, *How the World Began*, James Clarke, 1964.
JOHN HAPGOOD, *Religion and Science*, Mills and Boon, 1964.

A. R. VIDLER (ed.), *Soundings*, Cambridge University Press, 1964.

L. CHARLES BIRCH, *Nature and God*, S.C.M. Press, 1965.

PIERRE TEILLARD DE CHARDIN, *The Phenomenon of Man*, Collins, 1959.

God and morality

G. F. WOODS, *A Defence of Theological Ethics*, Cambridge University Press, 1966.

JOSEPH FLETCHER, *Situation Ethics*, S.C.M. Press, 1966.

CHARLES WILLIAMS, *Descent into Hell* and *All Hallows Eve*, Faber, 1949 and 1945.

C. S. LEWIS, *The Great Divorce*, Geoffrey Bles, 1945.

JOHN BAILLIE, *And the Life Everlasting*, Oxford University Press, 1934.

I. T. RAMSAY, *Freedom and Immortality*, S.C.M. Press, 1960.

God the Father

HELMUT THIELICKE, *The Waiting Father*, James Clarke, 1962.

JONATHAN GRAHAM, *He Came unto His Own*, The Faith Press, 1961.

J. A. T. ROBINSON, *Honest to God*, S.C.M. Press, 1963.

—— and DAVID L. EDWARDS, *The Honest to God Debate*, S.C.M. Press, 1963.

ANTHONY FLEW, *God and Philosophy*, Hutchinson, 1966.

PAUL TILLICH, *The Shaking of the Foundations*, Penguin, 1962.

I. T. RAMSAY, *Christian Discourse*, Oxford University Press, 1965.

JOHN MACQUARRIE, *God-Talk*, S.C.M. Press, 1967.

HUGH MONTEFIORE, *Awkward Questions on Christian Love*, Fontana Books, 1964.

C. S. LEWIS, *The Problem of Pain*, Fontana Books, 1957.

LADISLAUS BOROS, *Pain and Providence* and *The Moment of Truth*, Burns and Oates, 1966 and 1965.

WILLIAM TEMPLE, *Christus Veritas*, Macmillan, 1939.

D. W. D. SHAW, *Who is God?*, S.C.M. Press, 1968.

JOHN HICK (ed.), *The Existence of God*, Macmillan, 1964.